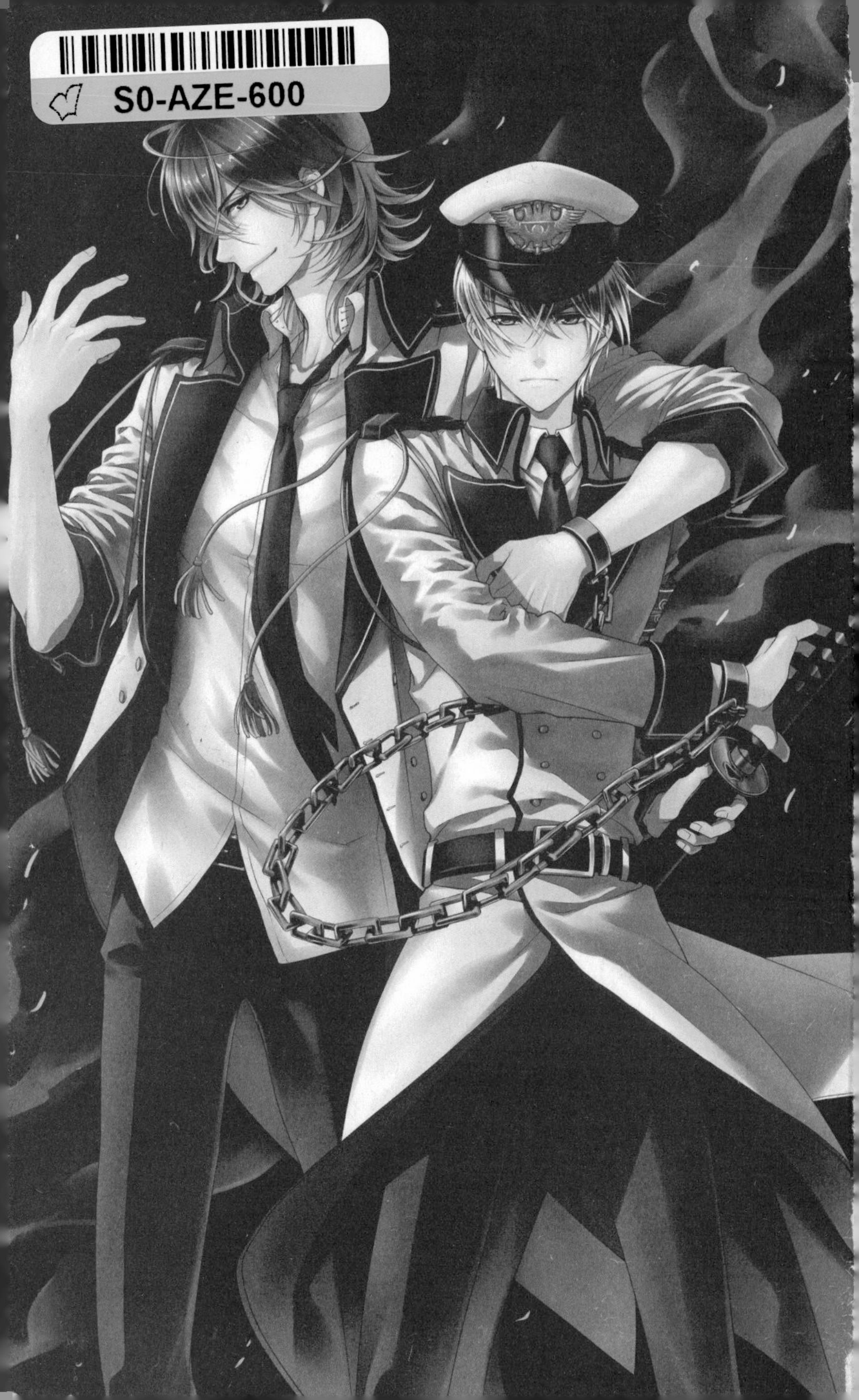

HANGER

Hirotaka Kisaragi

Table of Contents

Chapter 1

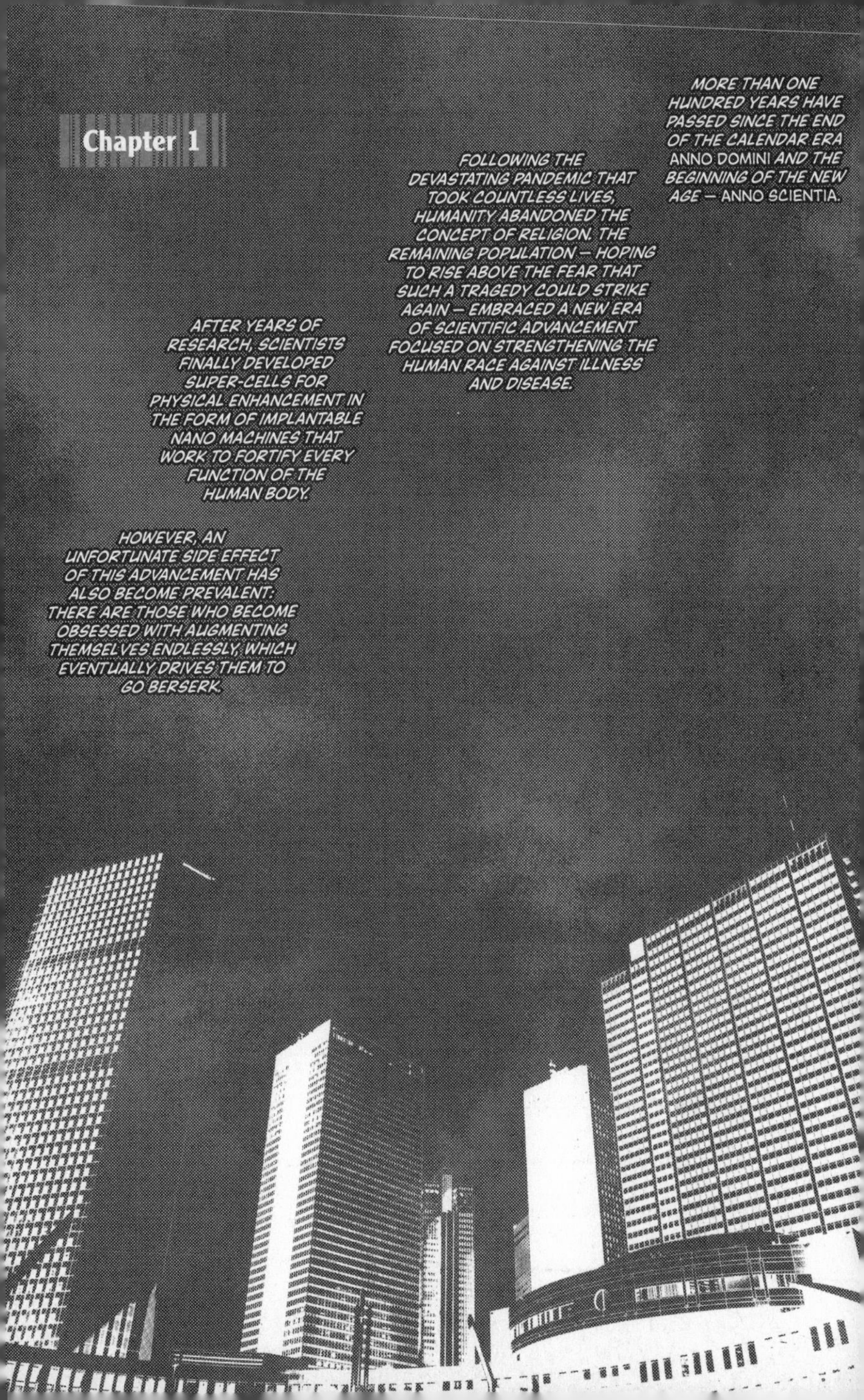
MORE THAN ONE HUNDRED YEARS HAVE PASSED SINCE THE END OF THE CALENDAR ERA ANNO DOMINI AND THE BEGINNING OF THE NEW AGE — ANNO SCIENTIA.
FOLLOWING THE DEVASTATING PANDEMIC THAT TOOK COUNTLESS LIVES, HUMANITY ABANDONED THE CONCEPT OF RELIGION. THE REMAINING POPULATION — HOPING TO RISE ABOVE THE FEAR THAT SUCH A TRAGEDY COULD STRIKE AGAIN — EMBRACED A NEW ERA OF SCIENTIFIC ADVANCEMENT FOCUSED ON STRENGTHENING THE HUMAN RACE AGAINST ILLNESS AND DISEASE.
AFTER YEARS OF RESEARCH, SCIENTISTS FINALLY DEVELOPED SUPER-CELLS FOR PHYSICAL ENHANCEMENT IN THE FORM OF IMPLANTABLE NANO MACHINES THAT WORK TO FORTIFY EVERY FUNCTION OF THE HUMAN BODY.
HOWEVER, AN UNFORTUNATE SIDE EFFECT OF THIS ADVANCEMENT HAS ALSO BECOME PREVALENT: THERE ARE THOSE WHO BECOME OBSESSED WITH AUGMENTING THEMSELVES ENDLESSLY, WHICH EVENTUALLY DRIVES THEM TO GO BERSERK.

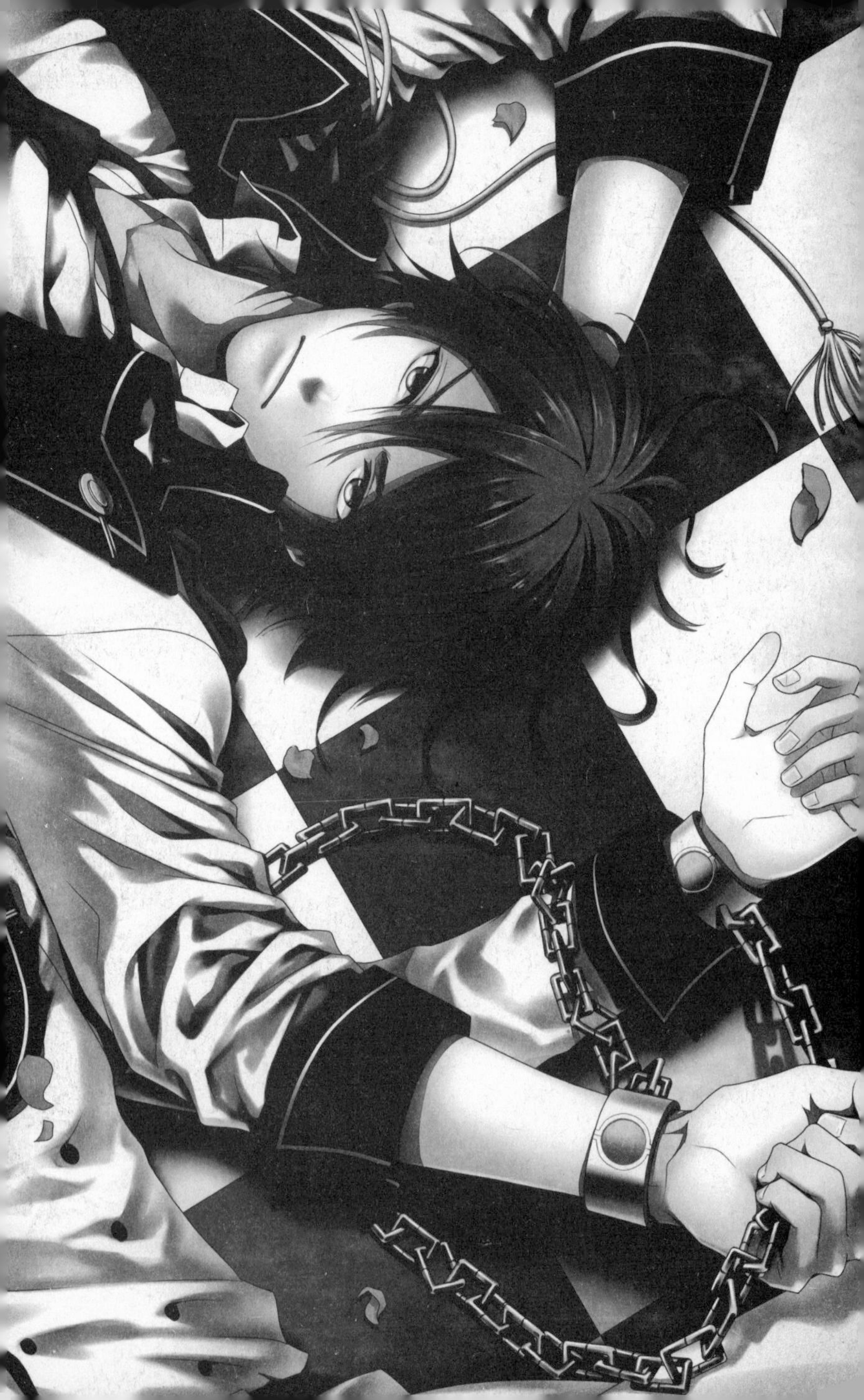

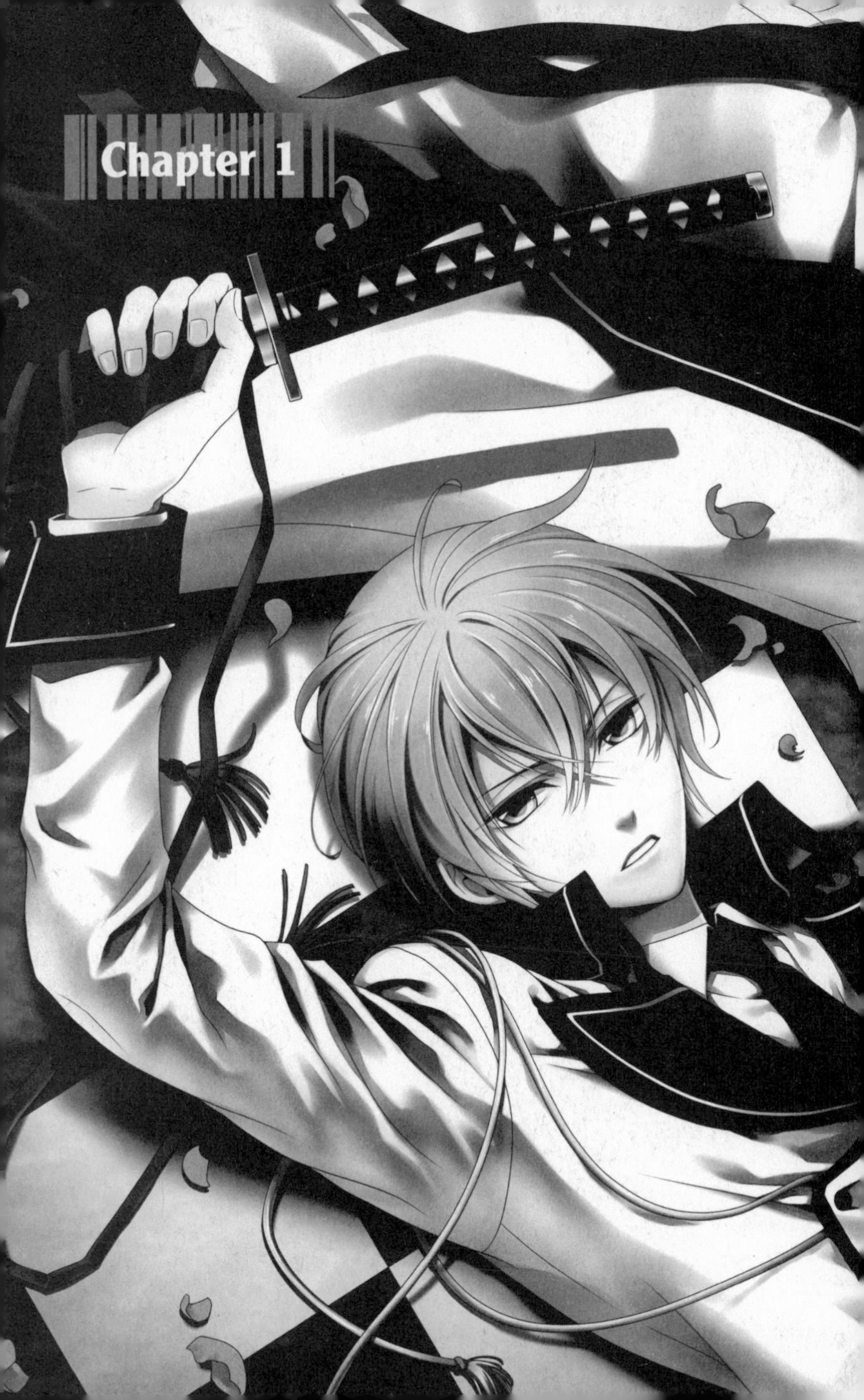
Chapter 1

HANGER

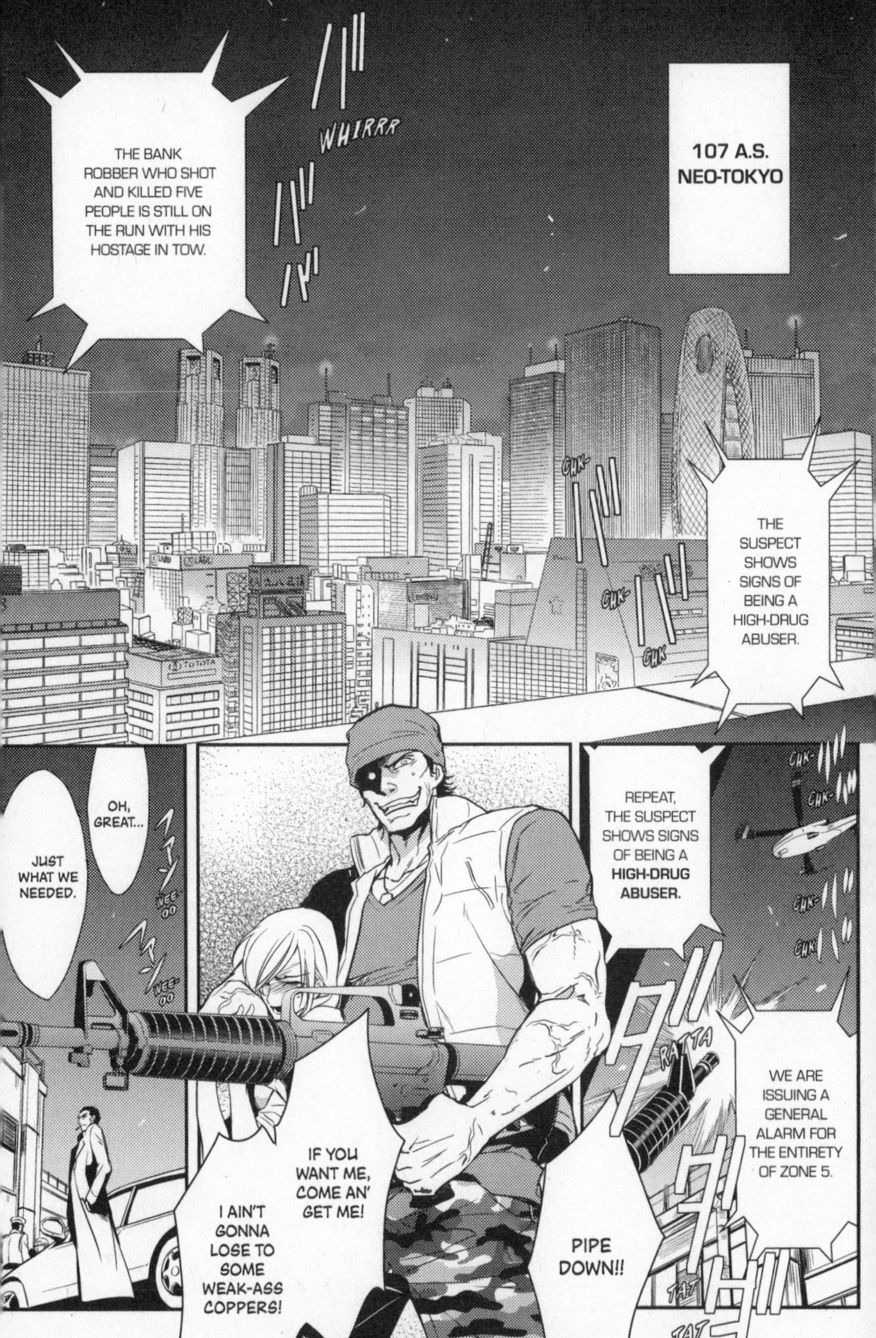
107 A.S.
NEO-TOKYO
WHIRRR
THE BANK ROBBER WHO SHOT AND KILLED FIVE PEOPLE IS STILL ON THE RUN WITH HIS HOSTAGE IN TOW.
THE SUSPECT SHOWS SIGNS OF BEING A HIGH-DRUG ABUSER.
CHK-
CHK-
CHK
REPEAT, THE SUSPECT SHOWS SIGNS OF BEING A **HIGH-DRUG ABUSER.**
CHK-
CHK-
CHK-
CHK
RATTA
WE ARE ISSUING A GENERAL ALARM FOR THE ENTIRETY OF ZONE 5.
PIPE DOWN!!
TAT
TAT
IF YOU WANT ME, COME AN' GET ME!
I AIN'T GONNA LOSE TO SOME WEAK-ASS COPPERS!
OH, GREAT...
JUST WHAT WE NEEDED.
WEE-OO
WEE-OO

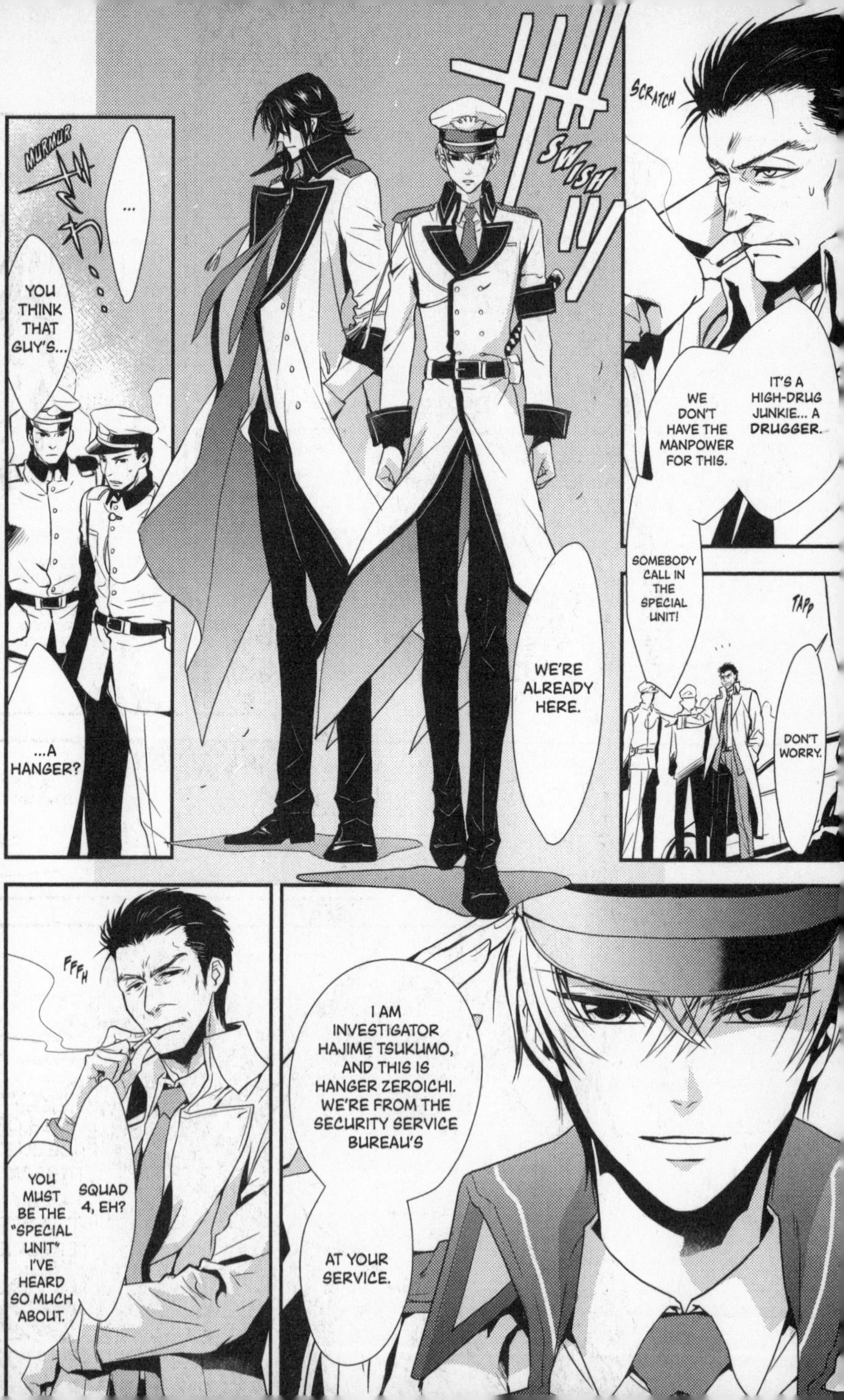
SCRATCH
IT'S A HIGH-DRUG JUNKIE... A DRUGGER.
WE DON'T HAVE THE MANPOWER FOR THIS.
SOMEBODY CALL IN THE SPECIAL UNIT!
TAPP
...
DON'T WORRY.
SWISH
WE'RE ALREADY HERE.
MURMUR
...
YOU THINK THAT GUY'S...
...A HANGER?
I AM INVESTIGATOR HAJIME TSUKUMO, AND THIS IS HANGER ZEROICHI. WE'RE FROM THE SECURITY SERVICE BUREAU'S
AT YOUR SERVICE.
FFFH
SQUAD 4, EH?
YOU MUST BE THE "SPECIAL UNIT" I'VE HEARD SO MUCH ABOUT.

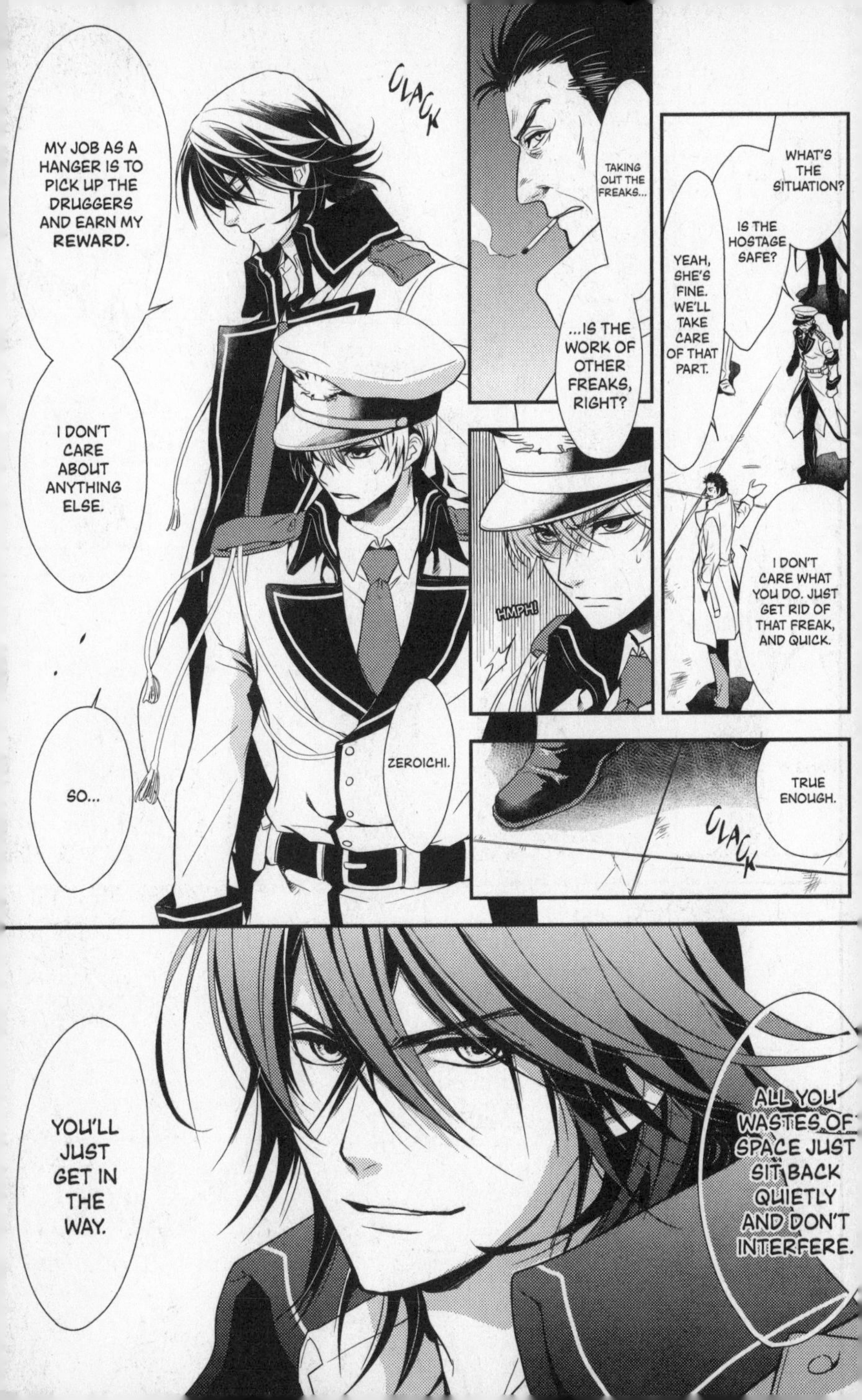
WHAT'S THE SITUATION?
IS THE HOSTAGE SAFE?
YEAH, SHE'S FINE. WE'LL TAKE CARE OF THAT PART.
I DON'T CARE WHAT YOU DO. JUST GET RID OF THAT FREAK, AND QUICK.
TAKING OUT THE FREAKS...
...IS THE WORK OF OTHER FREAKS, RIGHT?
HMPH!
TRUE ENOUGH.
CLACK
ZEROICHI.
CLACK
MY JOB AS A HANGER IS TO PICK UP THE DRUGGERS AND EARN MY REWARD.
I DON'T CARE ABOUT ANYTHING ELSE.
SO...
ALL YOU WASTES OF SPACE JUST SIT BACK QUIETLY AND DON'T INTERFERE.
YOU'LL JUST GET IN THE WAY.

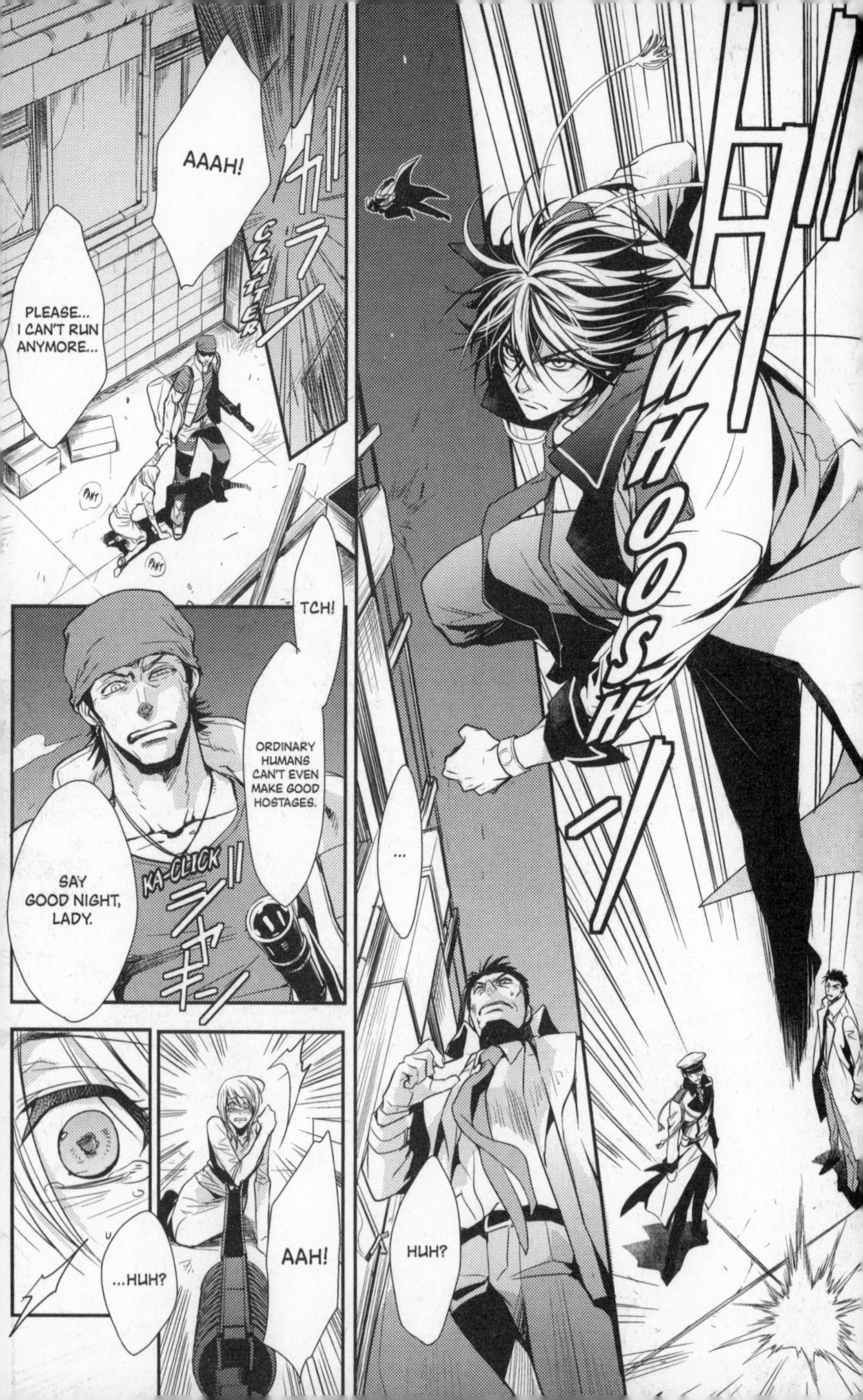
WHOOSH
...
HUH?
AAAH!
CLATTER
PLEASE... I CAN'T RUN ANYMORE...
PANT
PANT
TCH!
ORDINARY HUMANS CAN'T EVEN MAKE GOOD HOSTAGES.
KA-CLICK
SAY GOOD NIGHT, LADY.
AAH!
...HUH?

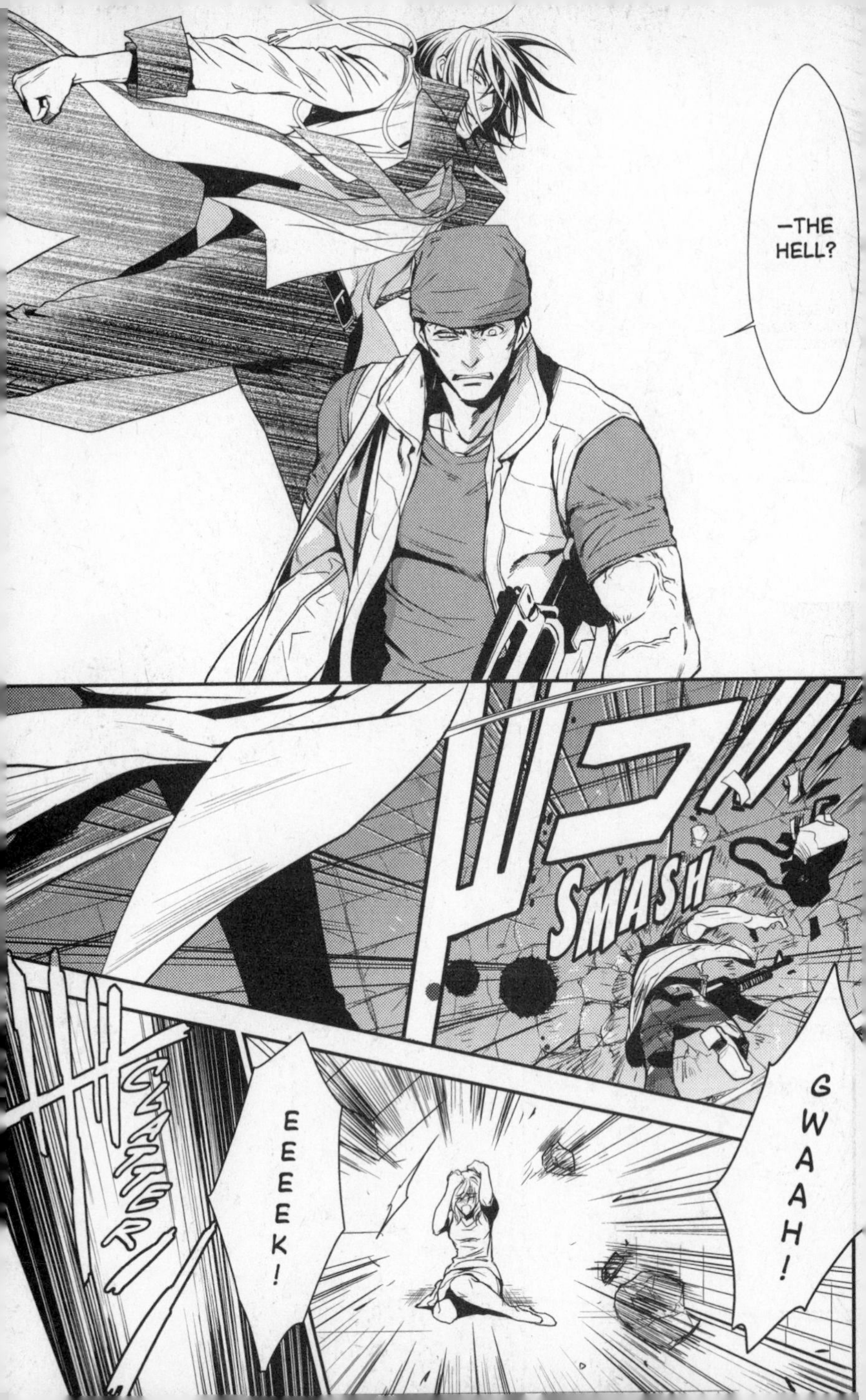
—THE HELL?
SMASH
GWAAH!
EEEEK!
CLATTER!

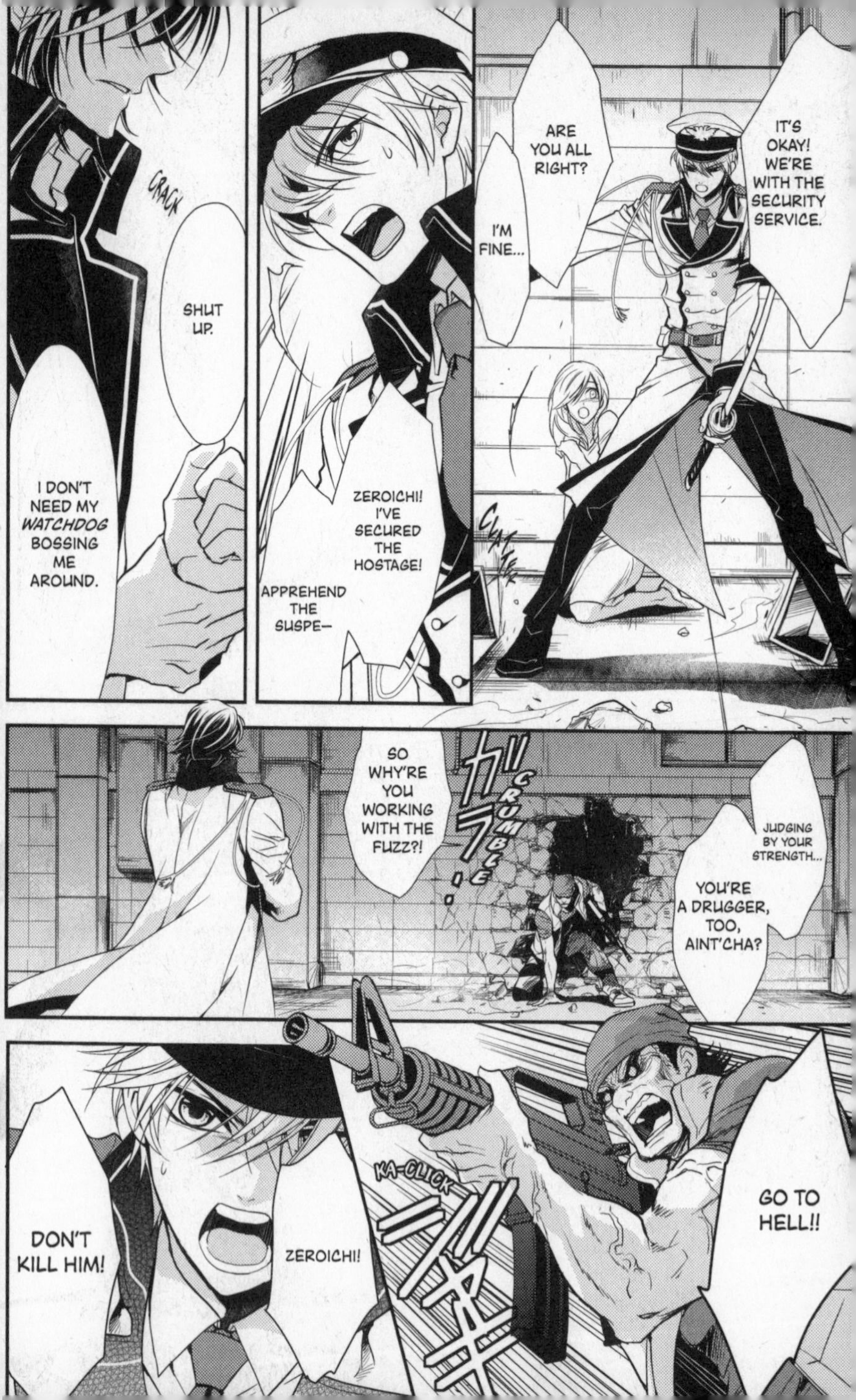
IT'S OKAY! WE'RE WITH THE SECURITY SERVICE.
ARE YOU ALL RIGHT?
I'M FINE...
CLATTER
ZEROICHI! I'VE SECURED THE HOSTAGE!
APPREHEND THE SUSPE—
CRACK
SHUT UP.
I DON'T NEED MY *WATCHDOG* BOSSING ME AROUND.
JUDGING BY YOUR STRENGTH...
YOU'RE A DRUGGER, TOO, AINT'CHA?
CRUMBLE
SO WHY'RE YOU WORKING WITH THE FUZZ?!
GO TO HELL!!
KA-CLICK
ZEROICHI!
DON'T KILL HIM!

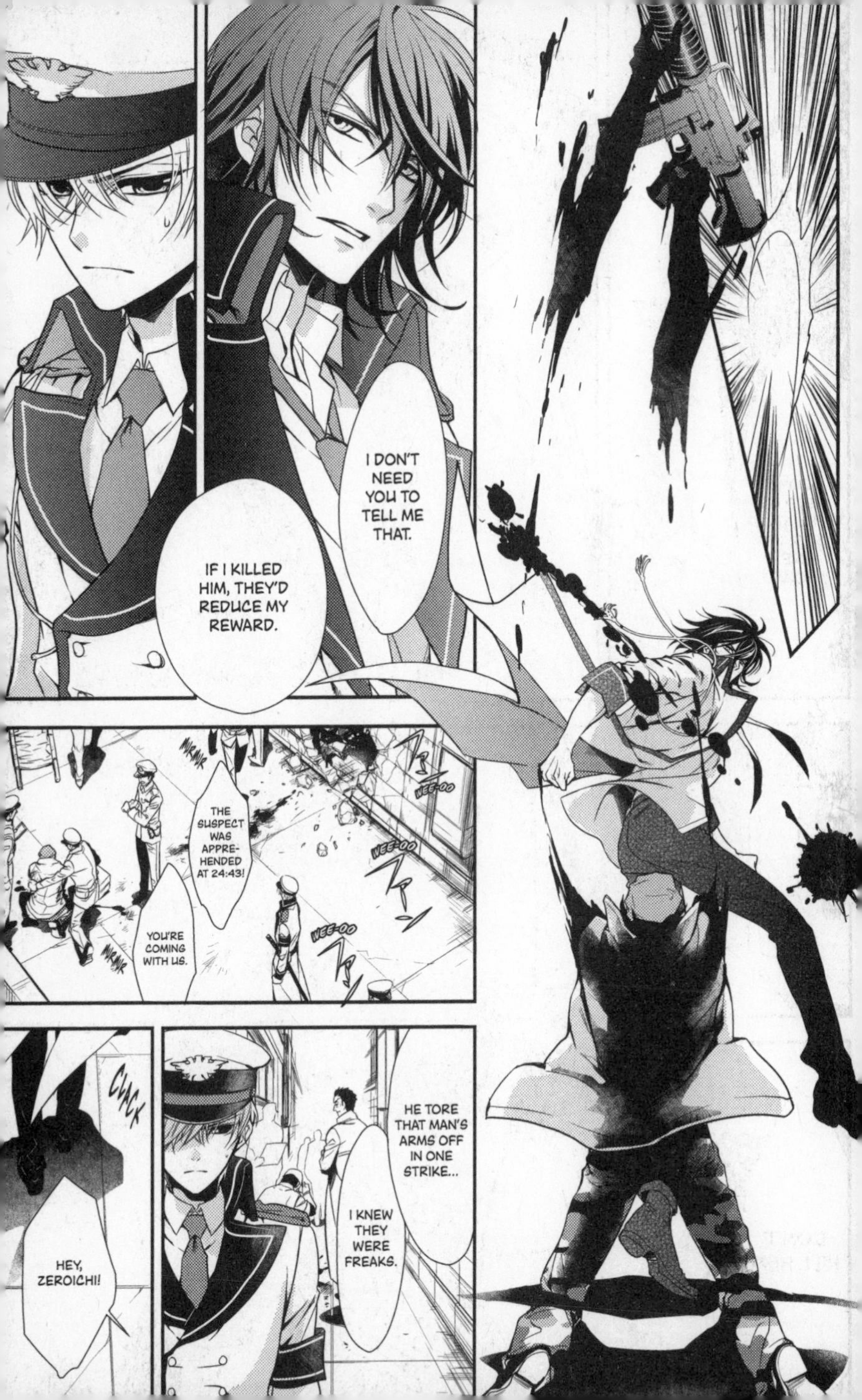
I DON'T NEED YOU TO TELL ME THAT.
IF I KILLED HIM, THEY'D REDUCE MY REWARD.
WEE-OO
WEE-OO
WEE-OO
THE SUSPECT WAS APPREHENDED AT 24:43!
MURMUR
YOU'RE COMING WITH US.
MURMUR
HE TORE THAT MAN'S ARMS OFF IN ONE STRIKE...
I KNEW THEY WERE FREAKS.
CLACK
HEY, ZEROICHI!

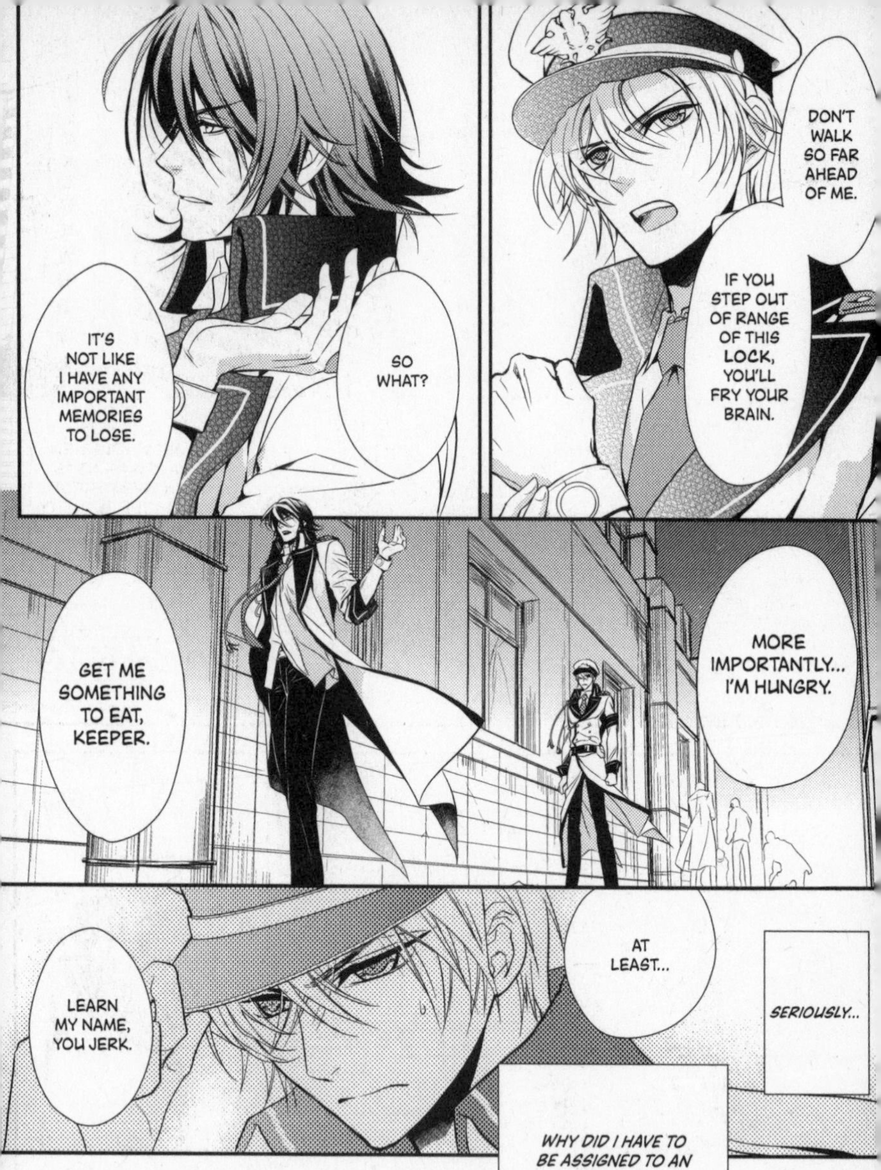
DON'T WALK SO FAR AHEAD OF ME.
IF YOU STEP OUT OF RANGE OF THIS LOCK, YOU'LL FRY YOUR BRAIN.
SO WHAT?
IT'S NOT LIKE I HAVE ANY IMPORTANT MEMORIES TO LOSE.
MORE IMPORTANTLY... I'M HUNGRY.
GET ME SOMETHING TO EAT, KEEPER.
SERIOUSLY...
AT LEAST...
LEARN MY NAME, YOU JERK.
WHY DID I HAVE TO BE ASSIGNED TO AN ASSHOLE LIKE HIM?

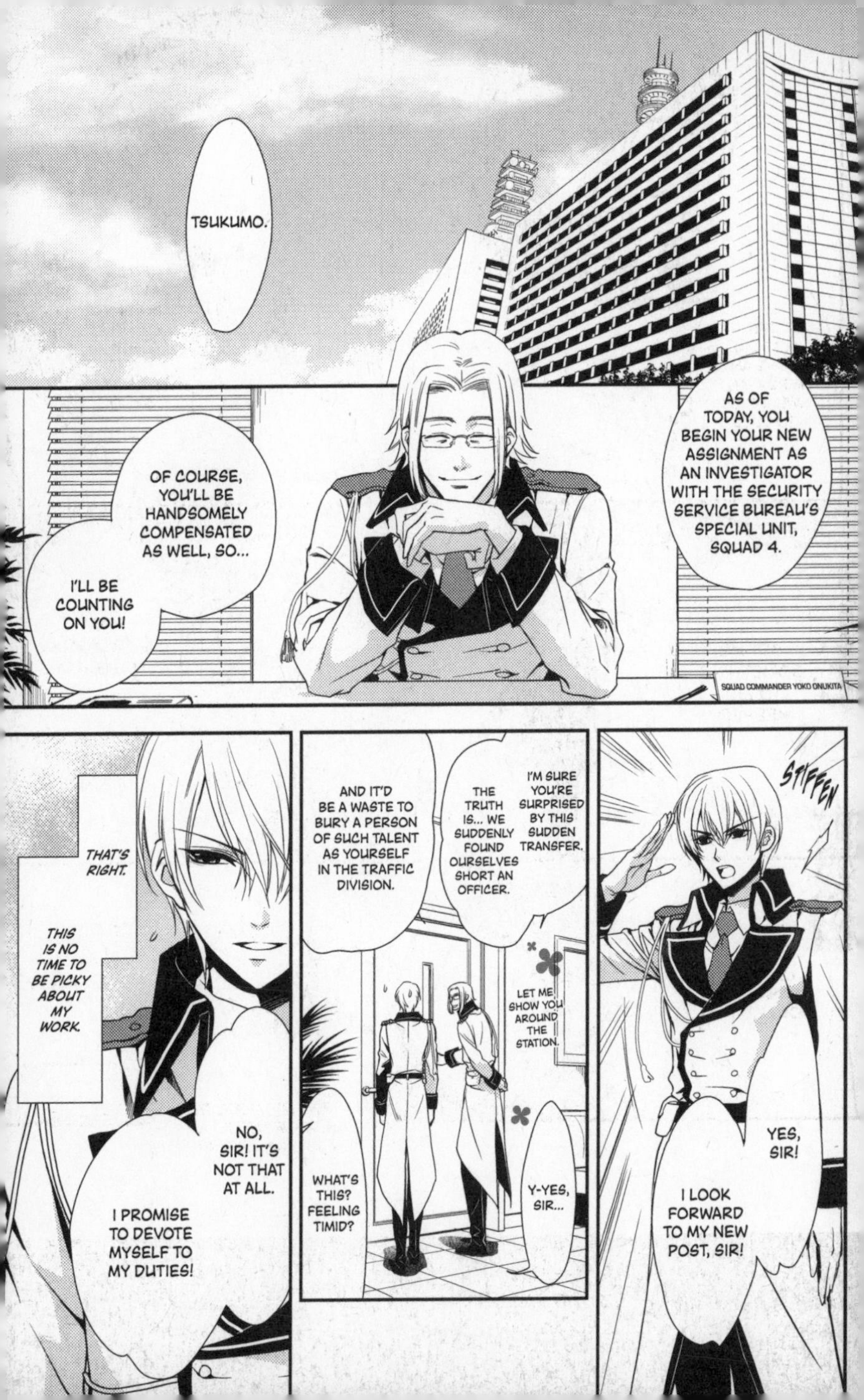
TSUKUMO.
AS OF TODAY, YOU BEGIN YOUR NEW ASSIGNMENT AS AN INVESTIGATOR WITH THE SECURITY SERVICE BUREAU'S SPECIAL UNIT, SQUAD 4.
OF COURSE, YOU'LL BE HANDSOMELY COMPENSATED AS WELL, SO...
I'LL BE COUNTING ON YOU!
SQUAD COMMANDER YOKO ONUKITA
STIFFEN
YES, SIR!
I LOOK FORWARD TO MY NEW POST, SIR!
I'M SURE YOU'RE SURPRISED BY THIS SUDDEN TRANSFER.
THE TRUTH IS... WE SUDDENLY FOUND OURSELVES SHORT AN OFFICER.
AND IT'D BE A WASTE TO BURY A PERSON OF SUCH TALENT AS YOURSELF IN THE TRAFFIC DIVISION.
LET ME SHOW YOU AROUND THE STATION.
Y-YES, SIR...
WHAT'S THIS? FEELING TIMID?
THAT'S RIGHT.
THIS IS NO TIME TO BE PICKY ABOUT MY WORK.
NO, SIR! IT'S NOT THAT AT ALL.
I PROMISE TO DEVOTE MYSELF TO MY DUTIES!

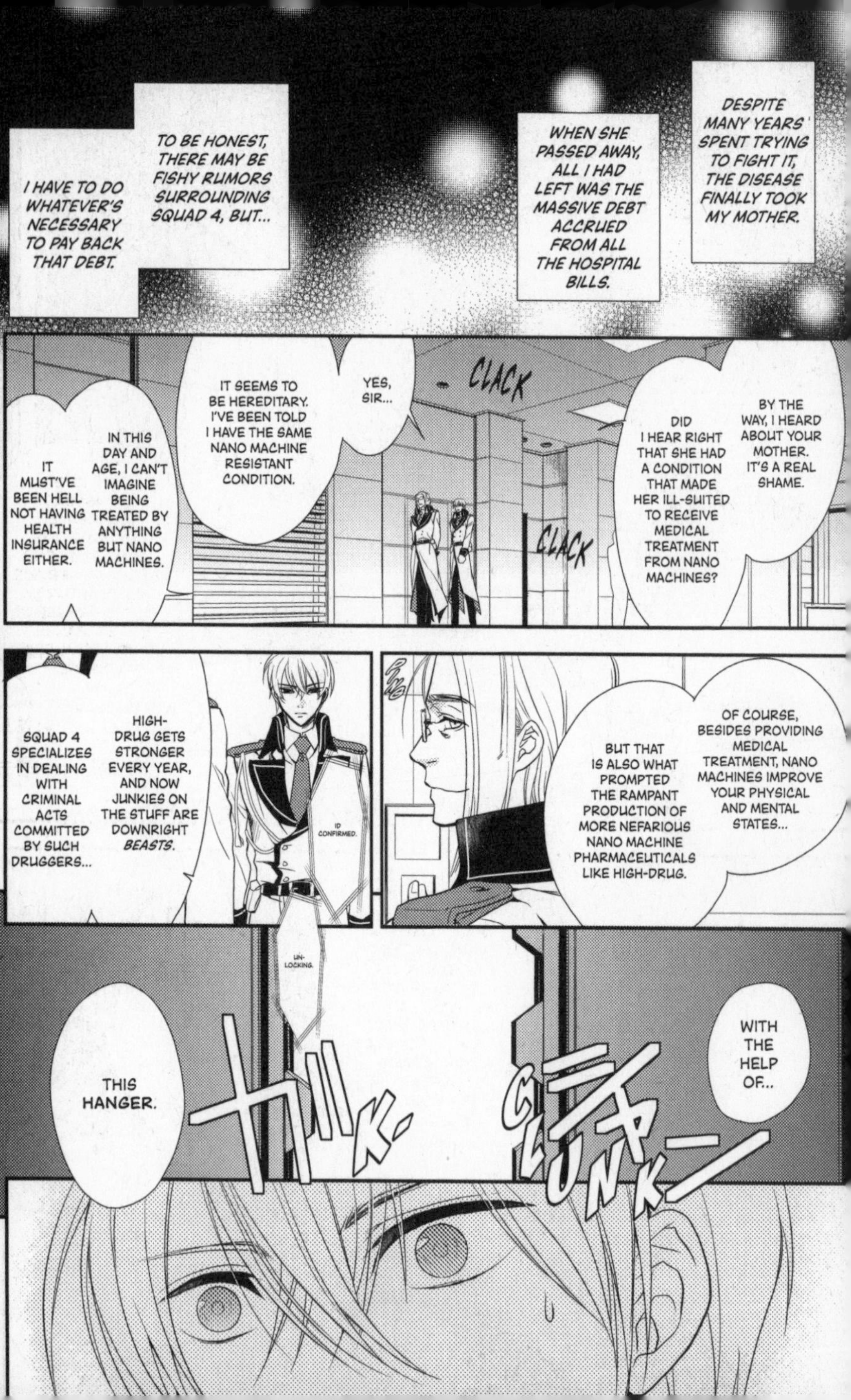
DESPITE MANY YEARS SPENT TRYING TO FIGHT IT, THE DISEASE FINALLY TOOK MY MOTHER.
WHEN SHE PASSED AWAY, ALL I HAD LEFT WAS THE MASSIVE DEBT ACCRUED FROM ALL THE HOSPITAL BILLS.
TO BE HONEST, THERE MAY BE FISHY RUMORS SURROUNDING SQUAD 4, BUT...
I HAVE TO DO WHATEVER'S NECESSARY TO PAY BACK THAT DEBT.
BY THE WAY, I HEARD ABOUT YOUR MOTHER. IT'S A REAL SHAME.
DID I HEAR RIGHT THAT SHE HAD A CONDITION THAT MADE HER ILL-SUITED TO RECEIVE MEDICAL TREATMENT FROM NANO MACHINES?
CLACK
CLACK
YES, SIR...
IT SEEMS TO BE HEREDITARY. I'VE BEEN TOLD I HAVE THE SAME NANO MACHINE RESISTANT CONDITION.
IN THIS DAY AND AGE, I CAN'T IMAGINE BEING TREATED BY ANYTHING BUT NANO MACHINES.
IT MUST'VE BEEN HELL NOT HAVING HEALTH INSURANCE EITHER.
OF COURSE, BESIDES PROVIDING MEDICAL TREATMENT, NANO MACHINES IMPROVE YOUR PHYSICAL AND MENTAL STATES...
BUT THAT IS ALSO WHAT PROMPTED THE RAMPANT PRODUCTION OF MORE NEFARIOUS NANO MACHINE PHARMACEUTICALS LIKE HIGH-DRUG.
HIGH-DRUG GETS STRONGER EVERY YEAR, AND NOW JUNKIES ON THE STUFF ARE DOWNRIGHT *BEASTS*.
SQUAD 4 SPECIALIZES IN DEALING WITH CRIMINAL ACTS COMMITTED BY SUCH DRUGGERS...
ID CONFIRMED.
WITH THE HELP OF...
CLUNK
UN-LOCKING.
K-
THIS HANGER.

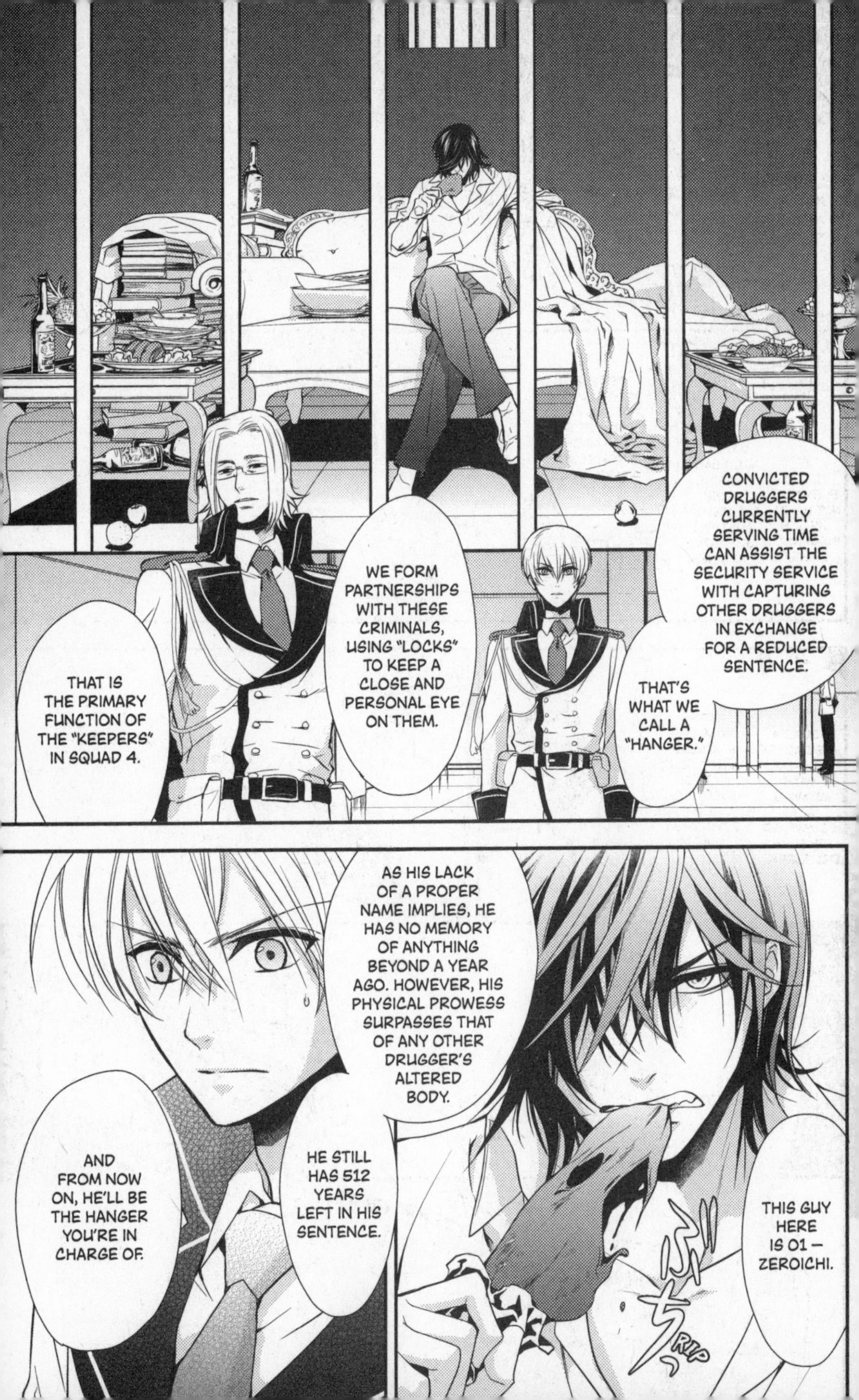

CONVICTED DRUGGERS CURRENTLY SERVING TIME CAN ASSIST THE SECURITY SERVICE WITH CAPTURING OTHER DRUGGERS IN EXCHANGE FOR A REDUCED SENTENCE.
THAT'S WHAT WE CALL A "HANGER."
WE FORM PARTNERSHIPS WITH THESE CRIMINALS, USING "LOCKS" TO KEEP A CLOSE AND PERSONAL EYE ON THEM.
THAT IS THE PRIMARY FUNCTION OF THE "KEEPERS" IN SQUAD 4.
THIS GUY HERE IS 01 — ZEROICHI.
RIP
AS HIS LACK OF A PROPER NAME IMPLIES, HE HAS NO MEMORY OF ANYTHING BEYOND A YEAR AGO. HOWEVER, HIS PHYSICAL PROWESS SURPASSES THAT OF ANY OTHER DRUGGER'S ALTERED BODY.
HE STILL HAS 512 YEARS LEFT IN HIS SENTENCE.
AND FROM NOW ON, HE'LL BE THE HANGER YOU'RE IN CHARGE OF.

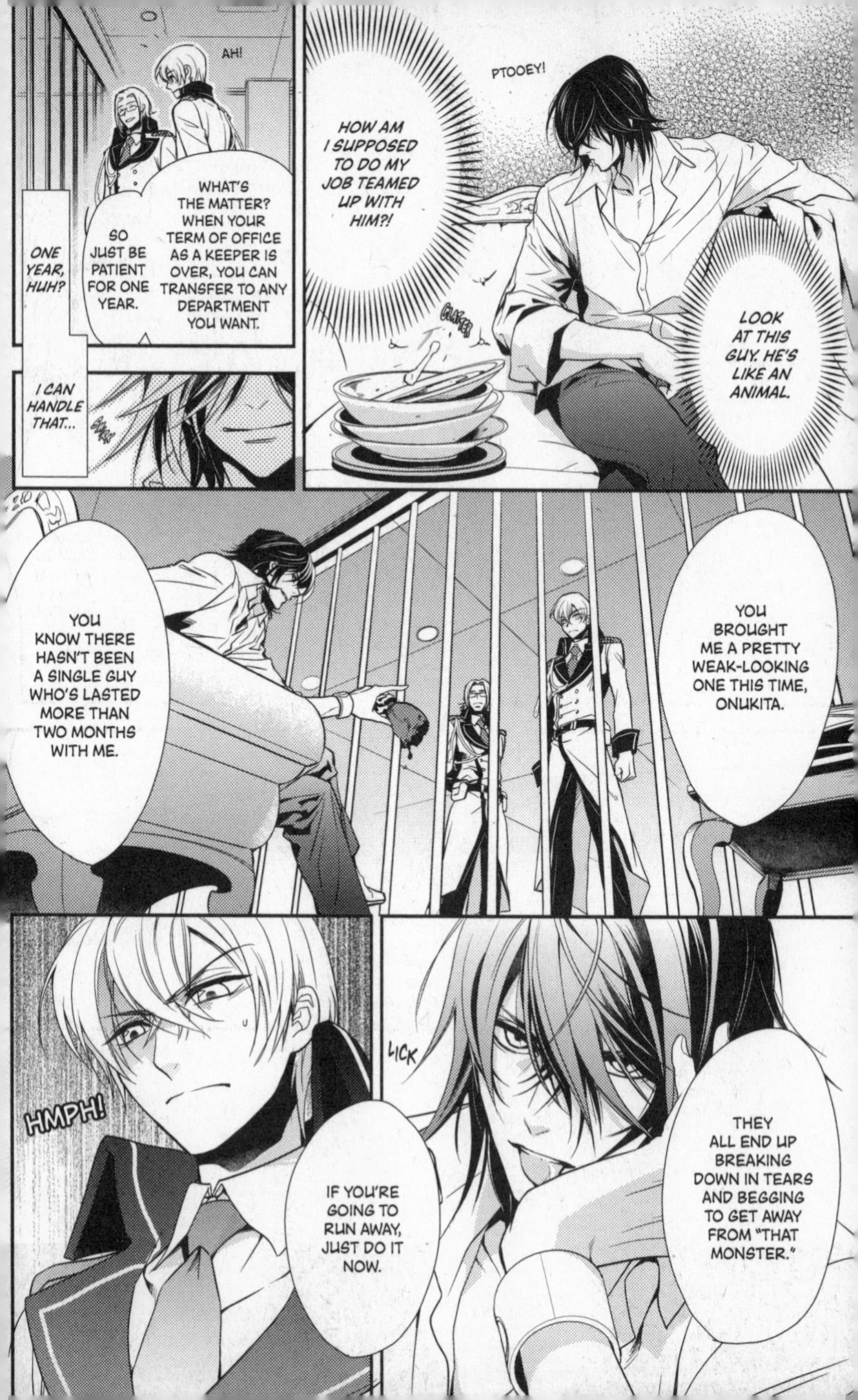
PTOOEY!
HOW AM I SUPPOSED TO DO MY JOB TEAMED UP WITH HIM?!
LOOK AT THIS GUY. HE'S LIKE AN ANIMAL.
CLATTER
AH!
WHAT'S THE MATTER? WHEN YOUR TERM OF OFFICE AS A KEEPER IS OVER, YOU CAN TRANSFER TO ANY DEPARTMENT YOU WANT.
SO JUST BE PATIENT FOR ONE YEAR.
ONE YEAR, HUH?
I CAN HANDLE THAT...
YOU BROUGHT ME A PRETTY WEAK-LOOKING ONE THIS TIME, ONUKITA.
YOU KNOW THERE HASN'T BEEN A SINGLE GUY WHO'S LASTED MORE THAN TWO MONTHS WITH ME.
LICK
THEY ALL END UP BREAKING DOWN IN TEARS AND BEGGING TO GET AWAY FROM "THAT MONSTER."
IF YOU'RE GOING TO RUN AWAY, JUST DO IT NOW.
HMPH!

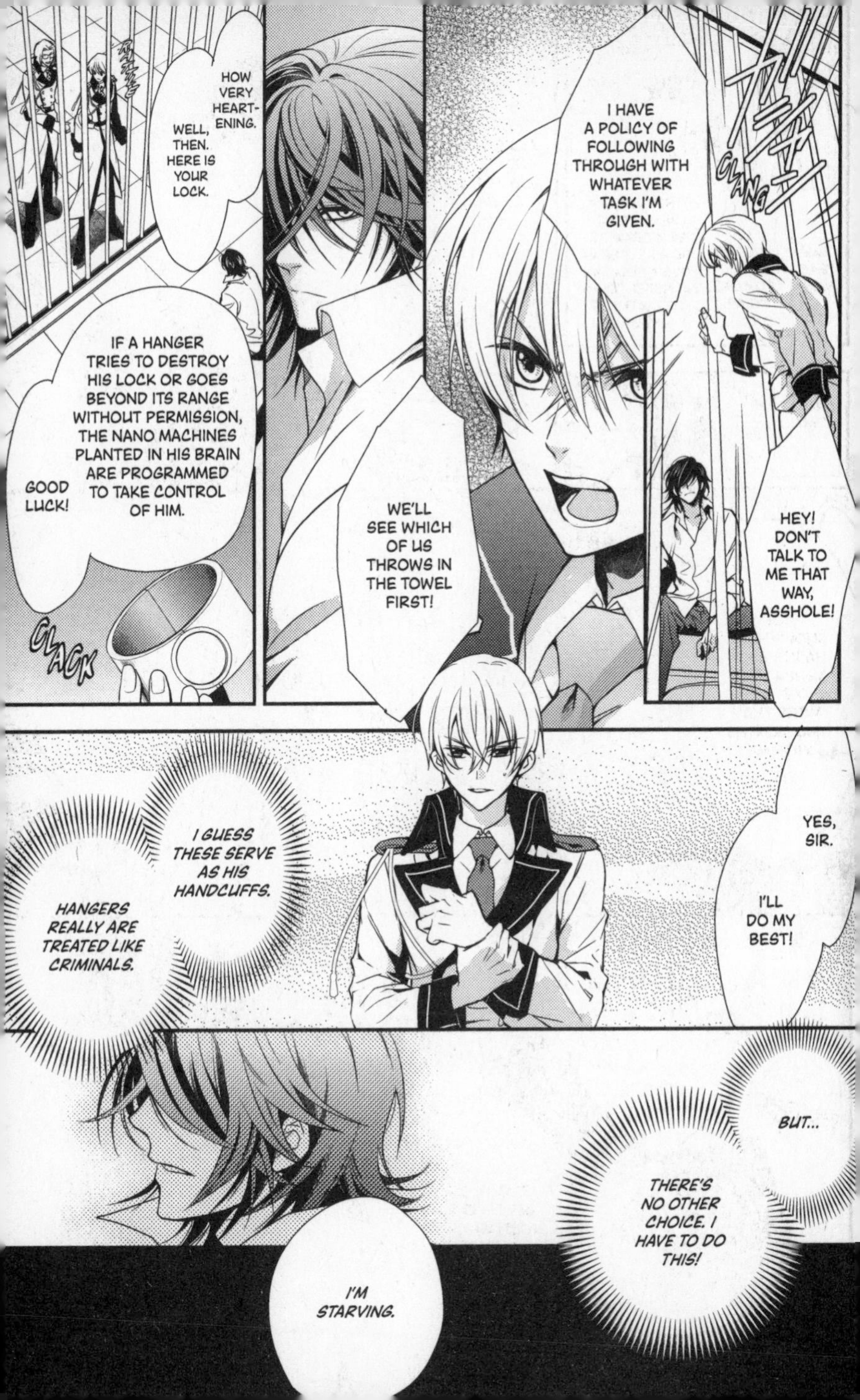
GWANG
I HAVE A POLICY OF FOLLOWING THROUGH WITH WHATEVER TASK I'M GIVEN.
HEY! DON'T TALK TO ME THAT WAY, ASSHOLE!
WE'LL SEE WHICH OF US THROWS IN THE TOWEL FIRST!
HOW VERY HEART-ENING.
WELL, THEN. HERE IS YOUR LOCK.
IF A HANGER TRIES TO DESTROY HIS LOCK OR GOES BEYOND ITS RANGE WITHOUT PERMISSION, THE NANO MACHINES PLANTED IN HIS BRAIN ARE PROGRAMMED TO TAKE CONTROL OF HIM.
GOOD LUCK!
CLACK
YES, SIR.
I'LL DO MY BEST!
I GUESS THESE SERVE AS HIS HANDCUFFS.
HANGERS REALLY ARE TREATED LIKE CRIMINALS.
BUT...
THERE'S NO OTHER CHOICE. I HAVE TO DO THIS!
I'M STARVING.

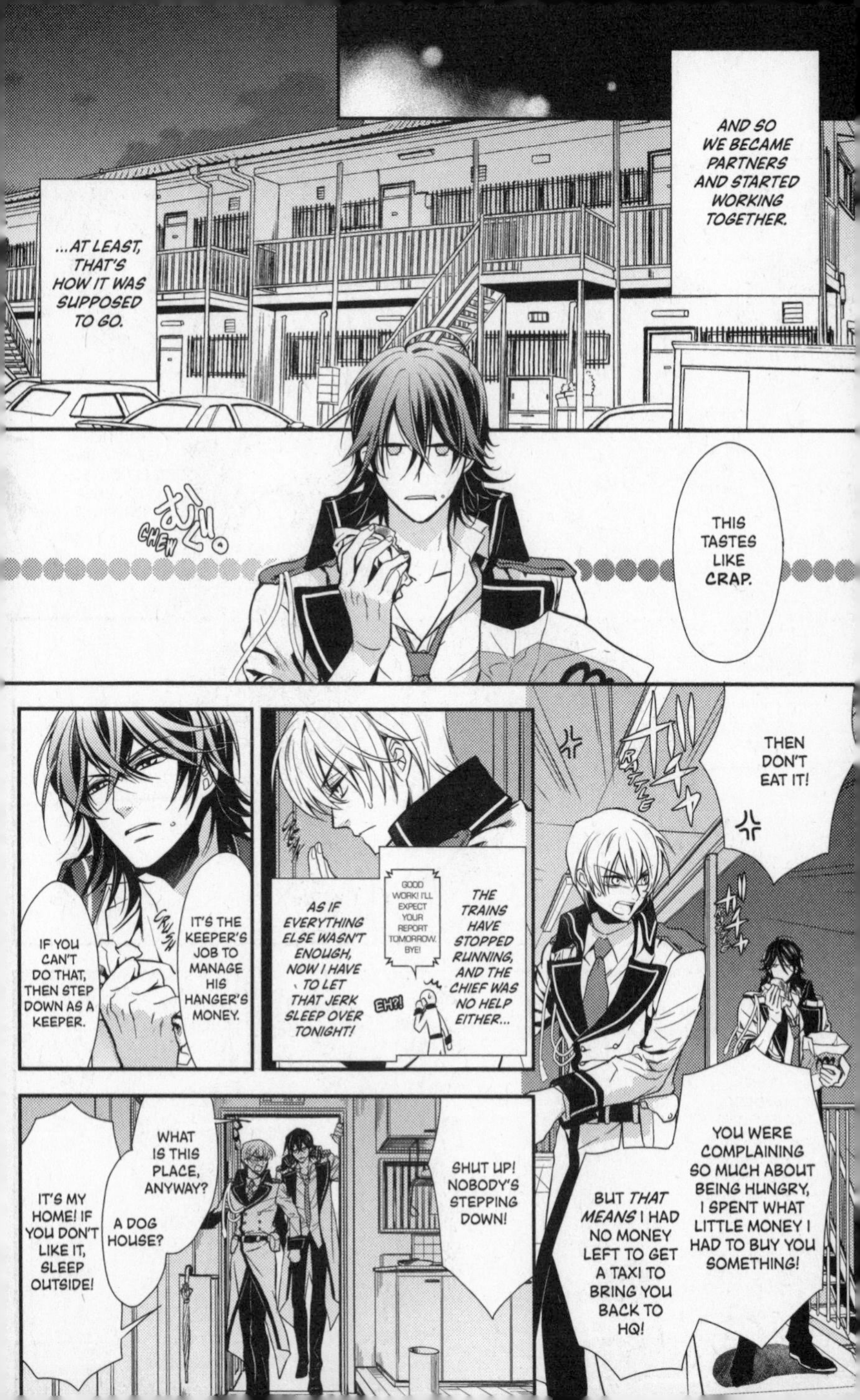
AND SO WE BECAME PARTNERS AND STARTED WORKING TOGETHER.
...AT LEAST, THAT'S HOW IT WAS SUPPOSED TO GO.
THIS TASTES LIKE CRAP.
むぐ!!
CHEW
THEN DON'T EAT IT!
RATTLE
YOU WERE COMPLAINING SO MUCH ABOUT BEING HUNGRY, I SPENT WHAT LITTLE MONEY I HAD TO BUY YOU SOMETHING!
BUT *THAT MEANS* I HAD NO MONEY LEFT TO GET A TAXI TO BRING YOU BACK TO HQ!
THE TRAINS HAVE STOPPED RUNNING, AND THE CHIEF WAS NO HELP EITHER...
GOOD WORK! I'LL EXPECT YOUR REPORT TOMORROW. BYE!
EH?!
AS IF EVERYTHING ELSE WASN'T ENOUGH, NOW I HAVE TO LET THAT JERK SLEEP OVER TONIGHT!
IT'S THE KEEPER'S JOB TO MANAGE HIS HANGER'S MONEY.
CRUSH
IF YOU CAN'T DO THAT, THEN STEP DOWN AS A KEEPER.
SHUT UP! NOBODY'S STEPPING DOWN!
WHAT IS THIS PLACE, ANYWAY?
A DOG HOUSE?
IT'S MY HOME! IF YOU DON'T LIKE IT, SLEEP OUTSIDE!

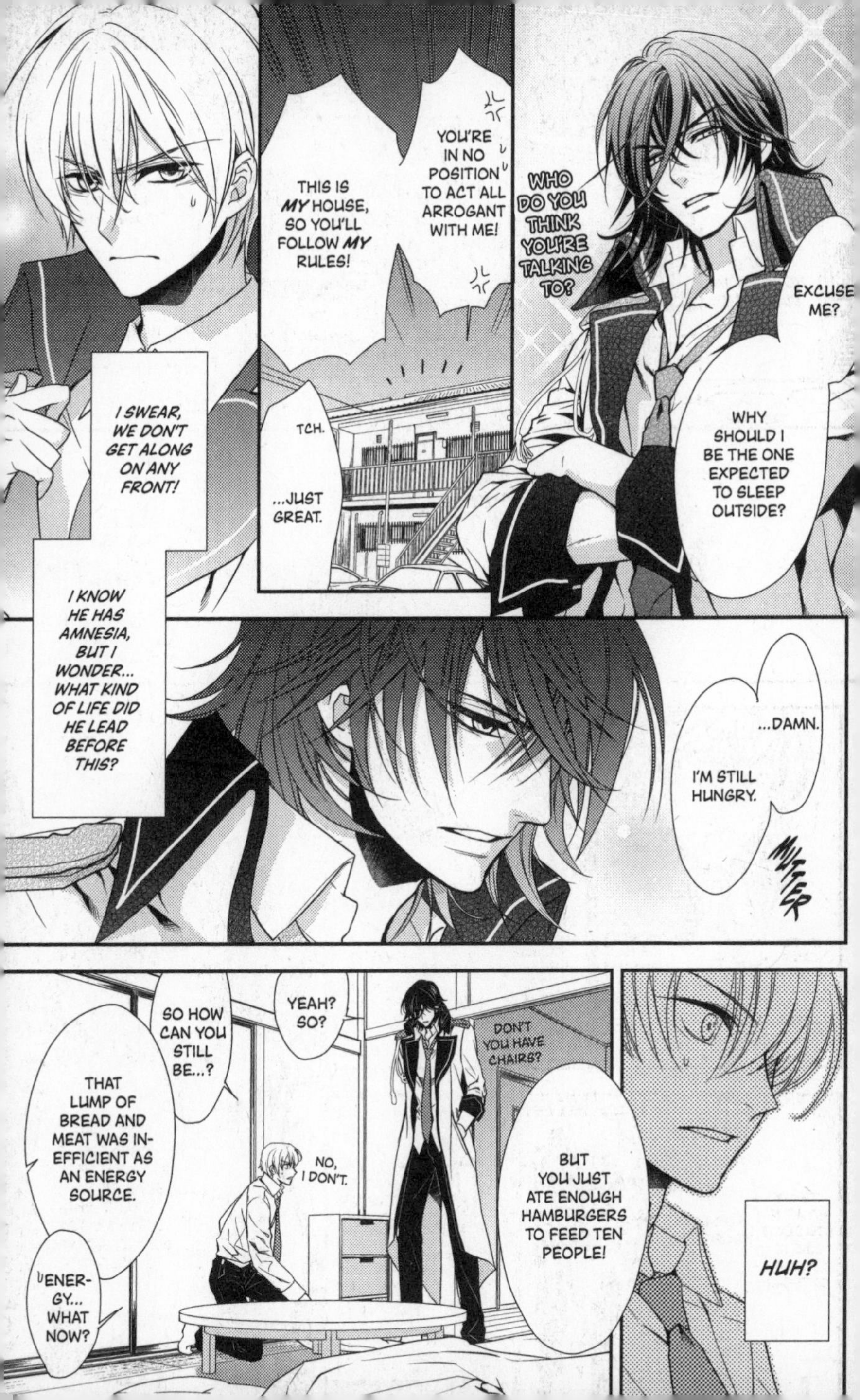
EXCUSE ME?
WHY SHOULD I BE THE ONE EXPECTED TO SLEEP OUTSIDE?
WHO DO YOU THINK YOU'RE TALKING TO?
YOU'RE IN NO POSITION TO ACT ALL ARROGANT WITH ME!
THIS IS *MY* HOUSE, SO YOU'LL FOLLOW *MY* RULES!
TCH.
...JUST GREAT.
I SWEAR, WE DON'T GET ALONG ON ANY FRONT!
...DAMN.
I'M STILL HUNGRY.
MUTTER
I KNOW HE HAS AMNESIA, BUT I WONDER... WHAT KIND OF LIFE DID HE LEAD BEFORE THIS?
HUH?
DON'T YOU HAVE CHAIRS?
NO, I DON'T.
BUT YOU JUST ATE ENOUGH HAMBURGERS TO FEED TEN PEOPLE!
YEAH? SO?
SO HOW CAN YOU STILL BE...?
THAT LUMP OF BREAD AND MEAT WAS IN-EFFICIENT AS AN ENERGY SOURCE.
ENER-GY... WHAT NOW?

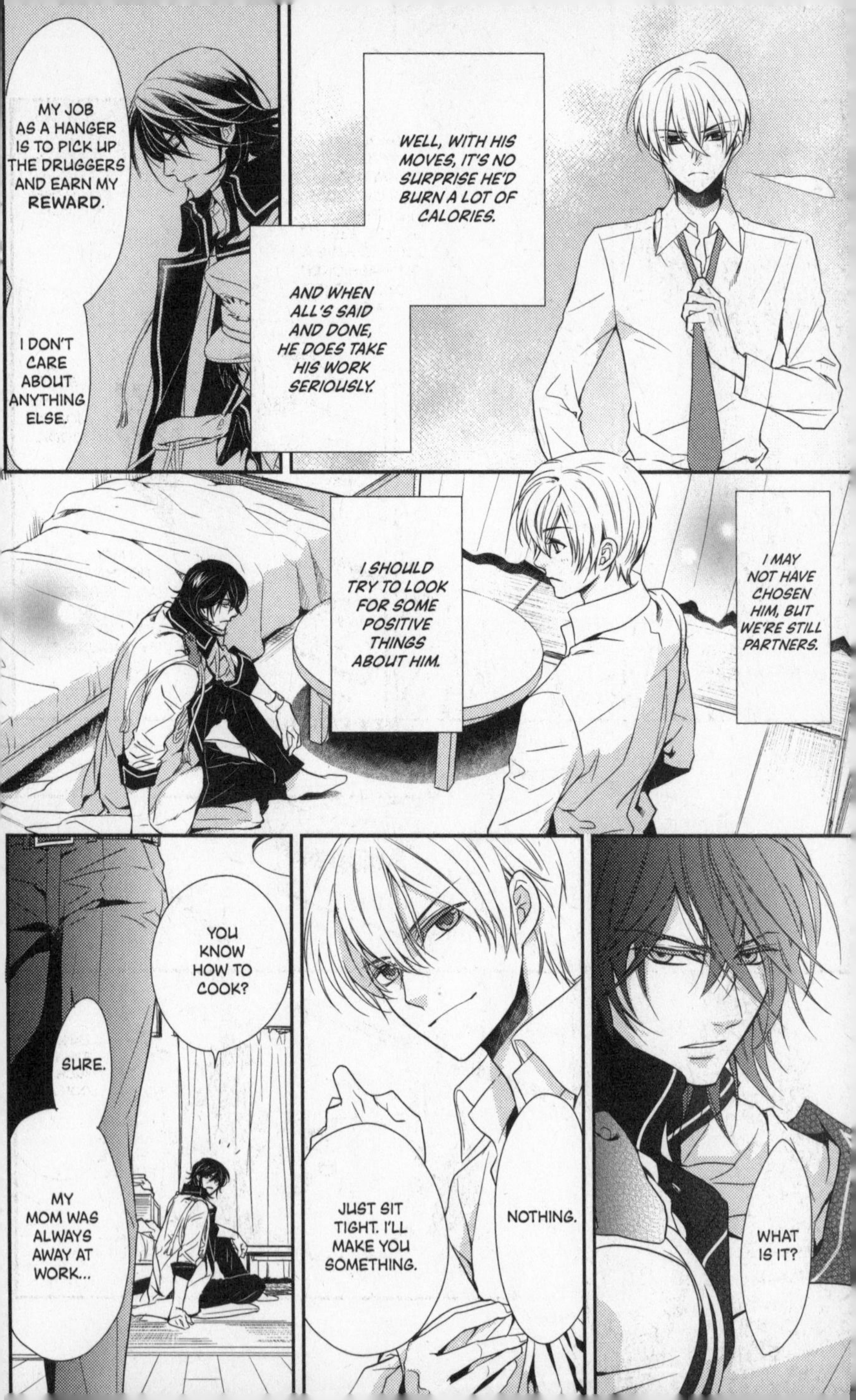
WELL, WITH HIS MOVES, IT'S NO SURPRISE HE'D BURN A LOT OF CALORIES.
AND WHEN ALL'S SAID AND DONE, HE DOES TAKE HIS WORK SERIOUSLY.
MY JOB AS A HANGER IS TO PICK UP THE DRUGGERS AND EARN MY REWARD.
I DON'T CARE ABOUT ANYTHING ELSE.
I MAY NOT HAVE CHOSEN HIM, BUT WE'RE STILL PARTNERS.
I SHOULD TRY TO LOOK FOR SOME POSITIVE THINGS ABOUT HIM.
WHAT IS IT?
NOTHING.
JUST SIT TIGHT. I'LL MAKE YOU SOMETHING.
YOU KNOW HOW TO COOK?
SURE.
MY MOM WAS ALWAYS AWAY AT WORK...

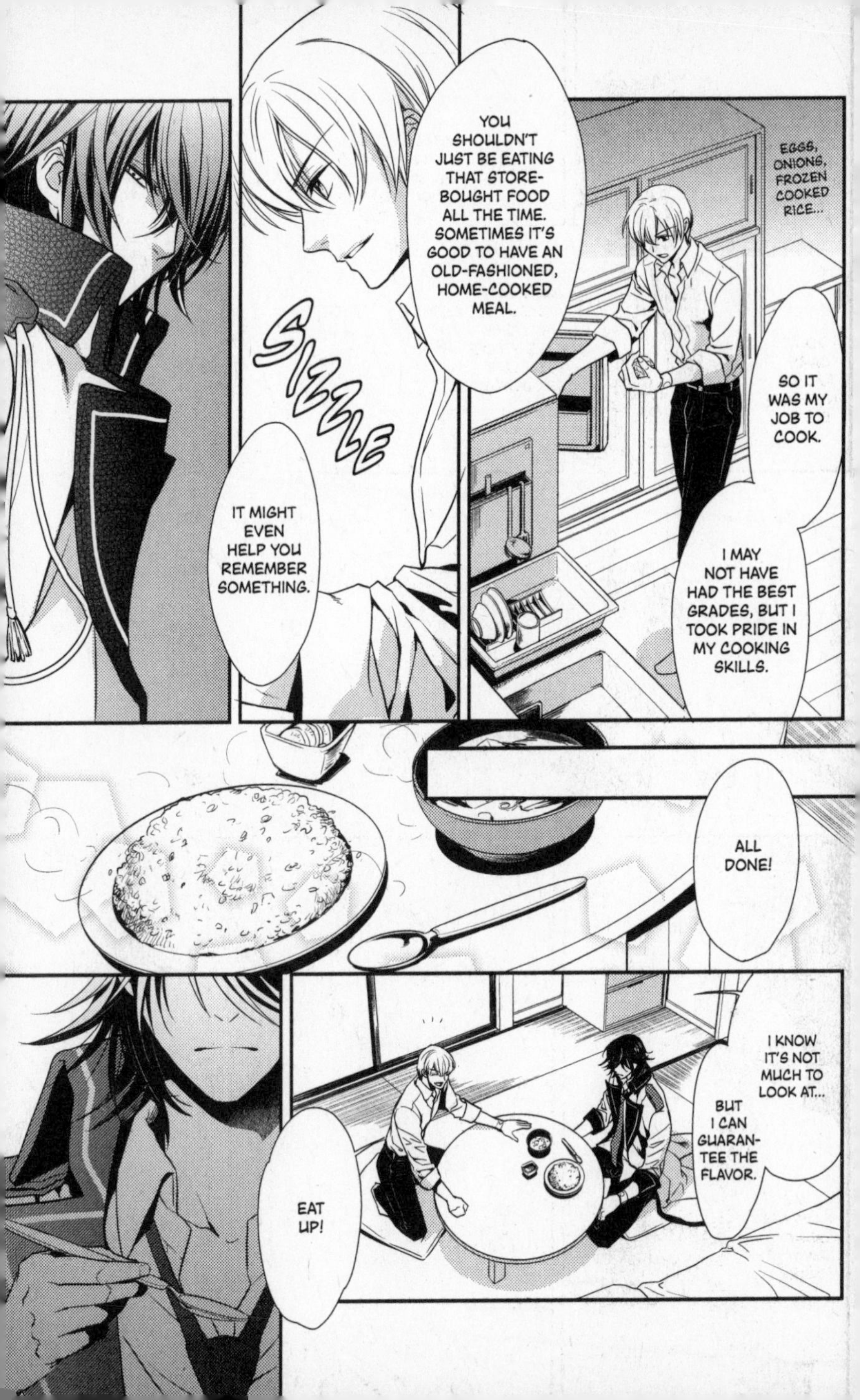
EGGS, ONIONS, FROZEN COOKED RICE...
SO IT WAS MY JOB TO COOK.
I MAY NOT HAVE HAD THE BEST GRADES, BUT I TOOK PRIDE IN MY COOKING SKILLS.
YOU SHOULDN'T JUST BE EATING THAT STORE-BOUGHT FOOD ALL THE TIME. SOMETIMES IT'S GOOD TO HAVE AN OLD-FASHIONED, HOME-COOKED MEAL.
SIZZLE
IT MIGHT EVEN HELP YOU REMEMBER SOMETHING.
ALL DONE!
I KNOW IT'S NOT MUCH TO LOOK AT...
BUT I CAN GUARANTEE THE FLAVOR.
EAT UP!

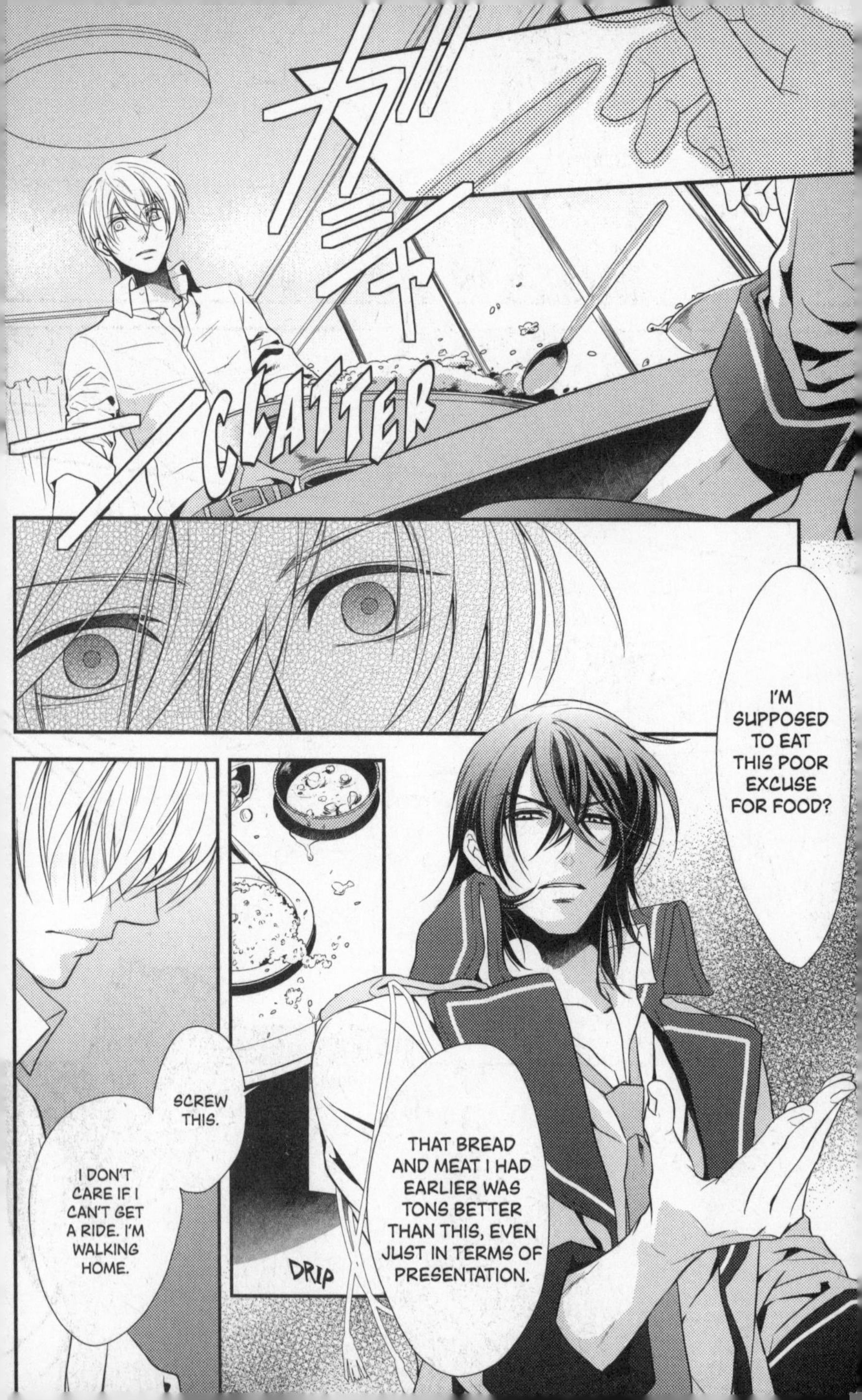
CLATTER
I'M SUPPOSED TO EAT THIS POOR EXCUSE FOR FOOD?
THAT BREAD AND MEAT I HAD EARLIER WAS TONS BETTER THAN THIS, EVEN JUST IN TERMS OF PRESENTATION.
DRIP
SCREW THIS.
I DON'T CARE IF I CAN'T GET A RIDE. I'M WALKING HOME.

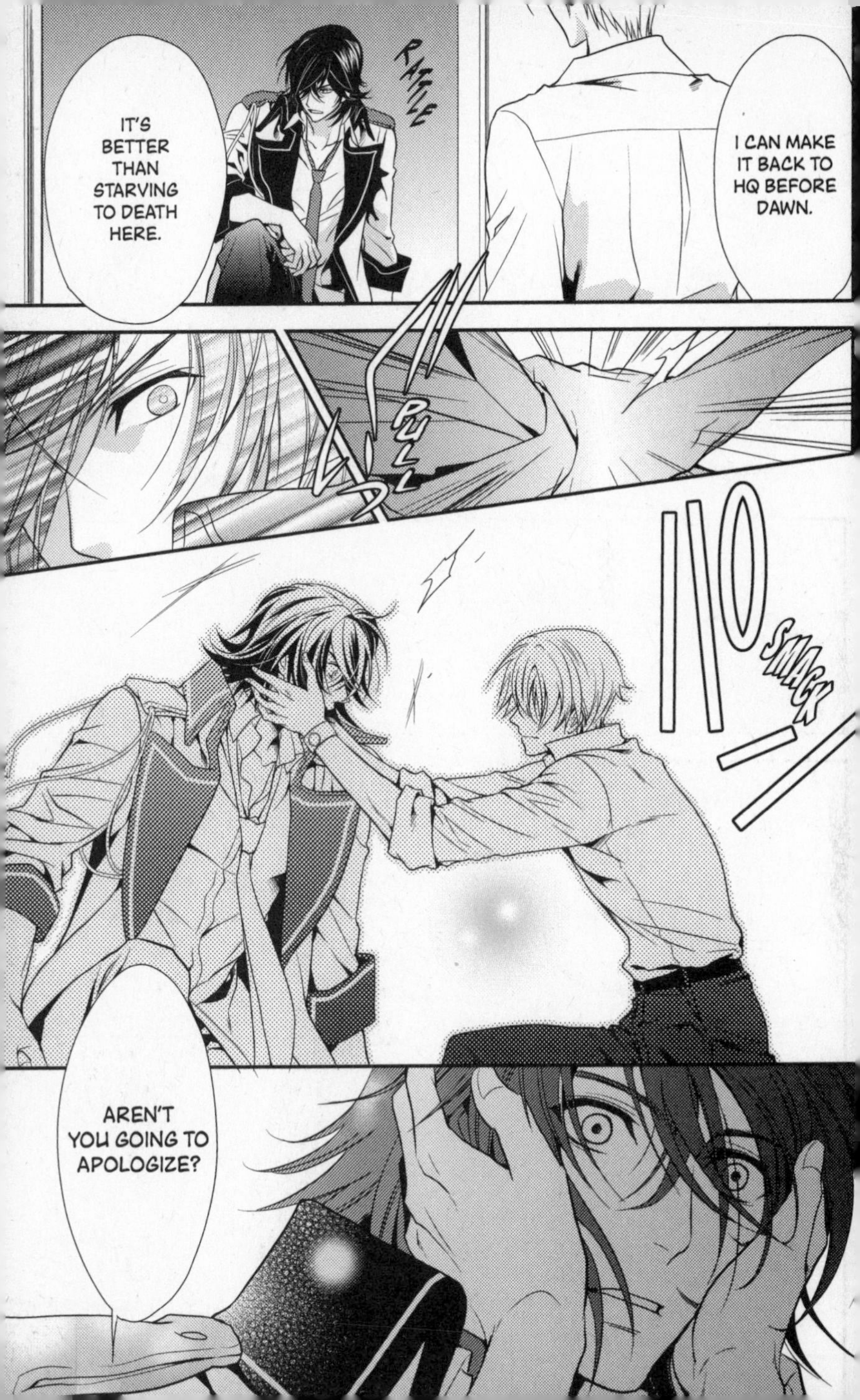
I CAN MAKE IT BACK TO HQ BEFORE DAWN.
RATTLE
IT'S BETTER THAN STARVING TO DEATH HERE.
PULL
SMACK
AREN'T YOU GOING TO APOLOGIZE?

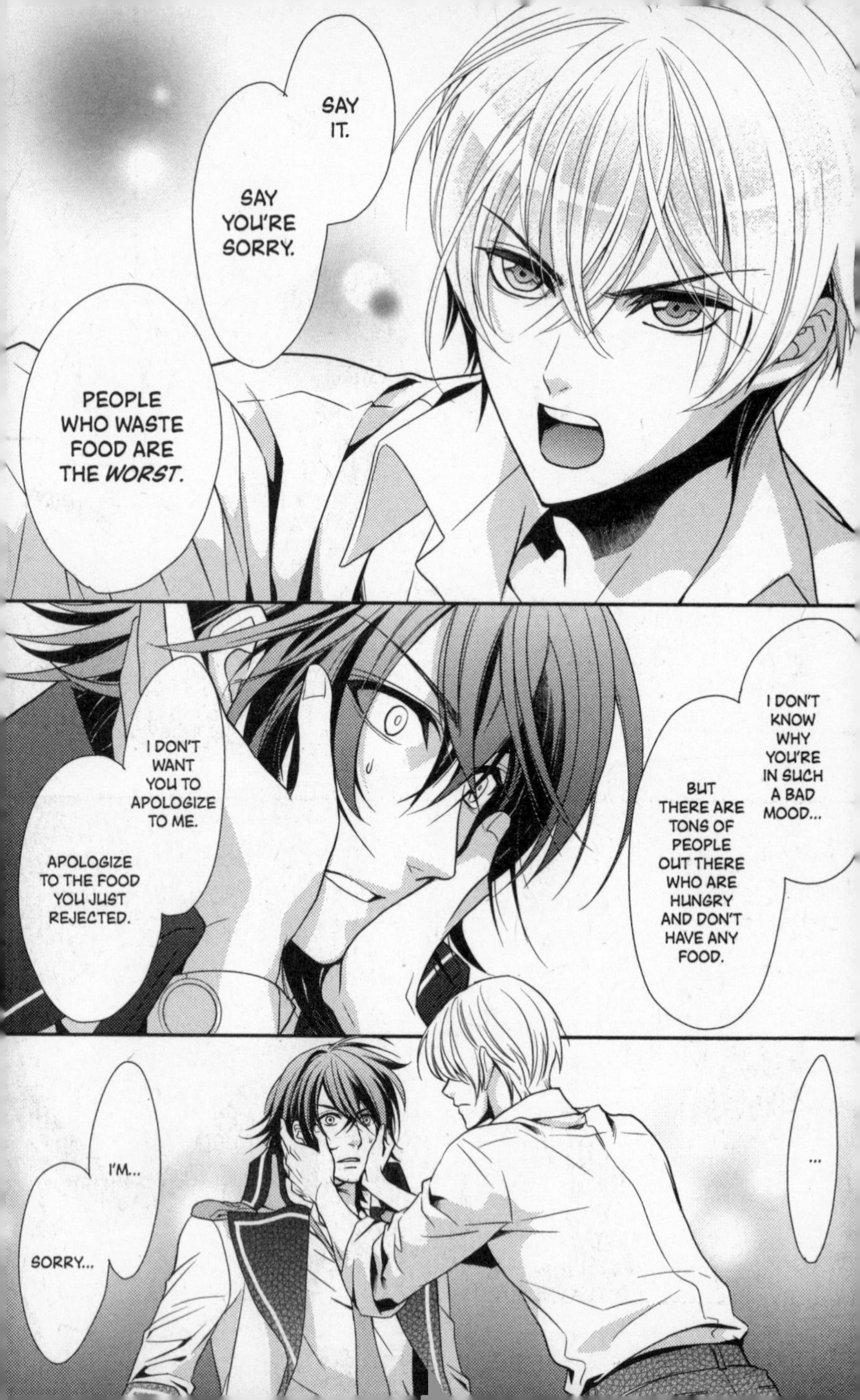
SAY IT.
SAY YOU'RE SORRY.
PEOPLE WHO WASTE FOOD ARE THE *WORST*.
I DON'T KNOW WHY YOU'RE IN SUCH A BAD MOOD...
BUT THERE ARE TONS OF PEOPLE OUT THERE WHO ARE HUNGRY AND DON'T HAVE ANY FOOD.
I DON'T WANT YOU TO APOLOGIZE TO ME.
APOLOGIZE TO THE FOOD YOU JUST REJECTED.
...
I'M...
SORRY...

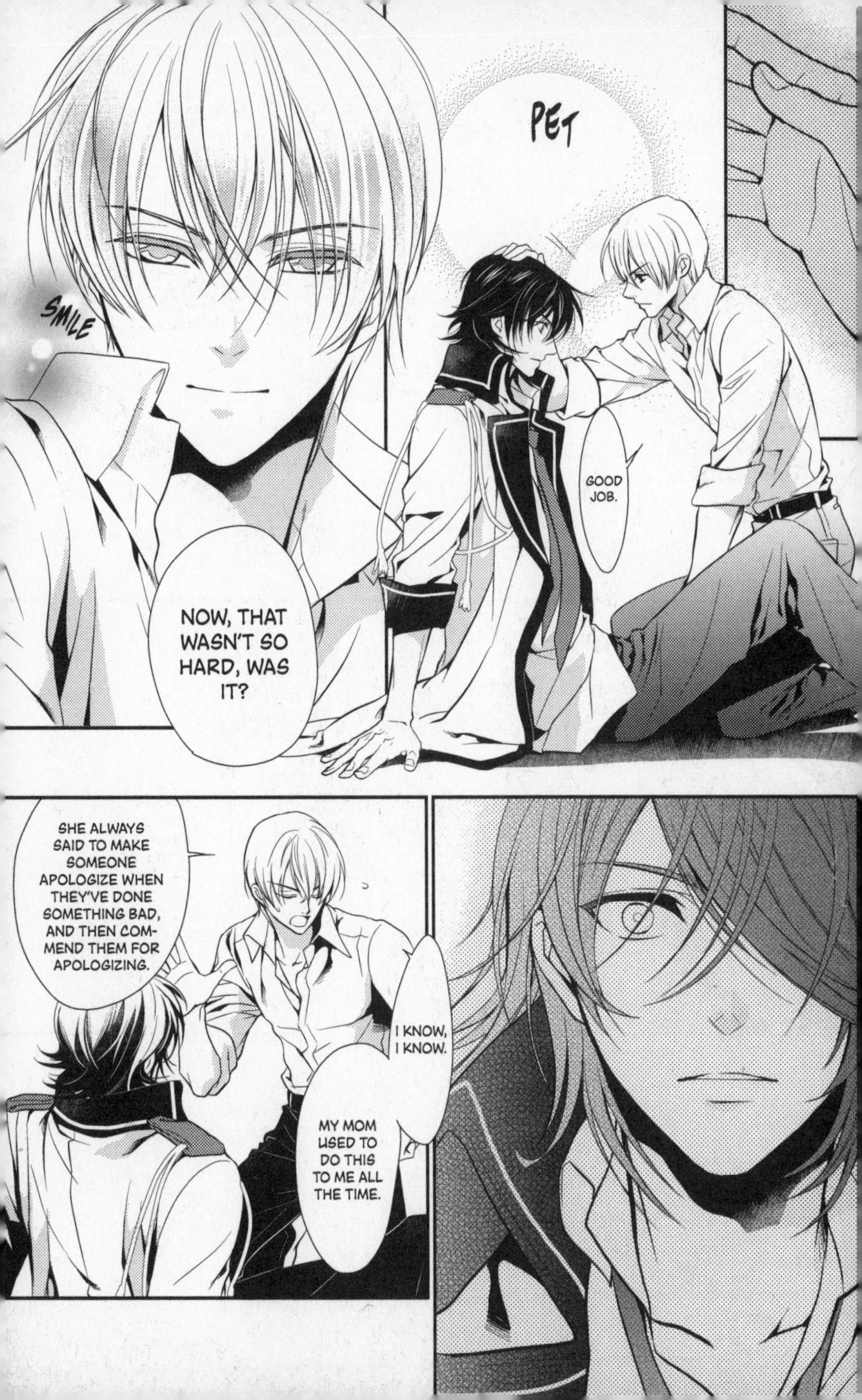
PET
GOOD JOB.
SMILE
NOW, THAT WASN'T SO HARD, WAS IT?
I KNOW, I KNOW.
MY MOM USED TO DO THIS TO ME ALL THE TIME.
SHE ALWAYS SAID TO MAKE SOMEONE APOLOGIZE WHEN THEY'VE DONE SOMETHING BAD, AND THEN COM-MEND THEM FOR APOLOGIZING.

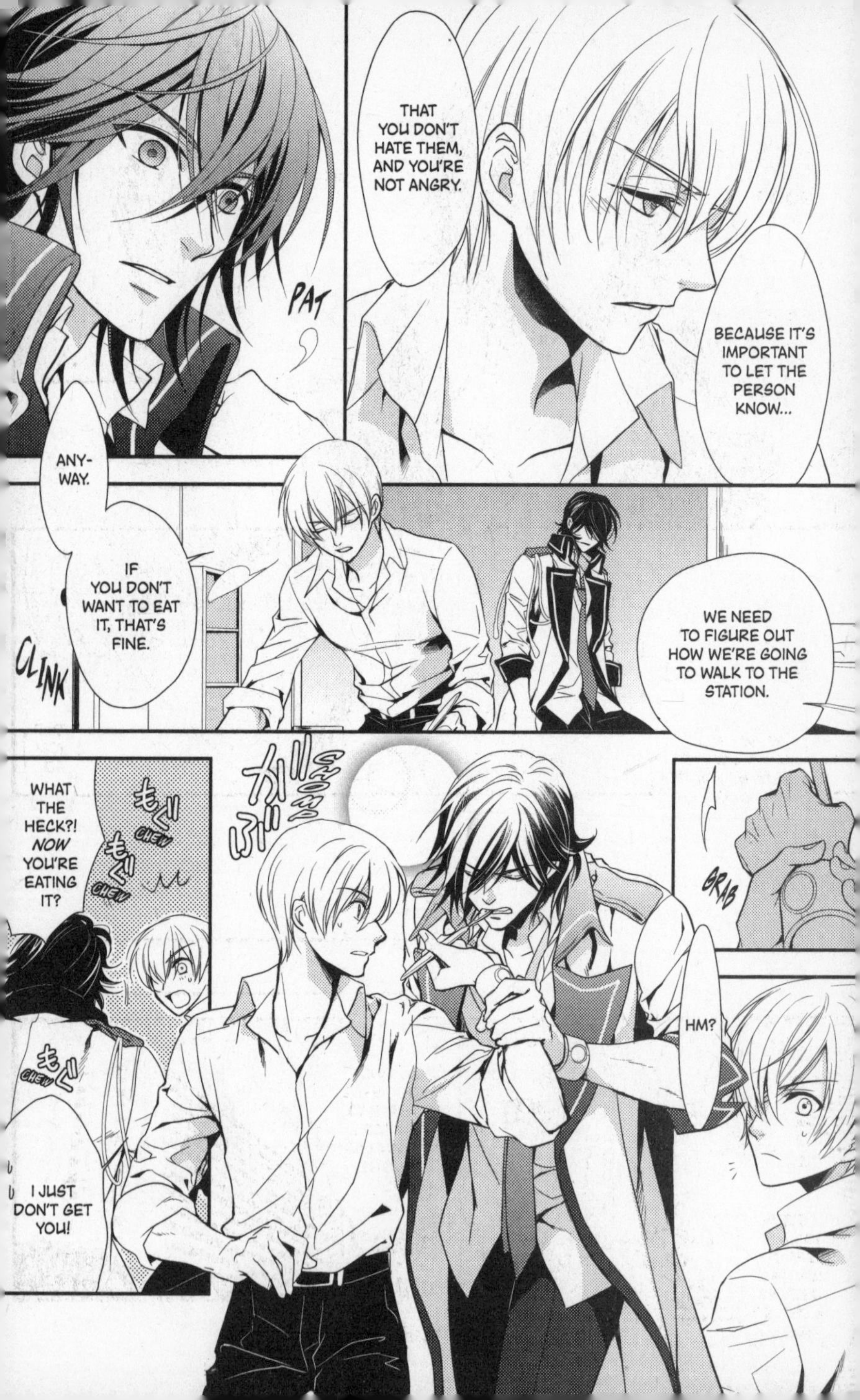
BECAUSE IT'S IMPORTANT TO LET THE PERSON KNOW...
THAT YOU DON'T HATE THEM, AND YOU'RE NOT ANGRY.
PAT
ANY-WAY.
IF YOU DON'T WANT TO EAT IT, THAT'S FINE.
CLINK
WE NEED TO FIGURE OUT HOW WE'RE GOING TO WALK TO THE STATION.
GRAB
HM?
かぷ CHOMP
もぐ CHEW
もぐ CHEW
WHAT THE HECK?! *NOW* YOU'RE EATING IT?
もぐ CHEW
I JUST DON'T GET YOU!

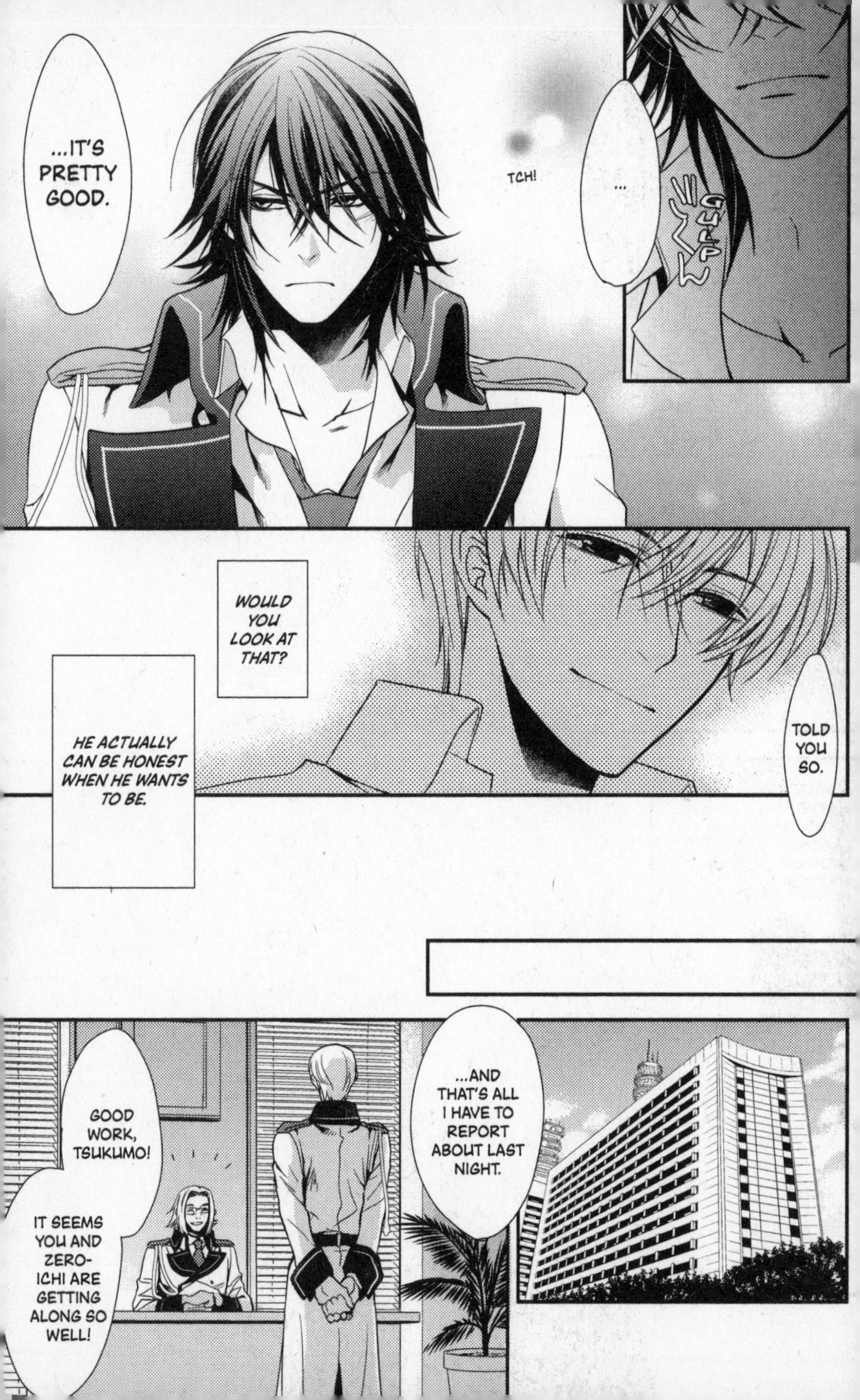
...
GULP
TCH!
...IT'S PRETTY GOOD.
TOLD YOU SO.
WOULD YOU LOOK AT THAT?
HE ACTUALLY CAN BE HONEST WHEN HE WANTS TO BE.
...AND THAT'S ALL I HAVE TO REPORT ABOUT LAST NIGHT.
GOOD WORK, TSUKUMO!
IT SEEMS YOU AND ZERO-ICHI ARE GETTING ALONG SO WELL!

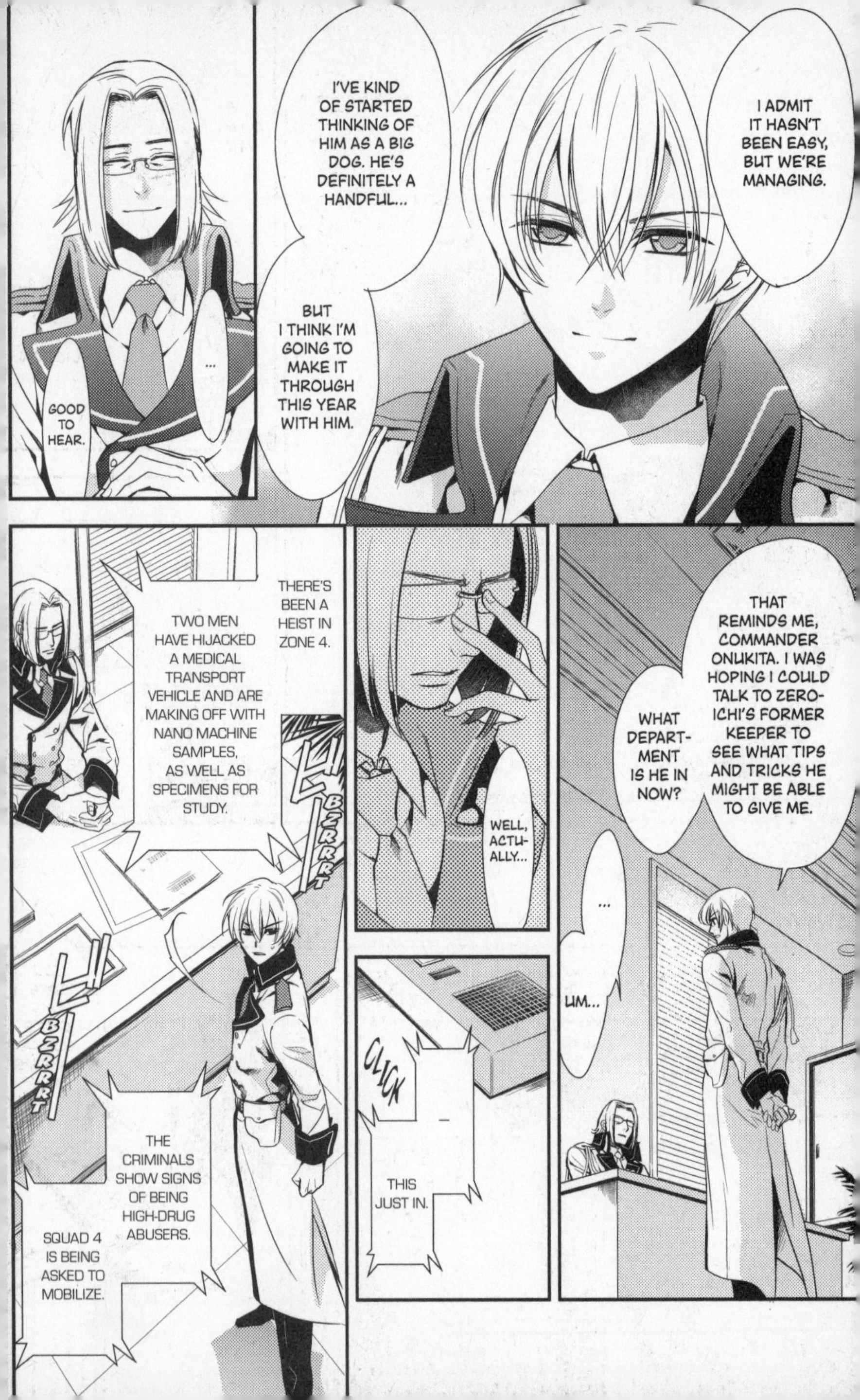
I ADMIT IT HASN'T BEEN EASY, BUT WE'RE MANAGING.
I'VE KIND OF STARTED THINKING OF HIM AS A BIG DOG. HE'S DEFINITELY A HANDFUL...
BUT I THINK I'M GOING TO MAKE IT THROUGH THIS YEAR WITH HIM.
...
GOOD TO HEAR.
THAT REMINDS ME, COMMANDER ONUKITA. I WAS HOPING I COULD TALK TO ZERO-ICHI'S FORMER KEEPER TO SEE WHAT TIPS AND TRICKS HE MIGHT BE ABLE TO GIVE ME.
WHAT DEPART-MENT IS HE IN NOW?
...
UM...
WELL, ACTU-ALLY...
CLICK
—
THIS JUST IN.
BZRRRT
THERE'S BEEN A HEIST IN ZONE 4.
TWO MEN HAVE HIJACKED A MEDICAL TRANSPORT VEHICLE AND ARE MAKING OFF WITH NANO MACHINE SAMPLES, AS WELL AS SPECIMENS FOR STUDY.
BZRRRT
THE CRIMINALS SHOW SIGNS OF BEING HIGH-DRUG ABUSERS.
SQUAD 4 IS BEING ASKED TO MOBILIZE.

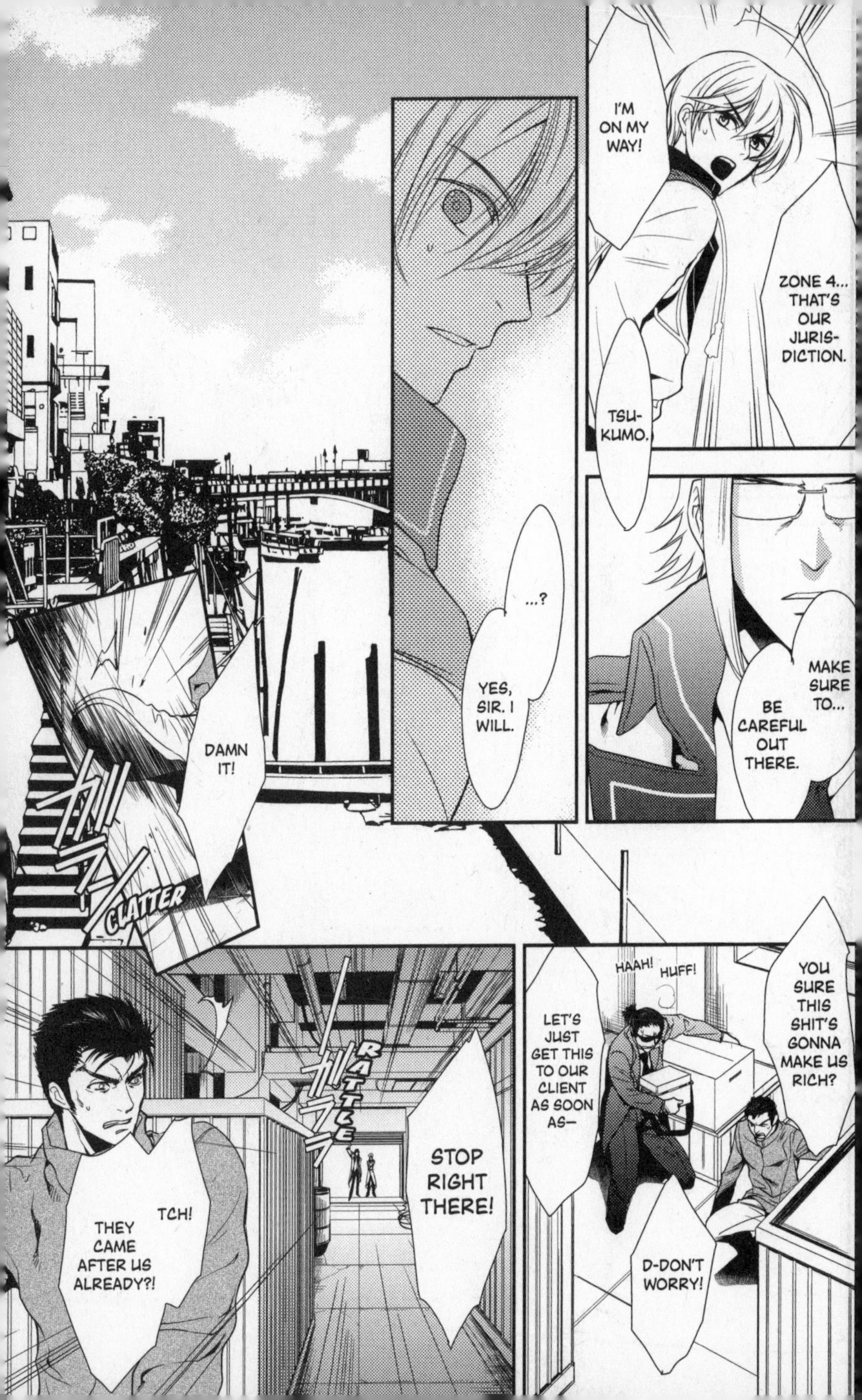
ZONE 4... THAT'S OUR JURISDICTION.
I'M ON MY WAY!
TSU-KUMO.
MAKE SURE TO...
BE CAREFUL OUT THERE.
...?
YES, SIR. I WILL.
DAMN IT!
CLATTER
YOU SURE THIS SHIT'S GONNA MAKE US RICH?
HUFF!
HAAH!
LET'S JUST GET THIS TO OUR CLIENT AS SOON AS–
D-DON'T WORRY!
STOP RIGHT THERE!
RATTLE
TCH!
THEY CAME AFTER US ALREADY?!

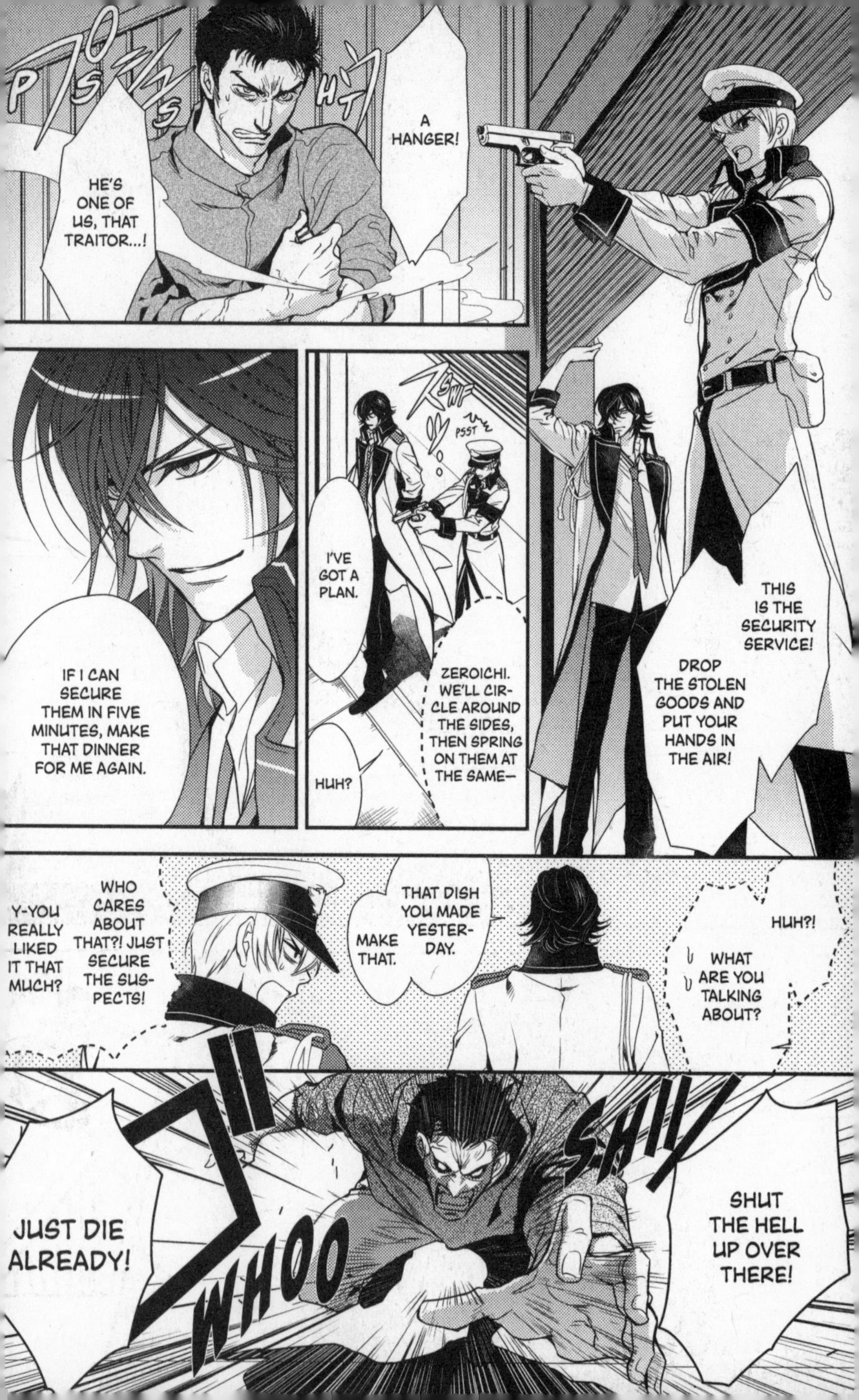
THIS IS THE SECURITY SERVICE!
DROP THE STOLEN GOODS AND PUT YOUR HANDS IN THE AIR!
PSSHHT
A HANGER!
HE'S ONE OF US, THAT TRAITOR...!
SWIF
PSST
ZEROICHI. WE'LL CIRCLE AROUND THE SIDES, THEN SPRING ON THEM AT THE SAME—
I'VE GOT A PLAN.
HUH?
IF I CAN SECURE THEM IN FIVE MINUTES, MAKE THAT DINNER FOR ME AGAIN.
HUH?!
WHAT ARE YOU TALKING ABOUT?
THAT DISH YOU MADE YESTERDAY.
MAKE THAT.
WHO CARES ABOUT THAT?! JUST SECURE THE SUSPECTS!
Y-YOU REALLY LIKED IT THAT MUCH?
SHUT THE HELL UP OVER THERE!
WHOOSH
JUST DIE ALREADY!

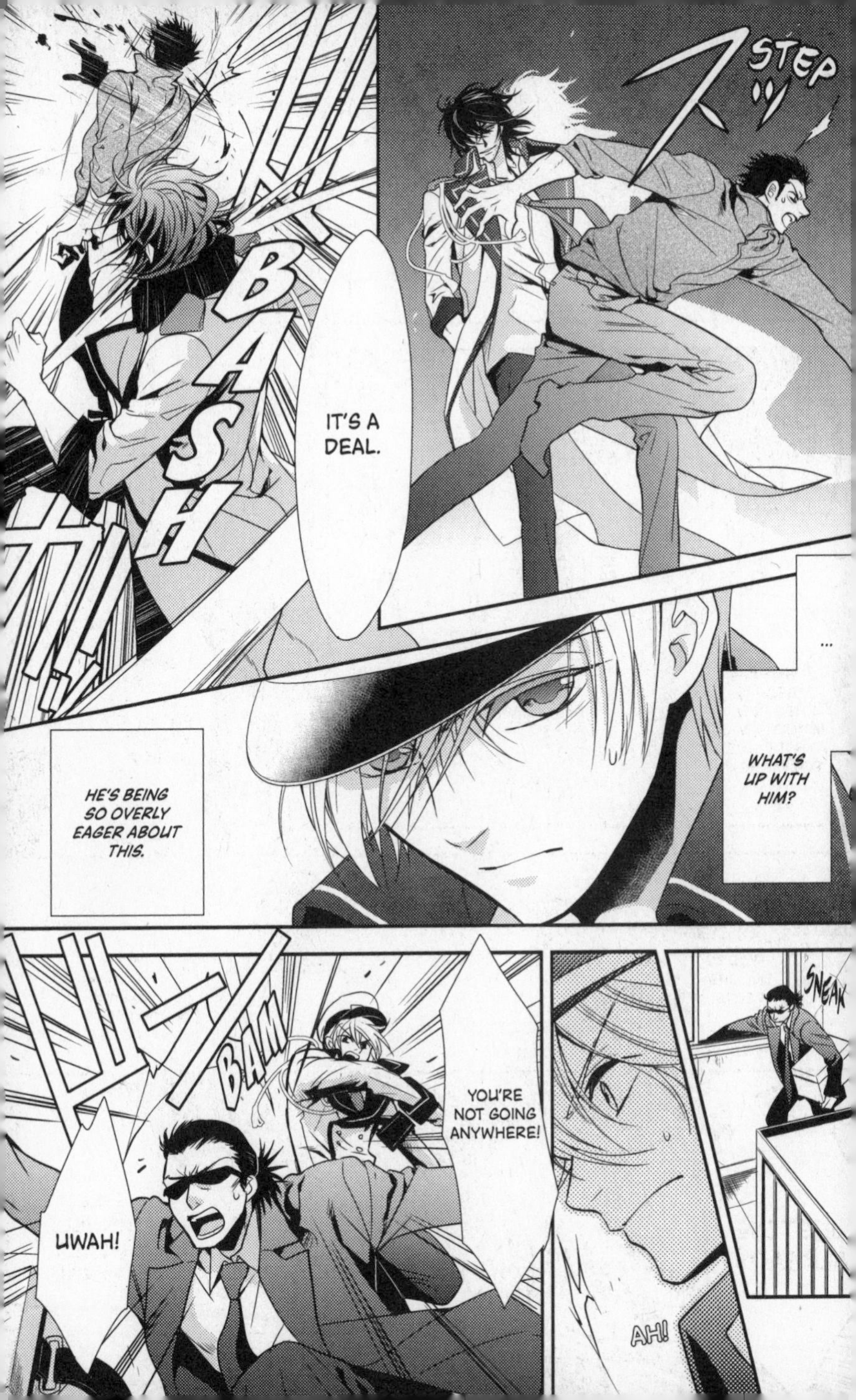
STEP
IT'S A DEAL.
BASH
...
WHAT'S UP WITH HIM?
HE'S BEING SO OVERLY EAGER ABOUT THIS.
SNEAK
AH!
BAM
YOU'RE NOT GOING ANYWHERE!
UWAH!

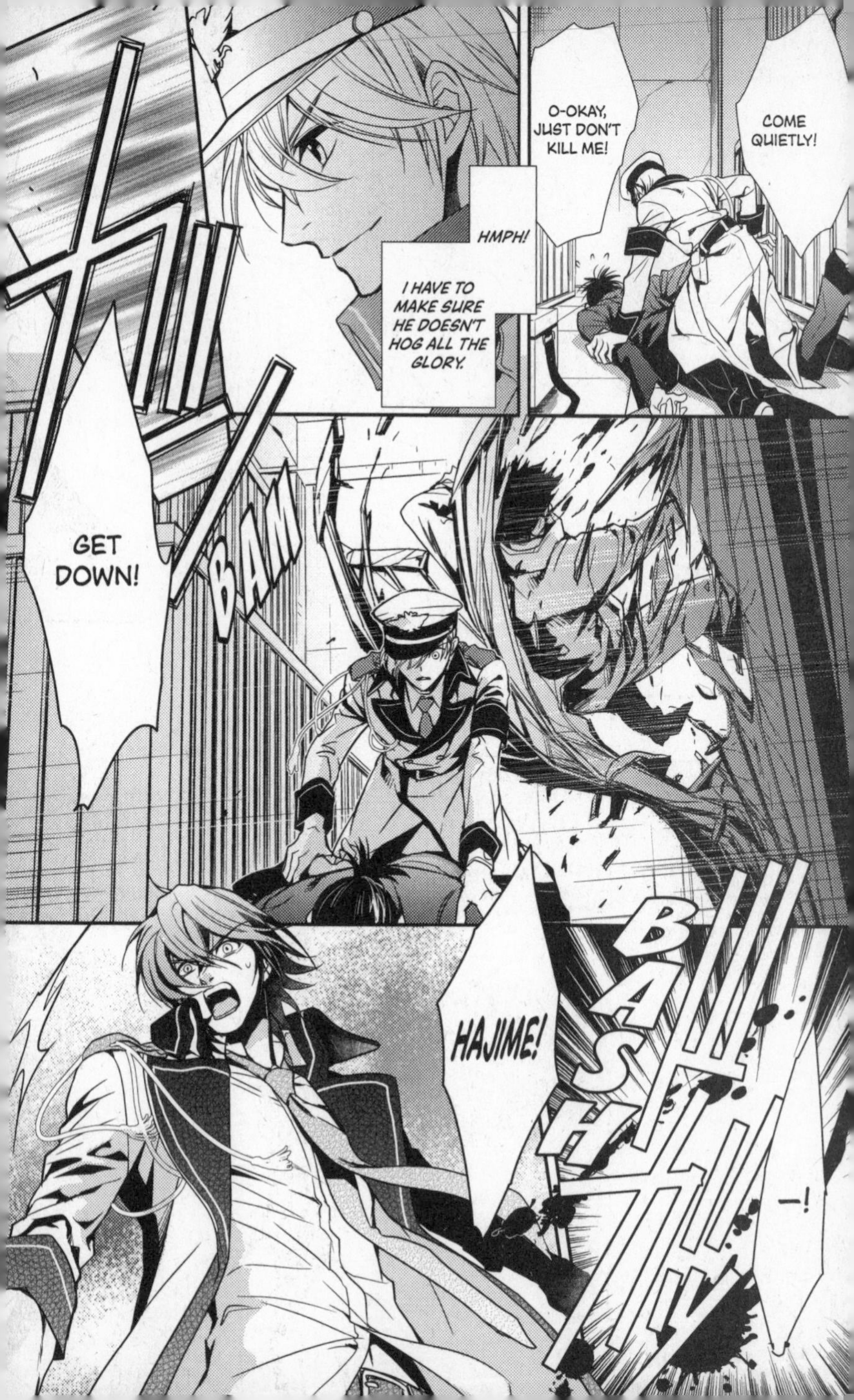
COME QUIETLY!
O-OKAY, JUST DON'T KILL ME!
HMPH!
I HAVE TO MAKE SURE HE DOESN'T HOG ALL THE GLORY.
BAM
GET DOWN!
BASHH
HAJIME!
—!

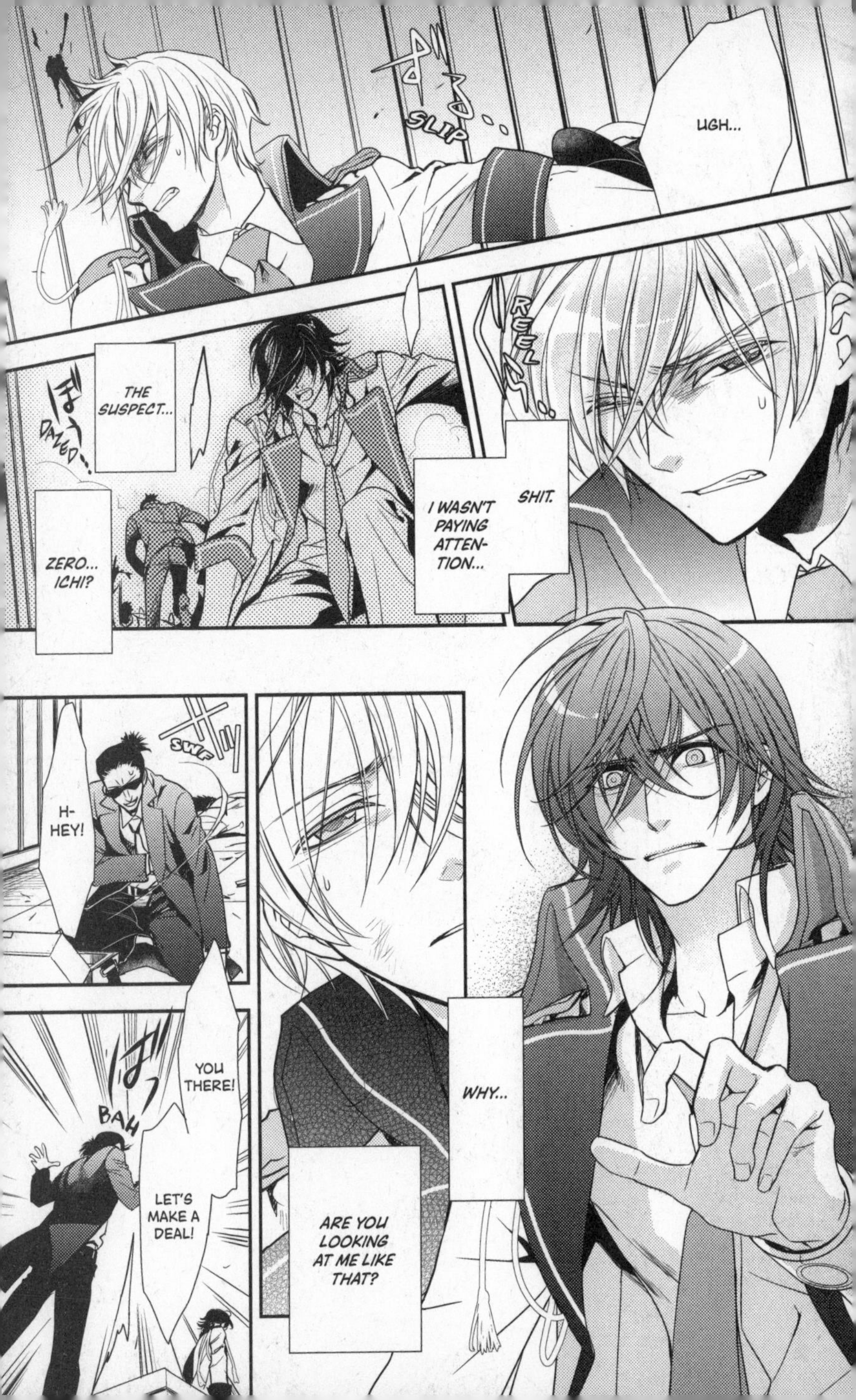

SLIP
UGH...
REEL
SHIT.
I WASN'T PAYING ATTENTION...
THE SUSPECT...
DAZED...
ZERO... ICHI?
WHY...
ARE YOU LOOKING AT ME LIKE THAT?
SWF
H-HEY!
BAH
YOU THERE!
LET'S MAKE A DEAL!

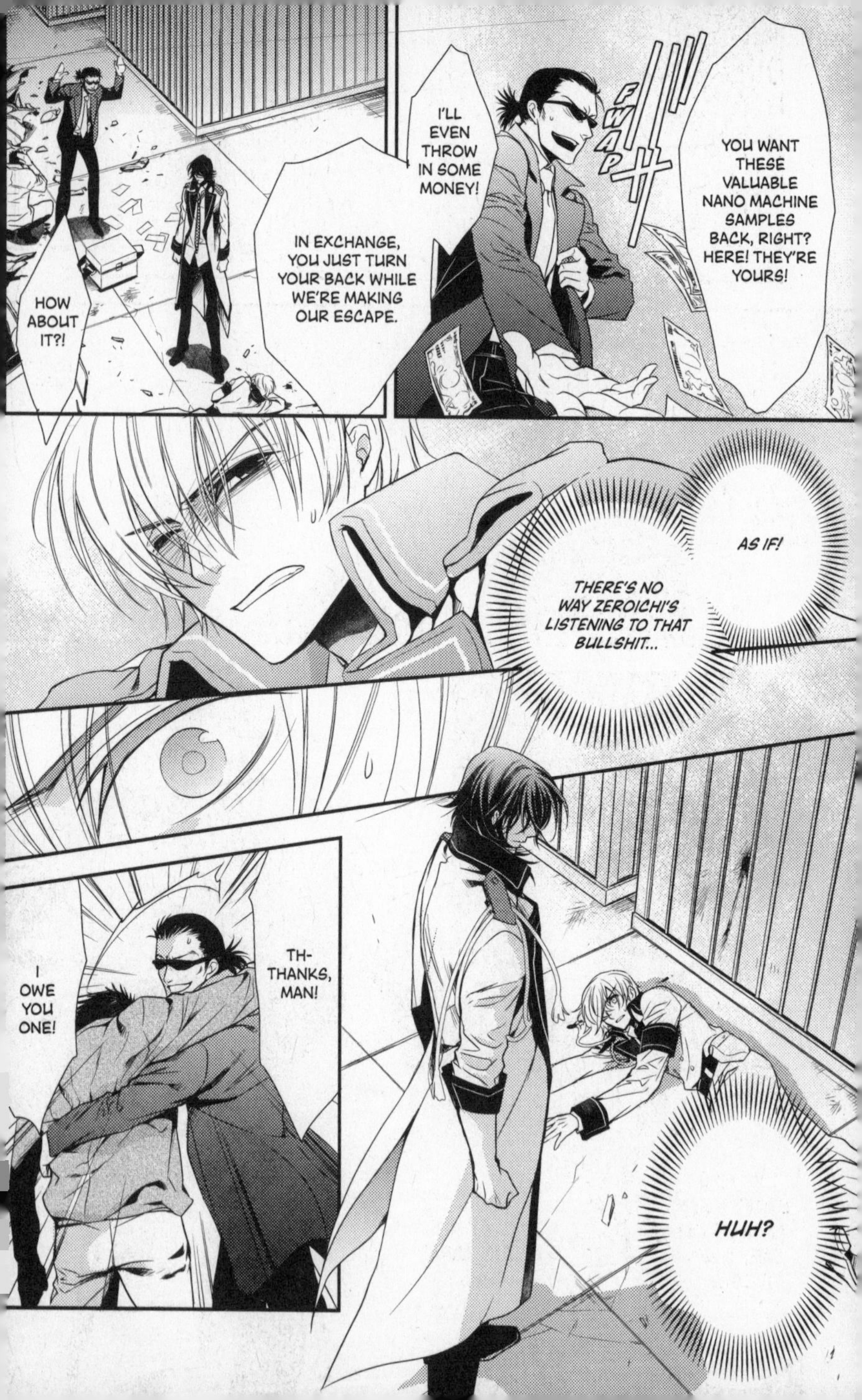
YOU WANT THESE VALUABLE NANO MACHINE SAMPLES BACK, RIGHT? HERE! THEY'RE YOURS!
FWAP
I'LL EVEN THROW IN SOME MONEY!
IN EXCHANGE, YOU JUST TURN YOUR BACK WHILE WE'RE MAKING OUR ESCAPE.
HOW ABOUT IT?!
AS IF!
THERE'S NO WAY ZEROICHI'S LISTENING TO THAT BULLSHIT...
HUH?
TH-THANKS, MAN!
I OWE YOU ONE!

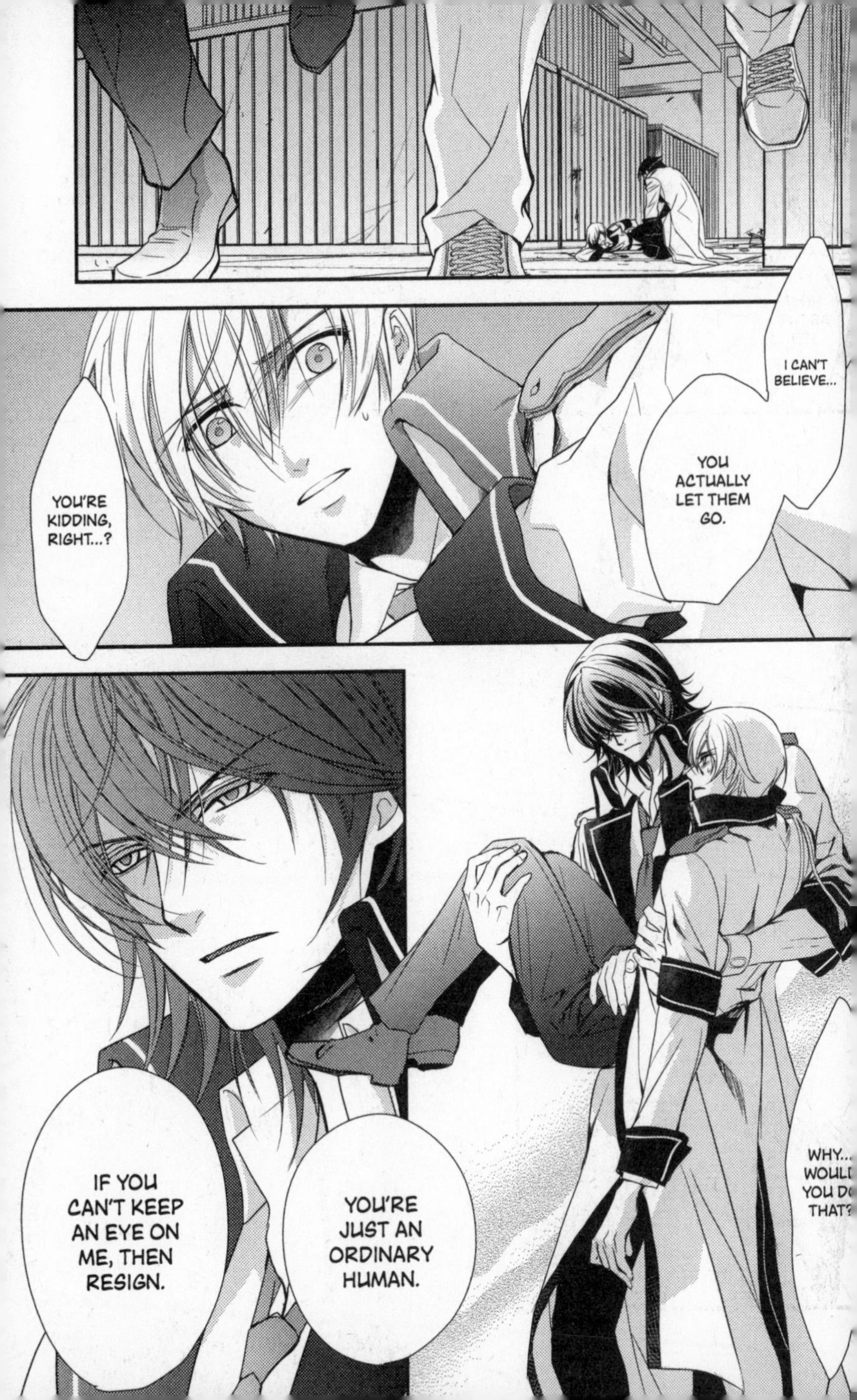
I CAN'T BELIEVE...
YOU ACTUALLY LET THEM GO.
YOU'RE KIDDING, RIGHT...?
WHY... WOUL YOU D THAT?
YOU'RE JUST AN ORDINARY HUMAN.
IF YOU CAN'T KEEP AN EYE ON ME, THEN RESIGN.

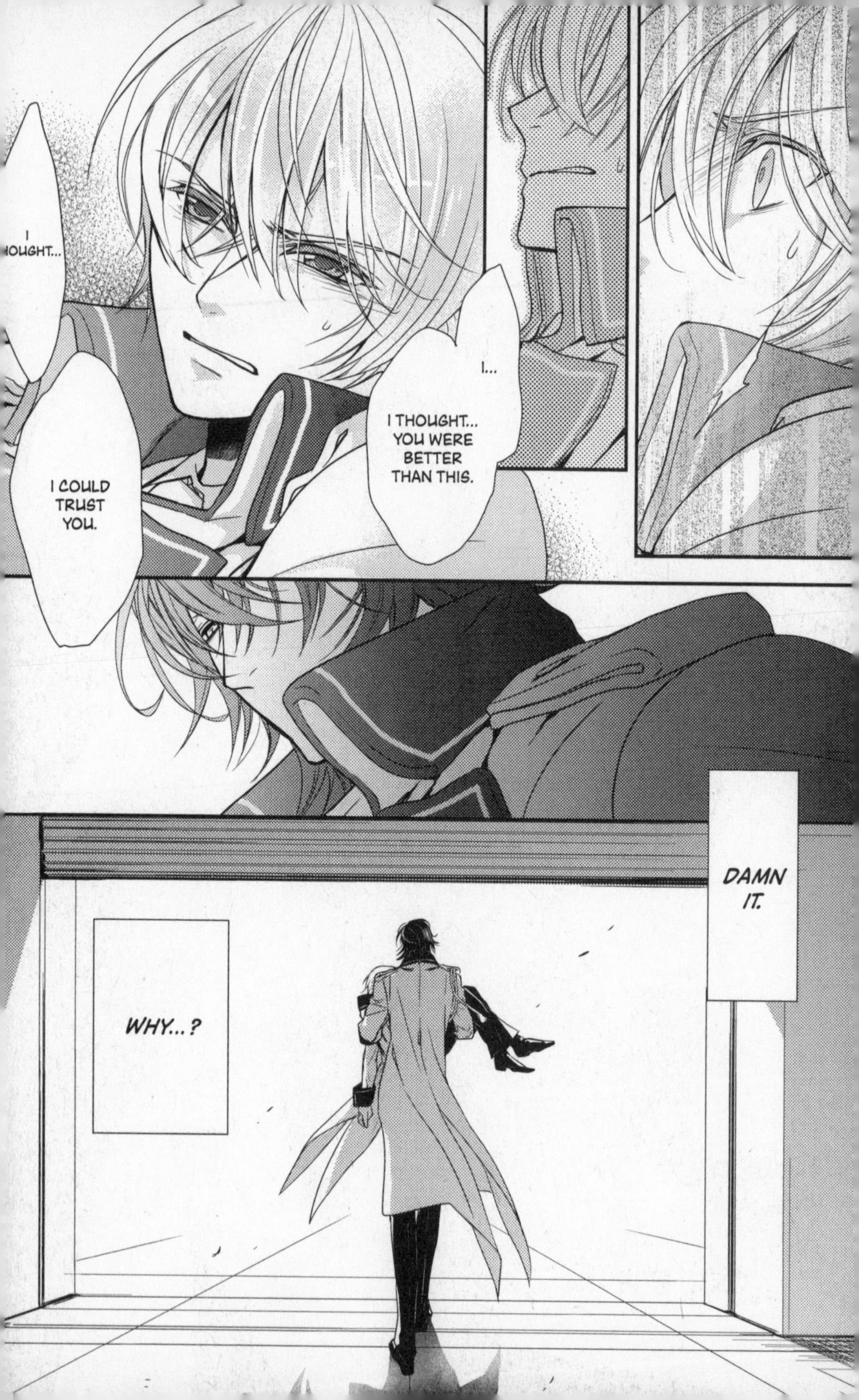
I...
I THOUGHT... YOU WERE BETTER THAN THIS.
I HOUGHT...
I COULD TRUST YOU.
DAMN IT.
WHY...?

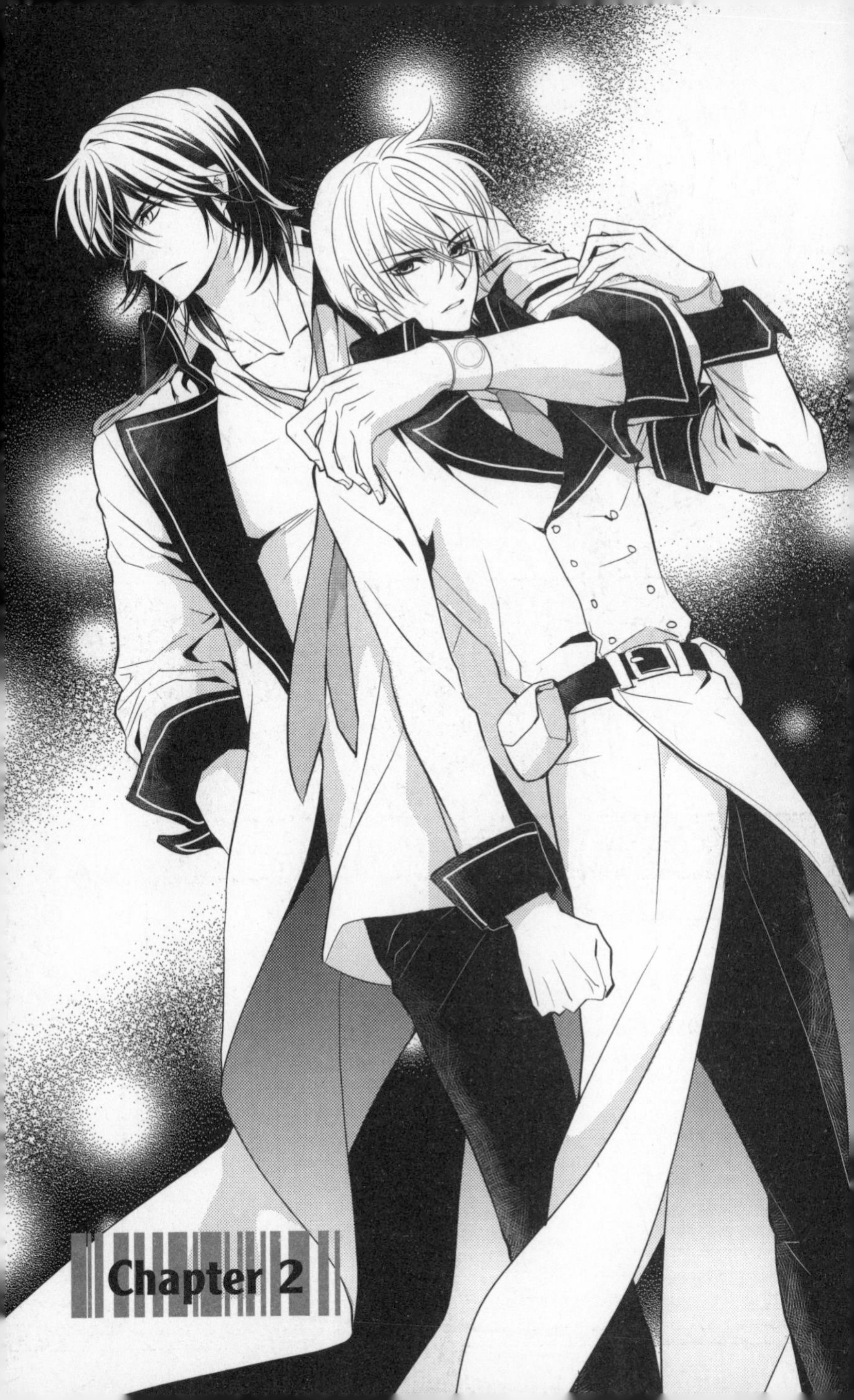
Chapter 2

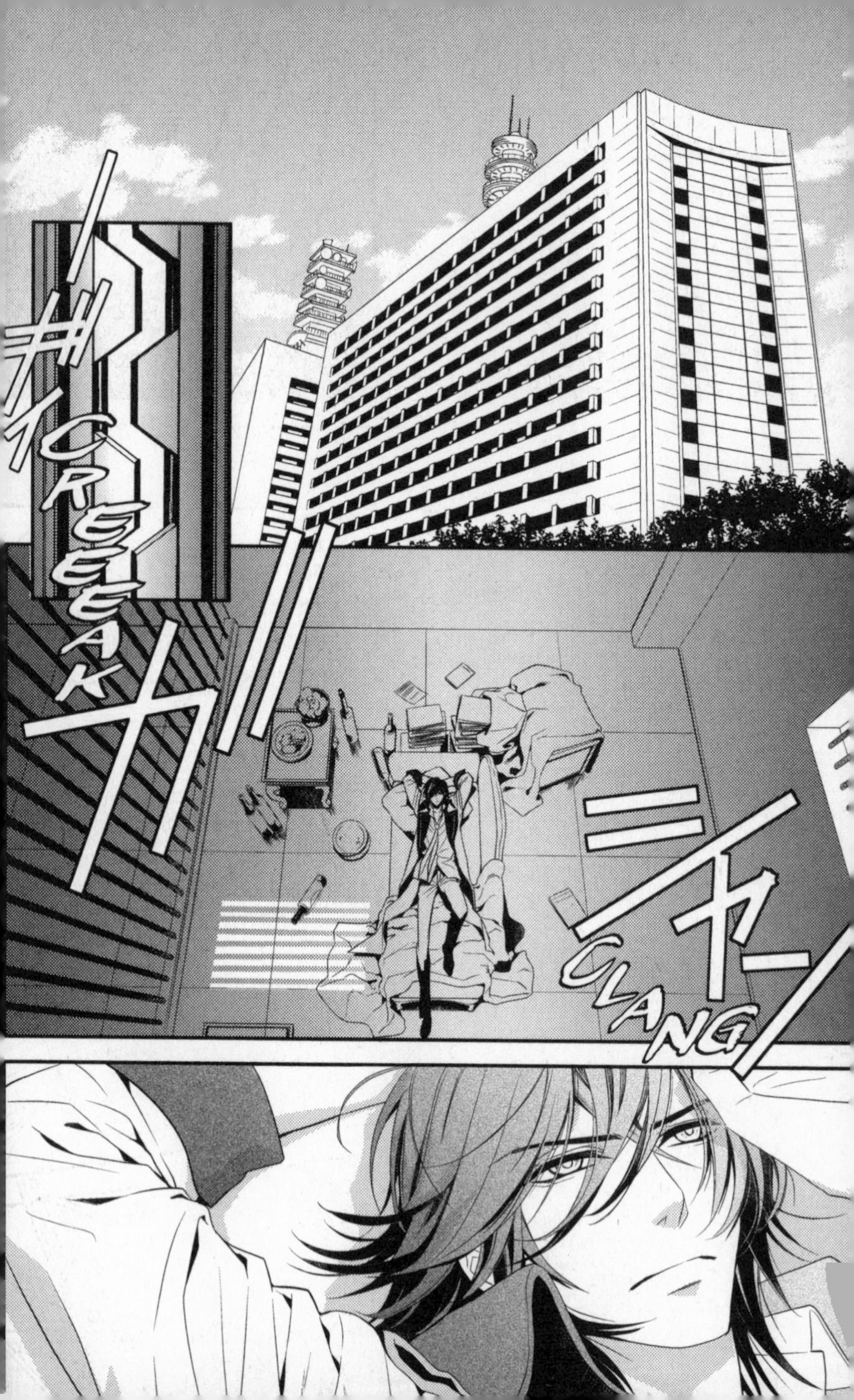
CREEEAK
CLANG

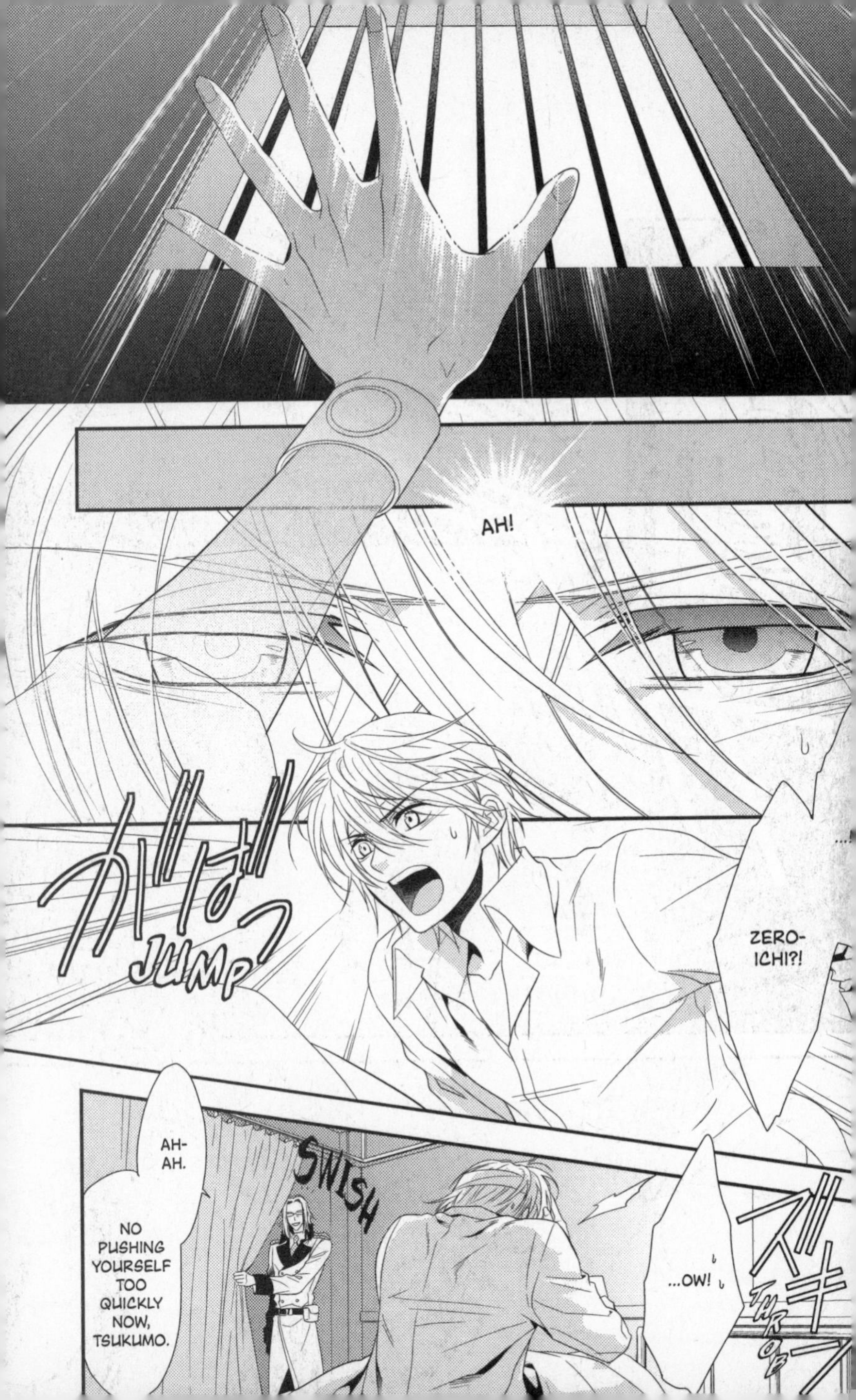

AH!
ZERO-ICHI?!
JUMP
THROB
...OW!
SWISH
AH-AH.
NO PUSHING YOURSELF TOO QUICKLY NOW, TSUKUMO.

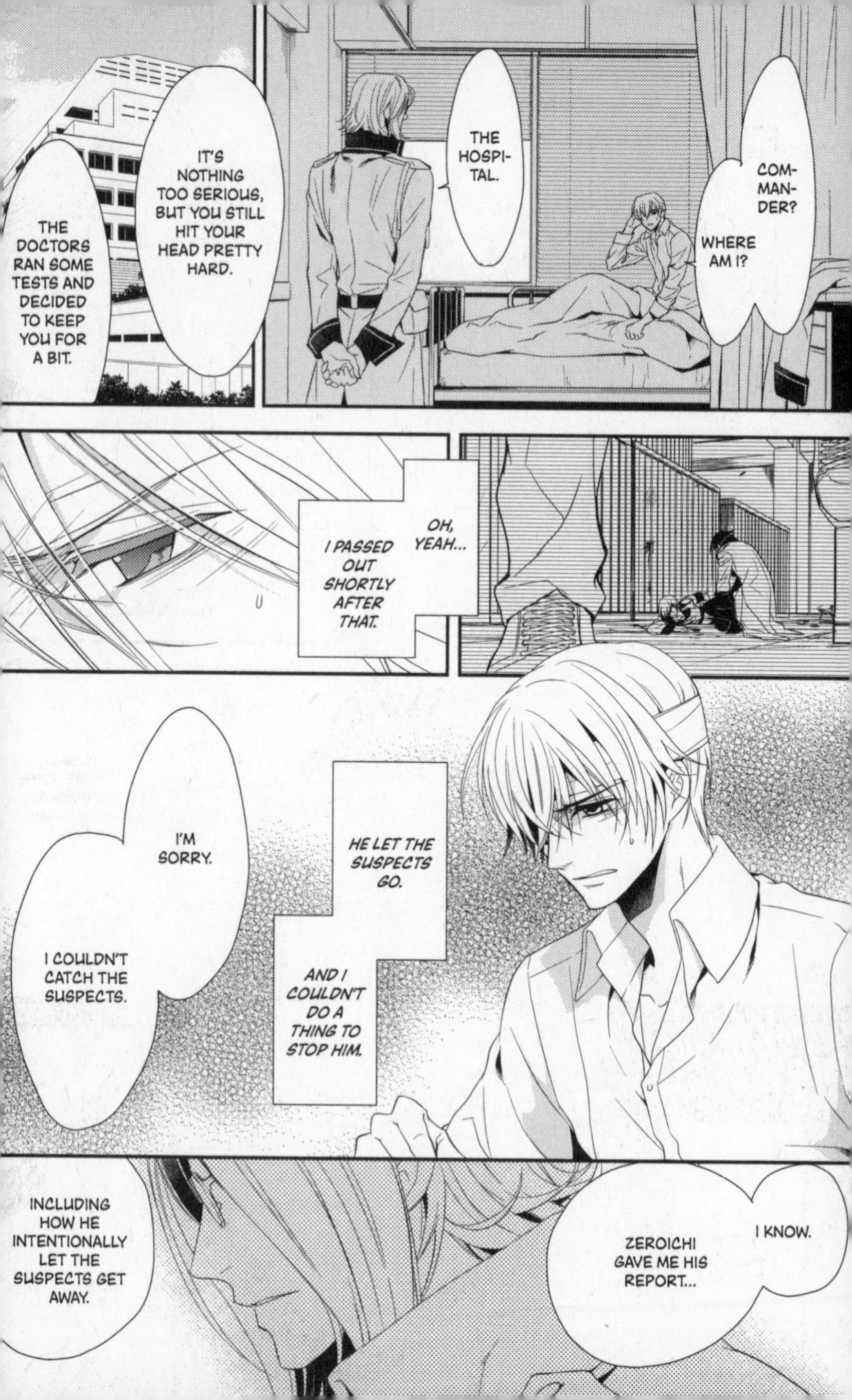
COMMANDER?
WHERE AM I?
THE HOSPITAL.
IT'S NOTHING TOO SERIOUS, BUT YOU STILL HIT YOUR HEAD PRETTY HARD.
THE DOCTORS RAN SOME TESTS AND DECIDED TO KEEP YOU FOR A BIT.
OH, YEAH...
I PASSED OUT SHORTLY AFTER THAT.
HE LET THE SUSPECTS GO.
AND I COULDN'T DO A THING TO STOP HIM.
I'M SORRY.
I COULDN'T CATCH THE SUSPECTS.
I KNOW.
ZEROICHI GAVE ME HIS REPORT...
INCLUDING HOW HE INTENTIONALLY LET THE SUSPECTS GET AWAY.

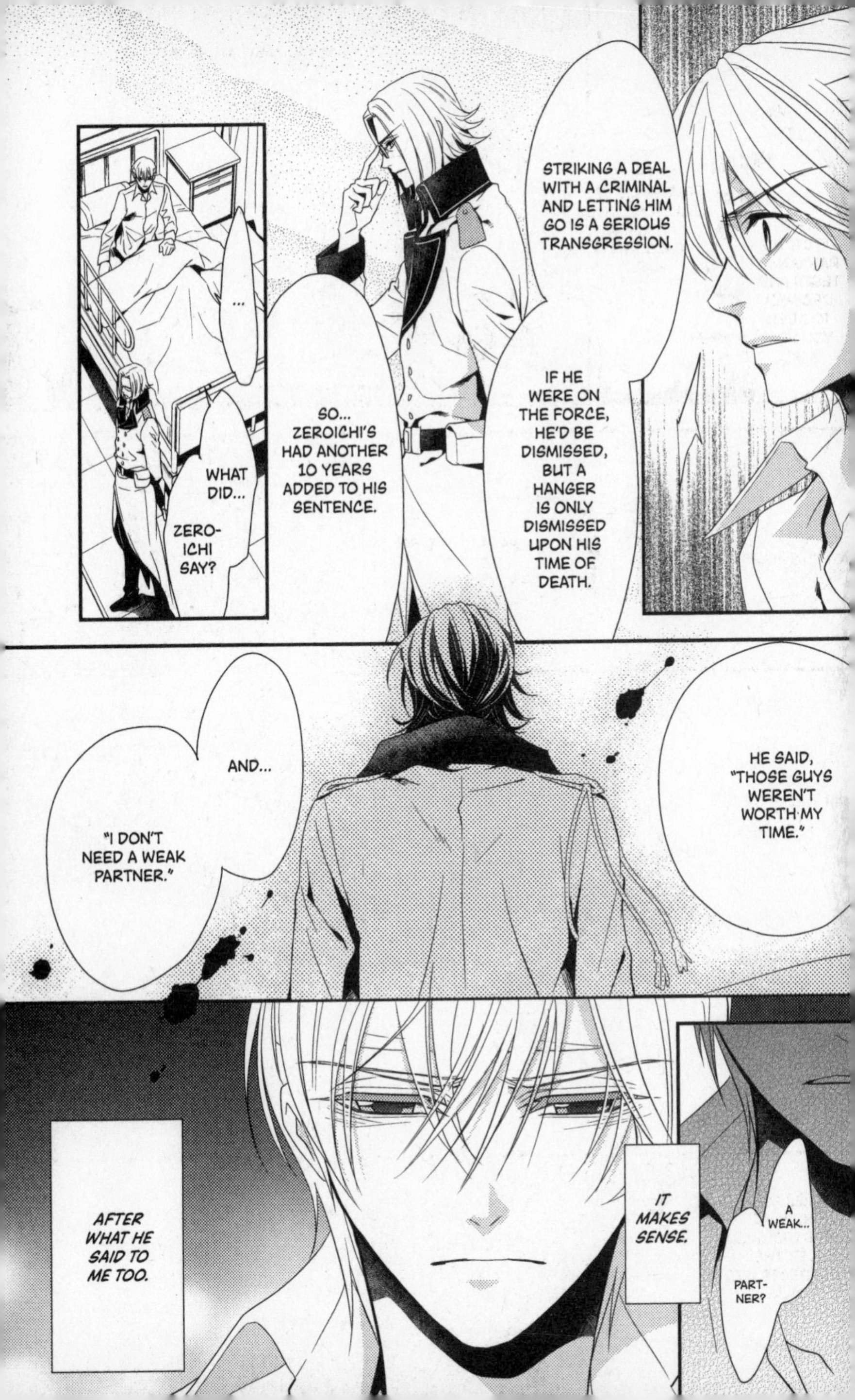
STRIKING A DEAL WITH A CRIMINAL AND LETTING HIM GO IS A SERIOUS TRANSGRESSION.
IF HE WERE ON THE FORCE, HE'D BE DISMISSED, BUT A HANGER IS ONLY DISMISSED UPON HIS TIME OF DEATH.
SO... ZEROICHI'S HAD ANOTHER 10 YEARS ADDED TO HIS SENTENCE.
...
WHAT DID... ZERO-ICHI SAY?
HE SAID, "THOSE GUYS WEREN'T WORTH MY TIME."
AND...
"I DON'T NEED A WEAK PARTNER."
A WEAK... PART-NER?
IT MAKES SENSE.
AFTER WHAT HE SAID TO ME TOO.

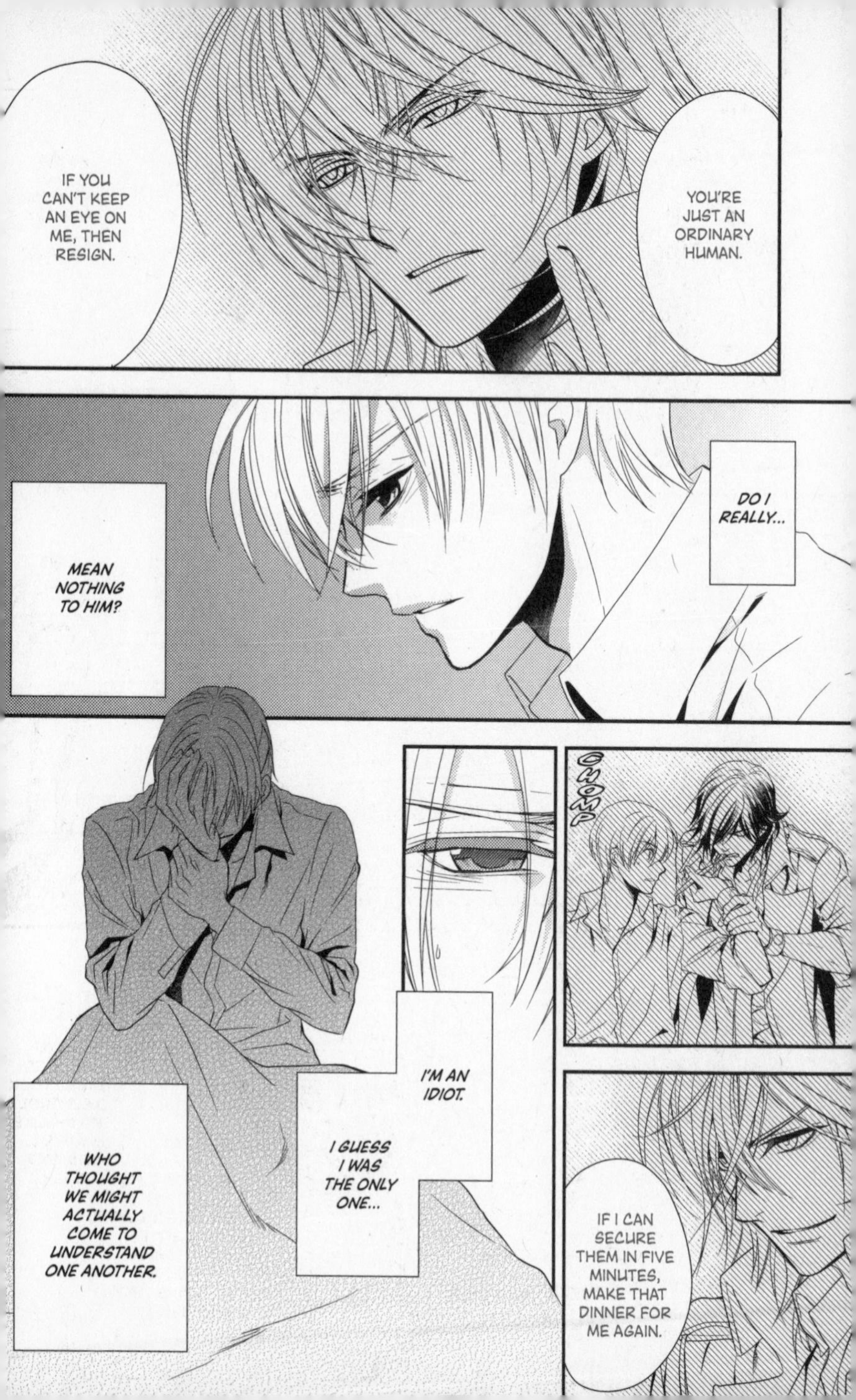
YOU'RE JUST AN ORDINARY HUMAN.
IF YOU CAN'T KEEP AN EYE ON ME, THEN RESIGN.
DO I REALLY...
MEAN NOTHING TO HIM?
CHOMP
IF I CAN SECURE THEM IN FIVE MINUTES, MAKE THAT DINNER FOR ME AGAIN.
I'M AN IDIOT.
I GUESS I WAS THE ONLY ONE...
WHO THOUGHT WE MIGHT ACTUALLY COME TO UNDERSTAND ONE ANOTHER.

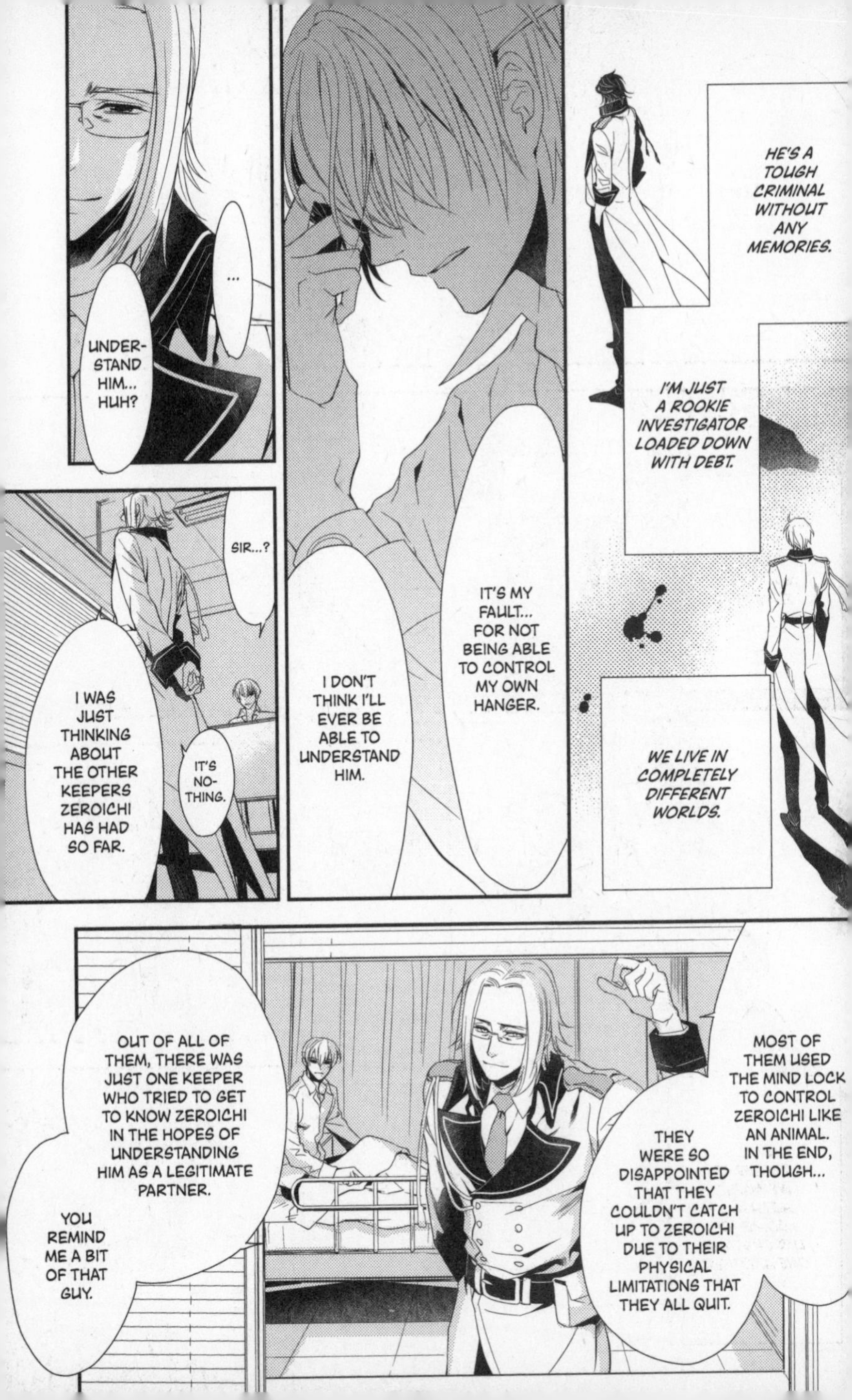
HE'S A TOUGH CRIMINAL WITHOUT ANY MEMORIES.
I'M JUST A ROOKIE INVESTIGATOR LOADED DOWN WITH DEBT.
WE LIVE IN COMPLETELY DIFFERENT WORLDS.
IT'S MY FAULT... FOR NOT BEING ABLE TO CONTROL MY OWN HANGER.
I DON'T THINK I'LL EVER BE ABLE TO UNDERSTAND HIM.
...
UNDER-STAND HIM... HUH?
SIR...?
IT'S NO-THING.
I WAS JUST THINKING ABOUT THE OTHER KEEPERS ZEROICHI HAS HAD SO FAR.
MOST OF THEM USED THE MIND LOCK TO CONTROL ZEROICHI LIKE AN ANIMAL. IN THE END, THOUGH...
THEY WERE SO DISAPPOINTED THAT THEY COULDN'T CATCH UP TO ZEROICHI DUE TO THEIR PHYSICAL LIMITATIONS THAT THEY ALL QUIT.
OUT OF ALL OF THEM, THERE WAS JUST ONE KEEPER WHO TRIED TO GET TO KNOW ZEROICHI IN THE HOPES OF UNDERSTANDING HIM AS A LEGITIMATE PARTNER.
YOU REMIND ME A BIT OF THAT GUY.

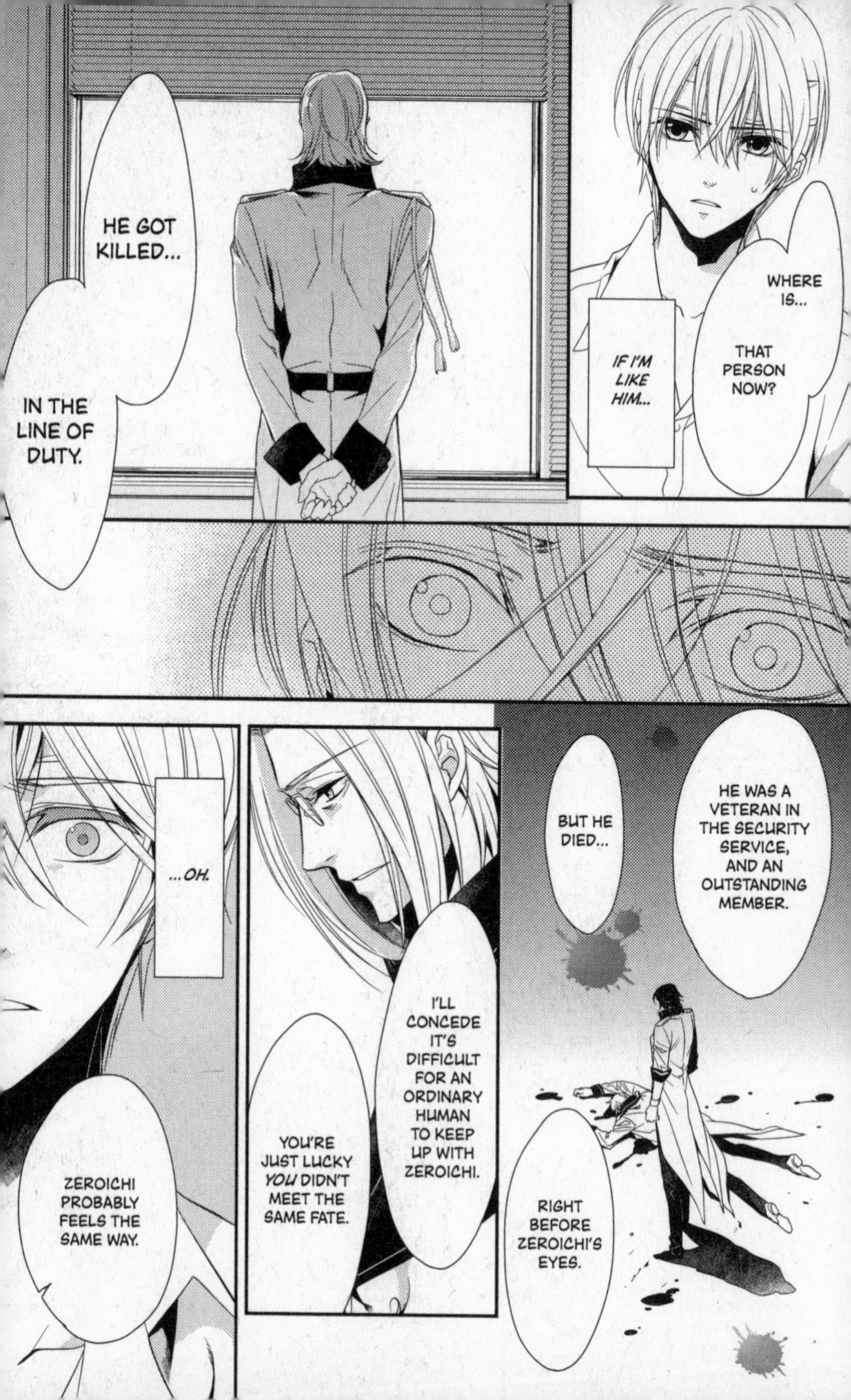
WHERE IS... THAT PERSON NOW?
IF I'M LIKE HIM...
HE GOT KILLED...
IN THE LINE OF DUTY.
HE WAS A VETERAN IN THE SECURITY SERVICE, AND AN OUTSTANDING MEMBER.
BUT HE DIED...
RIGHT BEFORE ZEROICHI'S EYES.
I'LL CONCEDE IT'S DIFFICULT FOR AN ORDINARY HUMAN TO KEEP UP WITH ZEROICHI.
YOU'RE JUST LUCKY *YOU* DIDN'T MEET THE SAME FATE.
...OH.
ZEROICHI PROBABLY FEELS THE SAME WAY.

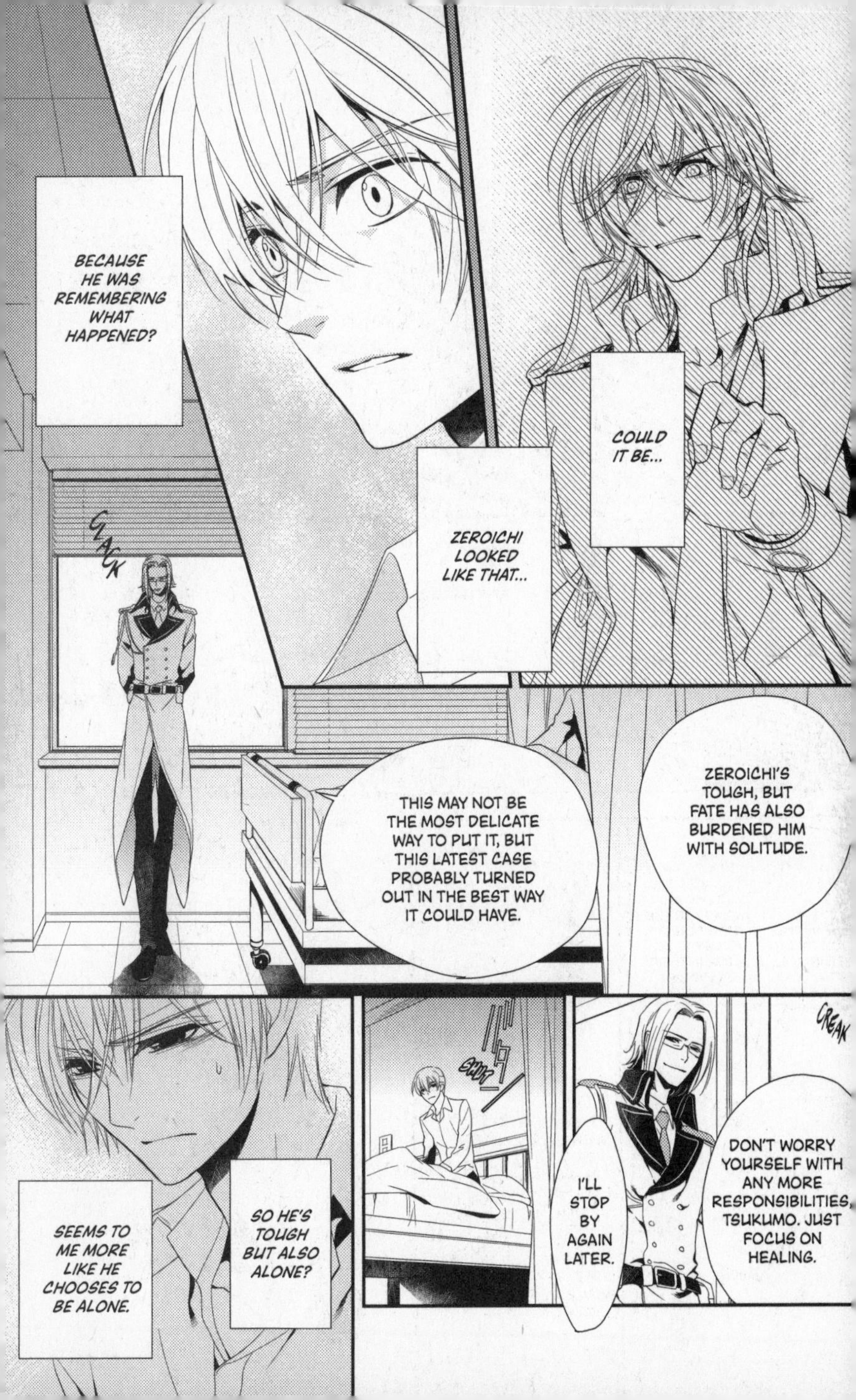
COULD IT BE...
ZEROICHI LOOKED LIKE THAT...
BECAUSE HE WAS REMEMBERING WHAT HAPPENED?
ZEROICHI'S TOUGH, BUT FATE HAS ALSO BURDENED HIM WITH SOLITUDE.
THIS MAY NOT BE THE MOST DELICATE WAY TO PUT IT, BUT THIS LATEST CASE PROBABLY TURNED OUT IN THE BEST WAY IT COULD HAVE.
CLACK
CREAK
DON'T WORRY YOURSELF WITH ANY MORE RESPONSIBILITIES, TSUKUMO. JUST FOCUS ON HEALING.
I'LL STOP BY AGAIN LATER.
SO HE'S TOUGH BUT ALSO ALONE?
SEEMS TO ME MORE LIKE HE CHOOSES TO BE ALONE.

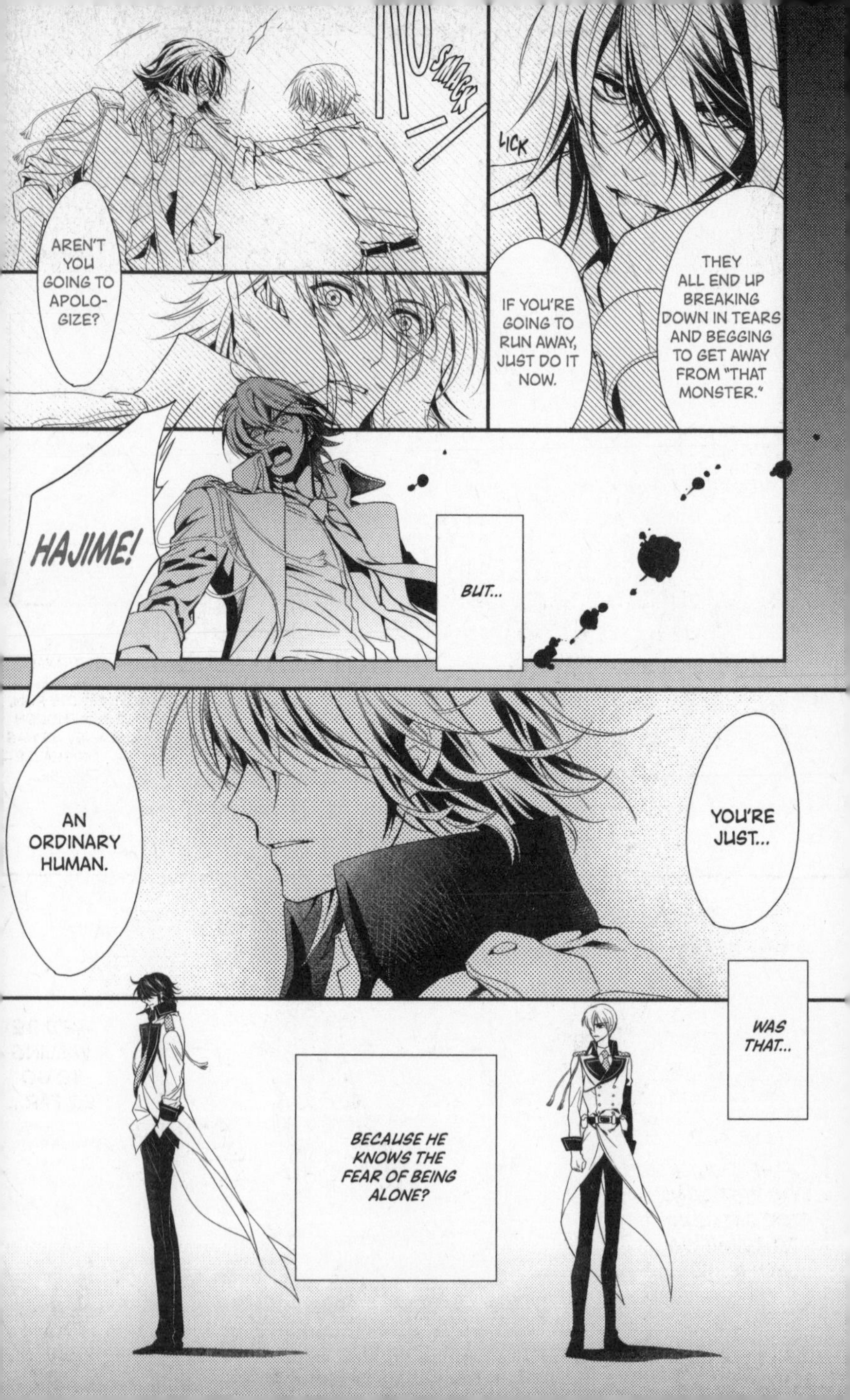
LICK
THEY ALL END UP BREAKING DOWN IN TEARS AND BEGGING TO GET AWAY FROM "THAT MONSTER."
IF YOU'RE GOING TO RUN AWAY, JUST DO IT NOW.
SMACK
AREN'T YOU GOING TO APOLO-GIZE?
BUT...
HAJIME!
YOU'RE JUST...
AN ORDINARY HUMAN.
WAS THAT...
BECAUSE HE KNOWS THE FEAR OF BEING ALONE?

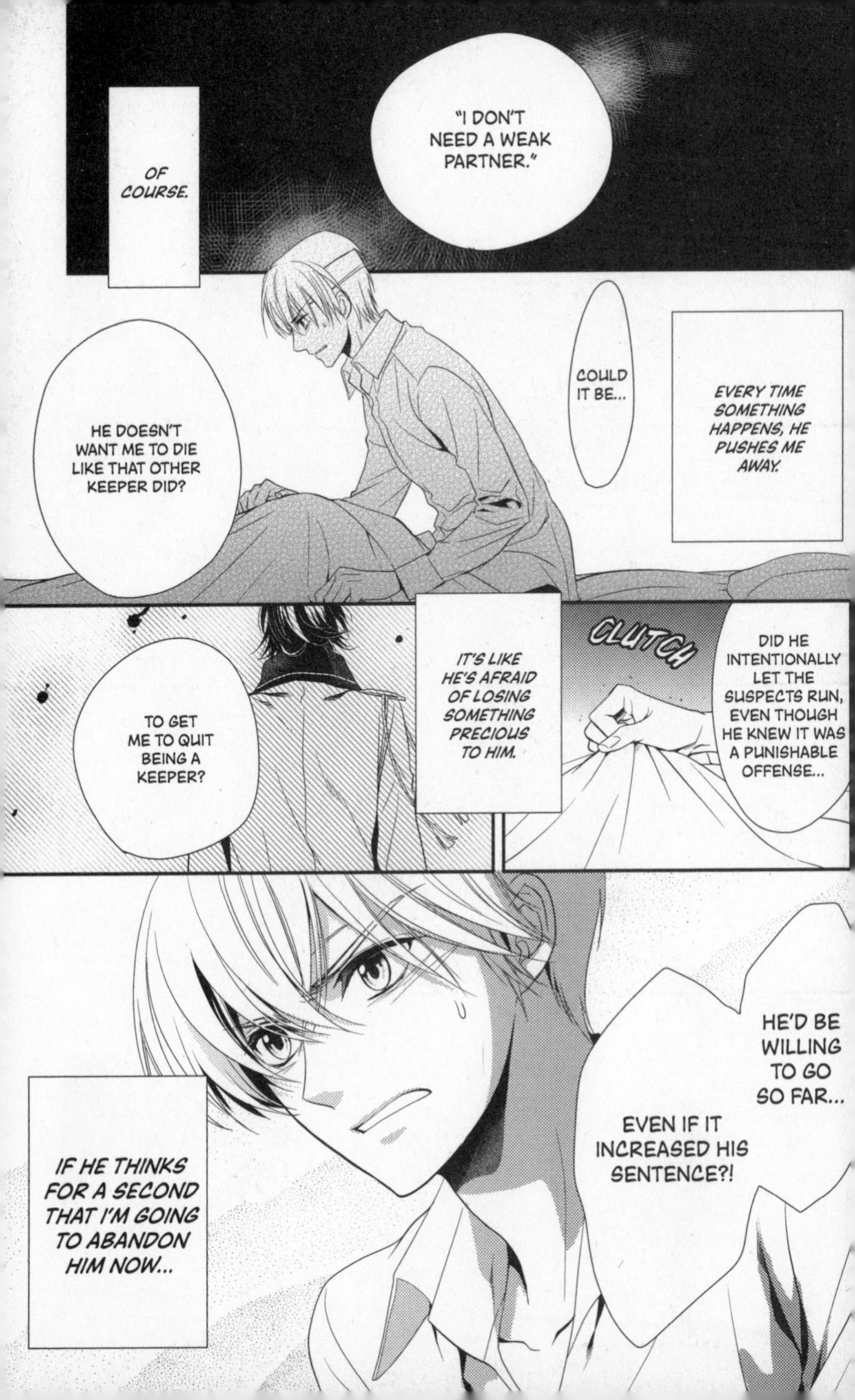
"I DON'T NEED A WEAK PARTNER."
OF COURSE.
EVERY TIME SOMETHING HAPPENS, HE PUSHES ME AWAY.
COULD IT BE...
HE DOESN'T WANT ME TO DIE LIKE THAT OTHER KEEPER DID?
DID HE INTENTIONALLY LET THE SUSPECTS RUN, EVEN THOUGH HE KNEW IT WAS A PUNISHABLE OFFENSE...
CLUTCH
IT'S LIKE HE'S AFRAID OF LOSING SOMETHING PRECIOUS TO HIM.
TO GET ME TO QUIT BEING A KEEPER?
HE'D BE WILLING TO GO SO FAR...
EVEN IF IT INCREASED HIS SENTENCE?!
IF HE THINKS FOR A SECOND THAT I'M GOING TO ABANDON HIM NOW...

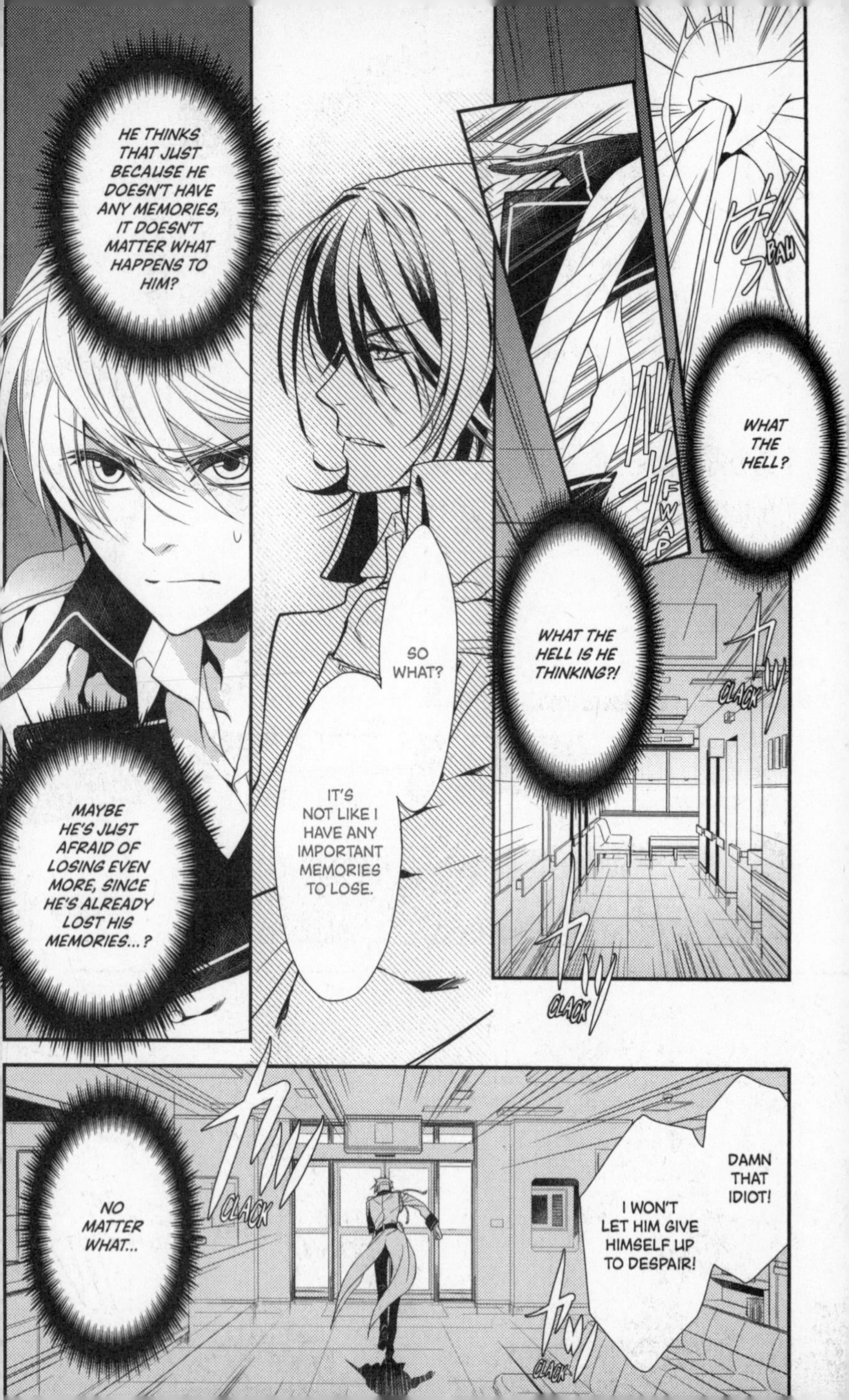
BAH
WHAT THE HELL?
FWAP
WHAT THE HELL IS HE THINKING?!
CLACK
SO WHAT?
IT'S NOT LIKE I HAVE ANY IMPORTANT MEMORIES TO LOSE.
CLACK
HE THINKS THAT JUST BECAUSE HE DOESN'T HAVE ANY MEMORIES, IT DOESN'T MATTER WHAT HAPPENS TO HIM?
MAYBE HE'S JUST AFRAID OF LOSING EVEN MORE, SINCE HE'S ALREADY LOST HIS MEMORIES...?
DAMN THAT IDIOT!
I WON'T LET HIM GIVE HIMSELF UP TO DESPAIR!
CLACK
CLACK
NO MATTER WHAT...

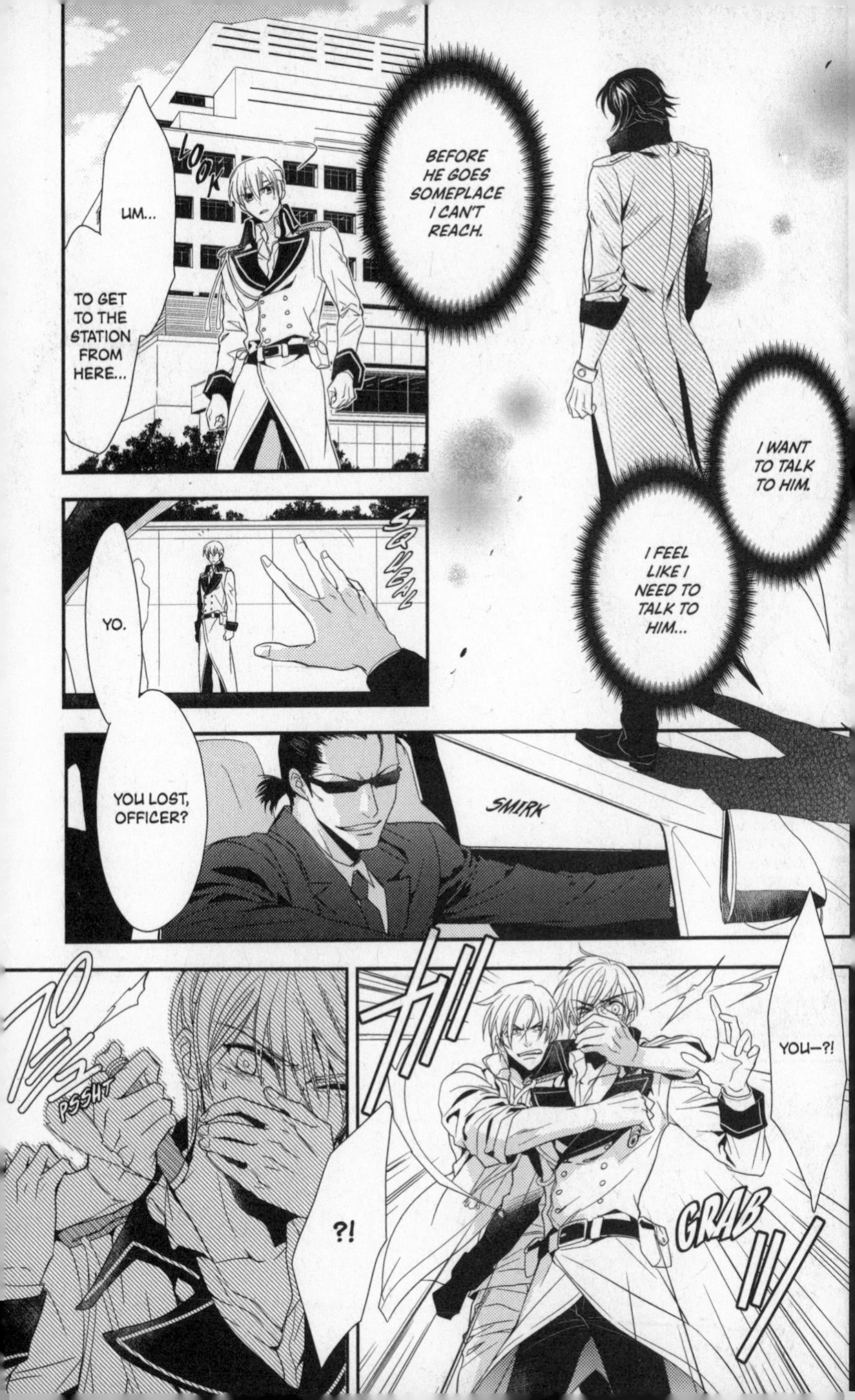
BEFORE HE GOES SOMEPLACE I CAN'T REACH.
I WANT TO TALK TO HIM.
I FEEL LIKE I NEED TO TALK TO HIM...
LOOK
UM...
TO GET TO THE STATION FROM HERE...
SQUEAL
YO.
SMIRK
YOU LOST, OFFICER?
YOU—?!
GRAB
PSSHT
?!

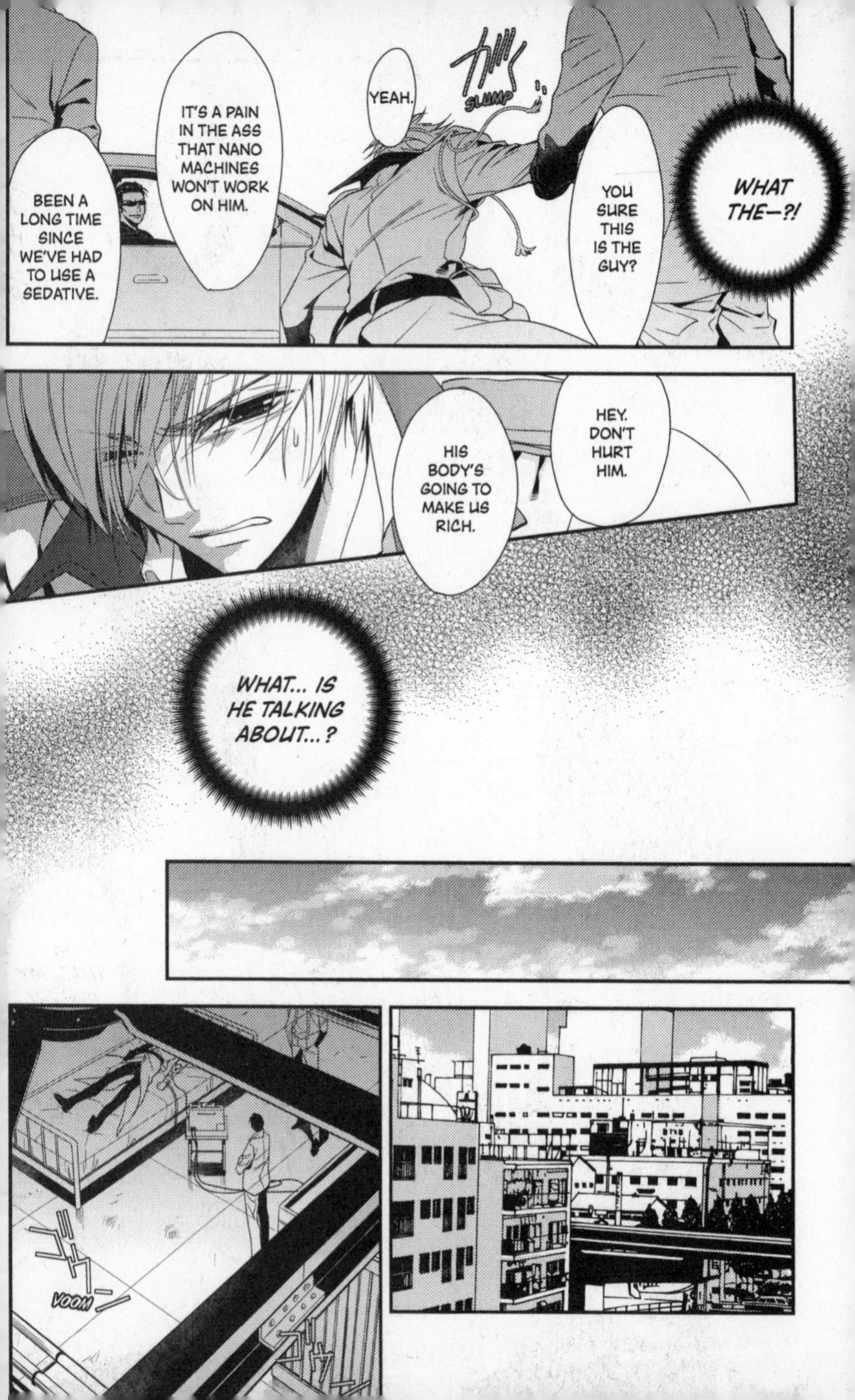
WHAT THE—?!
YOU SURE THIS IS THE GUY?
SLUMP
YEAH.
IT'S A PAIN IN THE ASS THAT NANO MACHINES WON'T WORK ON HIM.
BEEN A LONG TIME SINCE WE'VE HAD TO USE A SEDATIVE.
HEY. DON'T HURT HIM.
HIS BODY'S GOING TO MAKE US RICH.
WHAT... IS HE TALKING ABOUT...?
VOOM

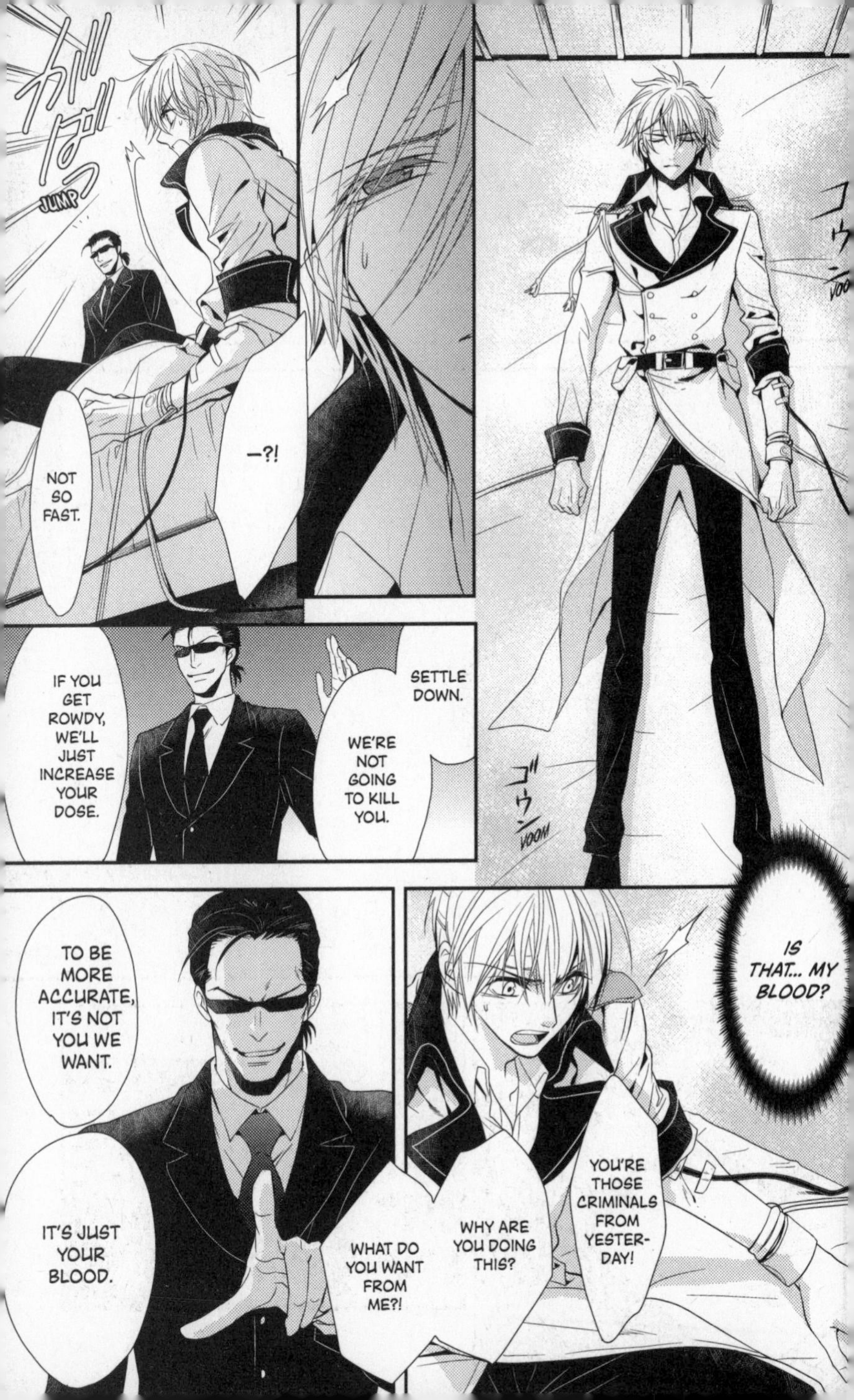
ゴウン
VOOM
ゴウン
VOOM
—?!
がばっ
JUMP
NOT SO FAST.
SETTLE DOWN.
WE'RE NOT GOING TO KILL YOU.
IF YOU GET ROWDY, WE'LL JUST INCREASE YOUR DOSE.
IS THAT... MY BLOOD?
YOU'RE THOSE CRIMINALS FROM YESTER-DAY!
WHY ARE YOU DOING THIS?
WHAT DO YOU WANT FROM ME?!
TO BE MORE ACCURATE, IT'S NOT YOU WE WANT.
IT'S JUST YOUR BLOOD.

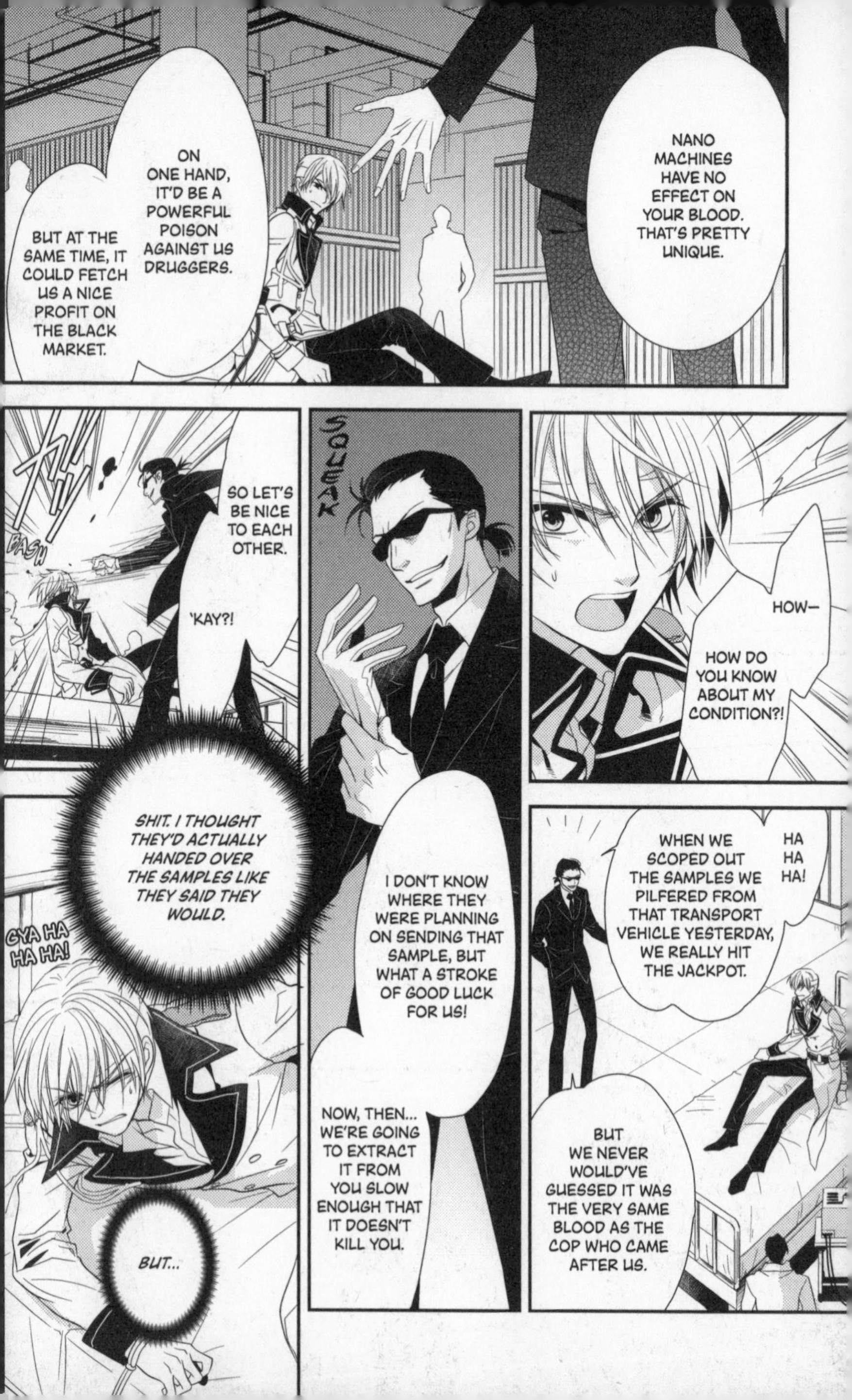
NANO MACHINES HAVE NO EFFECT ON YOUR BLOOD. THAT'S PRETTY UNIQUE.
ON ONE HAND, IT'D BE A POWERFUL POISON AGAINST US DRUGGERS.
BUT AT THE SAME TIME, IT COULD FETCH US A NICE PROFIT ON THE BLACK MARKET.
HOW—
HOW DO YOU KNOW ABOUT MY CONDITION?!
HA HA HA!
WHEN WE SCOPED OUT THE SAMPLES WE PILFERED FROM THAT TRANSPORT VEHICLE YESTERDAY, WE REALLY HIT THE JACKPOT.
BUT WE NEVER WOULD'VE GUESSED IT WAS THE VERY SAME BLOOD AS THE COP WHO CAME AFTER US.
SQUEAK
I DON'T KNOW WHERE THEY WERE PLANNING ON SENDING THAT SAMPLE, BUT WHAT A STROKE OF GOOD LUCK FOR US!
NOW, THEN... WE'RE GOING TO EXTRACT IT FROM YOU SLOW ENOUGH THAT IT DOESN'T KILL YOU.
SO LET'S BE NICE TO EACH OTHER.
'KAY?!
BASH
SHIT. I THOUGHT THEY'D ACTUALLY HANDED OVER THE SAMPLES LIKE THEY SAID THEY WOULD.
GYA HA HA HA!
BUT...

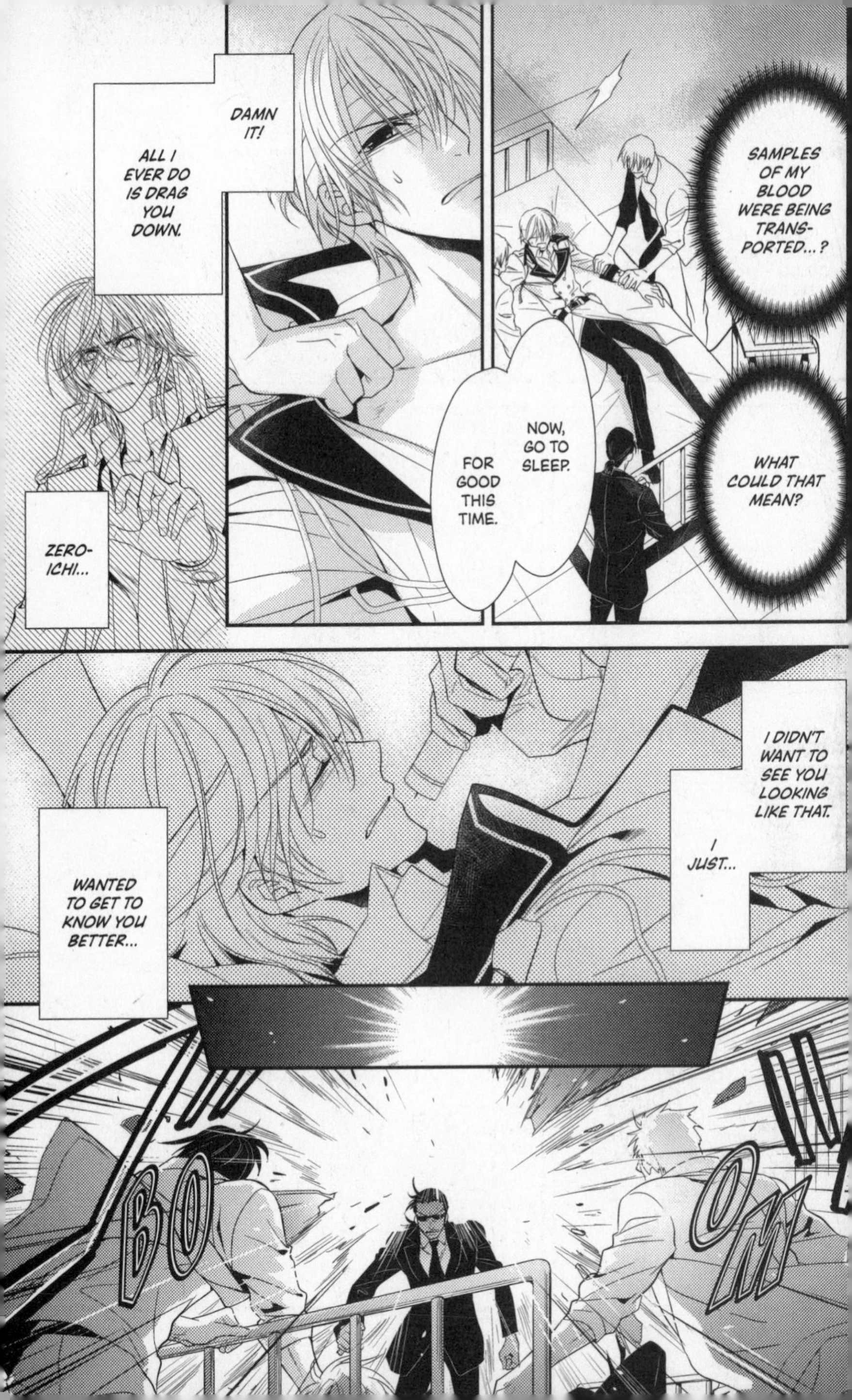
SAMPLES OF MY BLOOD WERE BEING TRANS-PORTED...?
WHAT COULD THAT MEAN?
NOW, GO TO SLEEP.
FOR GOOD THIS TIME.
DAMN IT!
ALL I EVER DO IS DRAG YOU DOWN.
ZERO-ICHI...
I DIDN'T WANT TO SEE YOU LOOKING LIKE THAT.
I JUST...
WANTED TO GET TO KNOW YOU BETTER...
BOOM

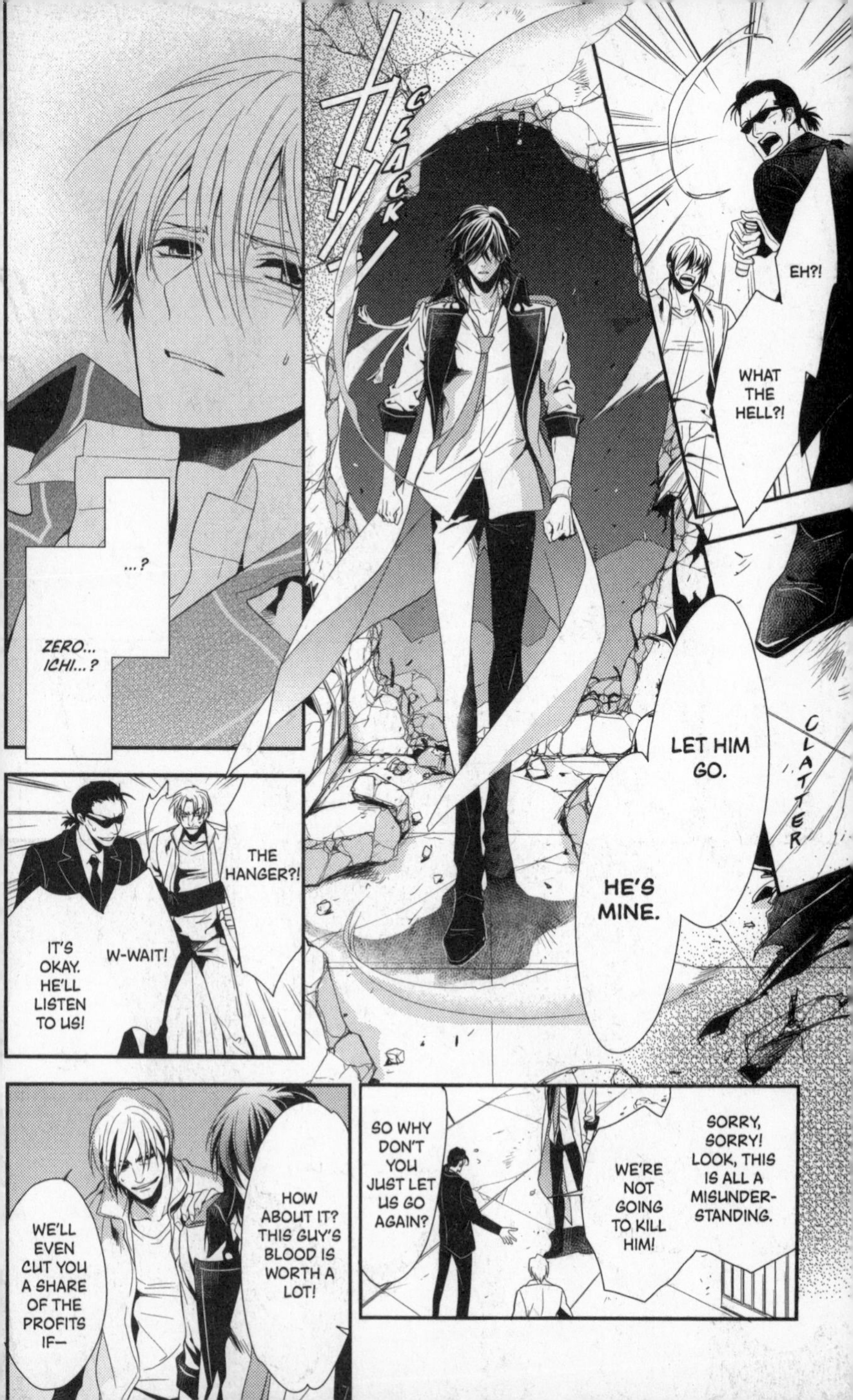
EH?!
WHAT THE HELL?!
CRACK
LET HIM GO.
HE'S MINE.
CLATTER
...?
ZERO... ICHI...?
THE HANGER?!
W-WAIT!
IT'S OKAY. HE'LL LISTEN TO US!
SORRY, SORRY! LOOK, THIS IS ALL A MISUNDER-STANDING.
WE'RE NOT GOING TO KILL HIM!
SO WHY DON'T YOU JUST LET US GO AGAIN?
HOW ABOUT IT? THIS GUY'S BLOOD IS WORTH A LOT!
WE'LL EVEN CUT YOU A SHARE OF THE PROFITS IF—

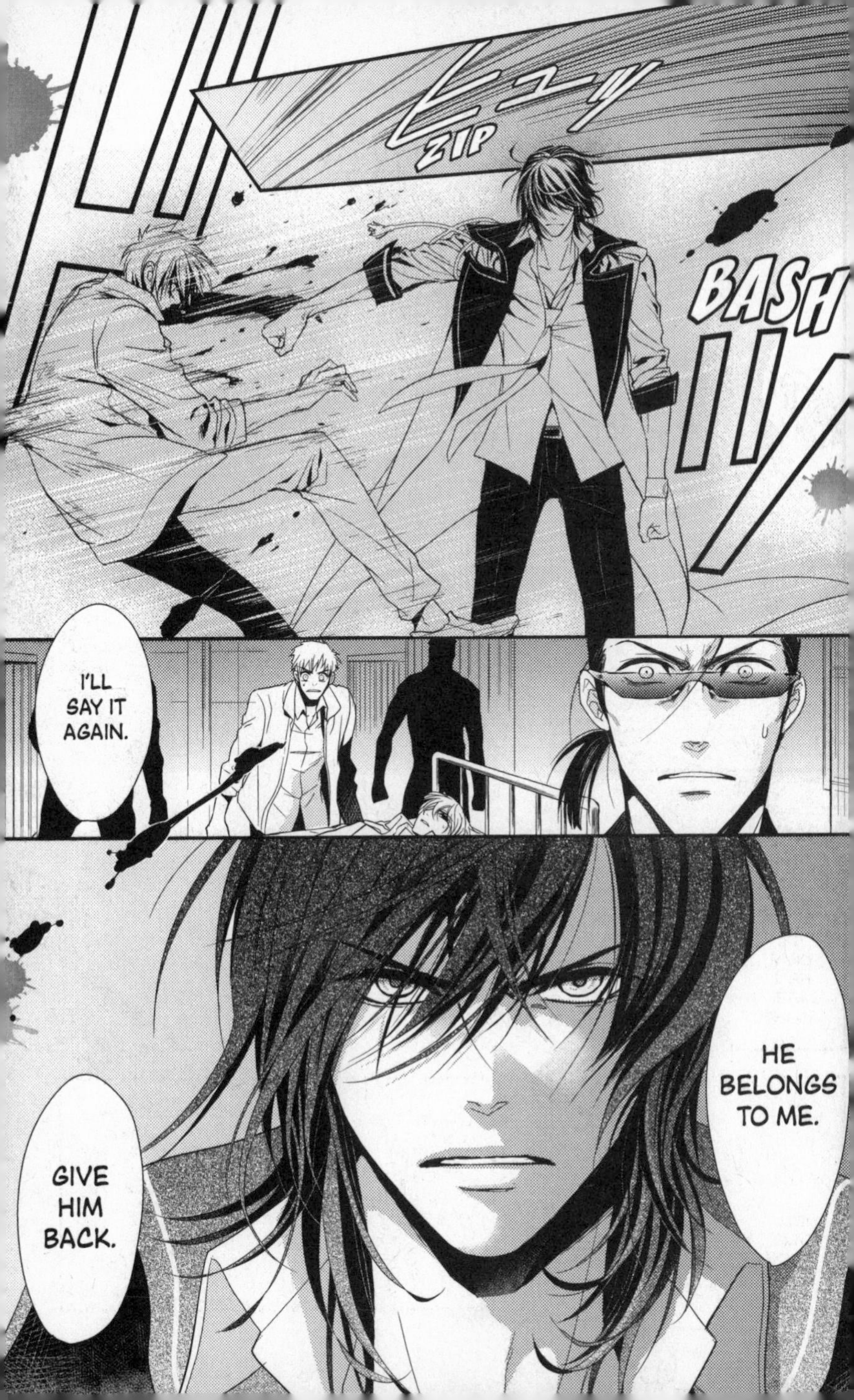
ヒュッ
ZIP
BASH
I'LL SAY IT AGAIN.
HE BELONGS TO ME.
GIVE HIM BACK.

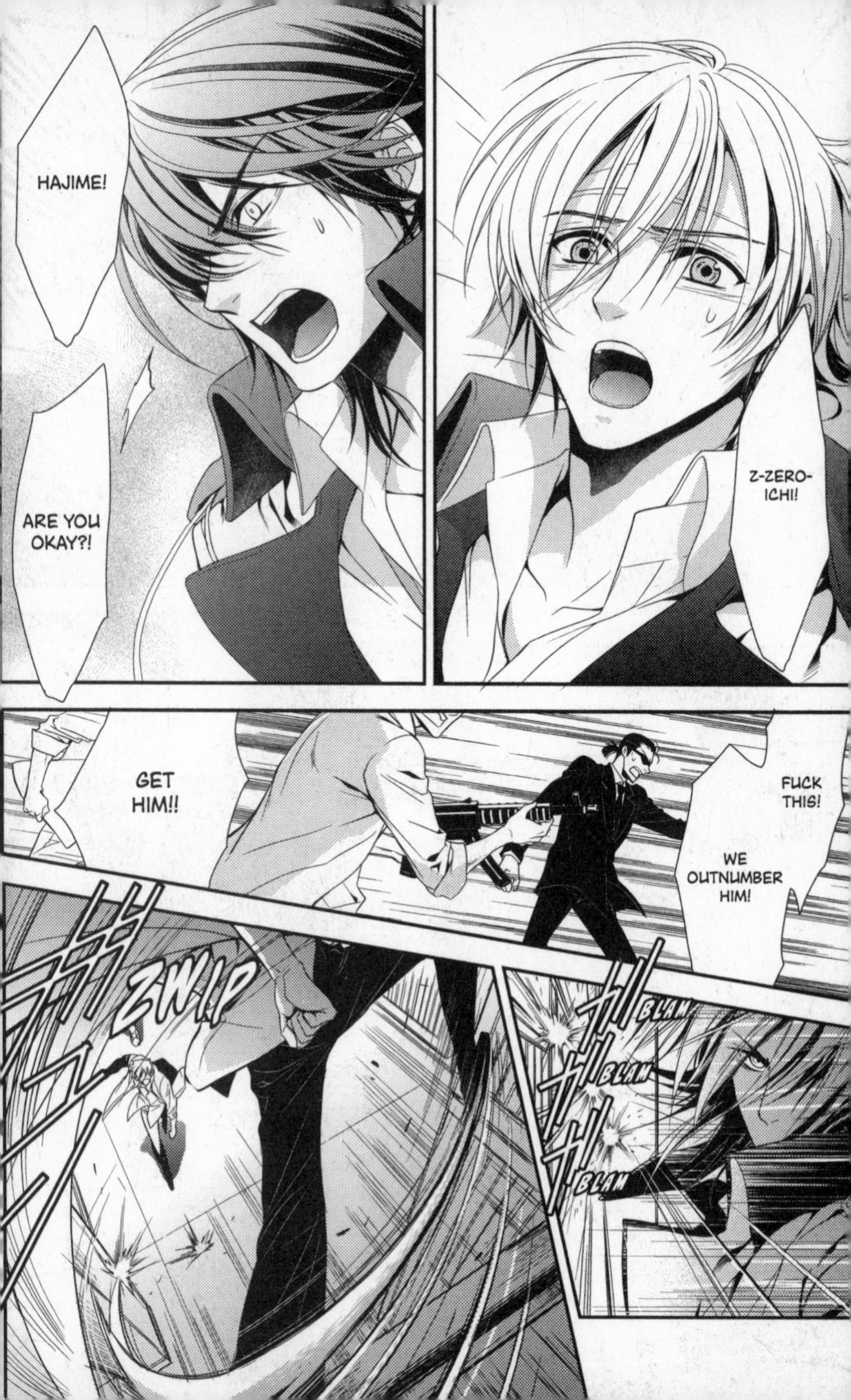
Z-ZERO-ICHI!
HAJIME!
ARE YOU OKAY?!
FUCK THIS!
WE OUTNUMBER HIM!
GET HIM!!
BLAM
BLAM
BLAM
ZWIP

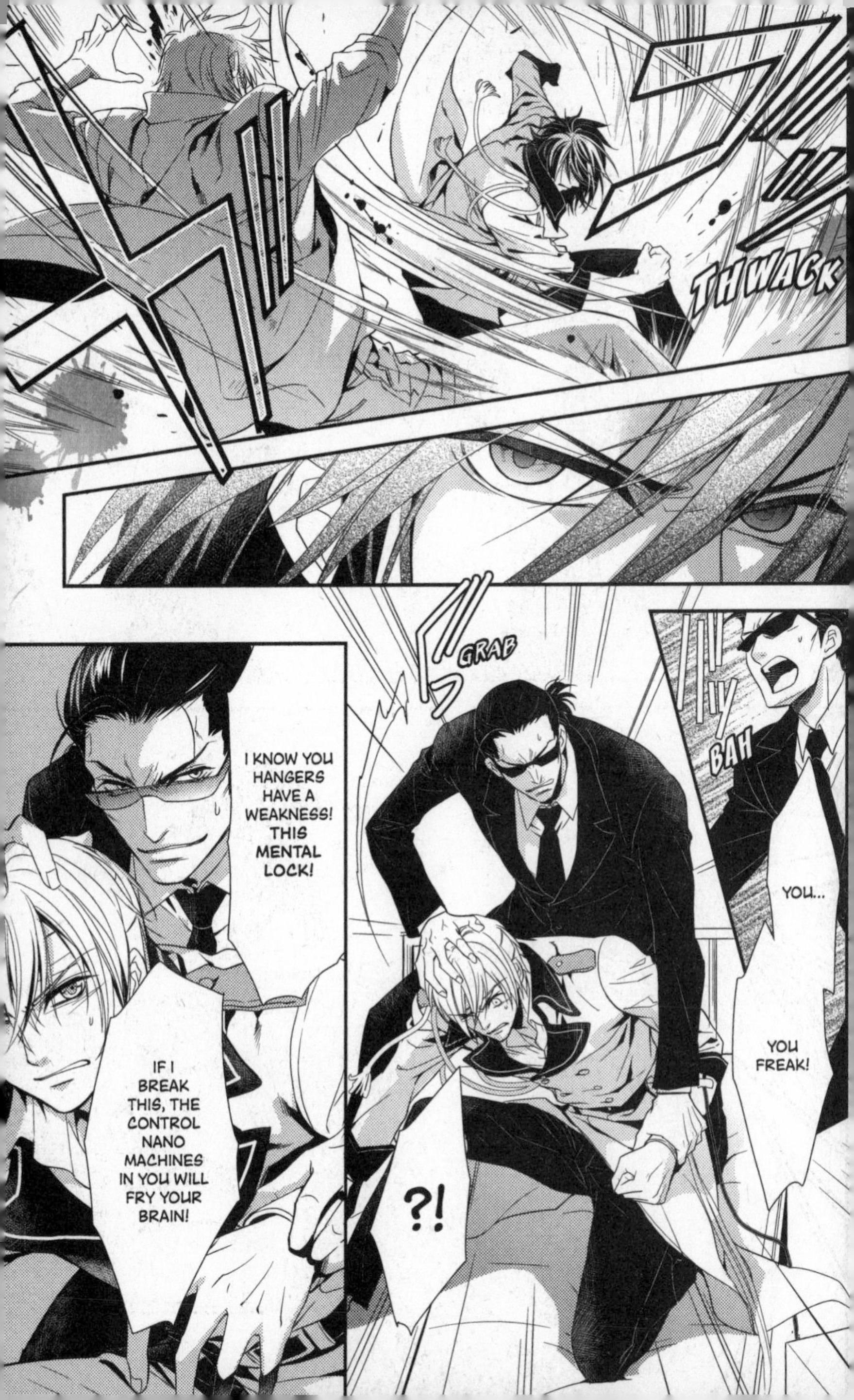
THWACK
BAH
YOU...
YOU FREAK!
GRAB
?!
I KNOW YOU HANGERS HAVE A WEAKNESS! THIS MENTAL LOCK!
IF I BREAK THIS, THE CONTROL NANO MACHINES IN YOU WILL FRY YOUR BRAIN!

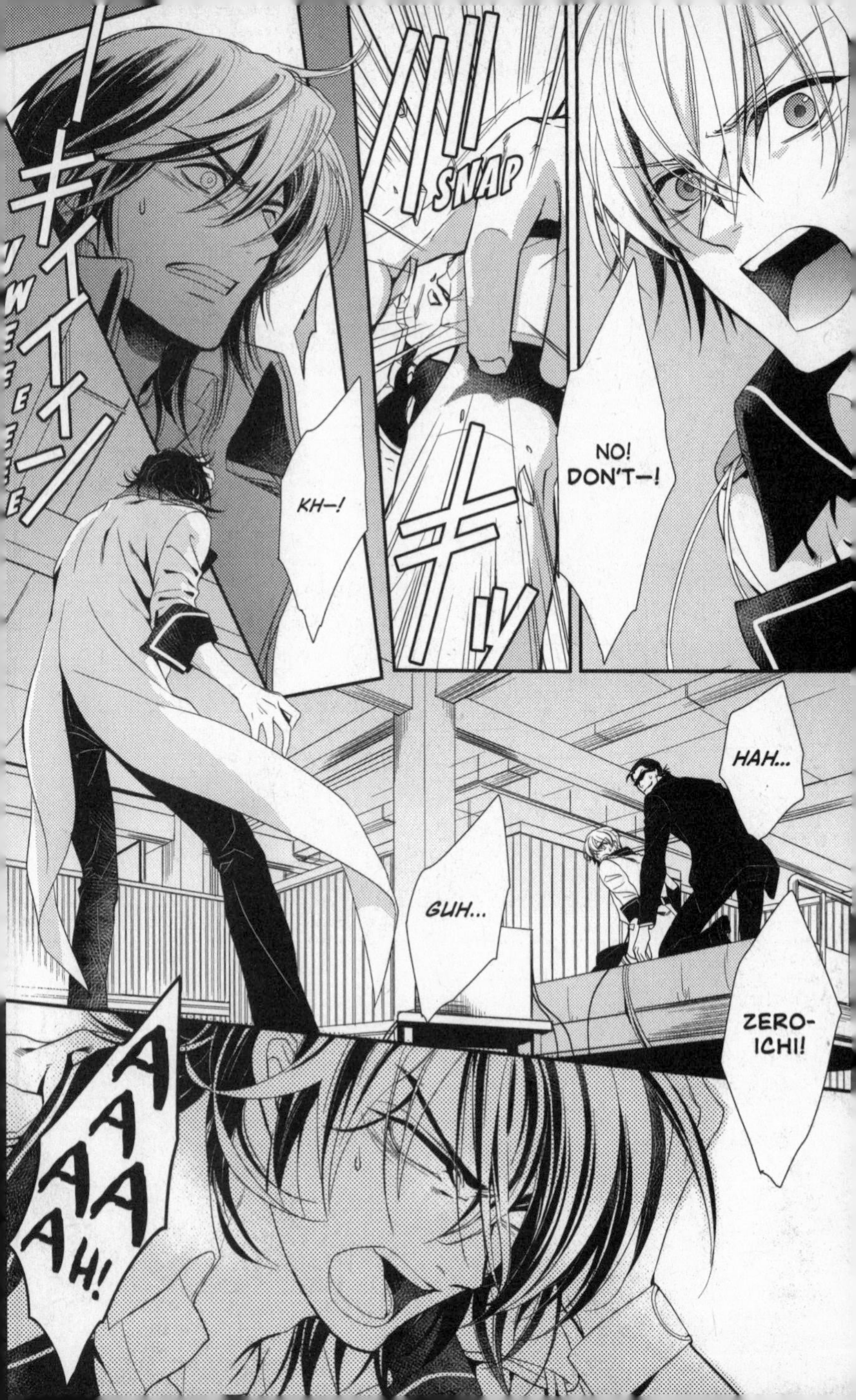
NO! DON'T—!
SNAP
KH—!
HAH...
GUH...
ZERO-ICHI!
AAAAAH!

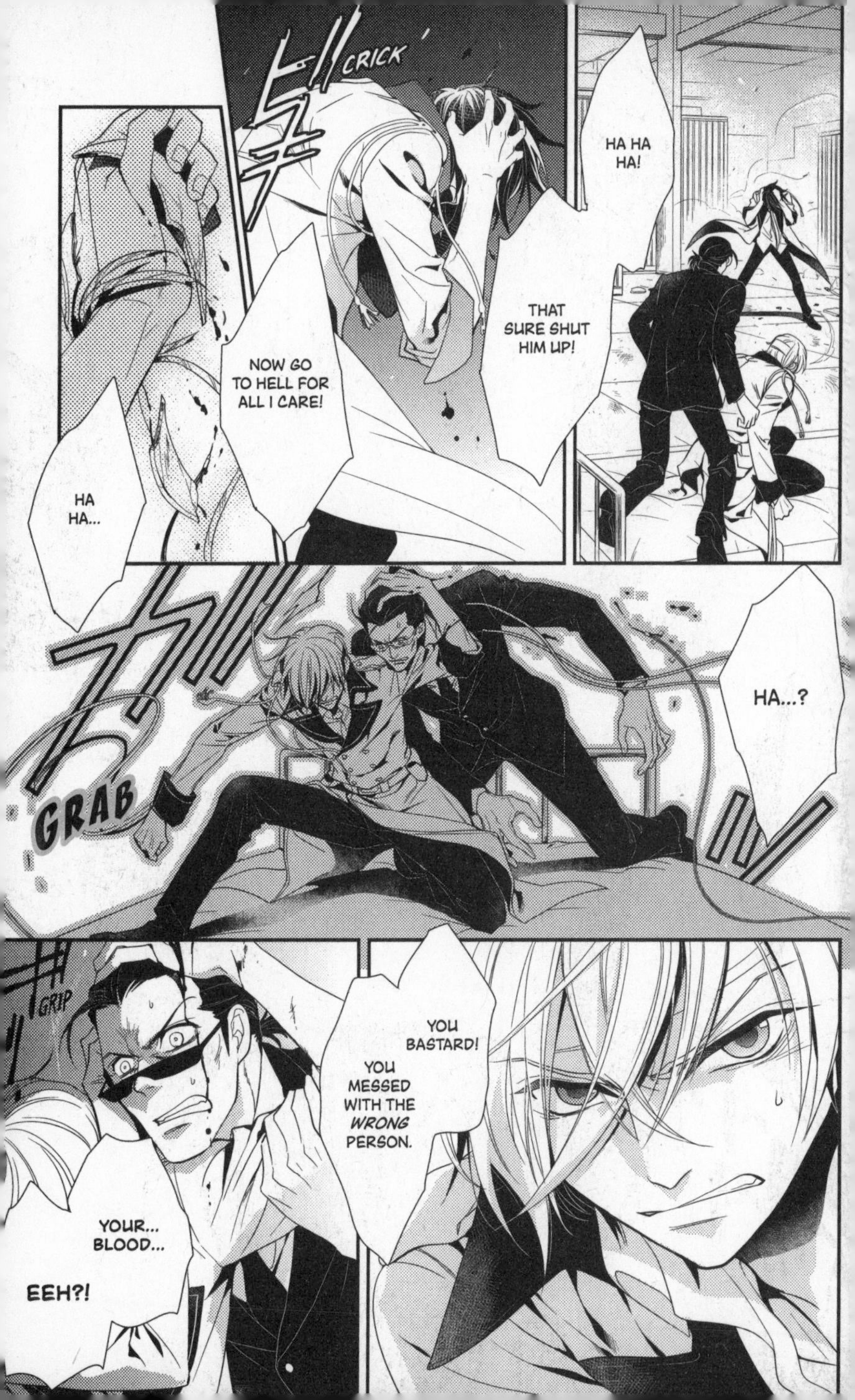
HA HA HA!
THAT SURE SHUT HIM UP!
CRICK
NOW GO TO HELL FOR ALL I CARE!
HA HA...
HA...?
GRAB
YOU BASTARD!
YOU MESSED WITH THE *WRONG* PERSON.
GRIP
YOUR... BLOOD...
EEH?!

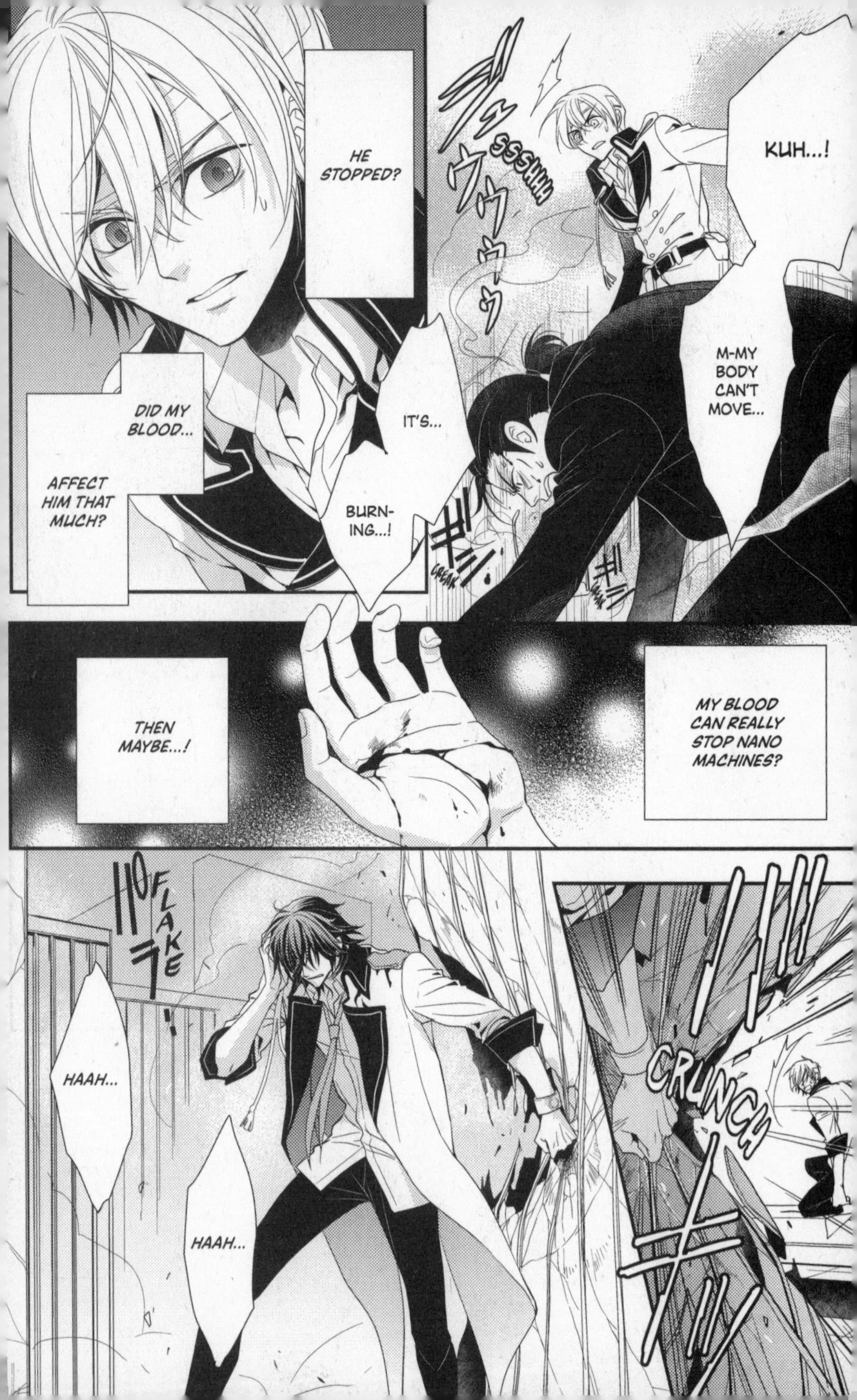
SSSSHHH
KUH...!
M-MY BODY CAN'T MOVE...
CREAK
CREAK
HE STOPPED?
IT'S...
BURNING...!
DID MY BLOOD...
AFFECT HIM THAT MUCH?
MY BLOOD CAN REALLY STOP NANO MACHINES?
THEN MAYBE...!
CRUNCH
FLAKE
HAAH...
HAAH...

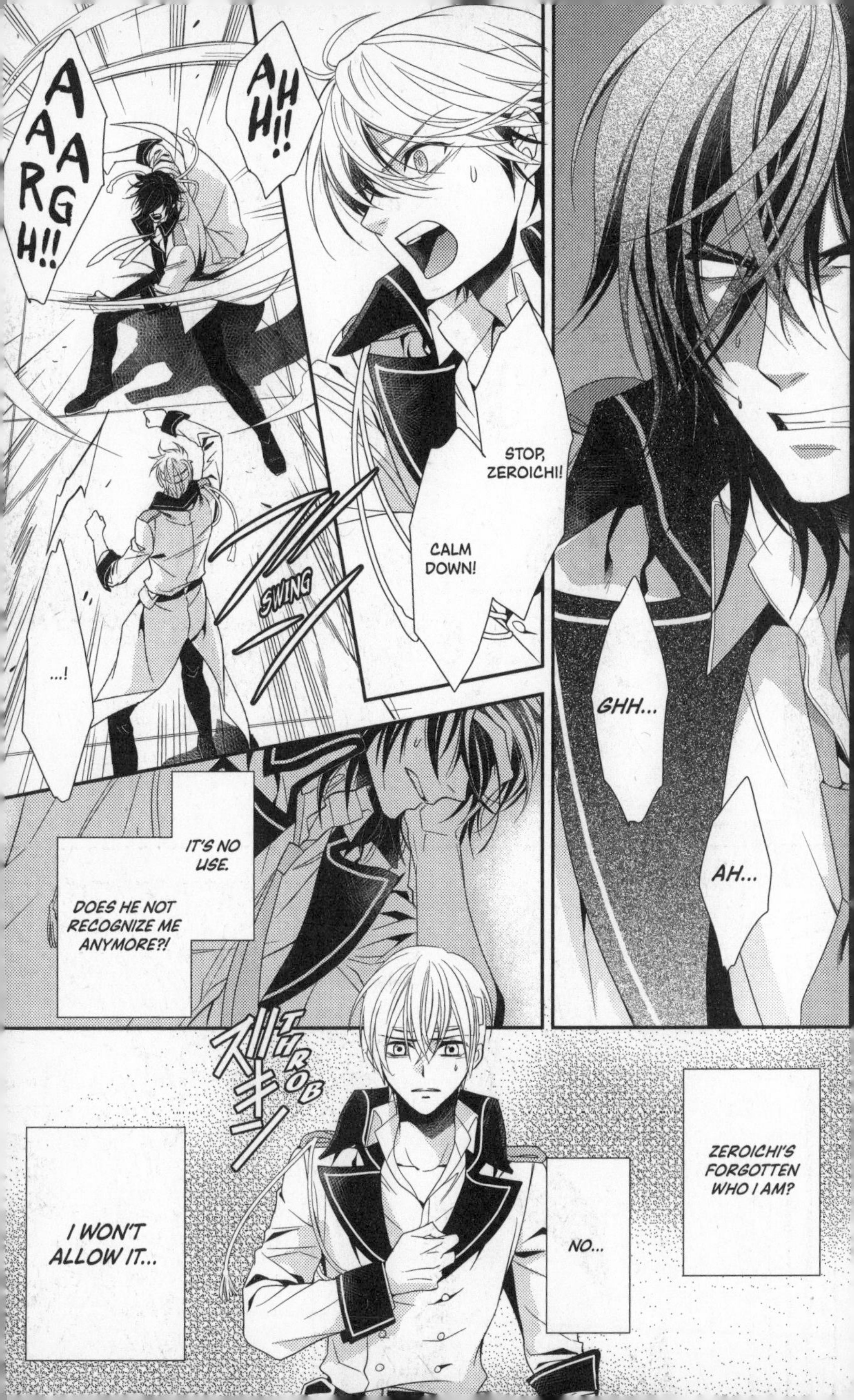
GHH...
AH...
AHH!!
STOP, ZEROICHI!
CALM DOWN!
AAARGH!!
SWING
...!
IT'S NO USE.
DOES HE NOT RECOGNIZE ME ANYMORE?!
ZEROICHI'S FORGOTTEN WHO I AM?
NO...
THROB
I WON'T ALLOW IT...

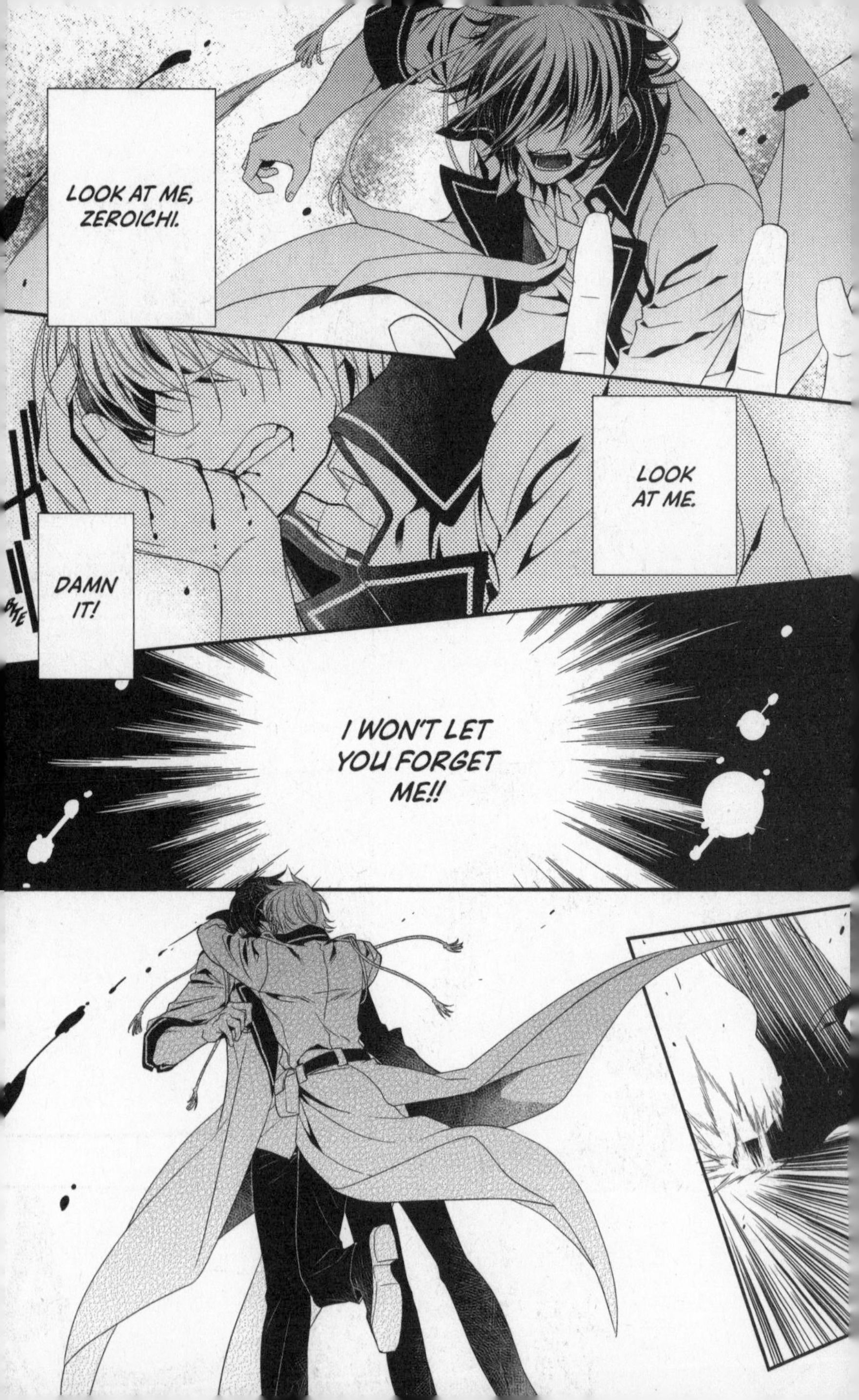
LOOK AT ME, ZEROICHI.
LOOK AT ME.
DAMN IT!
I WON'T LET YOU FORGET ME!!

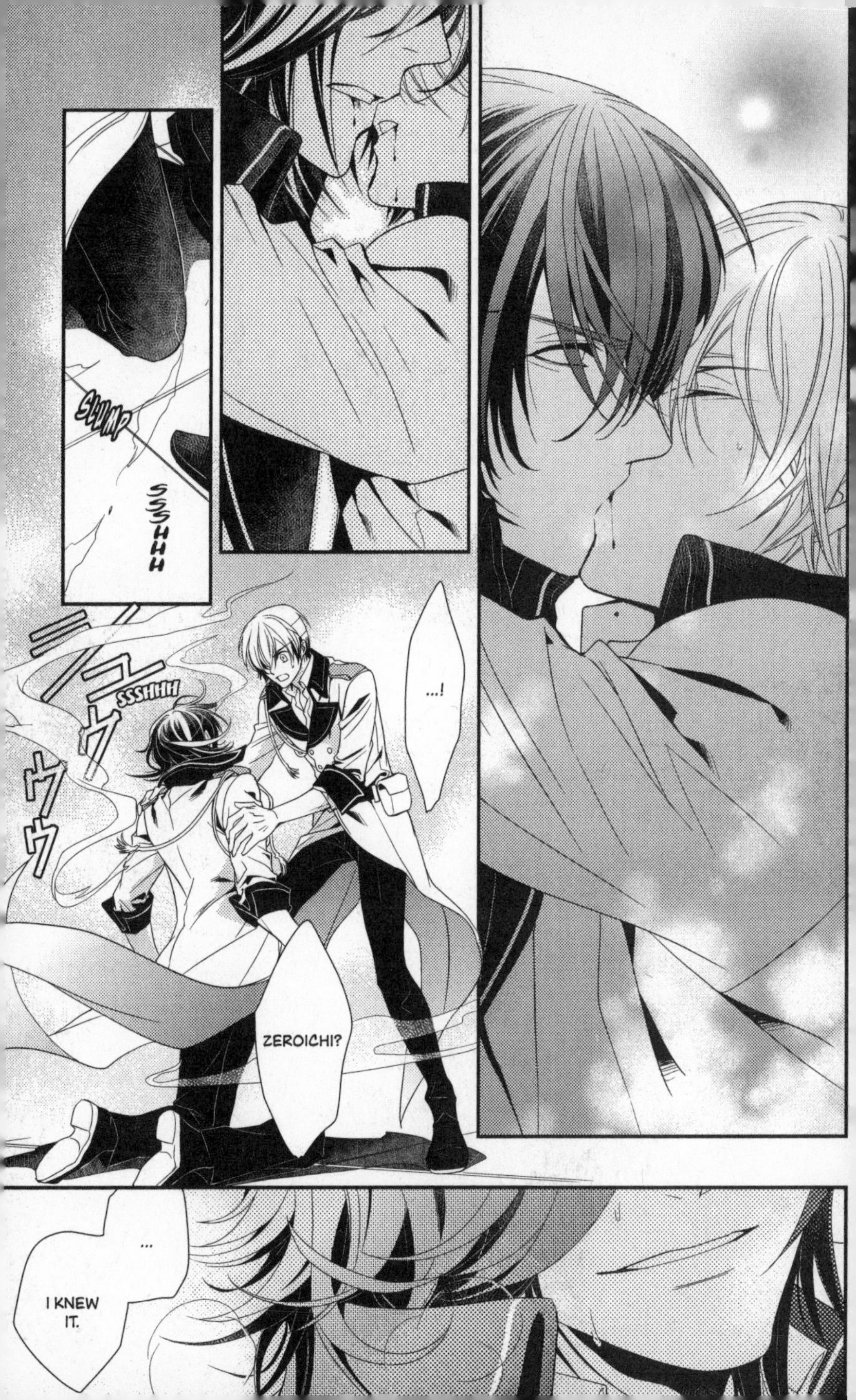
SLUMP
SSSHHH
...!
SSSHHH
シュウウウ
ZEROICHI?
...
I KNEW IT.

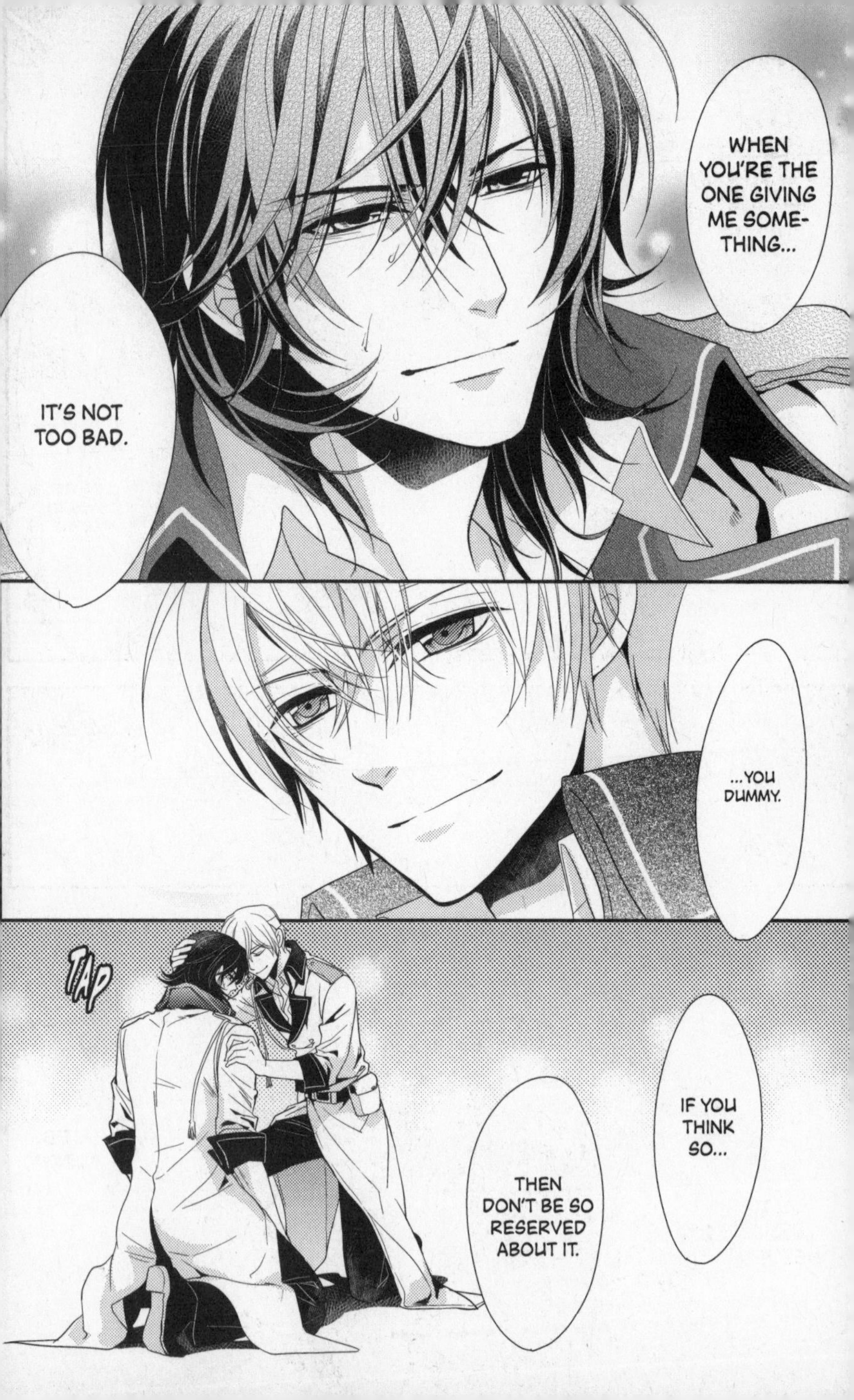
WHEN YOU'RE THE ONE GIVING ME SOME- THING...
IT'S NOT TOO BAD.
...YOU DUMMY.
IF YOU THINK SO...
THEN DON'T BE SO RESERVED ABOUT IT.
TAP

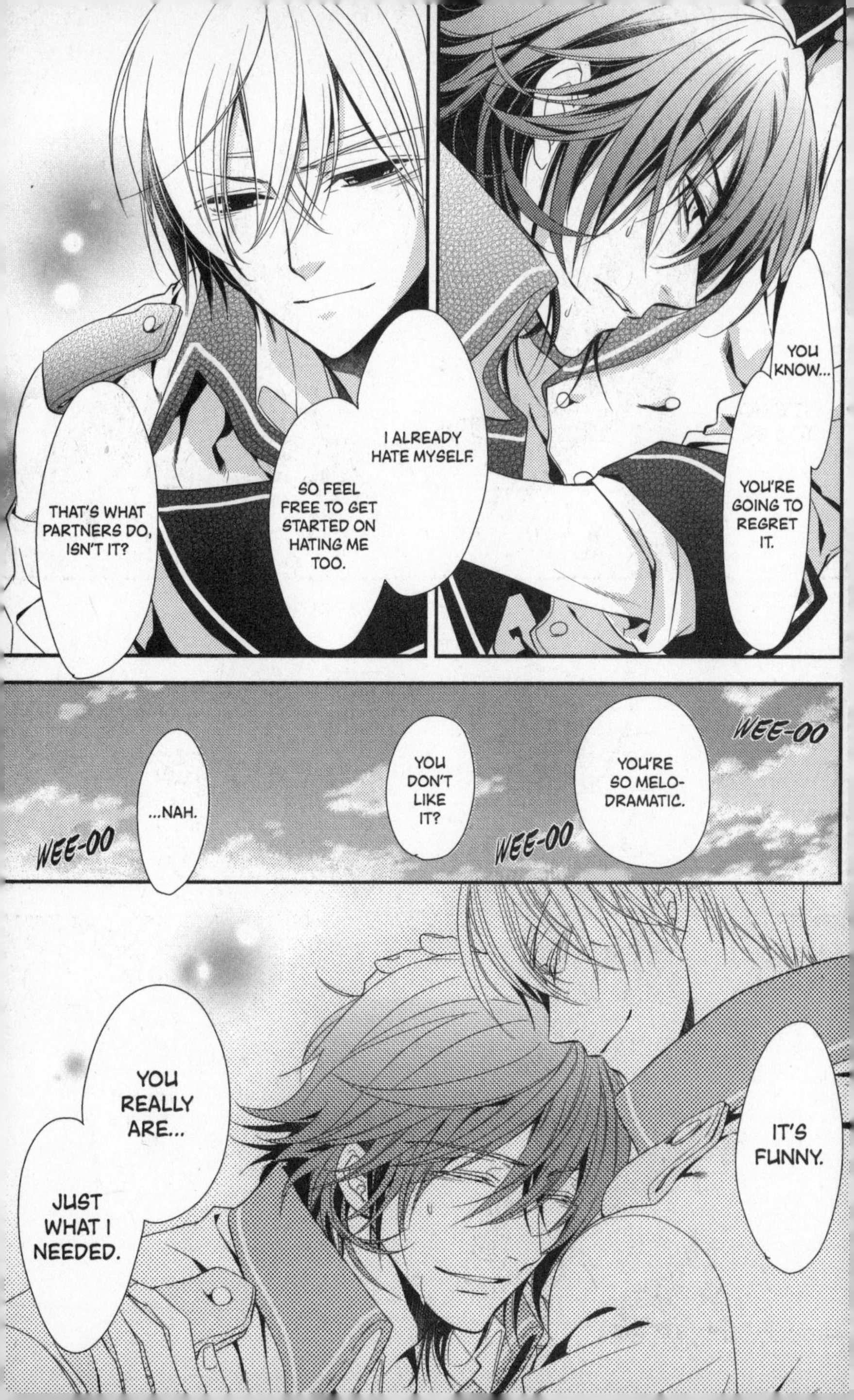
YOU KNOW...
YOU'RE GOING TO REGRET IT.
I ALREADY HATE MYSELF.
SO FEEL FREE TO GET STARTED ON HATING ME TOO.
THAT'S WHAT PARTNERS DO, ISN'T IT?
WEE-OO
YOU'RE SO MELO-DRAMATIC.
WEE-OO
YOU DON'T LIKE IT?
...NAH.
WEE-OO
IT'S FUNNY.
YOU REALLY ARE...
JUST WHAT I NEEDED.

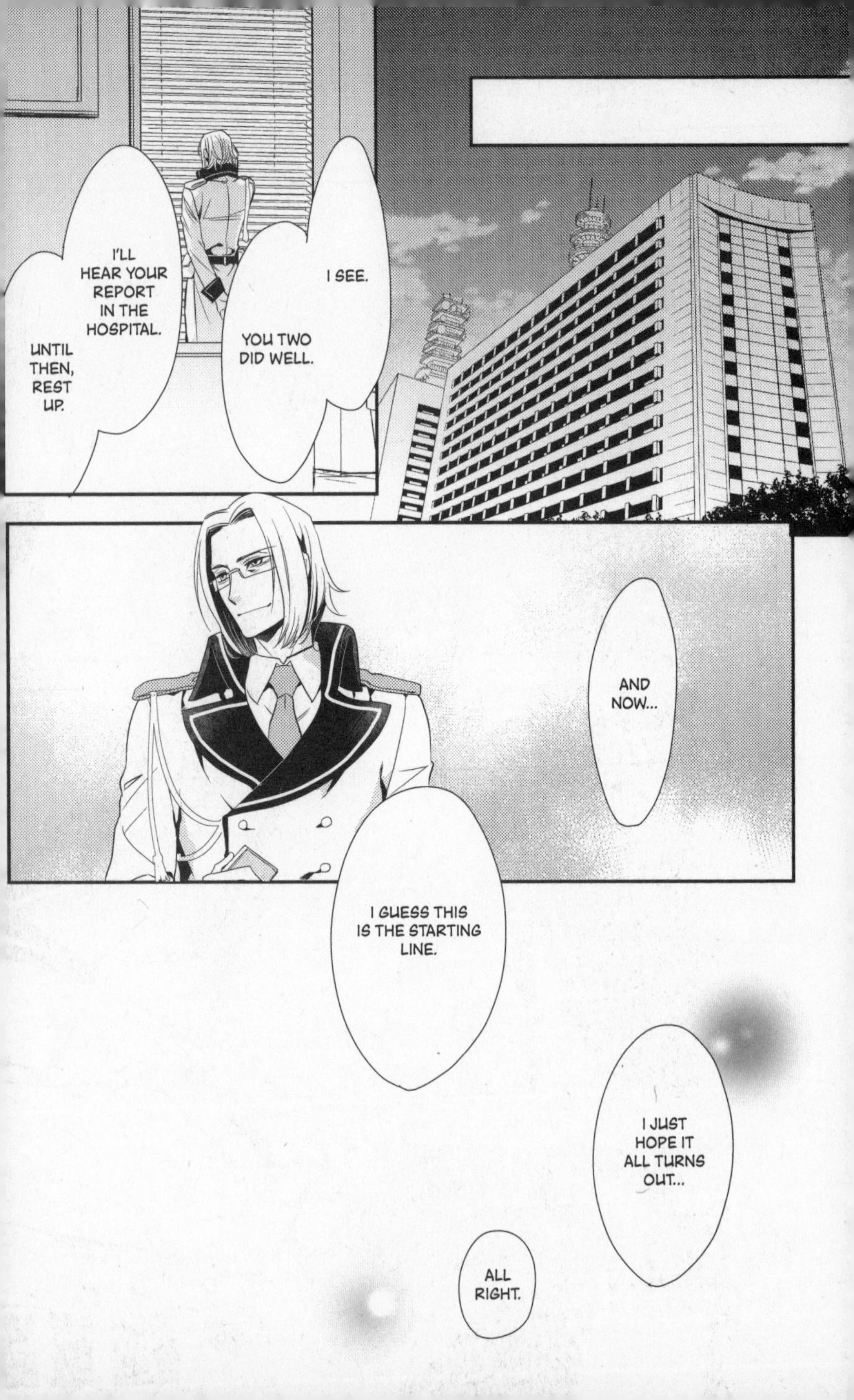
I SEE.
YOU TWO DID WELL.
I'LL HEAR YOUR REPORT IN THE HOSPITAL.
UNTIL THEN, REST UP.
AND NOW...
I GUESS THIS IS THE STARTING LINE.
I JUST HOPE IT ALL TURNS OUT...
ALL RIGHT.

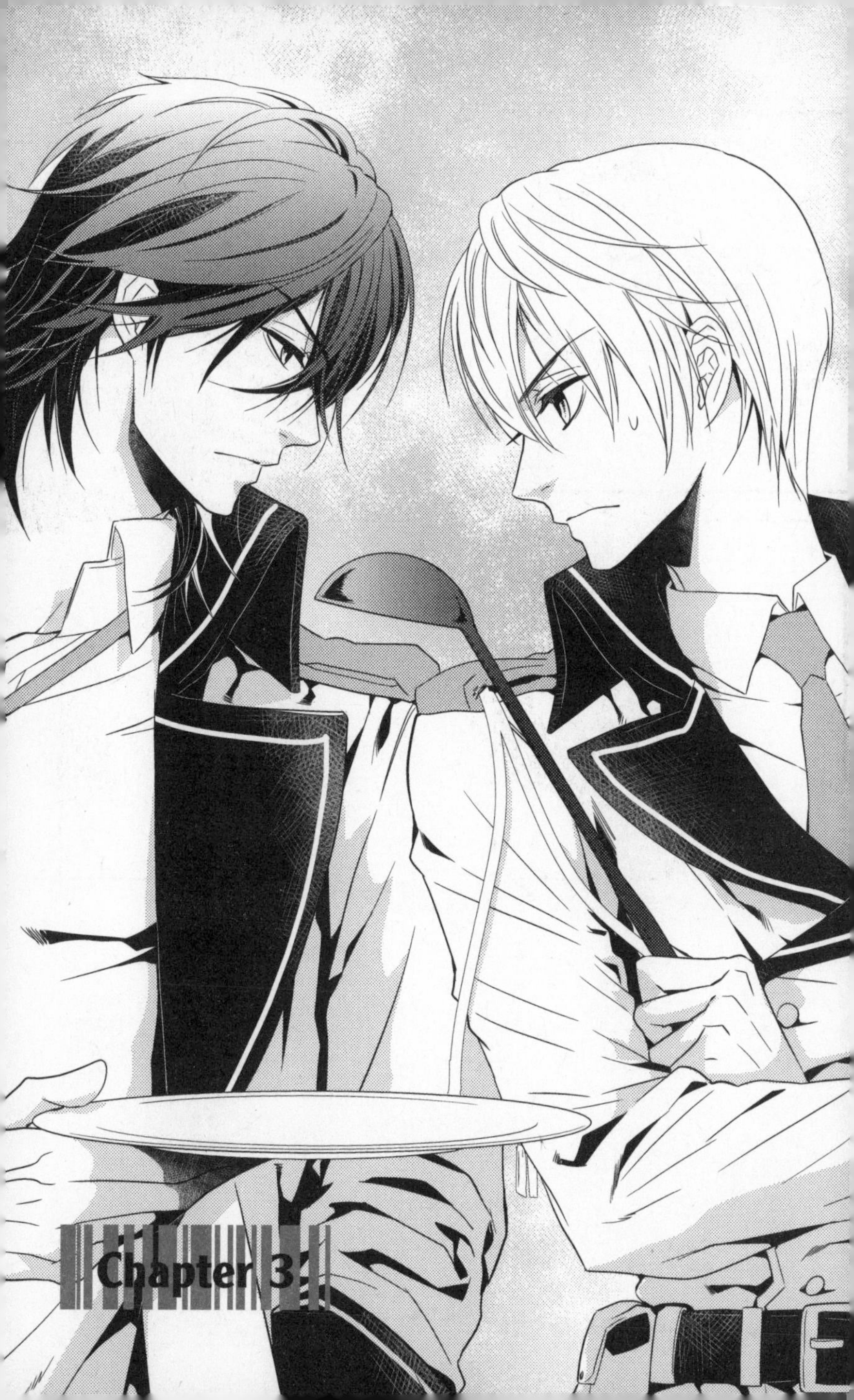
Chapter 3

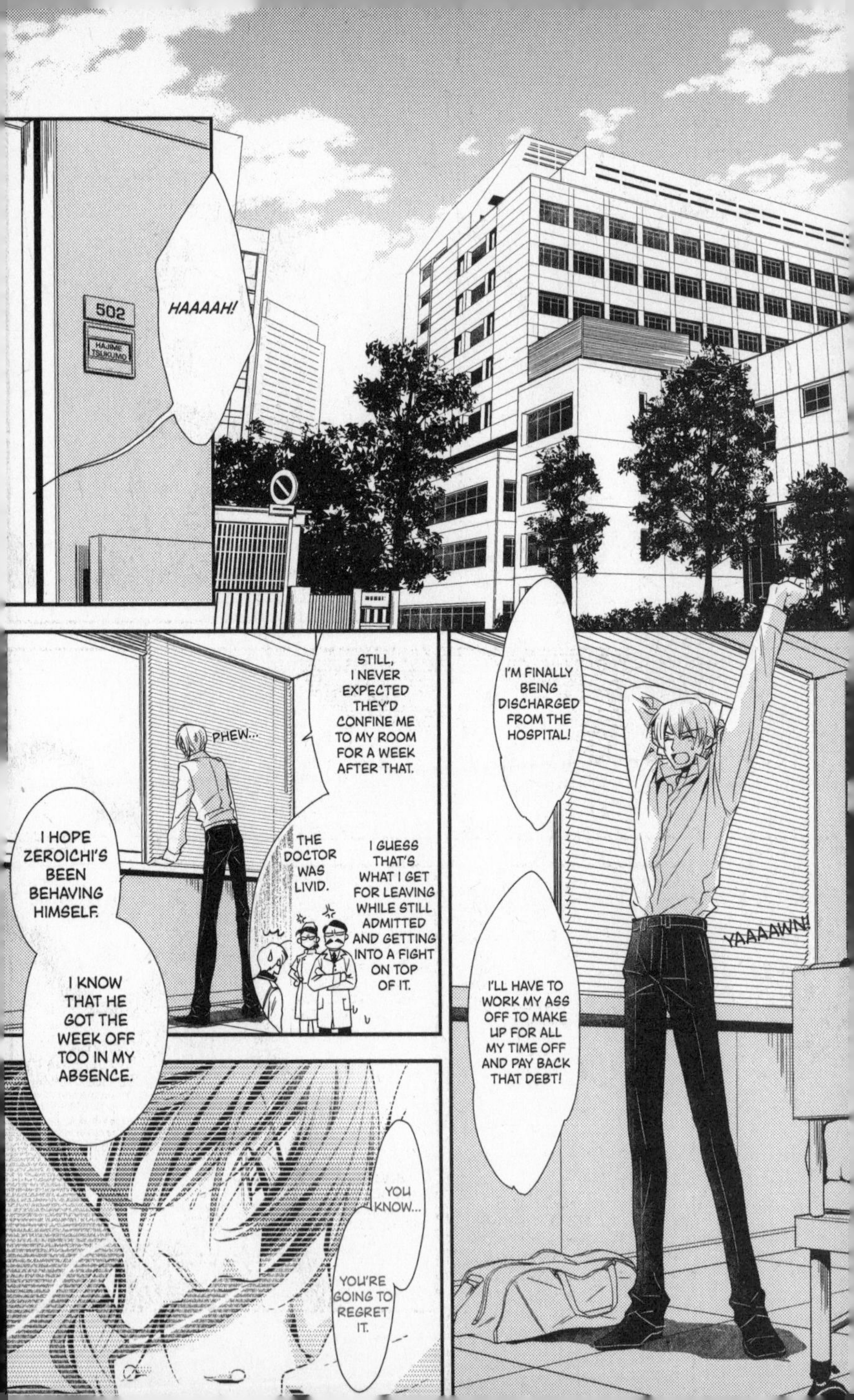
502
HAJIME TSUKUMO
HAAAAH!
I'M FINALLY BEING DISCHARGED FROM THE HOSPITAL!
YAAAAWN!
I'LL HAVE TO WORK MY ASS OFF TO MAKE UP FOR ALL MY TIME OFF AND PAY BACK THAT DEBT!
STILL, I NEVER EXPECTED THEY'D CONFINE ME TO MY ROOM FOR A WEEK AFTER THAT.
PHEW...
I GUESS THAT'S WHAT I GET FOR LEAVING WHILE STILL ADMITTED AND GETTING INTO A FIGHT ON TOP OF IT.
THE DOCTOR WAS LIVID.
I HOPE ZEROICHI'S BEEN BEHAVING HIMSELF.
I KNOW THAT HE GOT THE WEEK OFF TOO IN MY ABSENCE.
YOU KNOW...
YOU'RE GOING TO REGRET IT.

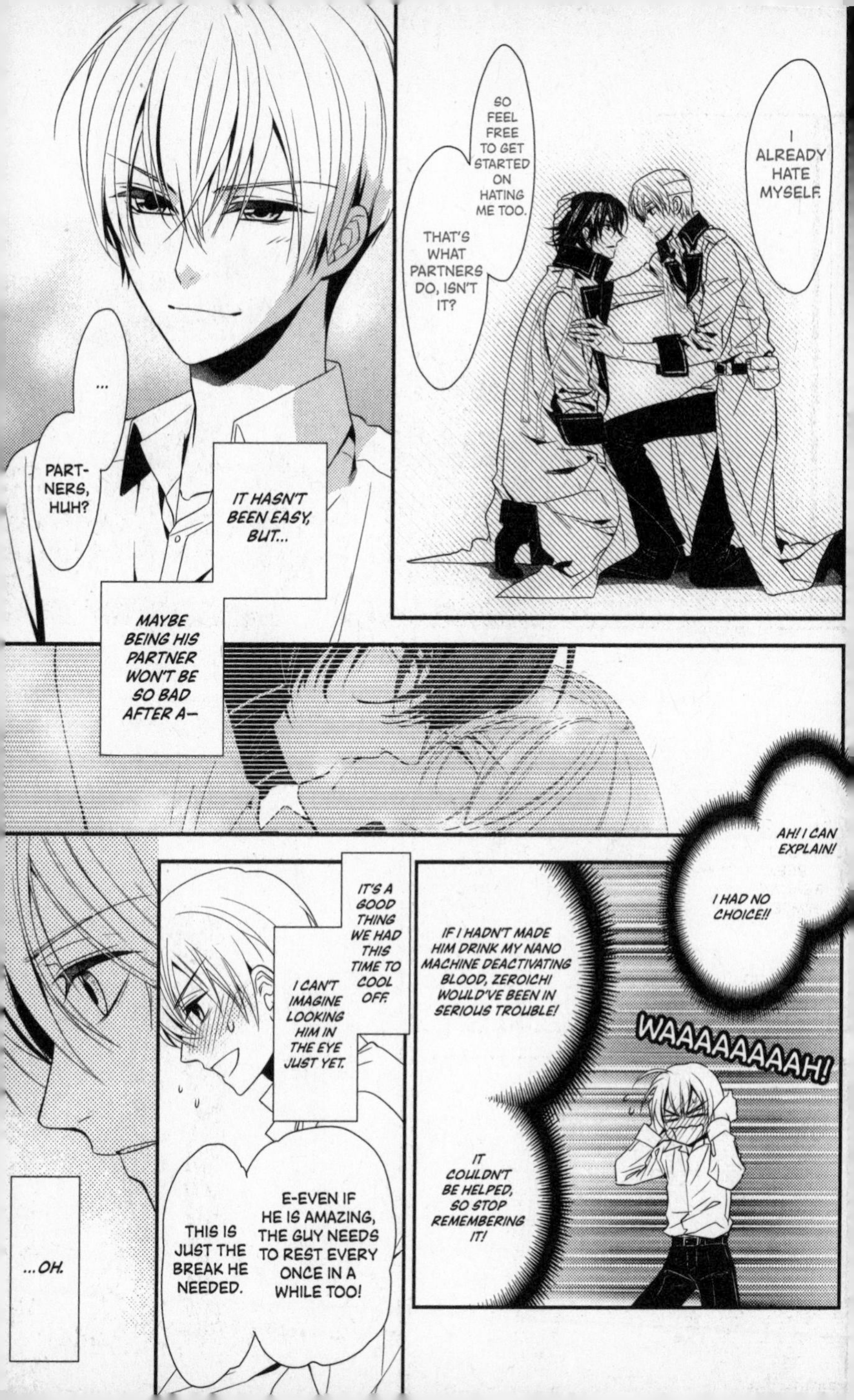
I ALREADY HATE MYSELF.
SO FEEL FREE TO GET STARTED ON HATING ME TOO.
THAT'S WHAT PARTNERS DO, ISN'T IT?
...
PARTNERS, HUH?
IT HASN'T BEEN EASY, BUT...
MAYBE BEING HIS PARTNER WON'T BE SO BAD AFTER A—
AH! I CAN EXPLAIN!
I HAD NO CHOICE!!
IF I HADN'T MADE HIM DRINK MY NANO MACHINE DEACTIVATING BLOOD, ZEROICHI WOULD'VE BEEN IN SERIOUS TROUBLE!
WAAAAAAAAAH!
IT COULDN'T BE HELPED, SO STOP REMEMBERING IT!
IT'S A GOOD THING WE HAD THIS TIME TO COOL OFF.
I CAN'T IMAGINE LOOKING HIM IN THE EYE JUST YET.
E-EVEN IF HE IS AMAZING, THE GUY NEEDS TO REST EVERY ONCE IN A WHILE TOO!
THIS IS JUST THE BREAK HE NEEDED.
...OH.

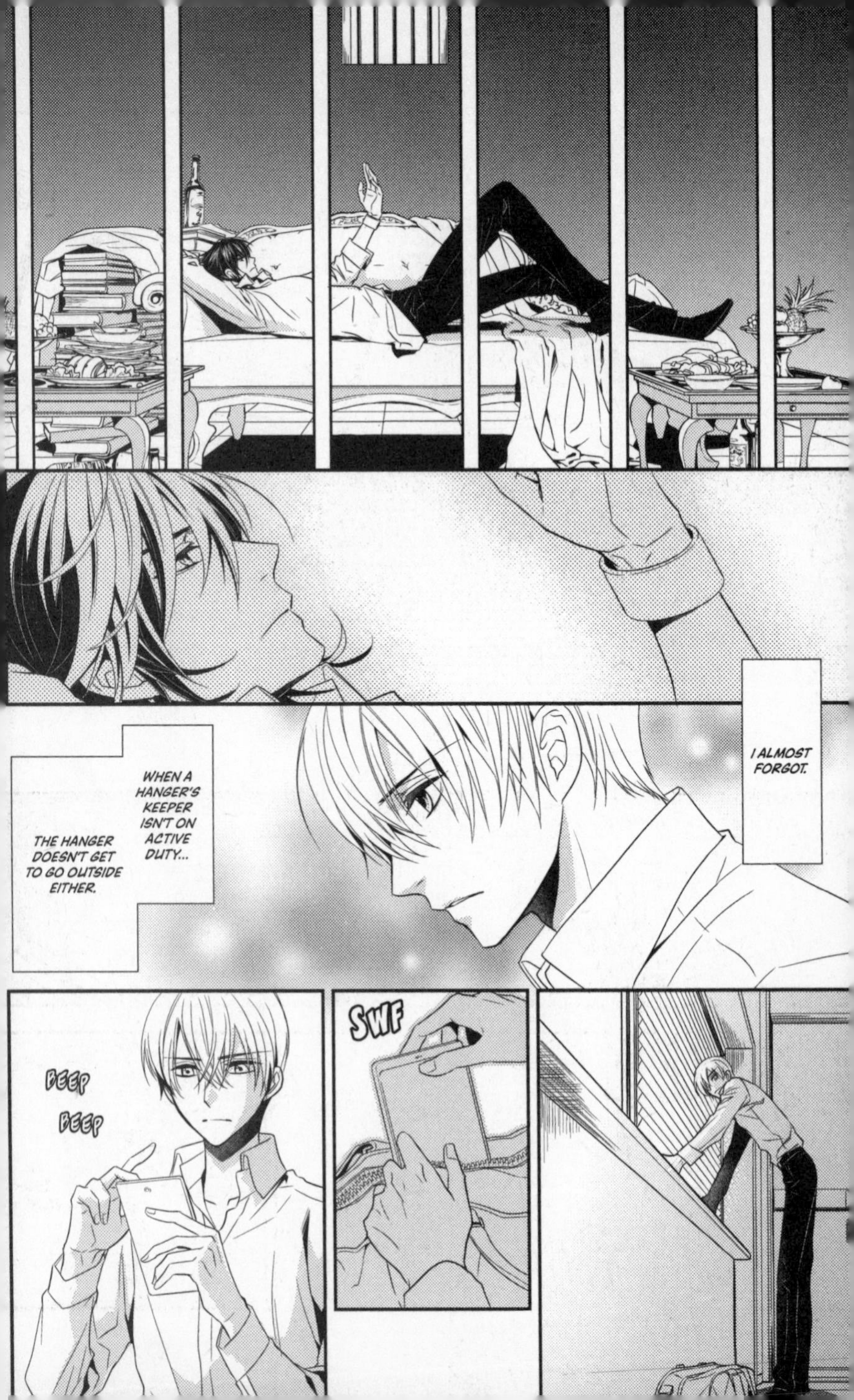
I ALMOST FORGOT.
WHEN A HANGER'S KEEPER ISN'T ON ACTIVE DUTY...
THE HANGER DOESN'T GET TO GO OUTSIDE EITHER.
SWF
BEEP
BEEP

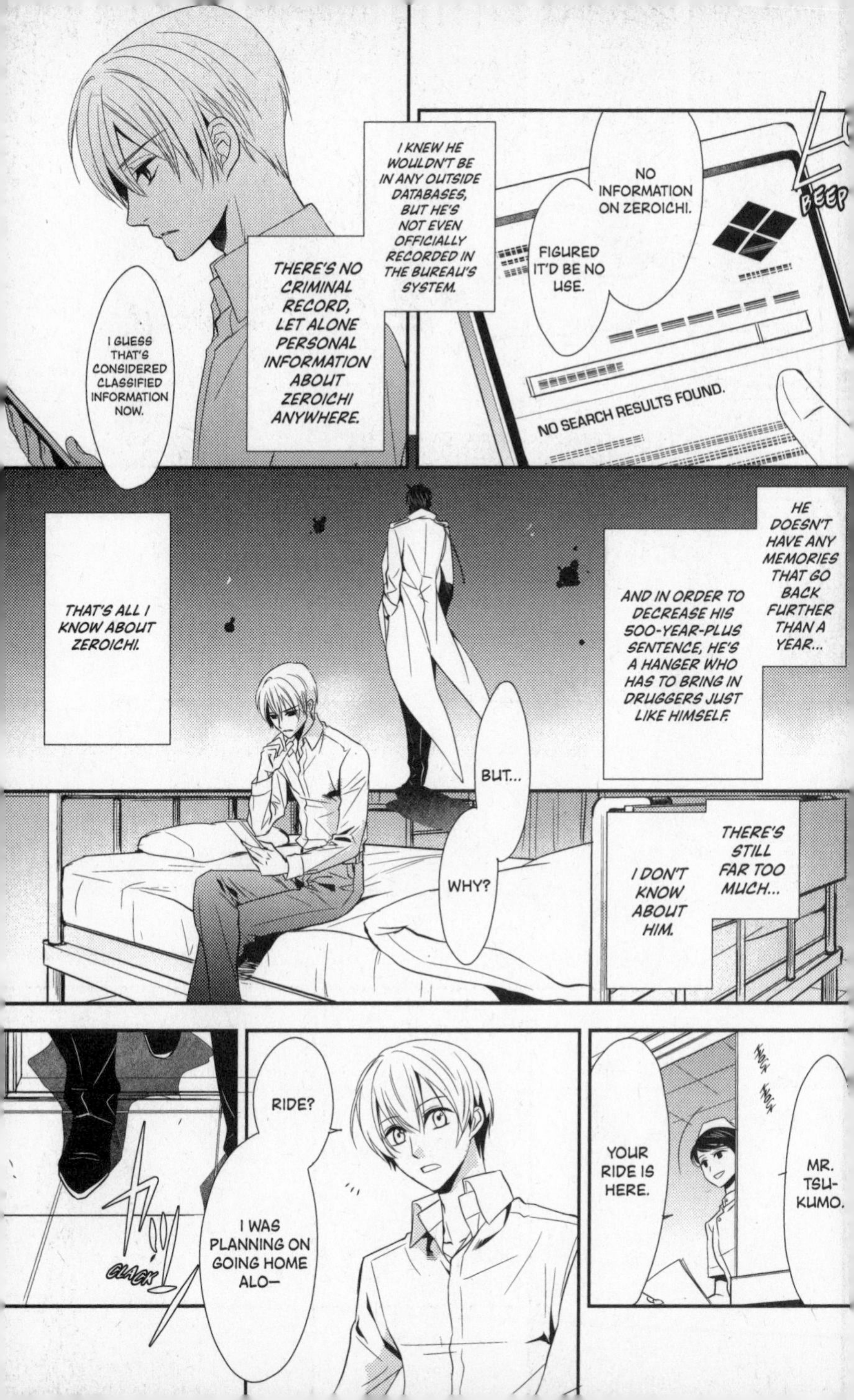

BEEP
NO INFORMATION ON ZEROICHI.
FIGURED IT'D BE NO USE.
NO SEARCH RESULTS FOUND.
I KNEW HE WOULDN'T BE IN ANY OUTSIDE DATABASES, BUT HE'S NOT EVEN OFFICIALLY RECORDED IN THE BUREAU'S SYSTEM.
THERE'S NO CRIMINAL RECORD, LET ALONE PERSONAL INFORMATION ABOUT ZEROICHI ANYWHERE.
I GUESS THAT'S CONSIDERED CLASSIFIED INFORMATION NOW.
HE DOESN'T HAVE ANY MEMORIES THAT GO BACK FURTHER THAN A YEAR...
AND IN ORDER TO DECREASE HIS 500-YEAR-PLUS SENTENCE, HE'S A HANGER WHO HAS TO BRING IN DRUGGERS JUST LIKE HIMSELF.
THAT'S ALL I KNOW ABOUT ZEROICHI.
BUT...
WHY?
THERE'S STILL FAR TOO MUCH...
I DON'T KNOW ABOUT HIM.
KNOCK KNOCK
MR. TSUKUMO.
YOUR RIDE IS HERE.
RIDE?
I WAS PLANNING ON GOING HOME ALO—
CLACK

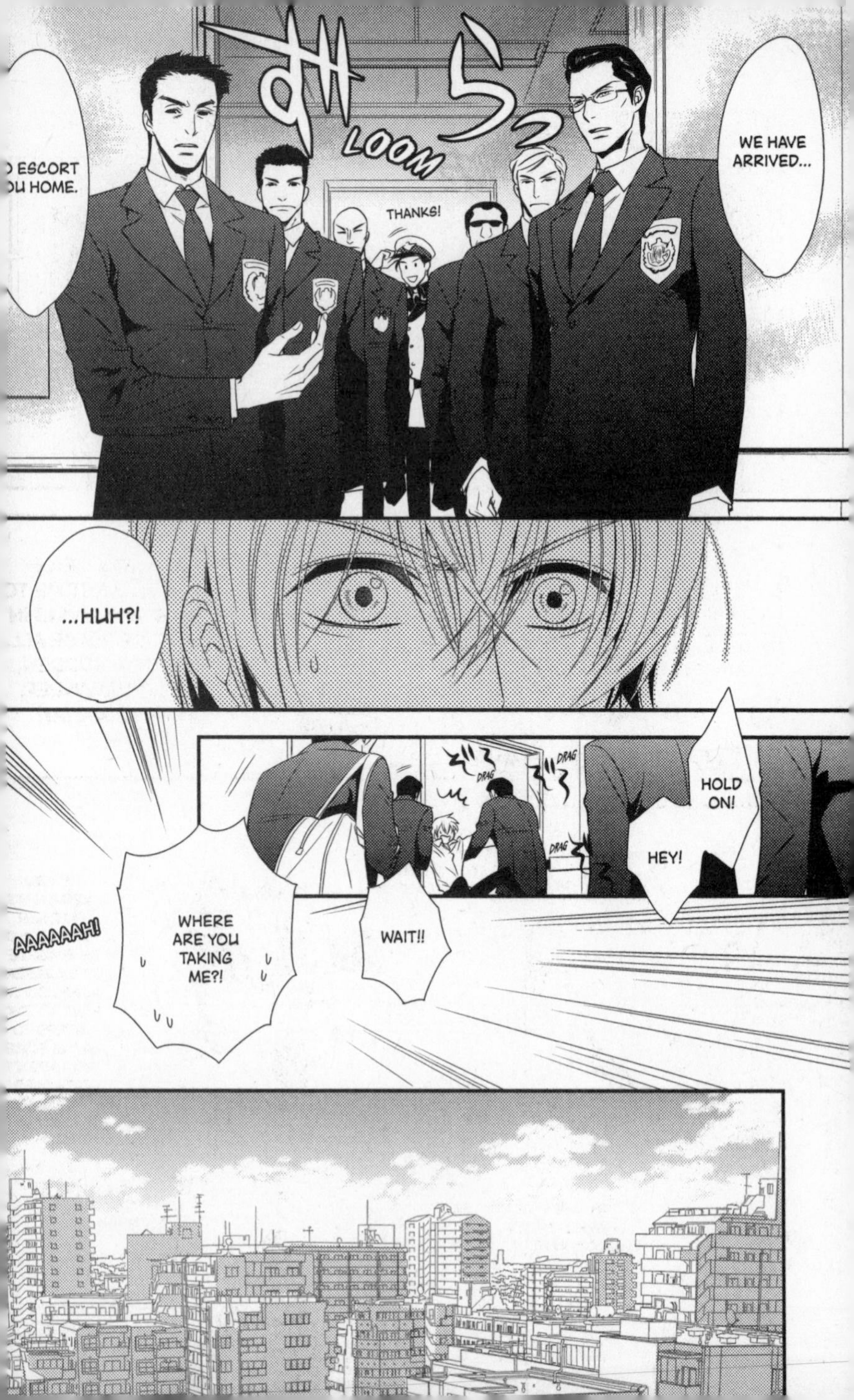
WE HAVE ARRIVED...
LOOM
THANKS!
O ESCORT OU HOME.
...HUH?!
HOLD ON!
HEY!
DRAG
DRAG
DRAG
WAIT!!
WHERE ARE YOU TAKING ME?!
AAAAAAH!

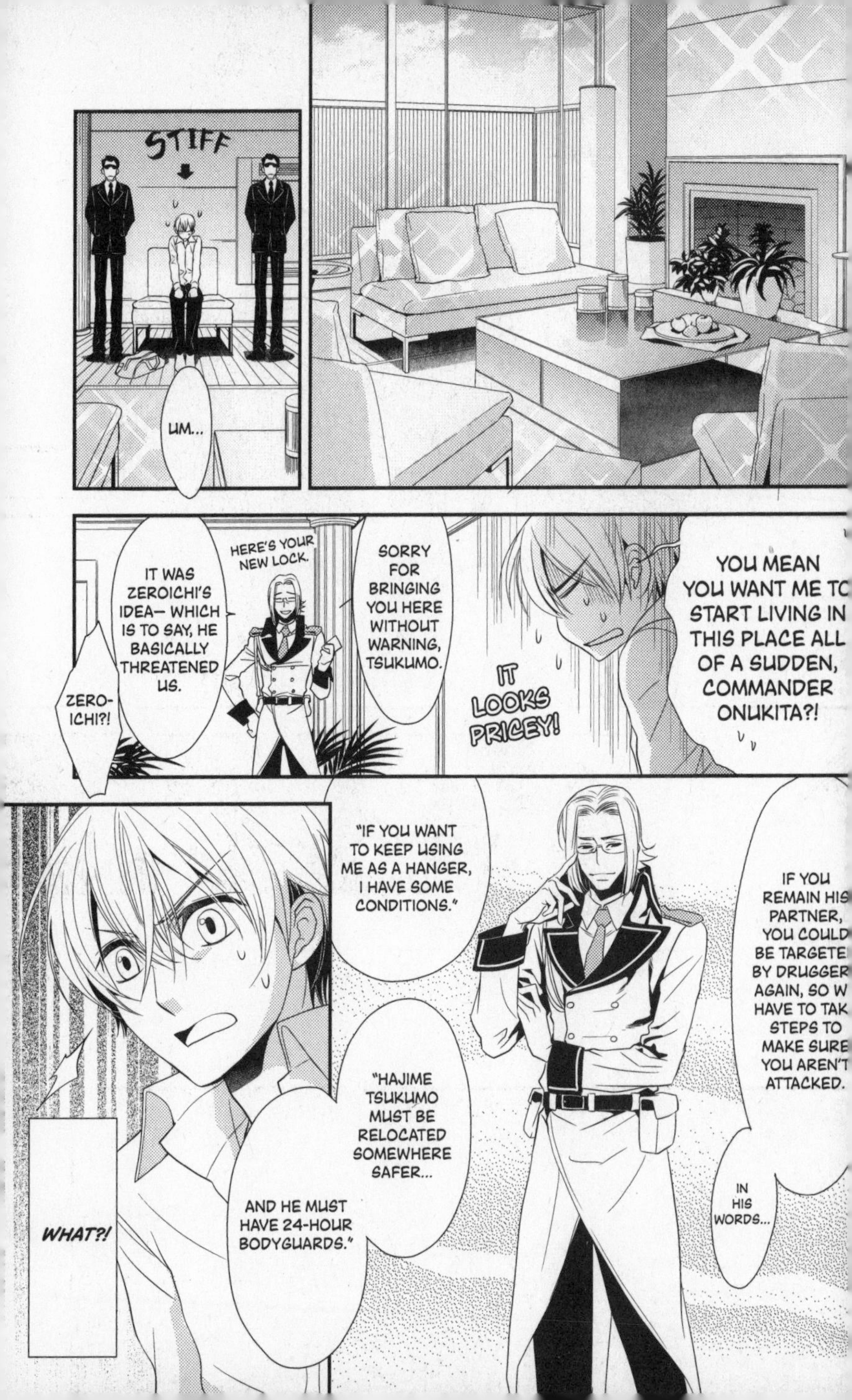
STIFF
UM...
YOU MEAN YOU WANT ME TO START LIVING IN THIS PLACE ALL OF A SUDDEN, COMMANDER ONUKITA?!
IT LOOKS PRICEY!
SORRY FOR BRINGING YOU HERE WITHOUT WARNING, TSUKUMO.
HERE'S YOUR NEW LOCK.
IT WAS ZEROICHI'S IDEA— WHICH IS TO SAY, HE BASICALLY THREATENED US.
ZERO-ICHI?!
IF YOU REMAIN HIS PARTNER, YOU COULD BE TARGETE BY DRUGGER AGAIN, SO W HAVE TO TAK STEPS TO MAKE SURE YOU AREN'T ATTACKED.
IN HIS WORDS...
"IF YOU WANT TO KEEP USING ME AS A HANGER, I HAVE SOME CONDITIONS."
"HAJIME TSUKUMO MUST BE RELOCATED SOMEWHERE SAFER...
AND HE MUST HAVE 24-HOUR BODYGUARDS."
WHAT?!

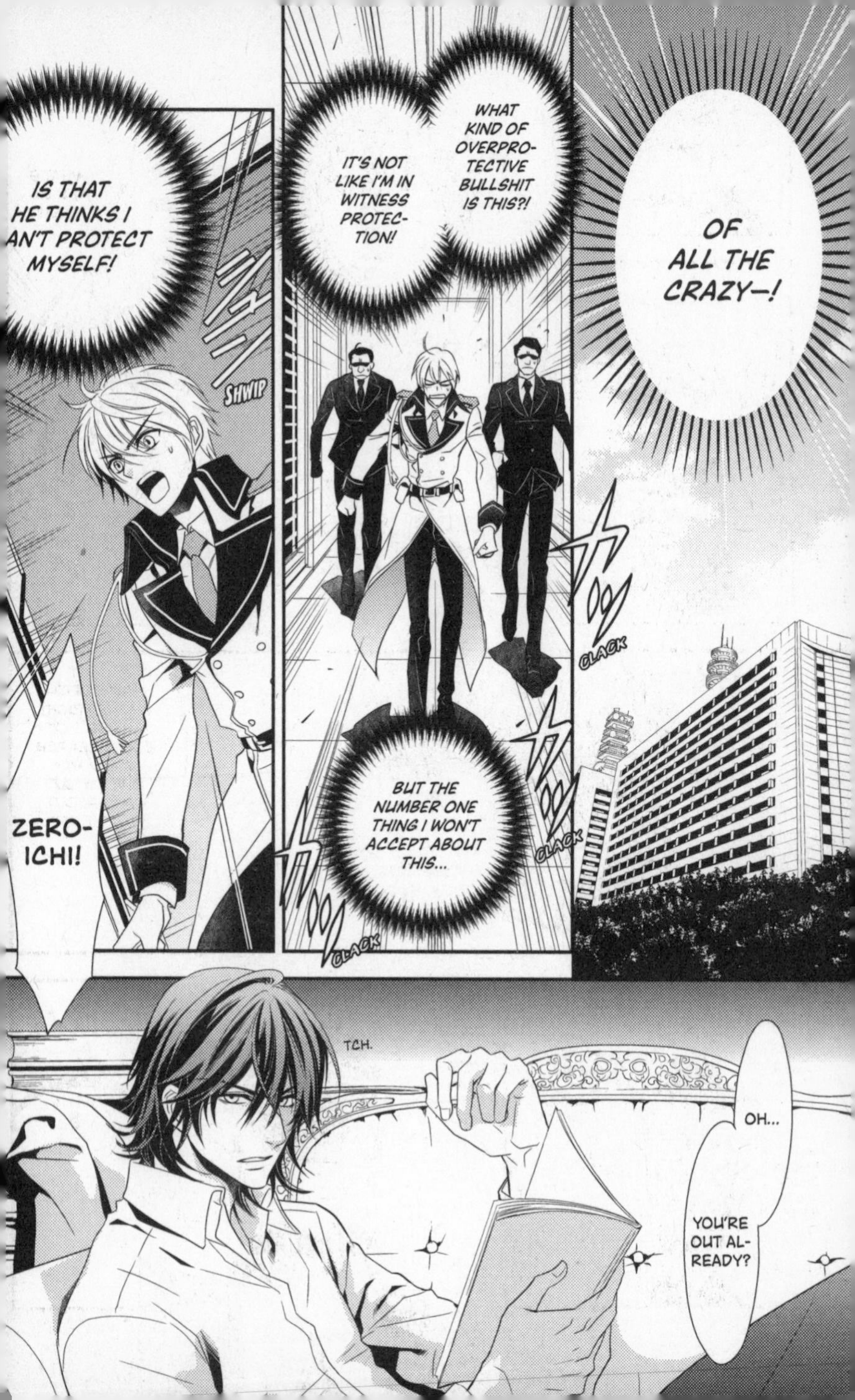
OF ALL THE CRAZY—!
WHAT KIND OF OVERPRO-TECTIVE BULLSHIT IS THIS?!
IT'S NOT LIKE I'M IN WITNESS PROTEC-TION!
CLACK
CLACK
CLACK
BUT THE NUMBER ONE THING I WON'T ACCEPT ABOUT THIS...
IS THAT HE THINKS I AN'T PROTECT MYSELF!
SHWIP
ZERO-ICHI!
OH...
YOU'RE OUT AL-READY?
TCH.

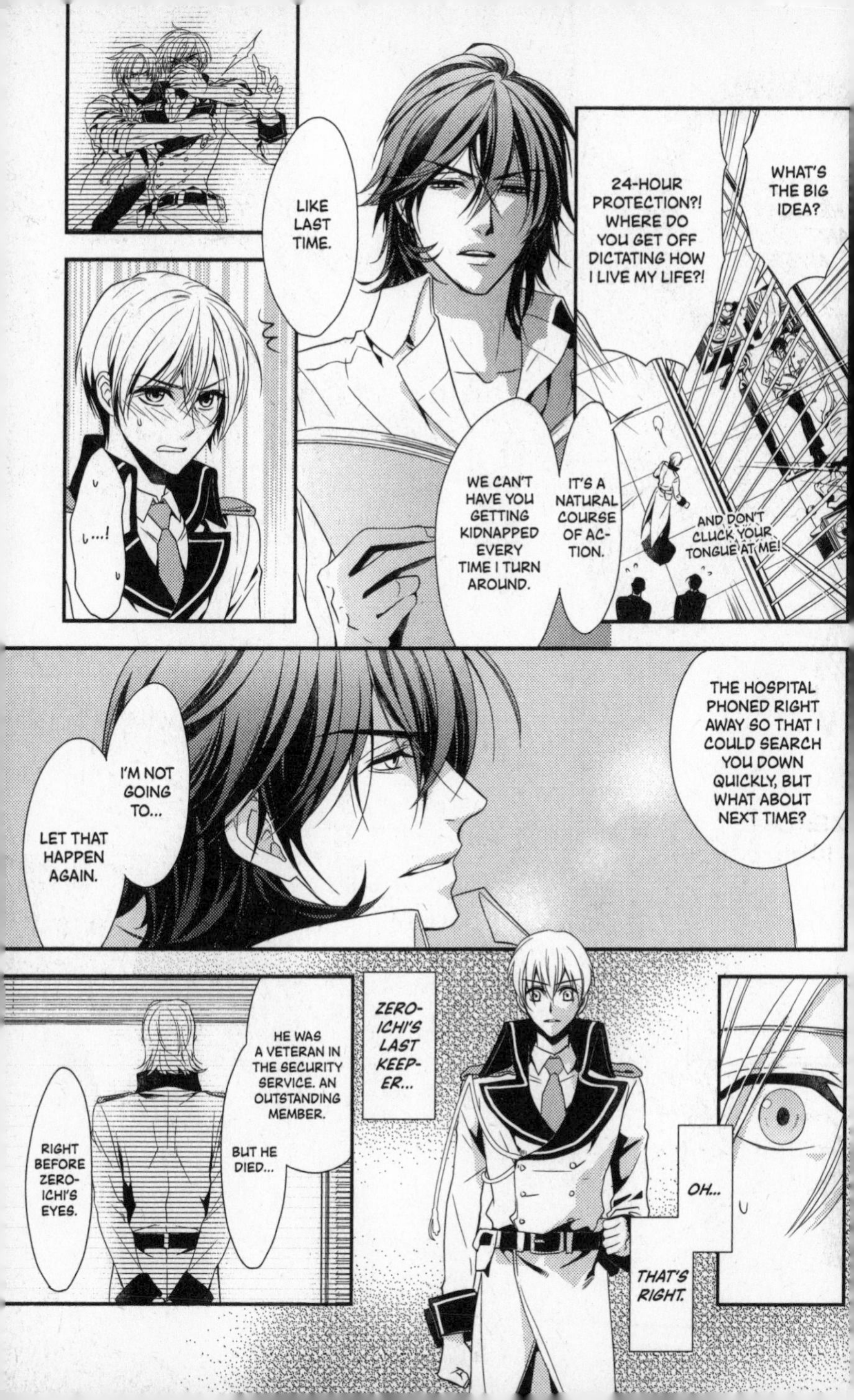
WHAT'S THE BIG IDEA?
24-HOUR PROTECTION?! WHERE DO YOU GET OFF DICTATING HOW I LIVE MY LIFE?!
AND DON'T CLUCK YOUR TONGUE AT ME!
IT'S A NATURAL COURSE OF AC-TION.
WE CAN'T HAVE YOU GETTING KIDNAPPED EVERY TIME I TURN AROUND.
LIKE LAST TIME.
L...!
THE HOSPITAL PHONED RIGHT AWAY SO THAT I COULD SEARCH YOU DOWN QUICKLY, BUT WHAT ABOUT NEXT TIME?
I'M NOT GOING TO...
LET THAT HAPPEN AGAIN.
OH...
THAT'S RIGHT.
ZERO-ICHI'S LAST KEEP-ER...
HE WAS A VETERAN IN THE SECURITY SERVICE. AN OUTSTANDING MEMBER.
BUT HE DIED...
RIGHT BEFORE ZERO-ICHI'S EYES.

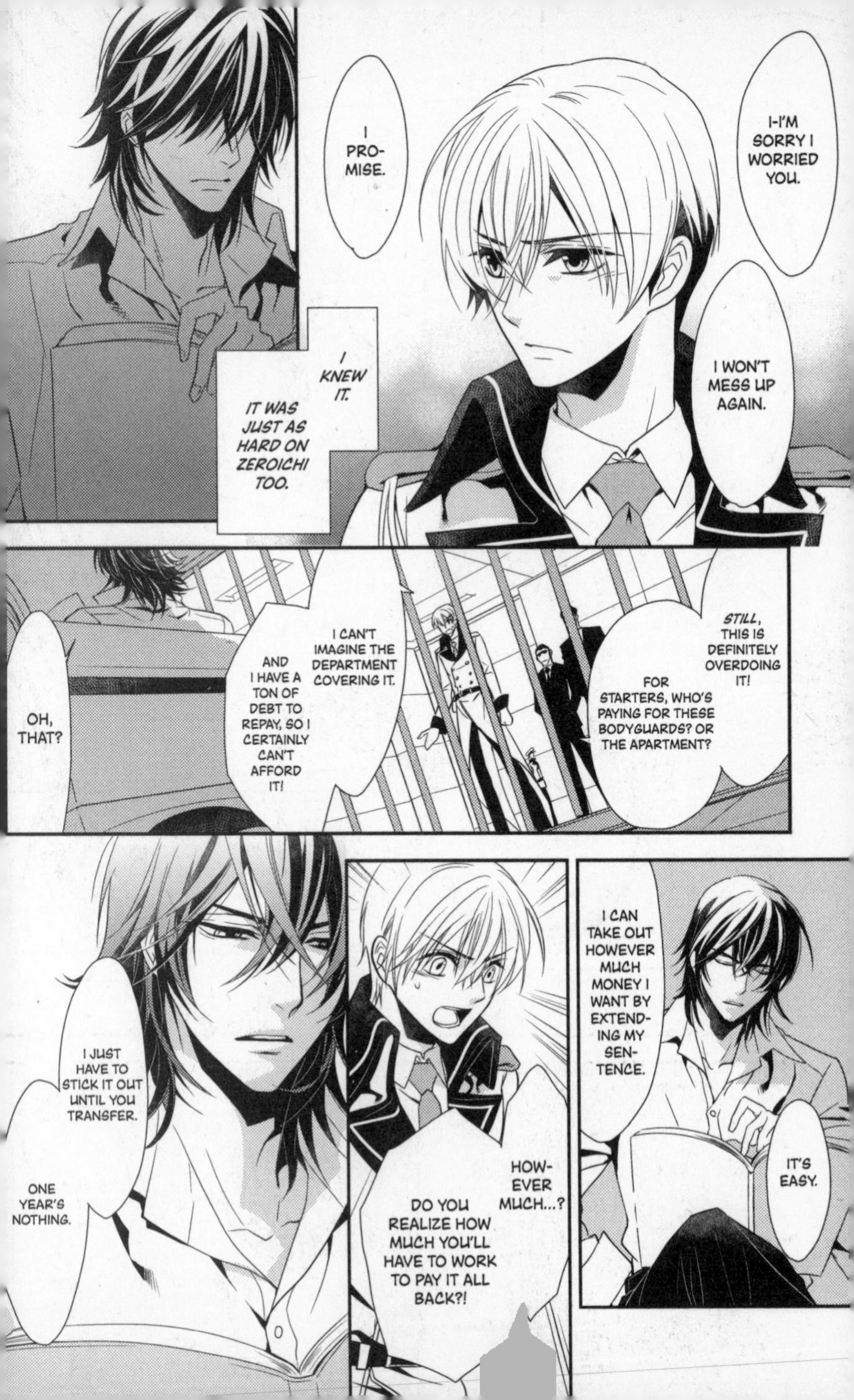
I-I'M SORRY I WORRIED YOU.
I WON'T MESS UP AGAIN.
I PROMISE.
I KNEW IT.
IT WAS JUST AS HARD ON ZEROICHI TOO.
STILL, THIS IS DEFINITELY OVERDOING IT!
FOR STARTERS, WHO'S PAYING FOR THESE BODYGUARDS? OR THE APARTMENT?
I CAN'T IMAGINE THE DEPARTMENT COVERING IT.
AND I HAVE A TON OF DEBT TO REPAY, SO I CERTAINLY CAN'T AFFORD IT!
OH, THAT?
I CAN TAKE OUT HOWEVER MUCH MONEY I WANT BY EXTENDING MY SENTENCE.
IT'S EASY.
HOWEVER MUCH...?
DO YOU REALIZE HOW MUCH YOU'LL HAVE TO WORK TO PAY IT ALL BACK?!
I JUST HAVE TO STICK IT OUT UNTIL YOU TRANSFER.
ONE YEAR'S NOTHING.

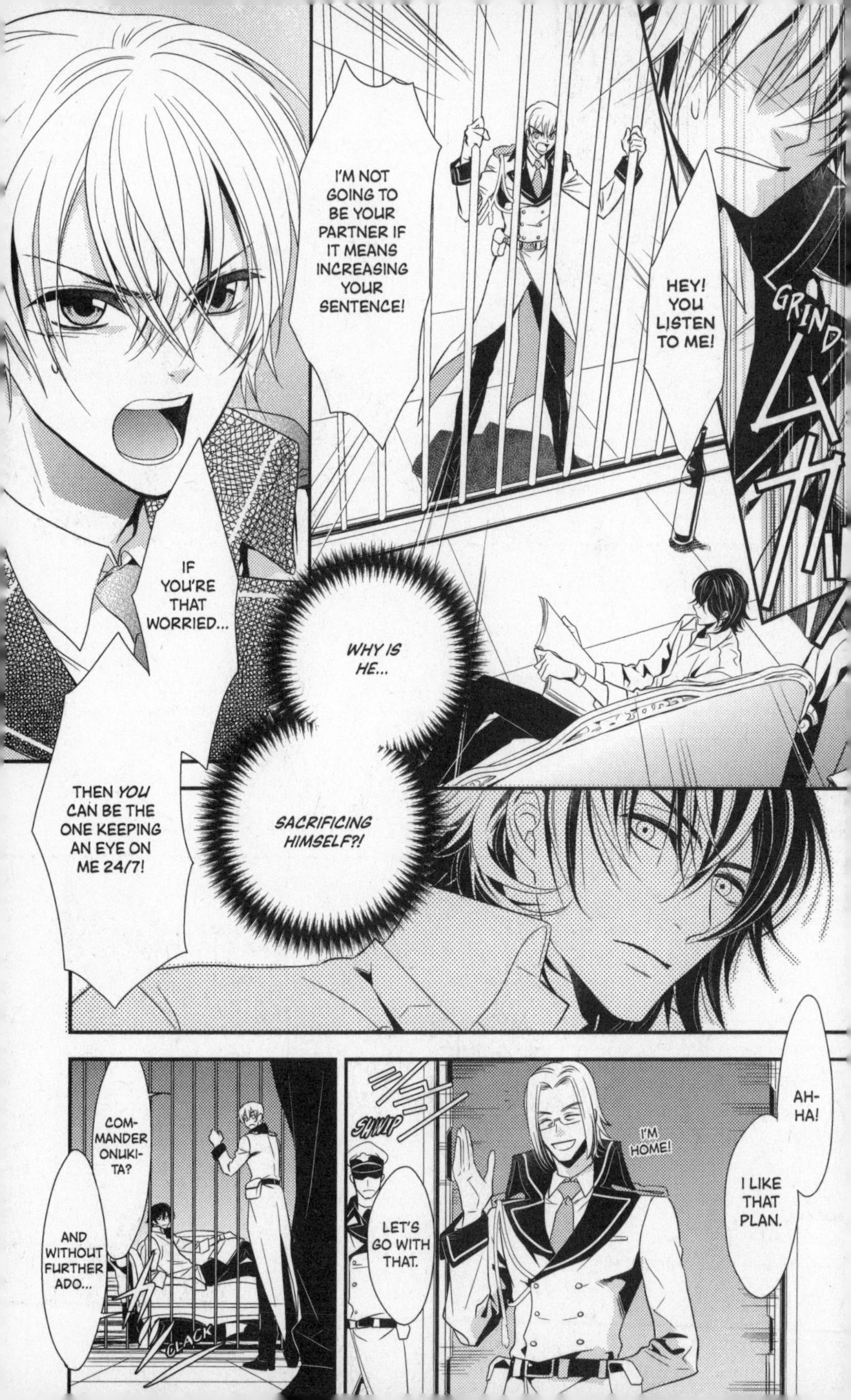
HEY! YOU LISTEN TO ME!
GRIND
I'M NOT GOING TO BE YOUR PARTNER IF IT MEANS INCREASING YOUR SENTENCE!
IF YOU'RE THAT WORRIED...
THEN *YOU* CAN BE THE ONE KEEPING AN EYE ON ME 24/7!
WHY IS HE...
SACRIFICING HIMSELF?!
AH-HA!
I LIKE THAT PLAN.
I'M HOME!
LET'S GO WITH THAT.
SHWIP
COM-MANDER ONUKI-TA?
AND WITHOUT FURTHER ADO...
CLACK

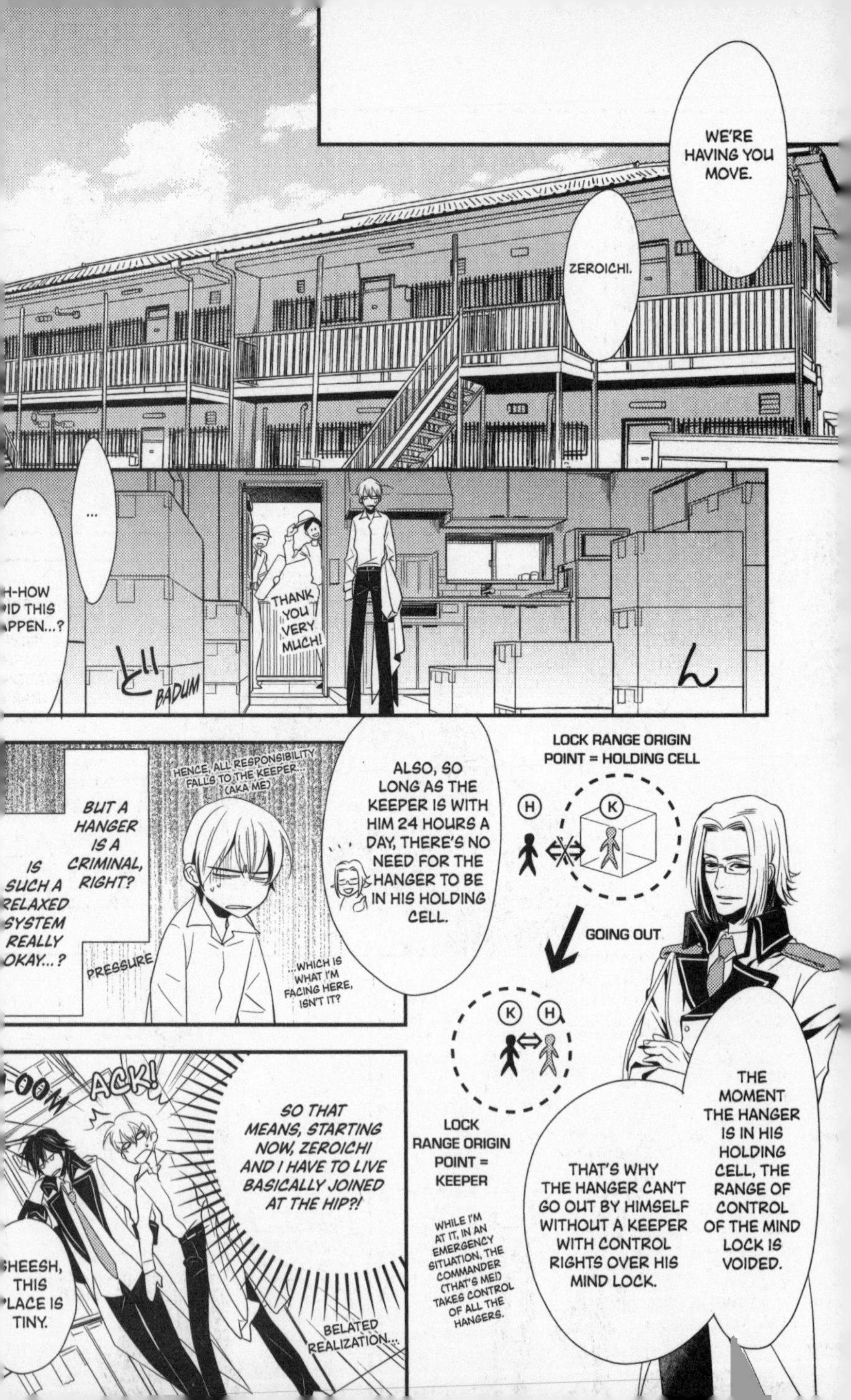
WE'RE HAVING YOU MOVE.
ZEROICHI.
ん
THANK YOU VERY MUCH!
BADUM
...
H-HOW
ID THIS
PPEN...?
LOCK RANGE ORIGIN POINT = HOLDING CELL
H
K
GOING OUT
K
H
LOCK RANGE ORIGIN POINT = KEEPER
ALSO, SO LONG AS THE KEEPER IS WITH HIM 24 HOURS A DAY, THERE'S NO NEED FOR THE HANGER TO BE IN HIS HOLDING CELL.
THE MOMENT THE HANGER IS IN HIS HOLDING CELL, THE RANGE OF CONTROL OF THE MIND LOCK IS VOIDED.
THAT'S WHY THE HANGER CAN'T GO OUT BY HIMSELF WITHOUT A KEEPER WITH CONTROL RIGHTS OVER HIS MIND LOCK.
WHILE I'M AT IT, IN AN EMERGENCY SITUATION, THE COMMANDER (THAT'S ME) TAKES CONTROL OF ALL THE HANGERS.
HENCE, ALL RESPONSIBILITY FALLS TO THE KEEPER... (AKA ME)
BUT A HANGER IS A CRIMINAL, RIGHT?
IS SUCH A
ELAXED SYSTEM REALLY
KAY...?
PRESSURE
...WHICH IS WHAT I'M FACING HERE, ISN'T IT?
SO THAT MEANS, STARTING NOW, ZEROICHI AND I HAVE TO LIVE BASICALLY JOINED AT THE HIP?!
ACK!
OOM
HEESH, THIS
LACE IS TINY.
BELATED REALIZATION...

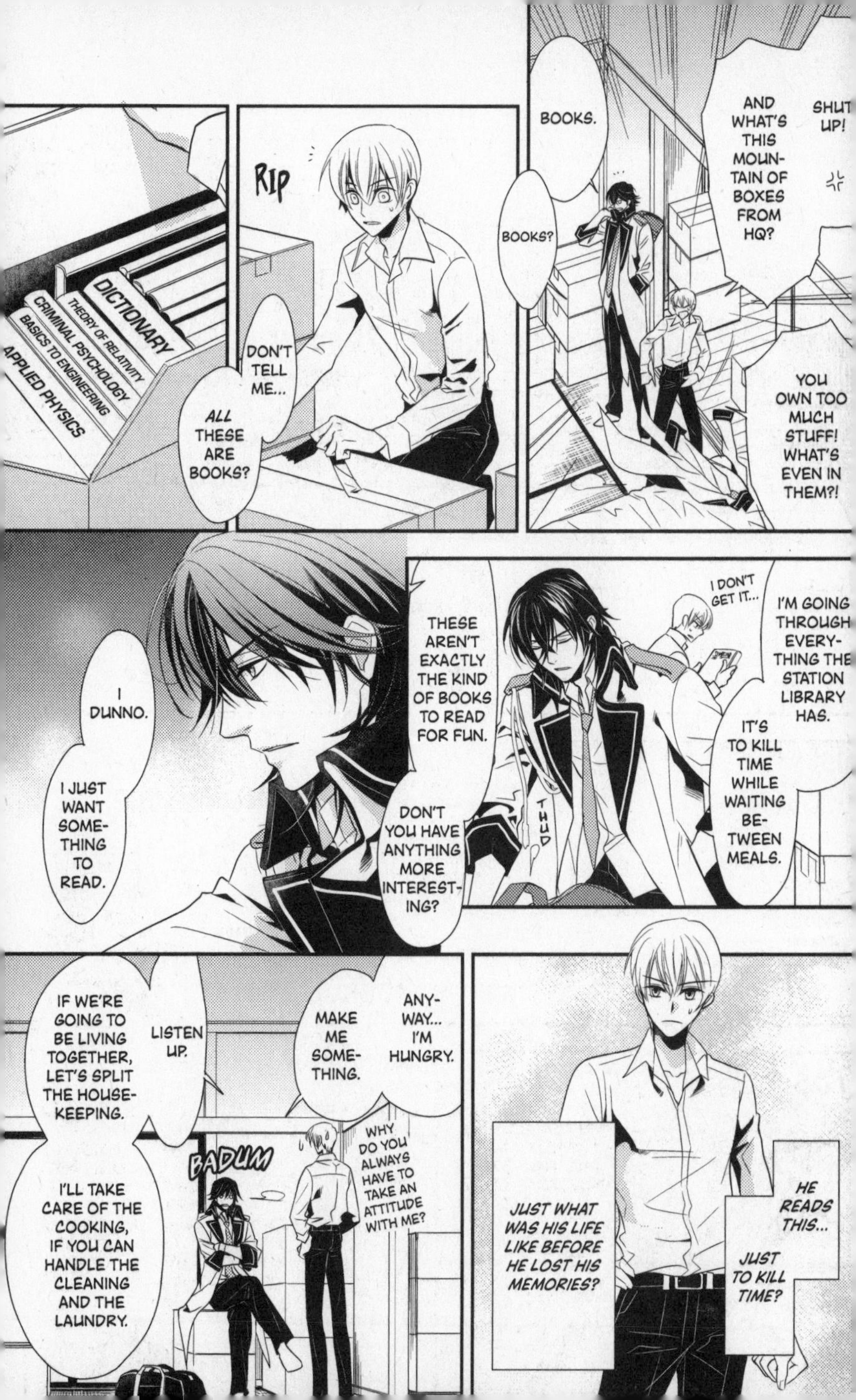
AND WHAT'S THIS MOUNTAIN OF BOXES FROM HQ?
SHUT UP!
YOU OWN TOO MUCH STUFF! WHAT'S EVEN IN THEM?!
BOOKS.
BOOKS?
RIP
DON'T TELL ME...
ALL THESE ARE BOOKS?
DICTIONARY
THEORY OF RELATIVITY
CRIMINAL PSYCHOLOGY
BASICS TO ENGINEERING
APPLIED PHYSICS
I DON'T GET IT...
I'M GOING THROUGH EVERYTHING THE STATION LIBRARY HAS.
IT'S TO KILL TIME WHILE WAITING BETWEEN MEALS.
THESE AREN'T EXACTLY THE KIND OF BOOKS TO READ FOR FUN.
THUD
DON'T YOU HAVE ANYTHING MORE INTERESTING?
I DUNNO.
I JUST WANT SOMETHING TO READ.
HE READS THIS...
JUST TO KILL TIME?
JUST WHAT WAS HIS LIFE LIKE BEFORE HE LOST HIS MEMORIES?
ANYWAY... I'M HUNGRY.
MAKE ME SOMETHING.
LISTEN UP.
IF WE'RE GOING TO BE LIVING TOGETHER, LET'S SPLIT THE HOUSEKEEPING.
WHY DO YOU ALWAYS HAVE TO TAKE AN ATTITUDE WITH ME?
BADUM
I'LL TAKE CARE OF THE COOKING, IF YOU CAN HANDLE THE CLEANING AND THE LAUNDRY.

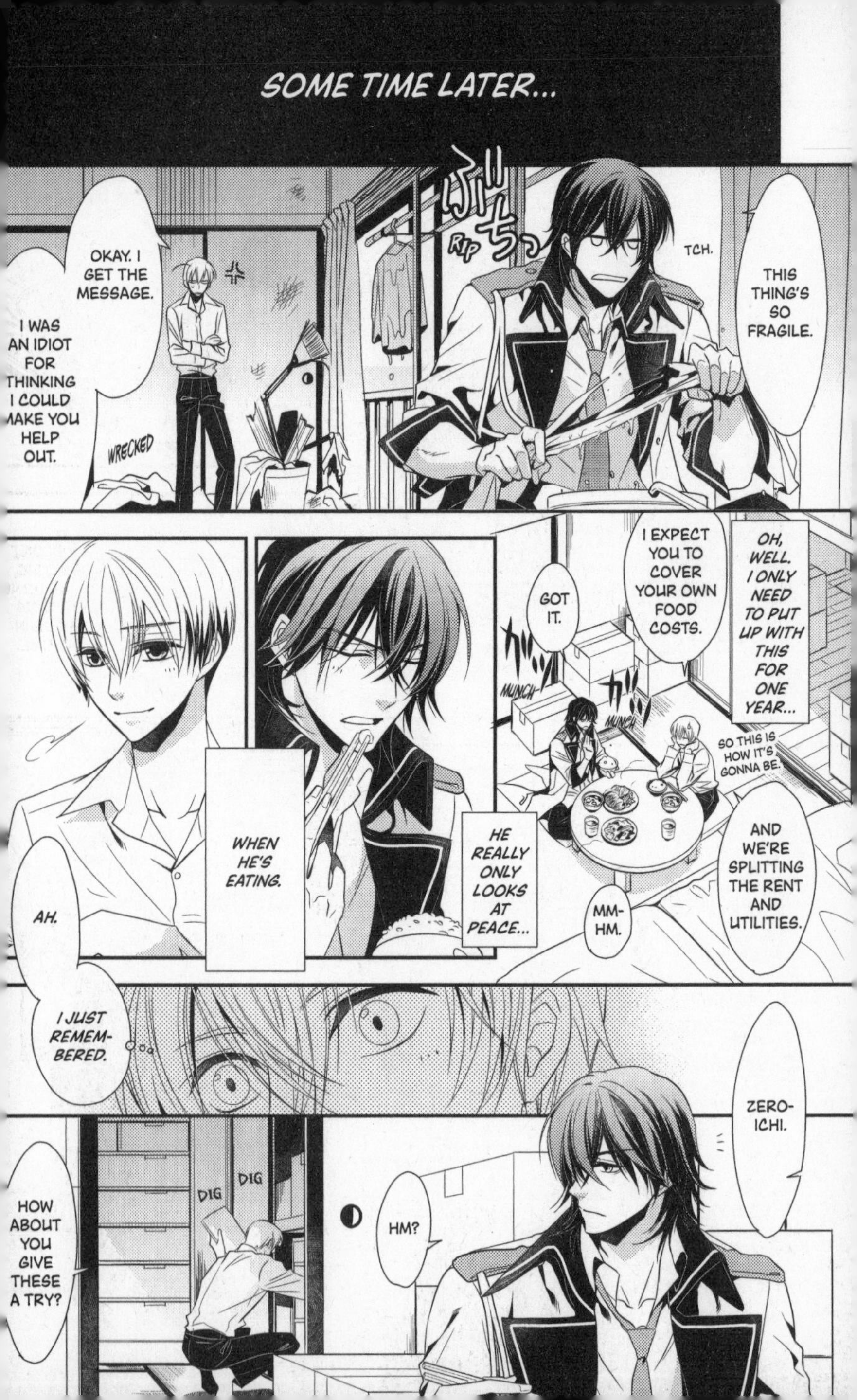
SOME TIME LATER...
THIS THING'S SO FRAGILE.
TCH.
RIP
OKAY. I GET THE MESSAGE.
I WAS AN IDIOT FOR THINKING I COULD MAKE YOU HELP OUT.
WRECKED
OH, WELL. I ONLY NEED TO PUT UP WITH THIS FOR ONE YEAR...
I EXPECT YOU TO COVER YOUR OWN FOOD COSTS.
GOT IT.
MUNCH
MUNCH
SO THIS IS HOW IT'S GONNA BE.
AND WE'RE SPLITTING THE RENT AND UTILITIES.
MM-HM.
HE REALLY ONLY LOOKS AT PEACE...
WHEN HE'S EATING.
AH.
ZERO-ICHI.
I JUST REMEMBERED.
HM?
DIG
DIG
HOW ABOUT YOU GIVE THESE A TRY?

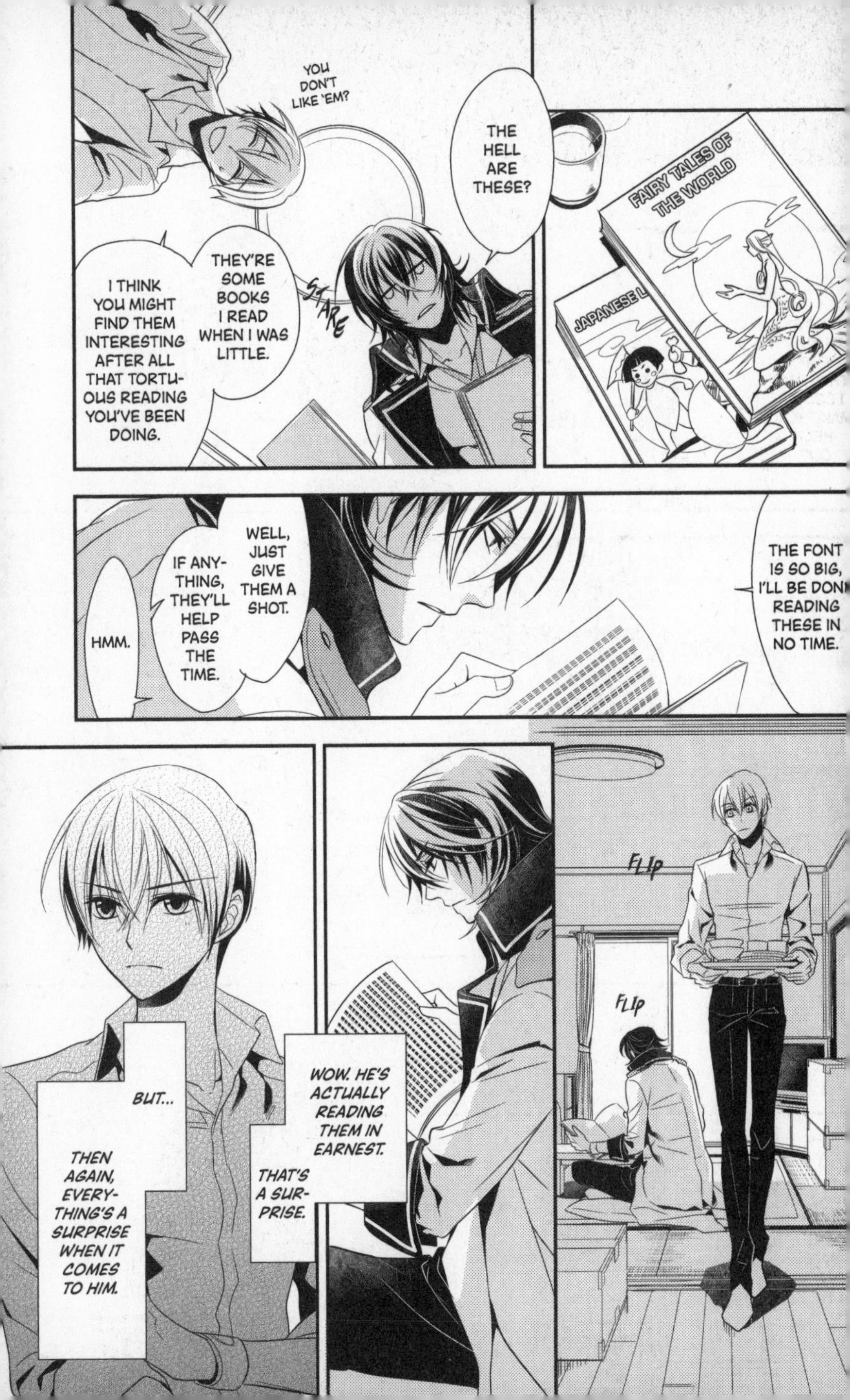
FAIRY TALES OF THE WORLD
JAPANESE L
THE HELL ARE THESE?
YOU DON'T LIKE 'EM?
THEY'RE SOME BOOKS I READ WHEN I WAS LITTLE.
STARE
I THINK YOU MIGHT FIND THEM INTERESTING AFTER ALL THAT TORTUOUS READING YOU'VE BEEN DOING.
THE FONT IS SO BIG, I'LL BE DON READING THESE IN NO TIME.
WELL, JUST GIVE THEM A SHOT.
IF ANYTHING, THEY'LL HELP PASS THE TIME.
HMM.
FLIP
FLIP
WOW. HE'S ACTUALLY READING THEM IN EARNEST.
THAT'S A SURPRISE.
BUT...
THEN AGAIN, EVERYTHING'S A SURPRISE WHEN IT COMES TO HIM.

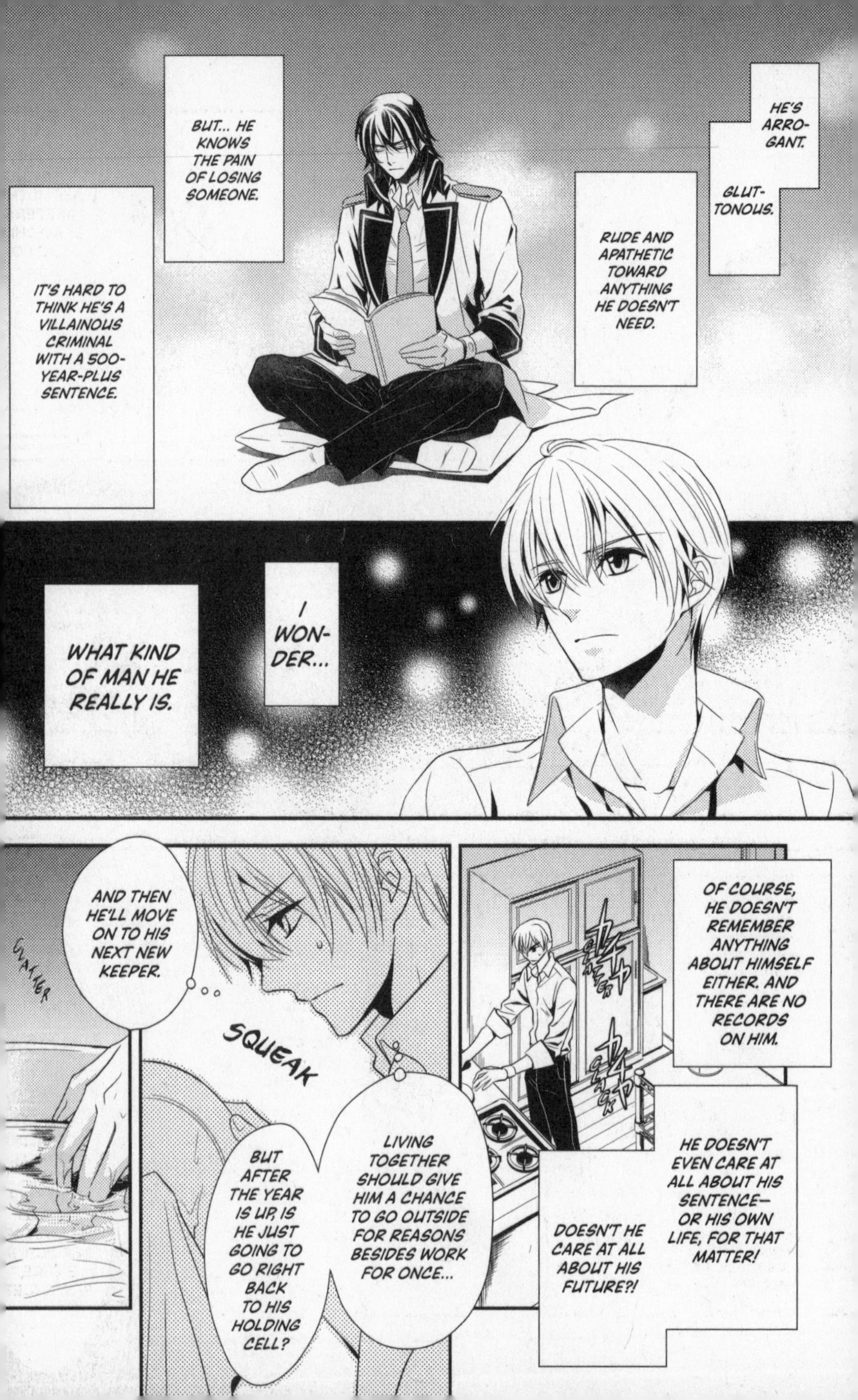
HE'S ARROGANT.
GLUTTONOUS.
RUDE AND APATHETIC TOWARD ANYTHING HE DOESN'T NEED.
BUT... HE KNOWS THE PAIN OF LOSING SOMEONE.
IT'S HARD TO THINK HE'S A VILLAINOUS CRIMINAL WITH A 500-YEAR-PLUS SENTENCE.
I WONDER...
WHAT KIND OF MAN HE REALLY IS.
OF COURSE, HE DOESN'T REMEMBER ANYTHING ABOUT HIMSELF EITHER. AND THERE ARE NO RECORDS ON HIM.
HE DOESN'T EVEN CARE AT ALL ABOUT HIS SENTENCE— OR HIS OWN LIFE, FOR THAT MATTER!
DOESN'T HE CARE AT ALL ABOUT HIS FUTURE?!
SQUEAK
LIVING TOGETHER SHOULD GIVE HIM A CHANCE TO GO OUTSIDE FOR REASONS BESIDES WORK FOR ONCE...
BUT AFTER THE YEAR IS UP, IS HE JUST GOING TO GO RIGHT BACK TO HIS HOLDING CELL?
AND THEN HE'LL MOVE ON TO HIS NEXT NEW KEEPER.
CLATTER

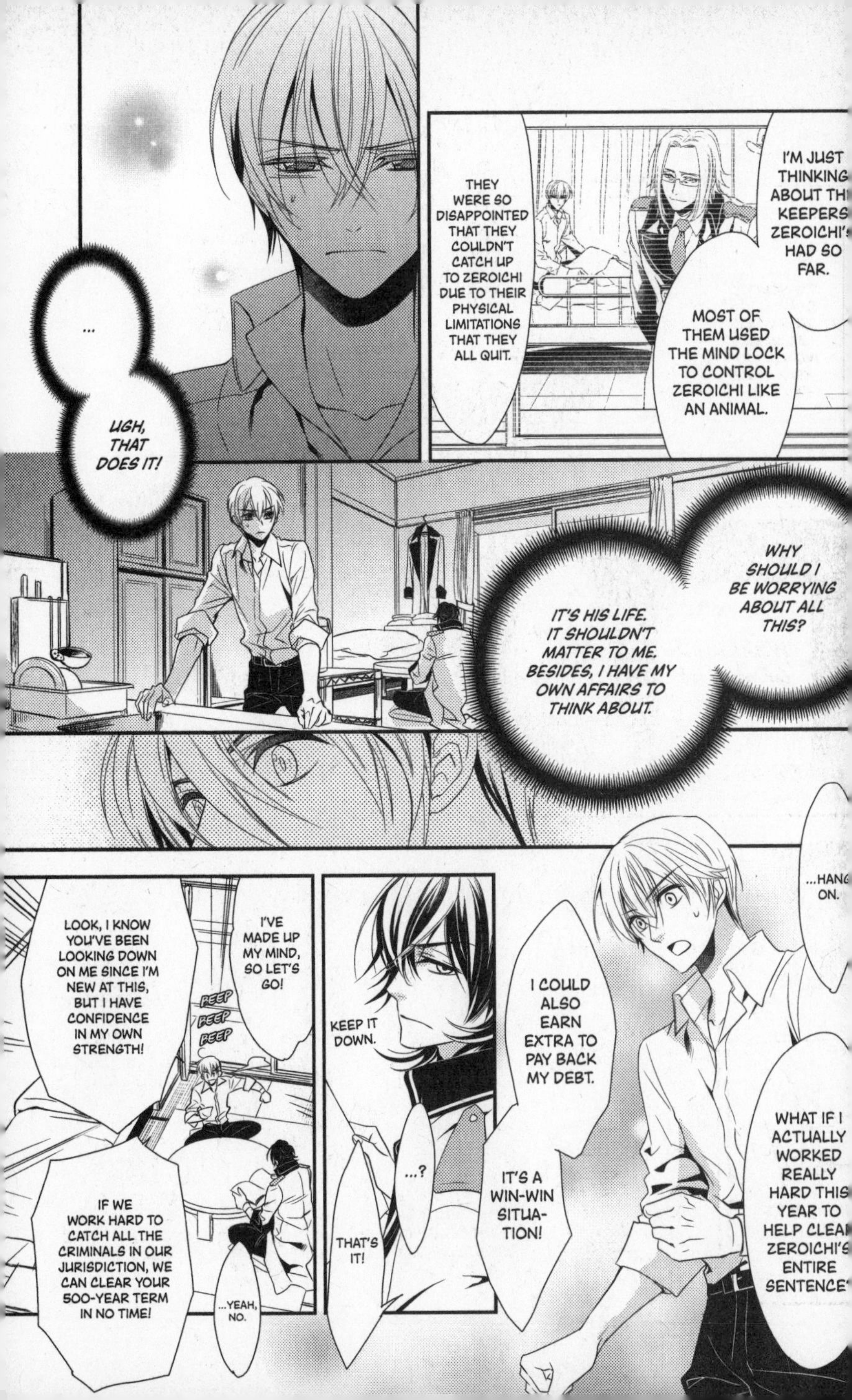
I'M JUST THINKING ABOUT TH KEEPERS ZEROICHI'S HAD SO FAR.
MOST OF THEM USED THE MIND LOCK TO CONTROL ZEROICHI LIKE AN ANIMAL.
THEY WERE SO DISAPPOINTED THAT THEY COULDN'T CATCH UP TO ZEROICHI DUE TO THEIR PHYSICAL LIMITATIONS THAT THEY ALL QUIT.
...
UGH, THAT DOES IT!
WHY SHOULD I BE WORRYING ABOUT ALL THIS?
IT'S HIS LIFE. IT SHOULDN'T MATTER TO ME. BESIDES, I HAVE MY OWN AFFAIRS TO THINK ABOUT.
...HANG ON.
WHAT IF I ACTUALLY WORKED REALLY HARD THIS YEAR TO HELP CLEA ZEROICHI'S ENTIRE SENTENCE
I COULD ALSO EARN EXTRA TO PAY BACK MY DEBT.
IT'S A WIN-WIN SITUA-TION!
KEEP IT DOWN.
...?
THAT'S IT!
I'VE MADE UP MY MIND, SO LET'S GO!
LOOK, I KNOW YOU'VE BEEN LOOKING DOWN ON ME SINCE I'M NEW AT THIS, BUT I HAVE CONFIDENCE IN MY OWN STRENGTH!
BEEP BEEP BEEP
IF WE WORK HARD TO CATCH ALL THE CRIMINALS IN OUR JURISDICTION, WE CAN CLEAR YOUR 500-YEAR TERM IN NO TIME!
...YEAH, NO.

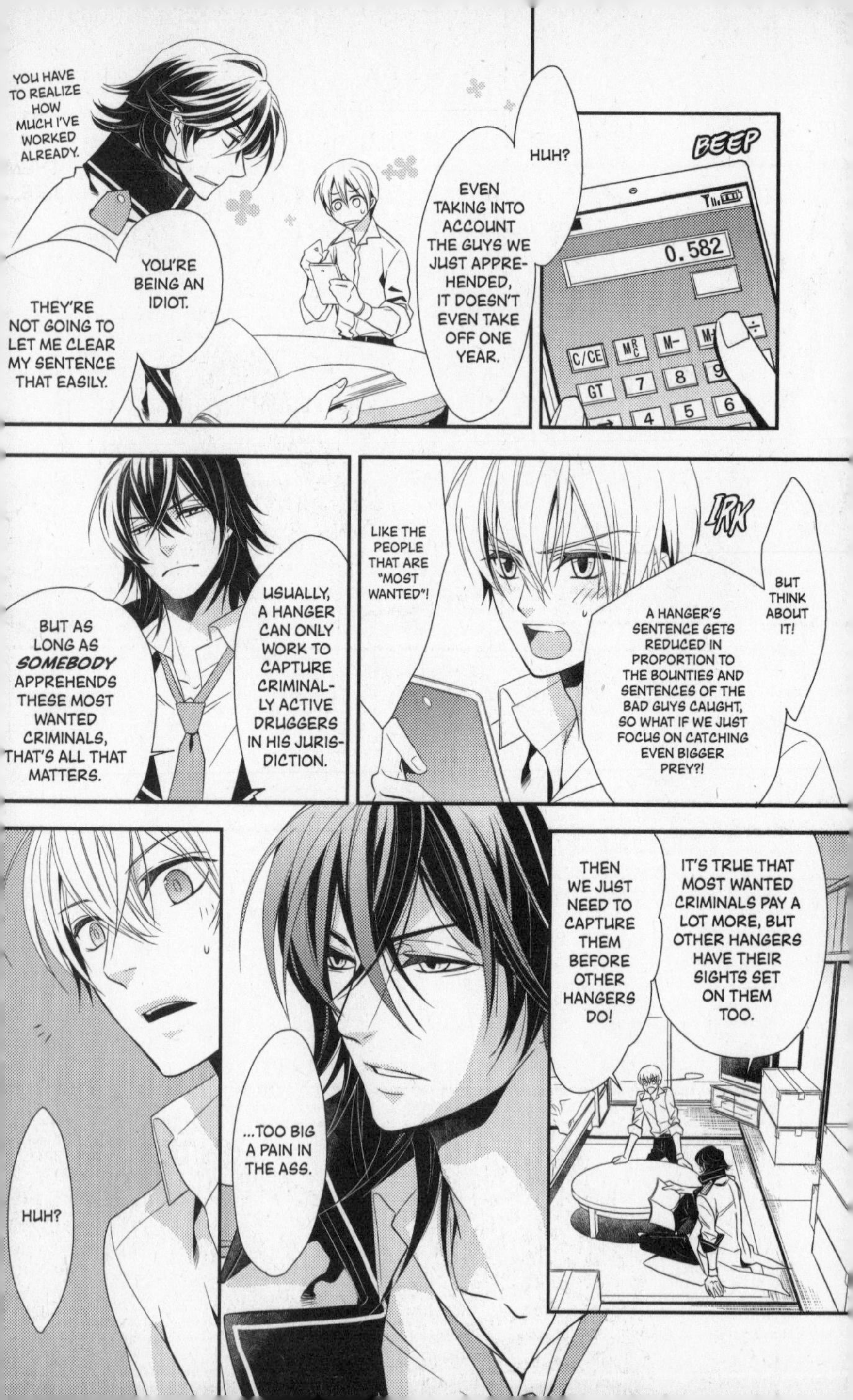
BEEP
0.582
HUH?
EVEN TAKING INTO ACCOUNT THE GUYS WE JUST APPREHENDED, IT DOESN'T EVEN TAKE OFF ONE YEAR.
YOU HAVE TO REALIZE HOW MUCH I'VE WORKED ALREADY.
YOU'RE BEING AN IDIOT.
THEY'RE NOT GOING TO LET ME CLEAR MY SENTENCE THAT EASILY.
IRK
BUT THINK ABOUT IT!
A HANGER'S SENTENCE GETS REDUCED IN PROPORTION TO THE BOUNTIES AND SENTENCES OF THE BAD GUYS CAUGHT, SO WHAT IF WE JUST FOCUS ON CATCHING EVEN BIGGER PREY?!
LIKE THE PEOPLE THAT ARE "MOST WANTED"!
USUALLY, A HANGER CAN ONLY WORK TO CAPTURE CRIMINALLY ACTIVE DRUGGERS IN HIS JURISDICTION.
BUT AS LONG AS *SOMEBODY* APPREHENDS THESE MOST WANTED CRIMINALS, THAT'S ALL THAT MATTERS.
IT'S TRUE THAT MOST WANTED CRIMINALS PAY A LOT MORE, BUT OTHER HANGERS HAVE THEIR SIGHTS SET ON THEM TOO.
THEN WE JUST NEED TO CAPTURE THEM BEFORE OTHER HANGERS DO!
...TOO BIG A PAIN IN THE ASS.
HUH?

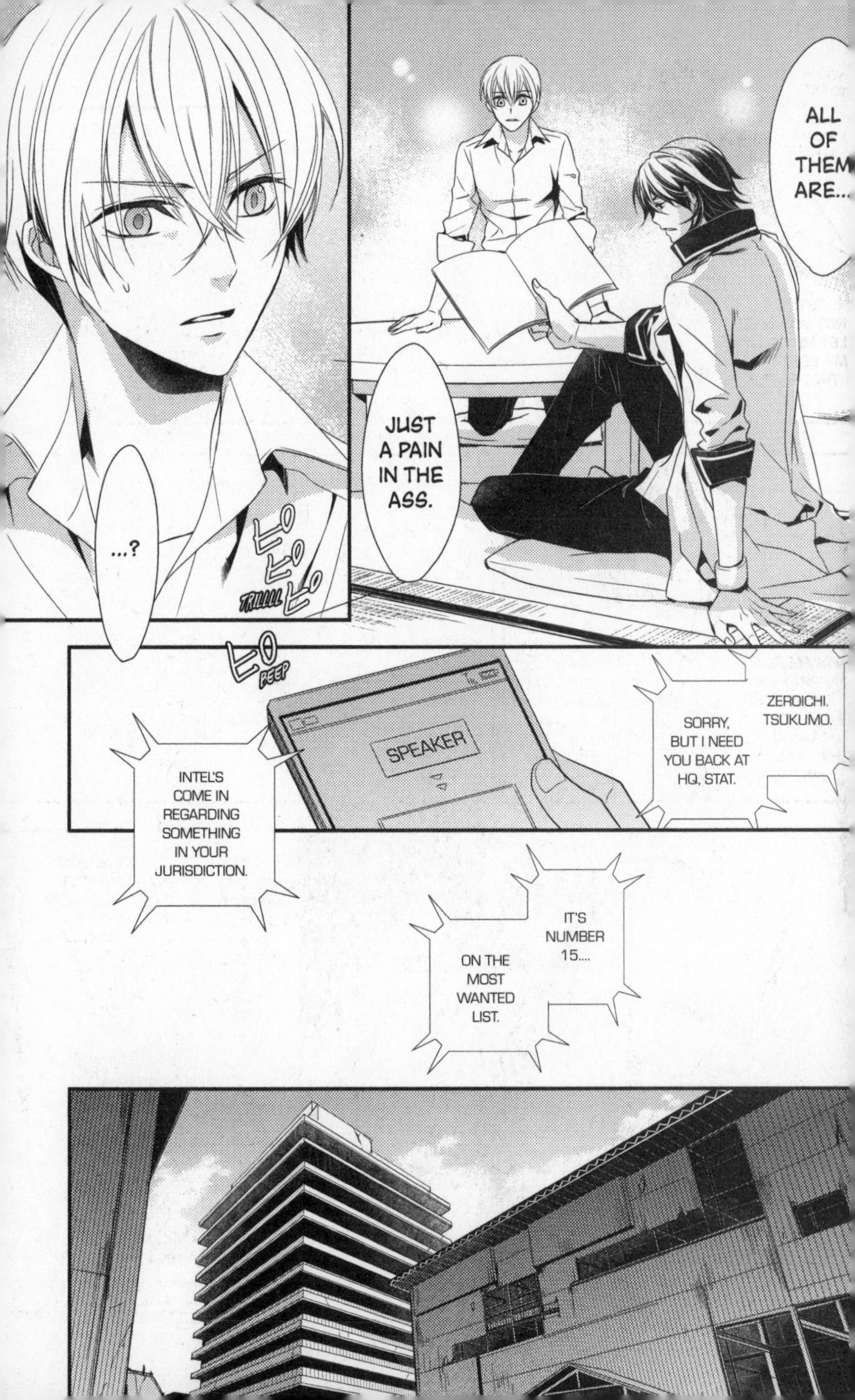
ALL OF THEM ARE...
JUST A PAIN IN THE ASS.
...?
TRILLLL
BEEP
ZEROICHI. TSUKUMO.
SORRY, BUT I NEED YOU BACK AT HQ, STAT.
SPEAKER
INTEL'S COME IN REGARDING SOMETHING IN YOUR JURISDICTION.
IT'S NUMBER 15....
ON THE MOST WANTED LIST.

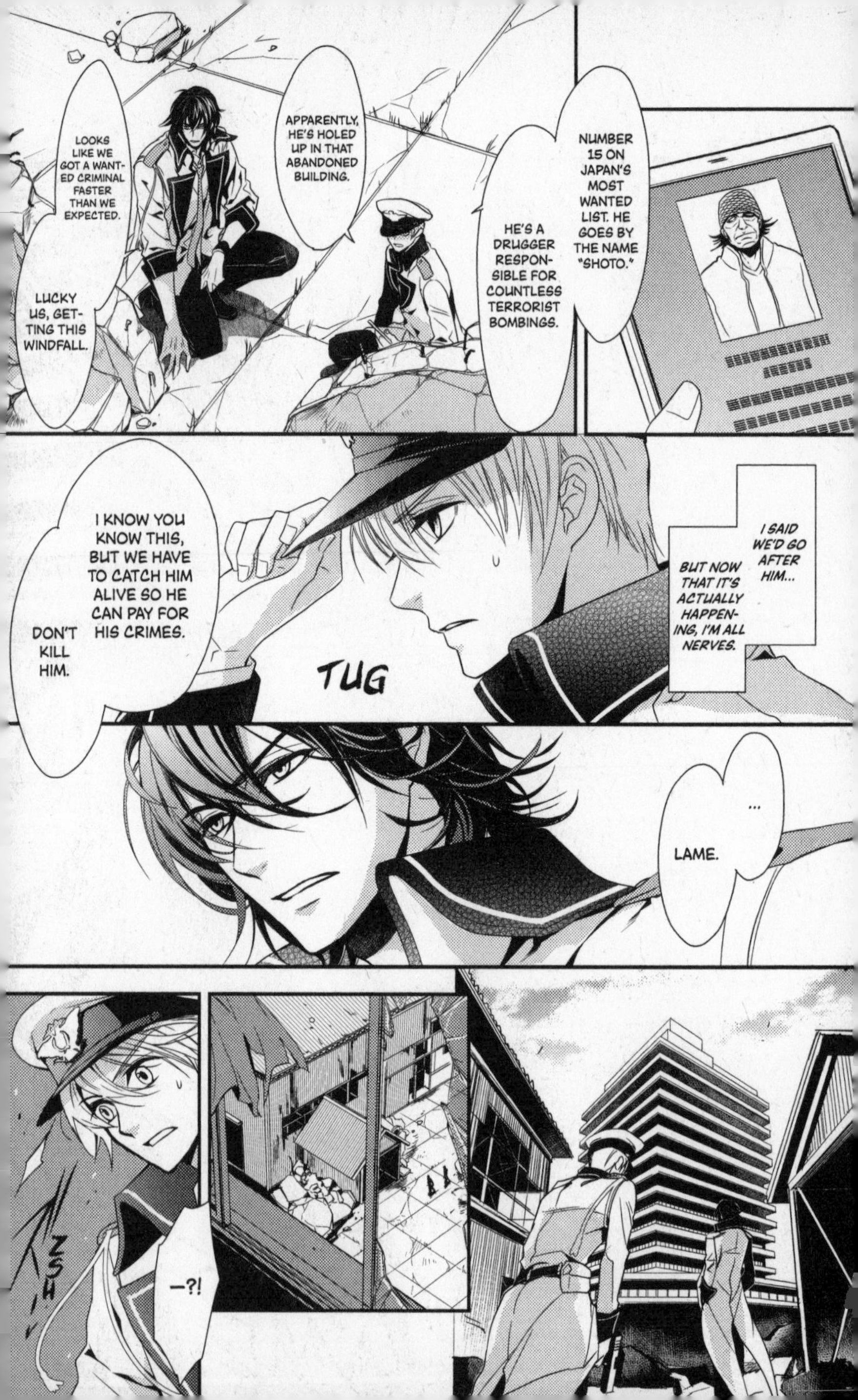
NUMBER 15 ON JAPAN'S MOST WANTED LIST. HE GOES BY THE NAME "SHOTO."
HE'S A DRUGGER RESPONSIBLE FOR COUNTLESS TERRORIST BOMBINGS.
APPARENTLY, HE'S HOLED UP IN THAT ABANDONED BUILDING.
LOOKS LIKE WE GOT A WANTED CRIMINAL FASTER THAN WE EXPECTED.
LUCKY US, GETTING THIS WINDFALL.
I SAID WE'D GO AFTER HIM...
BUT NOW THAT IT'S ACTUALLY HAPPENING, I'M ALL NERVES.
TUG
I KNOW YOU KNOW THIS, BUT WE HAVE TO CATCH HIM ALIVE SO HE CAN PAY FOR HIS CRIMES.
DON'T KILL HIM.
...
LAME.
ZSH
—?!

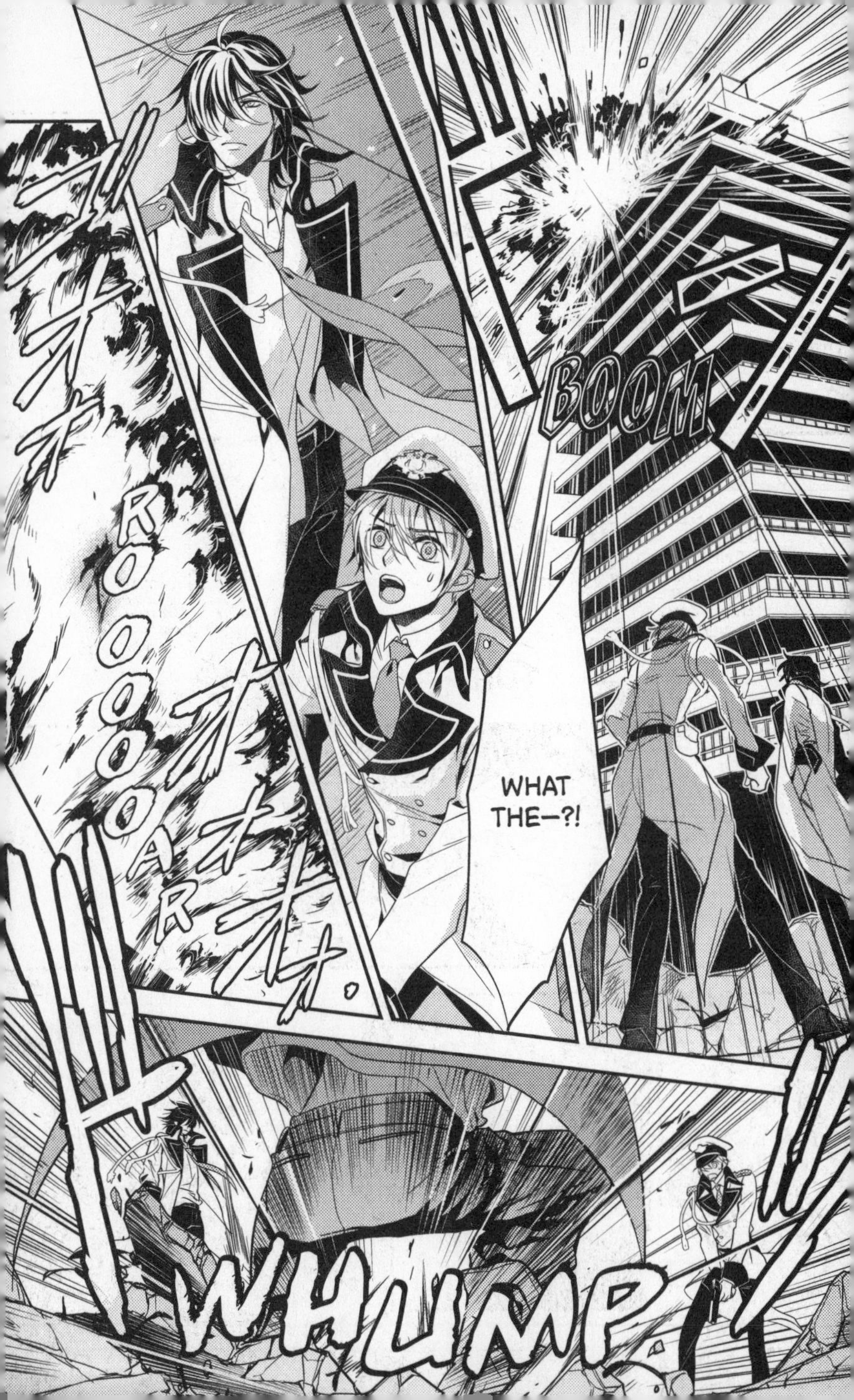
BOOM
WHAT THE—?!
ROOOOOAR
WHUMP!!

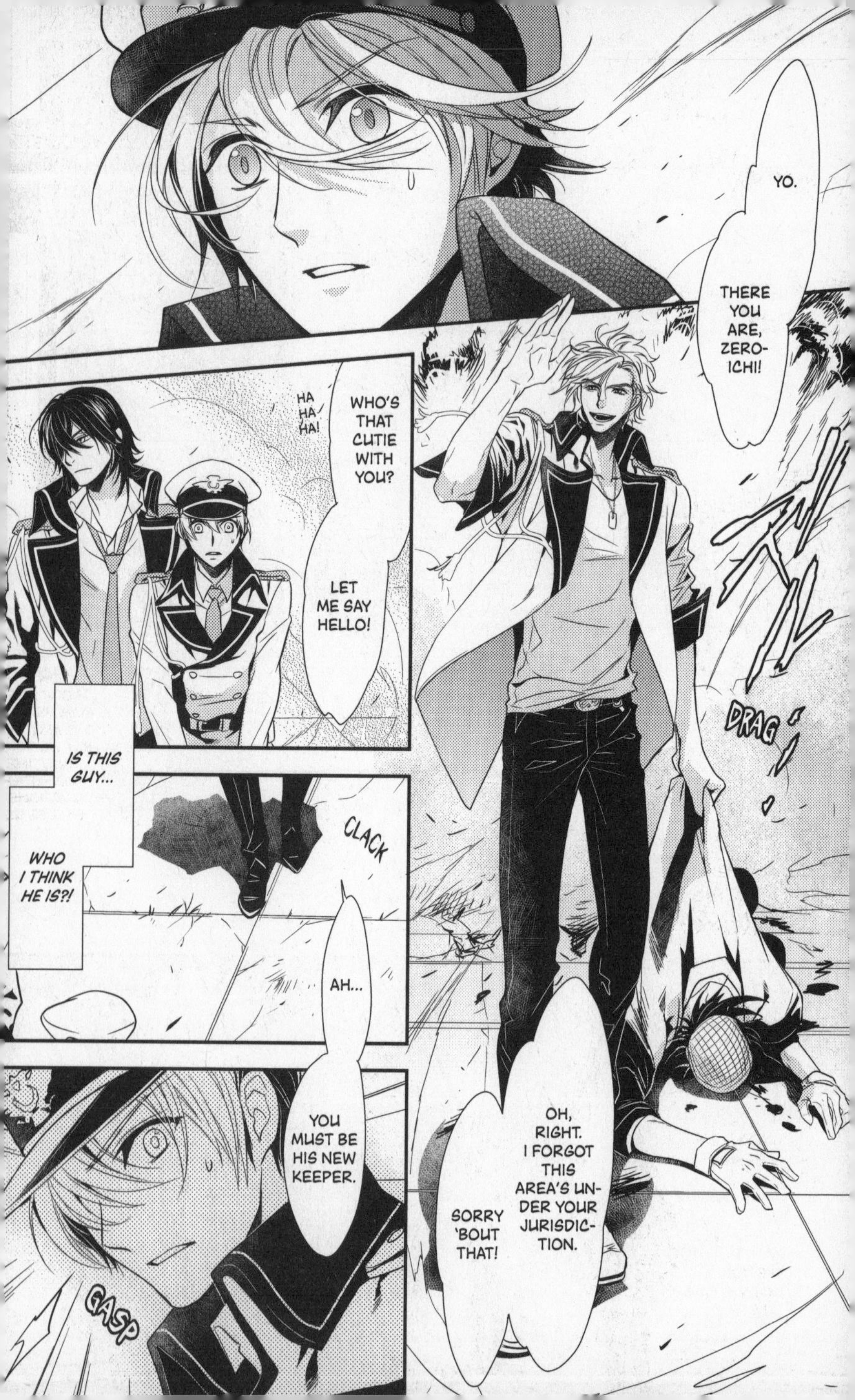

YO.
THERE YOU ARE, ZERO-ICHI!
DRAG
HA HA HA!
WHO'S THAT CUTIE WITH YOU?
LET ME SAY HELLO!
IS THIS GUY...
WHO I THINK HE IS?!
CLACK
AH...
YOU MUST BE HIS NEW KEEPER.
GASP
OH, RIGHT. I FORGOT THIS AREA'S UN-DER YOUR JURISDIC-TION.
SORRY 'BOUT THAT!

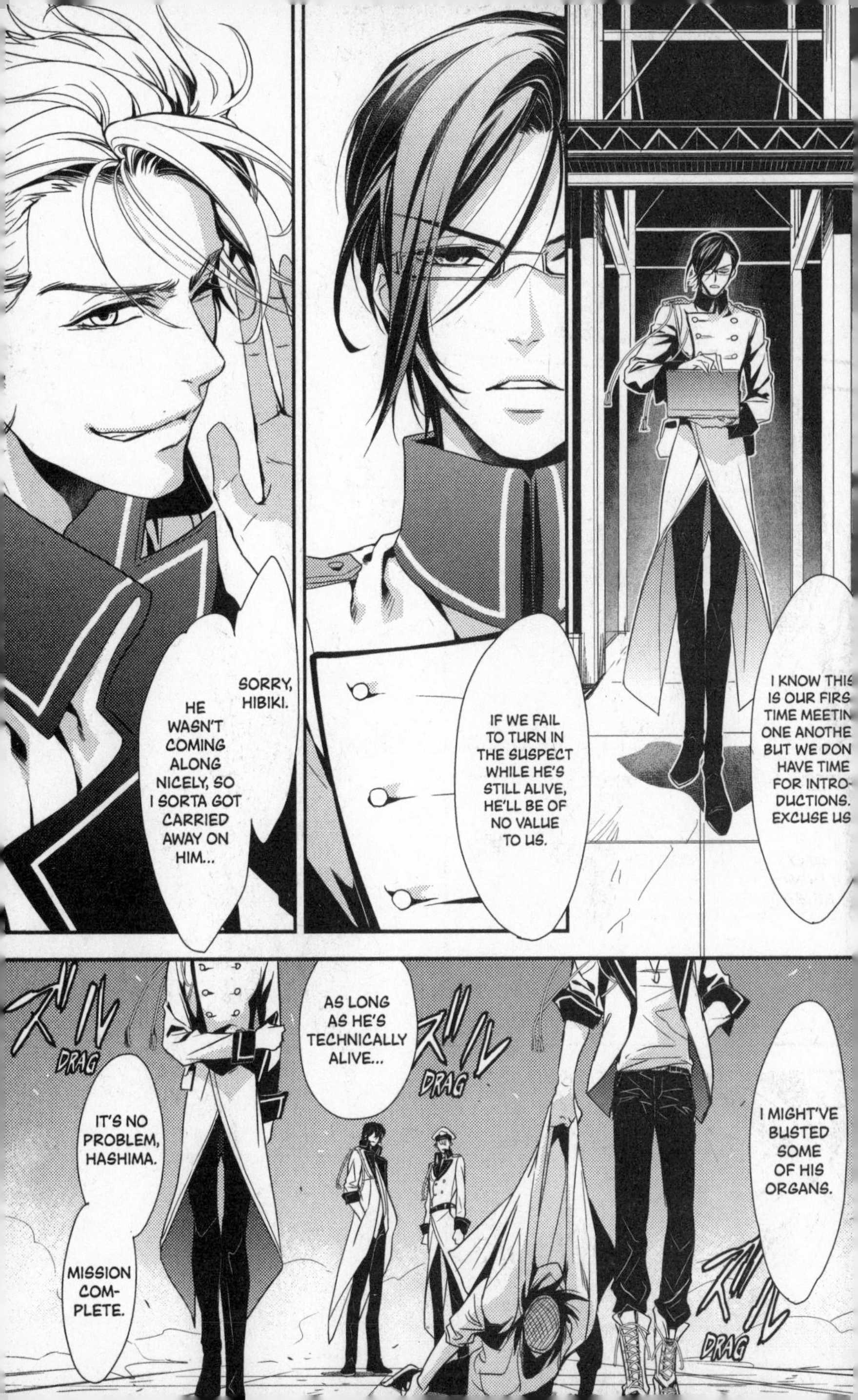
I KNOW THIS IS OUR FIRS TIME MEETIN ONE ANOTHE BUT WE DON HAVE TIME FOR INTRO-DUCTIONS. EXCUSE US
IF WE FAIL TO TURN IN THE SUSPECT WHILE HE'S STILL ALIVE, HE'LL BE OF NO VALUE TO US.
SORRY, HIBIKI.
HE WASN'T COMING ALONG NICELY, SO I SORTA GOT CARRIED AWAY ON HIM...
スル
DRAG
I MIGHT'VE BUSTED SOME OF HIS ORGANS.
スル
DRAG
AS LONG AS HE'S TECHNICALLY ALIVE...
スル
DRAG
IT'S NO PROBLEM, HASHIMA.
MISSION COM-PLETE.

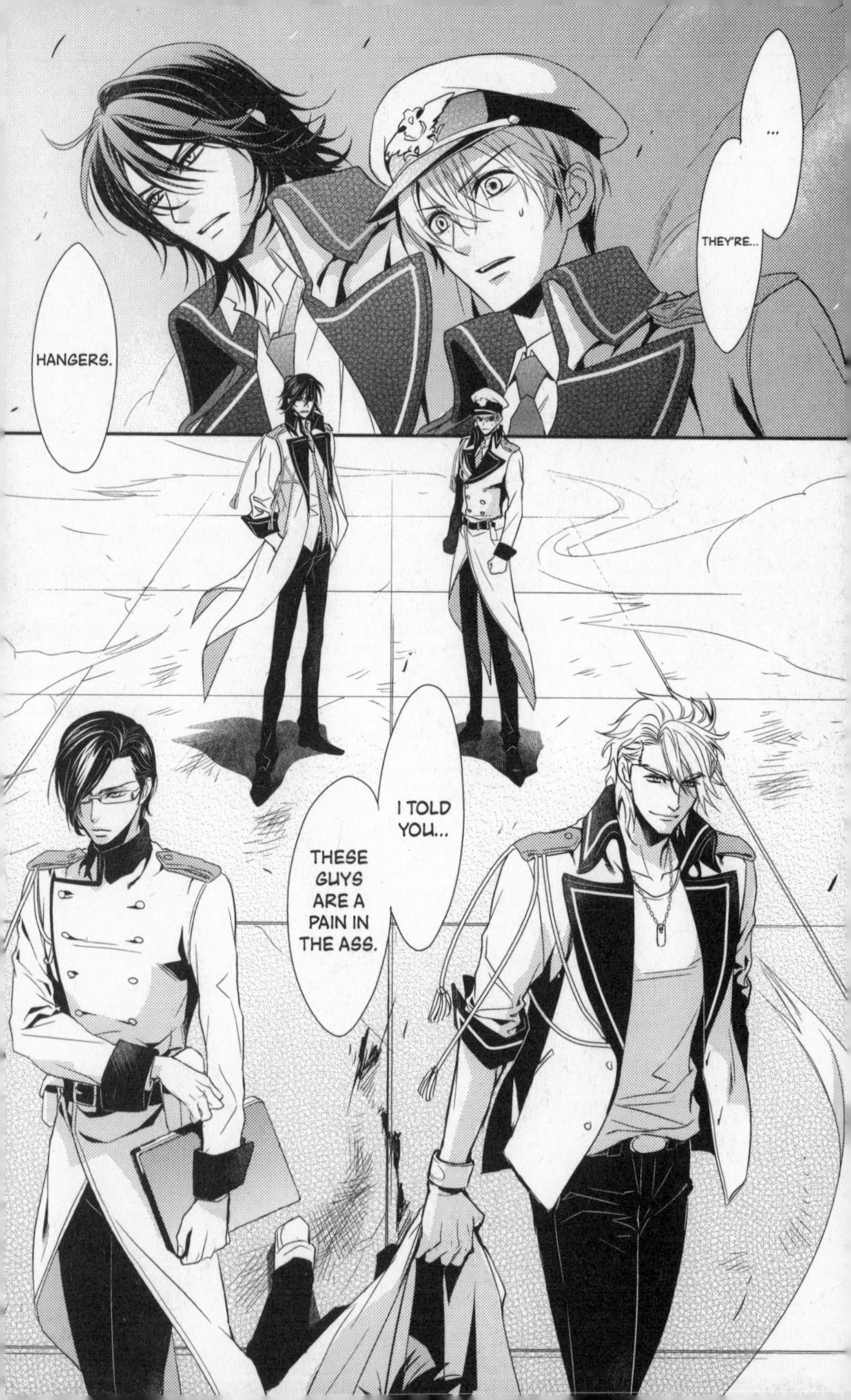
...
THEY'RE...
HANGERS.
I TOLD YOU...
THESE GUYS ARE A PAIN IN THE ASS.

Chapter 4

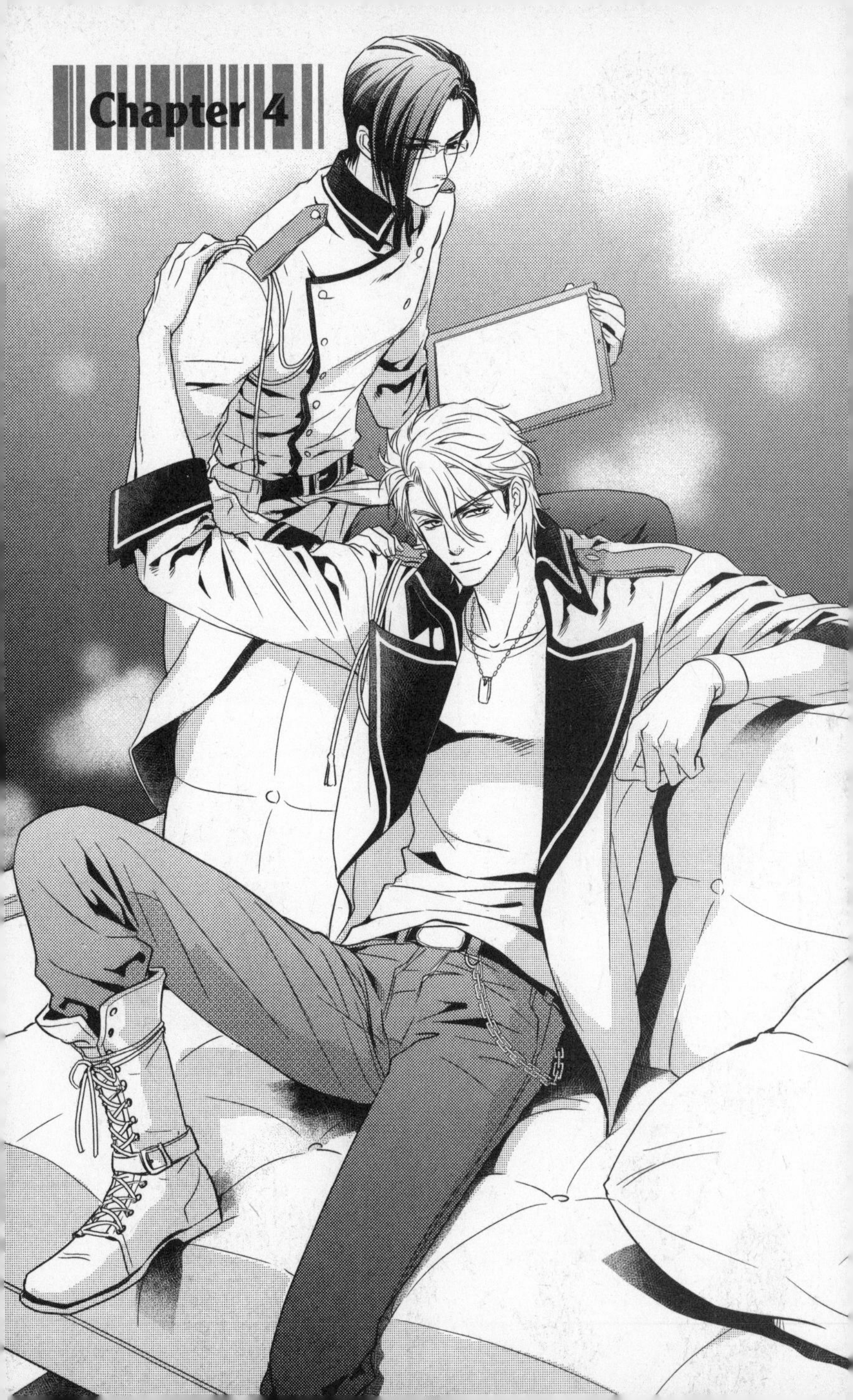

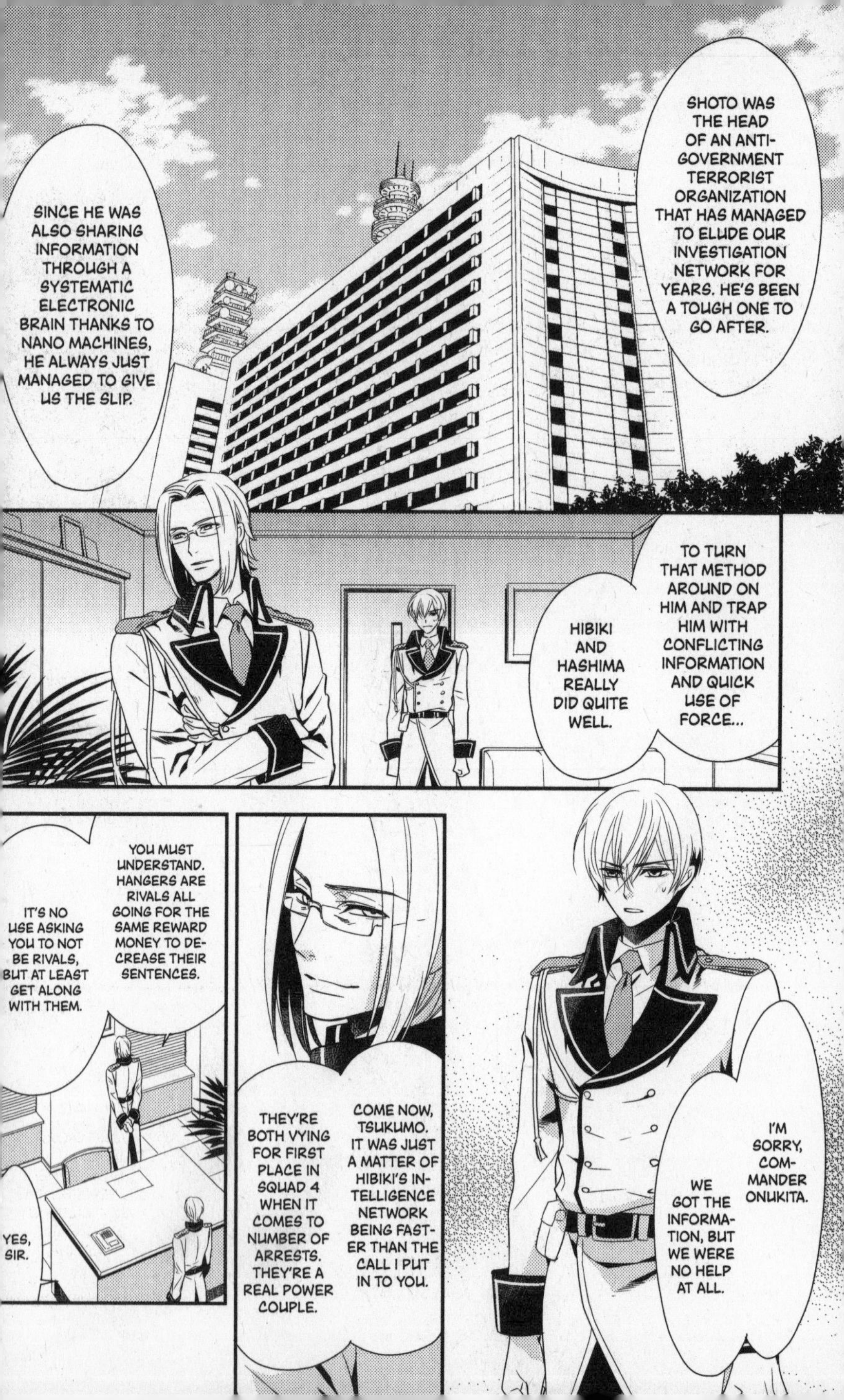
SHOTO WAS THE HEAD OF AN ANTI-GOVERNMENT TERRORIST ORGANIZATION THAT HAS MANAGED TO ELUDE OUR INVESTIGATION NETWORK FOR YEARS. HE'S BEEN A TOUGH ONE TO GO AFTER.
SINCE HE WAS ALSO SHARING INFORMATION THROUGH A SYSTEMATIC ELECTRONIC BRAIN THANKS TO NANO MACHINES, HE ALWAYS JUST MANAGED TO GIVE US THE SLIP.
TO TURN THAT METHOD AROUND ON HIM AND TRAP HIM WITH CONFLICTING INFORMATION AND QUICK USE OF FORCE...
HIBIKI AND HASHIMA REALLY DID QUITE WELL.
I'M SORRY, COMMANDER ONUKITA.
WE GOT THE INFORMATION, BUT WE WERE NO HELP AT ALL.
COME NOW, TSUKUMO. IT WAS JUST A MATTER OF HIBIKI'S INTELLIGENCE NETWORK BEING FASTER THAN THE CALL I PUT IN TO YOU.
THEY'RE BOTH VYING FOR FIRST PLACE IN SQUAD 4 WHEN IT COMES TO NUMBER OF ARRESTS. THEY'RE A REAL POWER COUPLE.
YOU MUST UNDERSTAND. HANGERS ARE RIVALS ALL GOING FOR THE SAME REWARD MONEY TO DECREASE THEIR SENTENCES.
IT'S NO USE ASKING YOU TO NOT BE RIVALS, BUT AT LEAST GET ALONG WITH THEM.
YES, SIR.

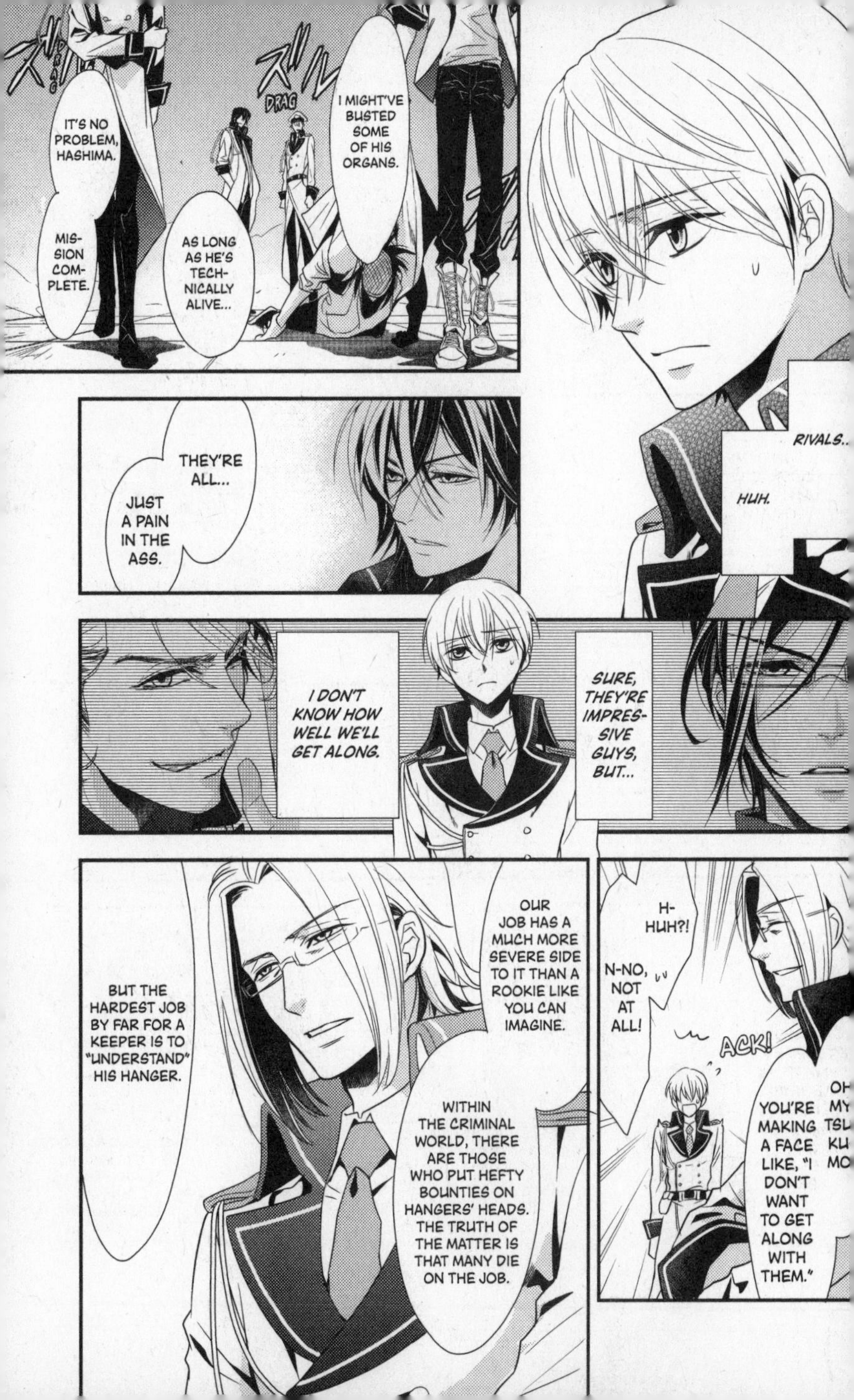
RIVALS...
HUH.
ズル DRAG
I MIGHT'VE BUSTED SOME OF HIS ORGANS.
ズル DRAG
IT'S NO PROBLEM, HASHIMA.
AS LONG AS HE'S TECHNICALLY ALIVE...
MISSION COMPLETE.
THEY'RE ALL...
JUST A PAIN IN THE ASS.
SURE, THEY'RE IMPRESSIVE GUYS, BUT...
I DON'T KNOW HOW WELL WE'LL GET ALONG.
YOU'RE MAKING A FACE LIKE, "I DON'T WANT TO GET ALONG WITH THEM."
ACK!
H-HUH?!
N-NO, NOT AT ALL!
OUR JOB HAS A MUCH MORE SEVERE SIDE TO IT THAN A ROOKIE LIKE YOU CAN IMAGINE.
WITHIN THE CRIMINAL WORLD, THERE ARE THOSE WHO PUT HEFTY BOUNTIES ON HANGERS' HEADS. THE TRUTH OF THE MATTER IS THAT MANY DIE ON THE JOB.
BUT THE HARDEST JOB BY FAR FOR A KEEPER IS TO "UNDERSTAND" HIS HANGER.

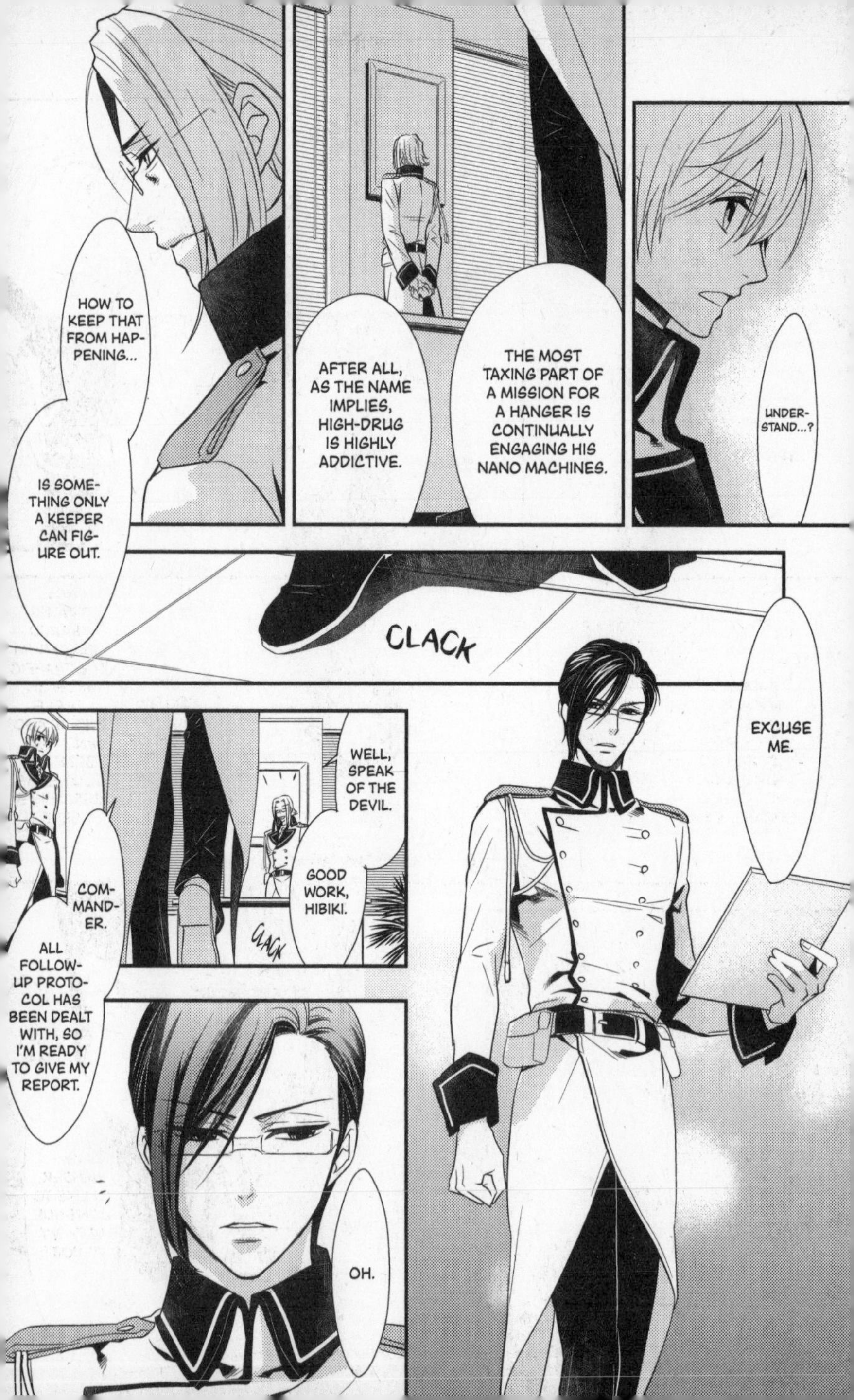
UNDER-STAND...?
THE MOST TAXING PART OF A MISSION FOR A HANGER IS CONTINUALLY ENGAGING HIS NANO MACHINES.
AFTER ALL, AS THE NAME IMPLIES, HIGH-DRUG IS HIGHLY ADDICTIVE.
HOW TO KEEP THAT FROM HAP-PENING...
IS SOME-THING ONLY A KEEPER CAN FIG-URE OUT.
CLACK
EXCUSE ME.
WELL, SPEAK OF THE DEVIL.
GOOD WORK, HIBIKI.
CLACK
COM-MAND-ER.
ALL FOLLOW-UP PROTO-COL HAS BEEN DEALT WITH, SO I'M READY TO GIVE MY REPORT.
OH.

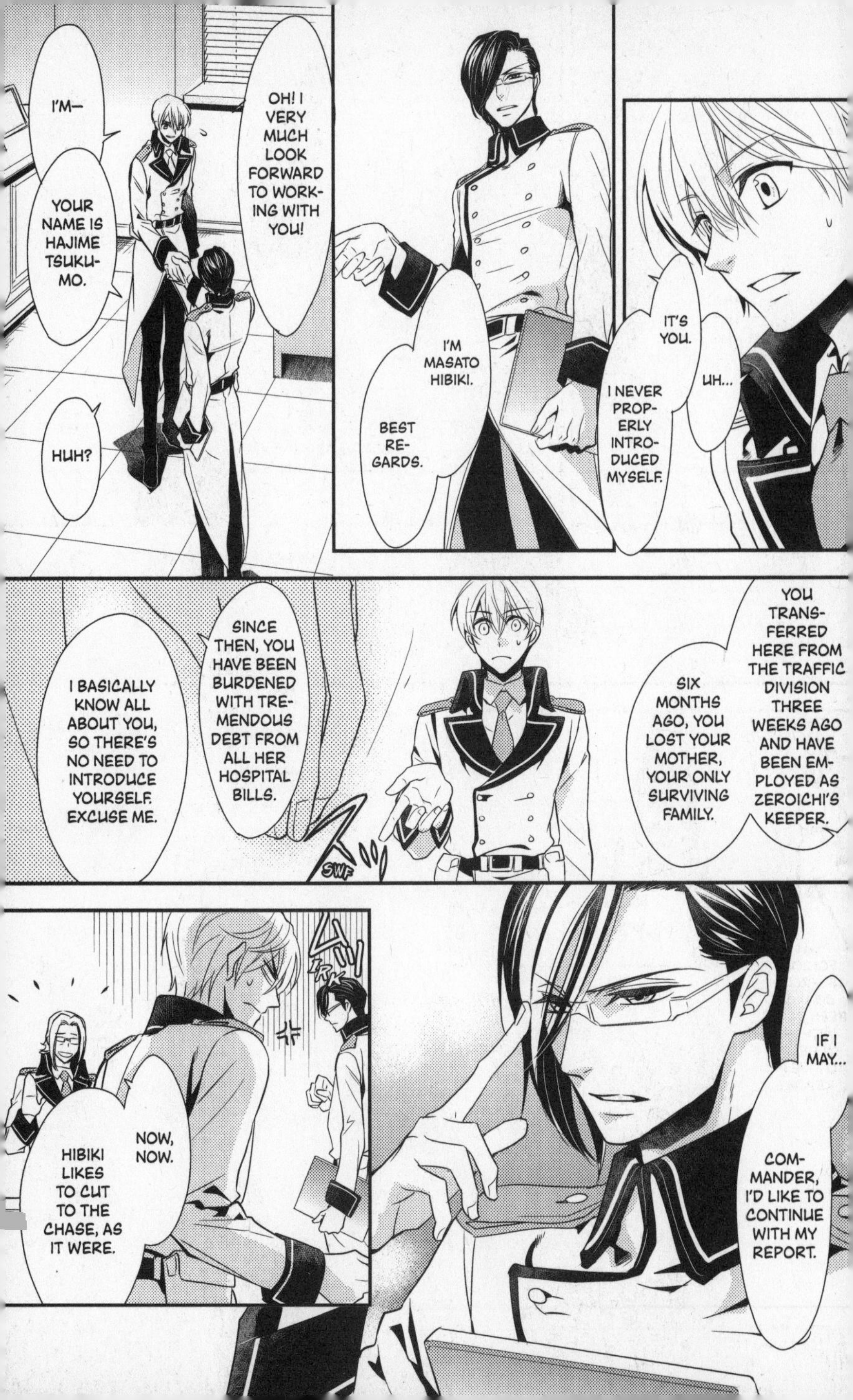
IT'S YOU.
UH...
I NEVER PROPERLY INTRODUCED MYSELF.
I'M MASATO HIBIKI.
BEST REGARDS.
OH! I VERY MUCH LOOK FORWARD TO WORKING WITH YOU!
I'M—
YOUR NAME IS HAJIME TSUKUMO.
HUH?
YOU TRANSFERRED HERE FROM THE TRAFFIC DIVISION THREE WEEKS AGO AND HAVE BEEN EMPLOYED AS ZEROICHI'S KEEPER.
SIX MONTHS AGO, YOU LOST YOUR MOTHER, YOUR ONLY SURVIVING FAMILY.
SINCE THEN, YOU HAVE BEEN BURDENED WITH TREMENDOUS DEBT FROM ALL HER HOSPITAL BILLS.
I BASICALLY KNOW ALL ABOUT YOU, SO THERE'S NO NEED TO INTRODUCE YOURSELF. EXCUSE ME.
SWF
IF I MAY...
COMMANDER, I'D LIKE TO CONTINUE WITH MY REPORT.
IRK
NOW, NOW.
HIBIKI LIKES TO CUT TO THE CHASE, AS IT WERE.

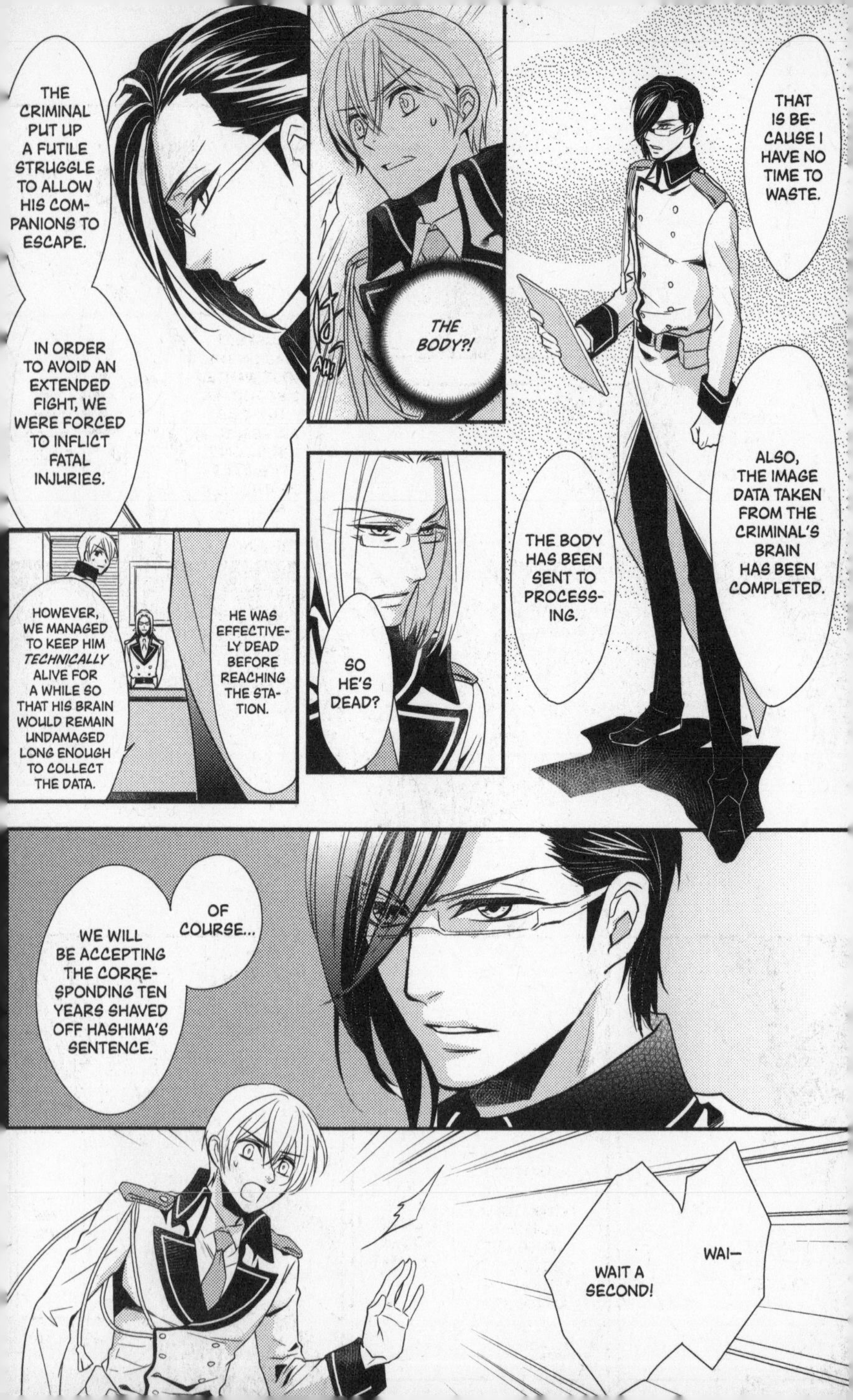
THAT IS BE-CAUSE I HAVE NO TIME TO WASTE.
ALSO, THE IMAGE DATA TAKEN FROM THE CRIMINAL'S BRAIN HAS BEEN COMPLETED.
THE BODY HAS BEEN SENT TO PROCESS-ING.
THE BODY?!
AH!
SO HE'S DEAD?
THE CRIMINAL PUT UP A FUTILE STRUGGLE TO ALLOW HIS COM-PANIONS TO ESCAPE.
IN ORDER TO AVOID AN EXTENDED FIGHT, WE WERE FORCED TO INFLICT FATAL INJURIES.
HE WAS EFFECTIVE-LY DEAD BEFORE REACHING THE STA-TION.
HOWEVER, WE MANAGED TO KEEP HIM *TECHNICALLY* ALIVE FOR A WHILE SO THAT HIS BRAIN WOULD REMAIN UNDAMAGED LONG ENOUGH TO COLLECT THE DATA.
OF COURSE...
WE WILL BE ACCEPTING THE CORRE-SPONDING TEN YEARS SHAVED OFF HASHIMA'S SENTENCE.
WAI—
WAIT A SECOND!

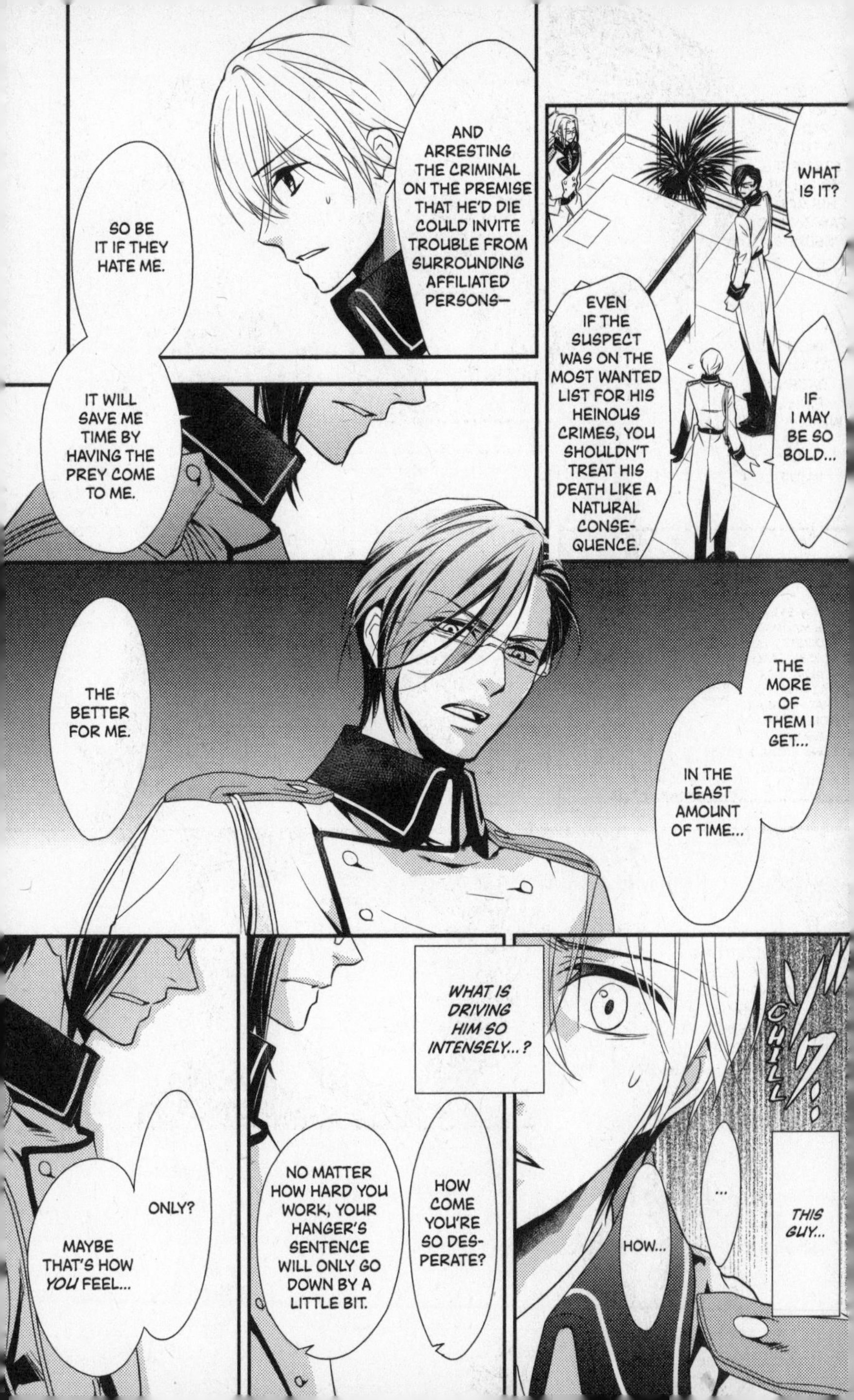
WHAT IS IT?
IF I MAY BE SO BOLD...
EVEN IF THE SUSPECT WAS ON THE MOST WANTED LIST FOR HIS HEINOUS CRIMES, YOU SHOULDN'T TREAT HIS DEATH LIKE A NATURAL CONSE-QUENCE.
AND ARRESTING THE CRIMINAL ON THE PREMISE THAT HE'D DIE COULD INVITE TROUBLE FROM SURROUNDING AFFILIATED PERSONS—
SO BE IT IF THEY HATE ME.
IT WILL SAVE ME TIME BY HAVING THE PREY COME TO ME.
THE MORE OF THEM I GET...
IN THE LEAST AMOUNT OF TIME...
THE BETTER FOR ME.
CHILL
THIS GUY...
...
HOW...
WHAT IS DRIVING HIM SO INTENSELY...?
HOW COME YOU'RE SO DES-PERATE?
NO MATTER HOW HARD YOU WORK, YOUR HANGER'S SENTENCE WILL ONLY GO DOWN BY A LITTLE BIT.
ONLY?
MAYBE THAT'S HOW YOU FEEL...

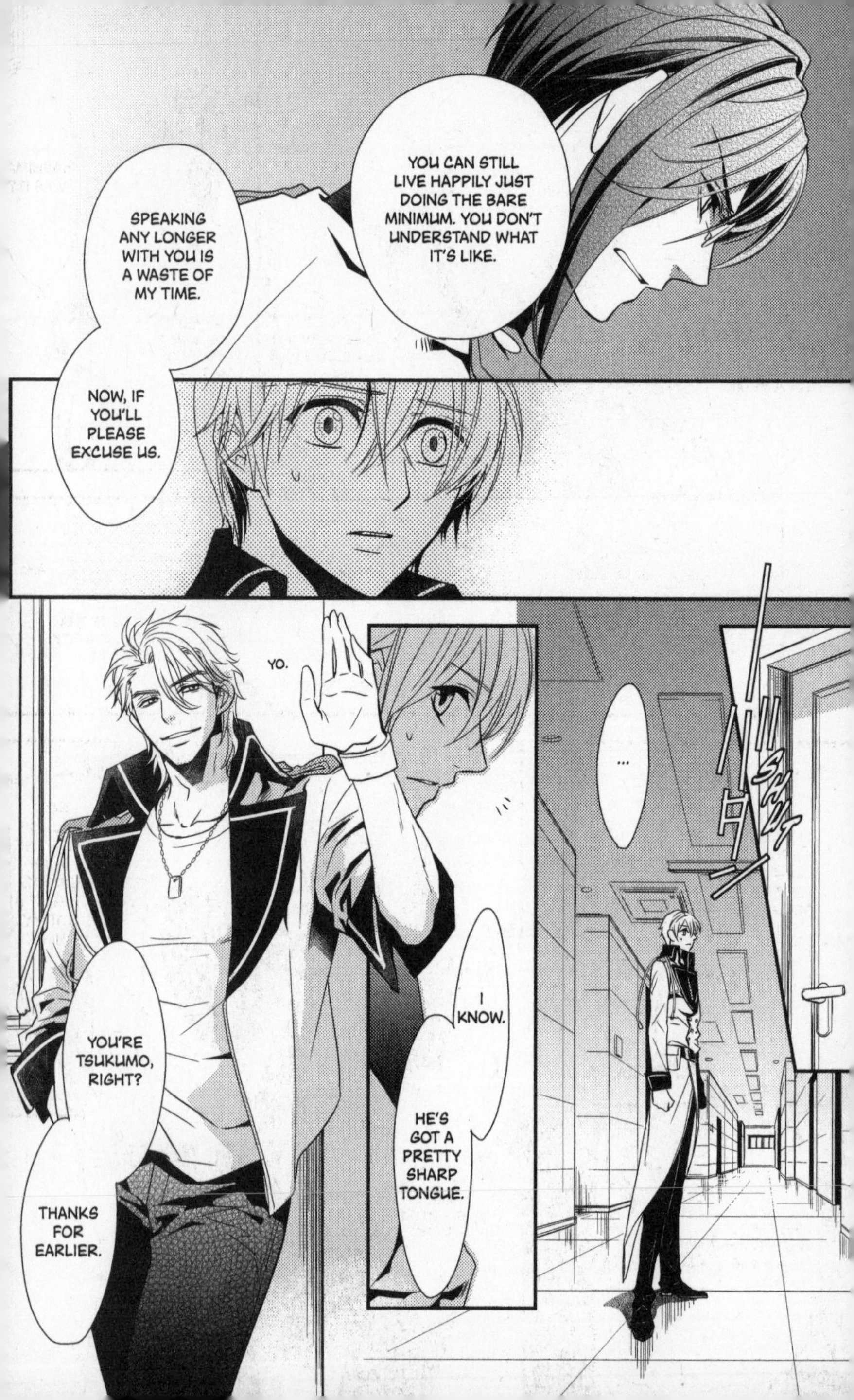
YOU CAN STILL LIVE HAPPILY JUST DOING THE BARE MINIMUM. YOU DON'T UNDERSTAND WHAT IT'S LIKE.
SPEAKING ANY LONGER WITH YOU IS A WASTE OF MY TIME.
NOW, IF YOU'LL PLEASE EXCUSE US.
SHUT
...
YO.
I KNOW.
HE'S GOT A PRETTY SHARP TONGUE.
YOU'RE TSUKUMO, RIGHT?
THANKS FOR EARLIER.

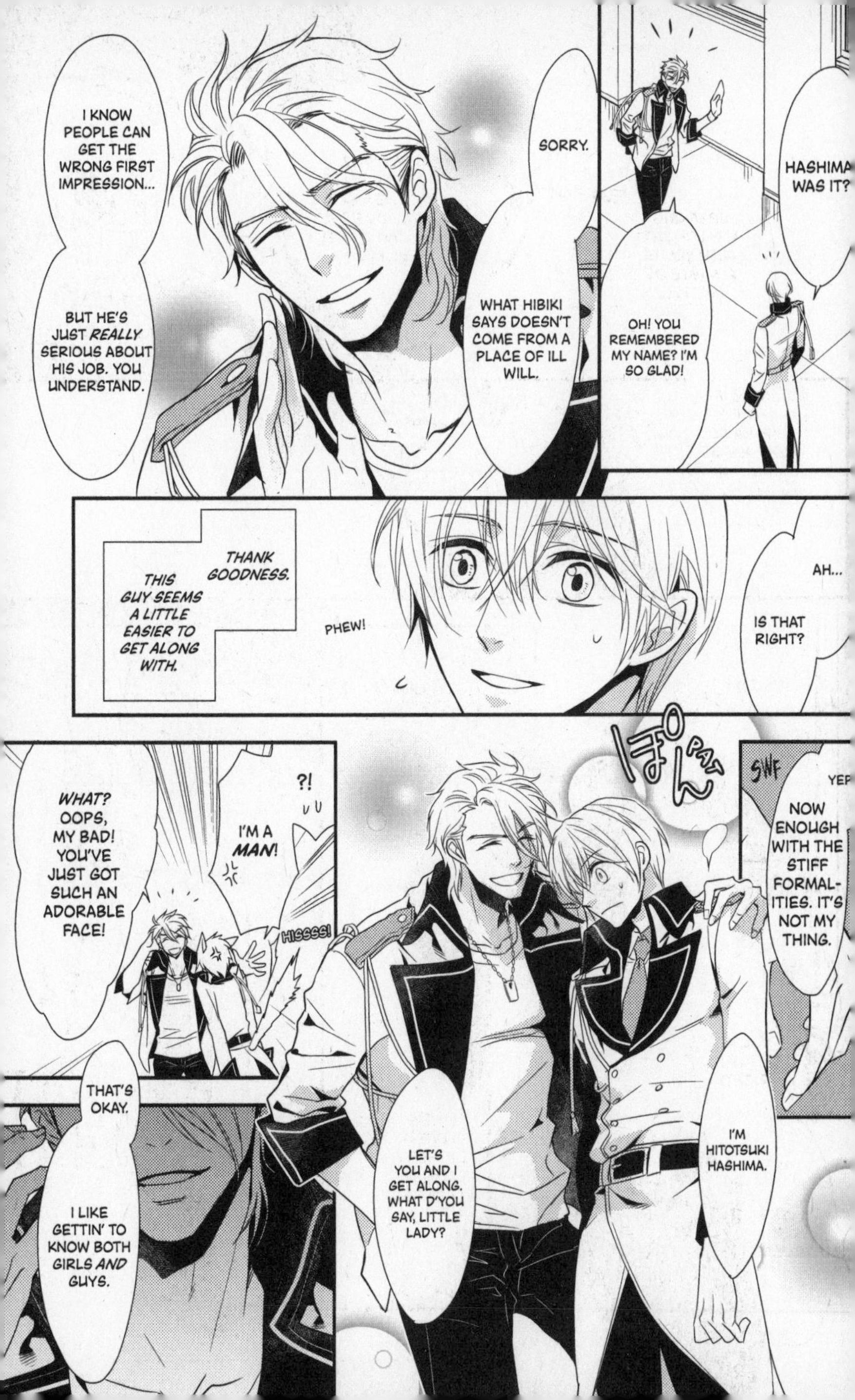
HASHIMA WAS IT?
OH! YOU REMEMBERED MY NAME? I'M SO GLAD!
SORRY.
WHAT HIBIKI SAYS DOESN'T COME FROM A PLACE OF ILL WILL.
I KNOW PEOPLE CAN GET THE WRONG FIRST IMPRESSION...
BUT HE'S JUST *REALLY* SERIOUS ABOUT HIS JOB. YOU UNDERSTAND.
AH...
IS THAT RIGHT?
PHEW!
THANK GOODNESS.
THIS GUY SEEMS A LITTLE EASIER TO GET ALONG WITH.
SNF
YEP
NOW ENOUGH WITH THE STIFF FORMAL-ITIES. IT'S NOT MY THING.
ぽん
PAT
I'M HITOTSUKI HASHIMA.
LET'S YOU AND I GET ALONG. WHAT D'YOU SAY, LITTLE LADY?
?!
I'M A *MAN*!
HISSSS!
WHAT? OOPS, MY BAD! YOU'VE JUST GOT SUCH AN ADORABLE FACE!
THAT'S OKAY.
I LIKE GETTIN' TO KNOW BOTH GIRLS *AND* GUYS.

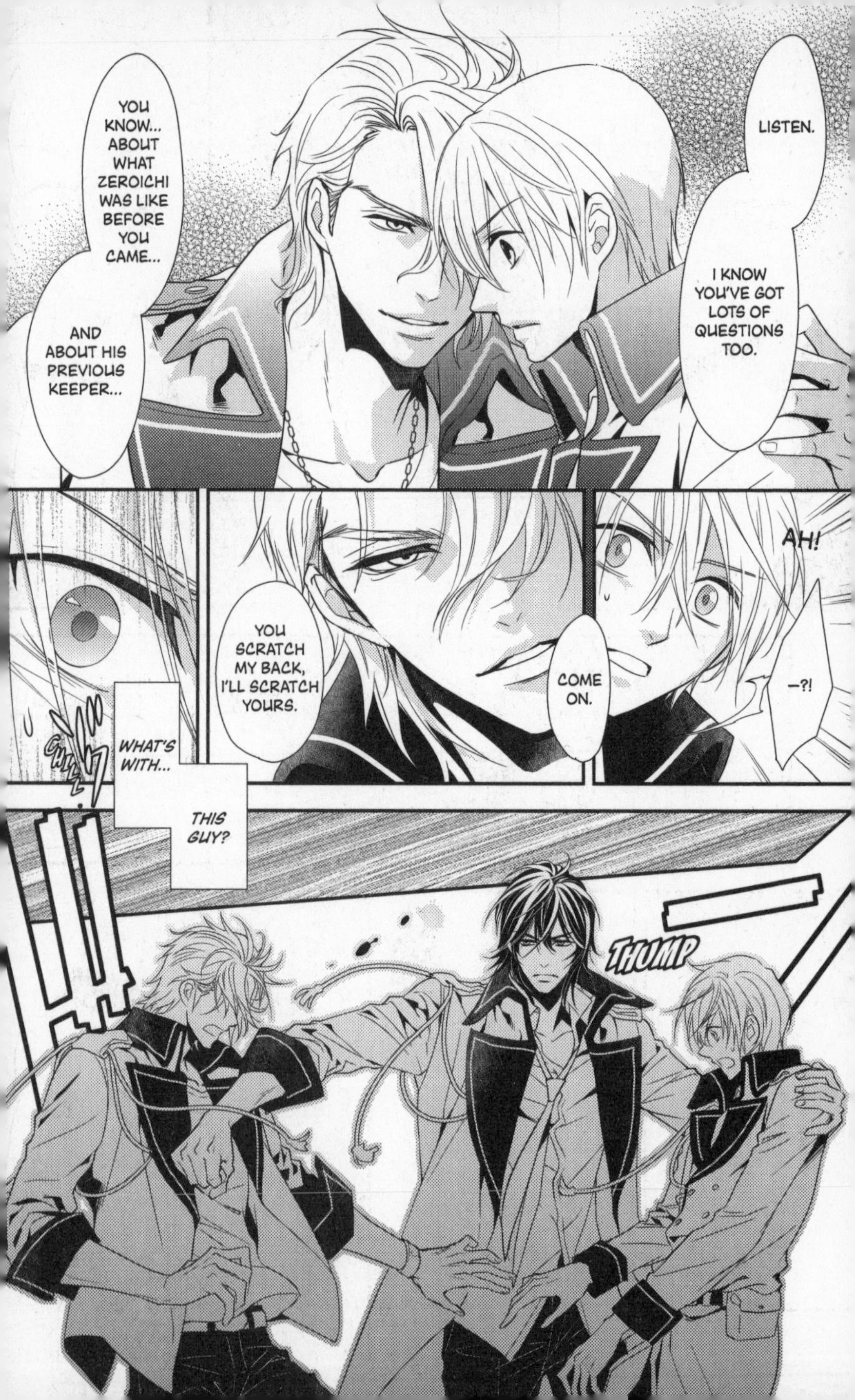
LISTEN.
I KNOW YOU'VE GOT LOTS OF QUESTIONS TOO.
YOU KNOW... ABOUT WHAT ZEROICHI WAS LIKE BEFORE YOU CAME...
AND ABOUT HIS PREVIOUS KEEPER...
AH!
—?!
COME ON.
YOU SCRATCH MY BACK, I'LL SCRATCH YOURS.
CHILL
WHAT'S WITH...
THIS GUY?
THUMP

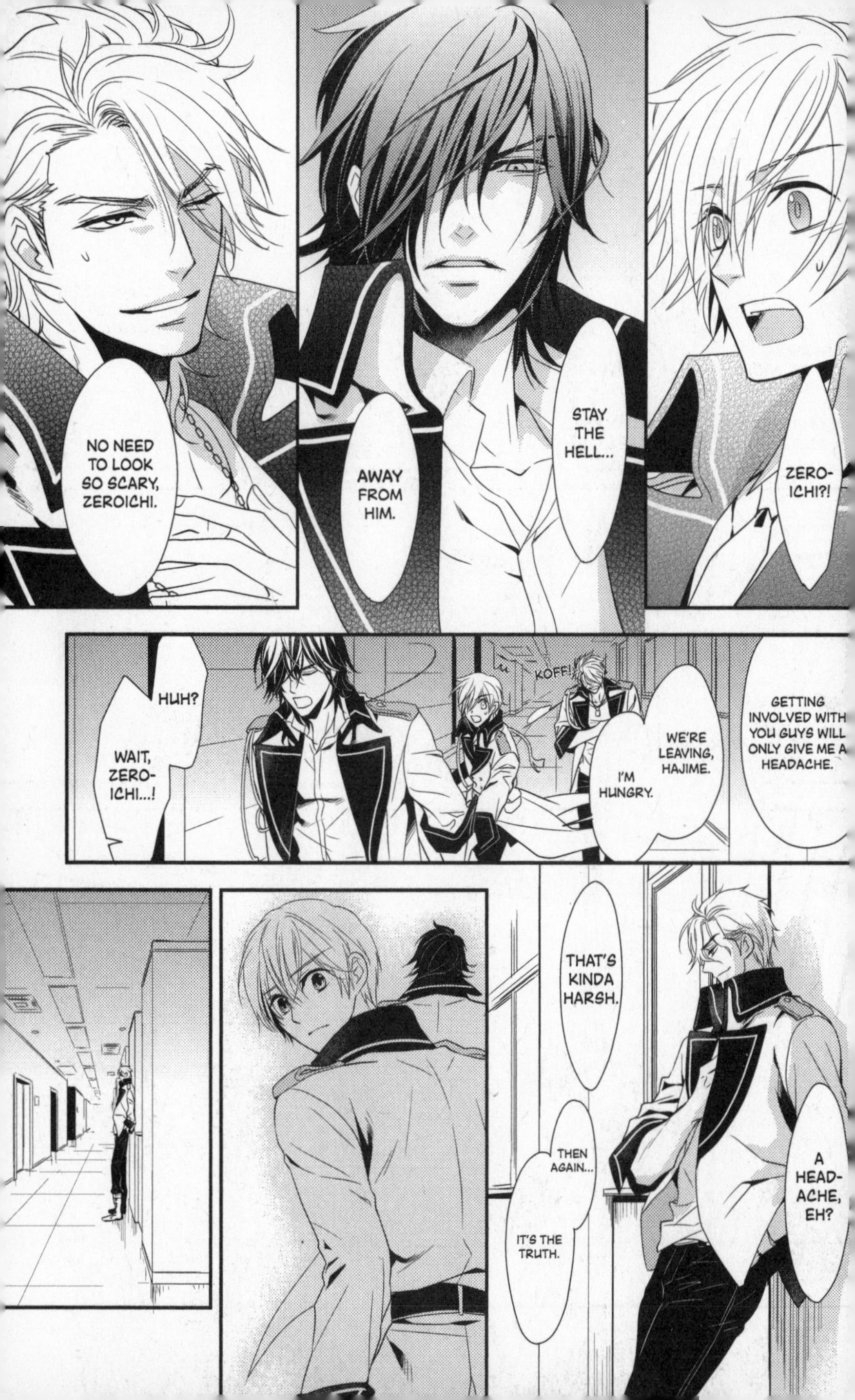
ZERO-ICHI?!
STAY THE HELL...
AWAY FROM HIM.
NO NEED TO LOOK SO SCARY, ZEROICHI.
GETTING INVOLVED WITH YOU GUYS WILL ONLY GIVE ME A HEADACHE.
WE'RE LEAVING, HAJIME.
I'M HUNGRY.
KOFF!
HUH?
WAIT, ZERO-ICHI...!
A HEAD-ACHE, EH?
THAT'S KINDA HARSH.
THEN AGAIN...
IT'S THE TRUTH.

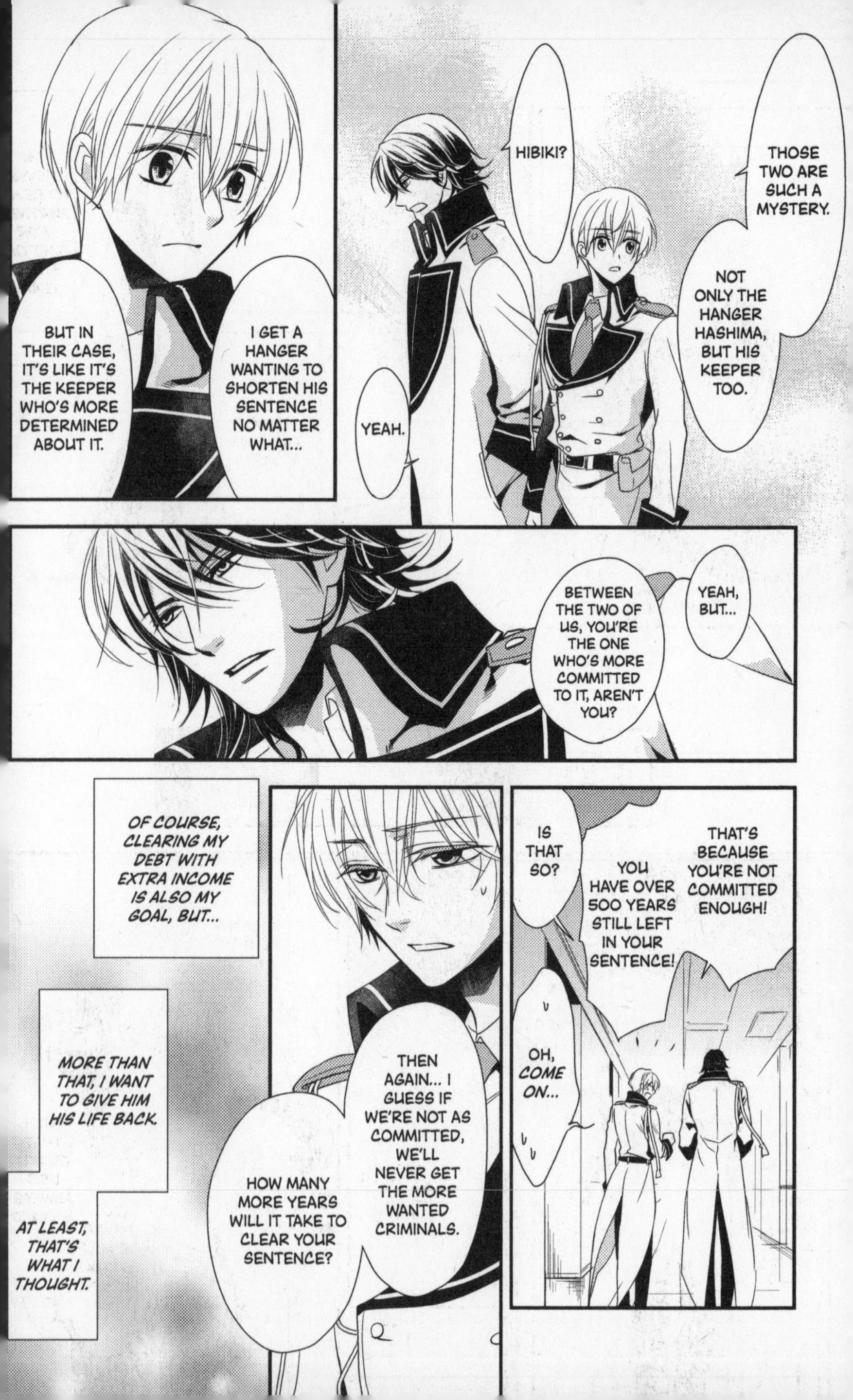
THOSE TWO ARE SUCH A MYSTERY.
NOT ONLY THE HANGER HASHIMA, BUT HIS KEEPER TOO.
HIBIKI?
YEAH.
I GET A HANGER WANTING TO SHORTEN HIS SENTENCE NO MATTER WHAT...
BUT IN THEIR CASE, IT'S LIKE IT'S THE KEEPER WHO'S MORE DETERMINED ABOUT IT.
YEAH, BUT...
BETWEEN THE TWO OF US, YOU'RE THE ONE WHO'S MORE COMMITTED TO IT, AREN'T YOU?
THAT'S BECAUSE YOU'RE NOT COMMITTED ENOUGH!
YOU HAVE OVER 500 YEARS STILL LEFT IN YOUR SENTENCE!
IS THAT SO?
OH, COME ON...
THEN AGAIN... I GUESS IF WE'RE NOT AS COMMITTED, WE'LL NEVER GET THE MORE WANTED CRIMINALS.
HOW MANY MORE YEARS WILL IT TAKE TO CLEAR YOUR SENTENCE?
OF COURSE, CLEARING MY DEBT WITH EXTRA INCOME IS ALSO MY GOAL, BUT...
MORE THAN THAT, I WANT TO GIVE HIM HIS LIFE BACK.
AT LEAST, THAT'S WHAT I THOUGHT.

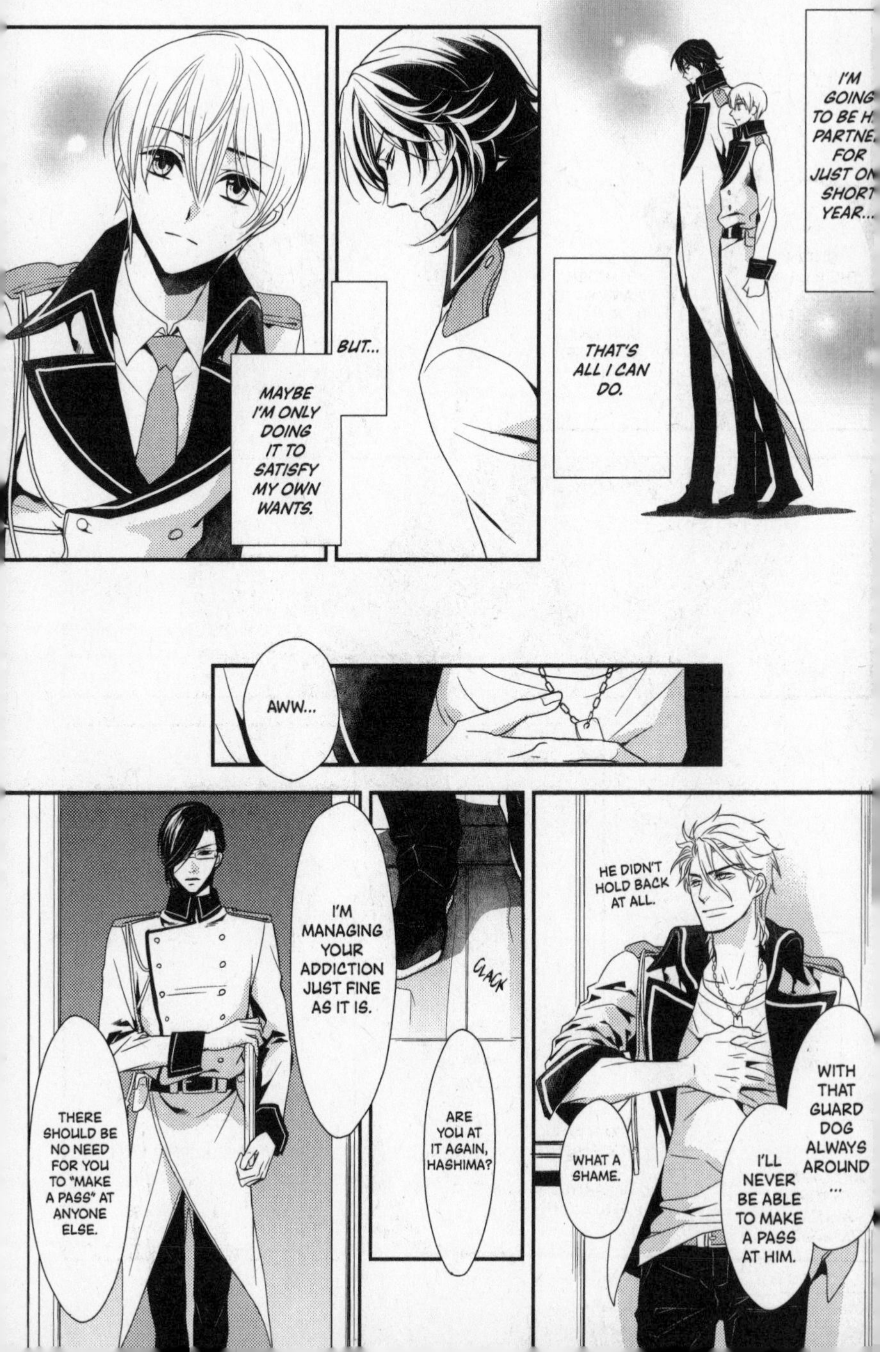
I'M GOING TO BE H PARTNE FOR JUST ON SHORT YEAR...
THAT'S ALL I CAN DO.
BUT...
MAYBE I'M ONLY DOING IT TO SATISFY MY OWN WANTS.
AWW...
HE DIDN'T HOLD BACK AT ALL.
WITH THAT GUARD DOG ALWAYS AROUND...
I'LL NEVER BE ABLE TO MAKE A PASS AT HIM.
WHAT A SHAME.
CLACK
ARE YOU AT IT AGAIN, HASHIMA?
I'M MANAGING YOUR ADDICTION JUST FINE AS IT IS.
THERE SHOULD BE NO NEED FOR YOU TO "MAKE A PASS" AT ANYONE ELSE.

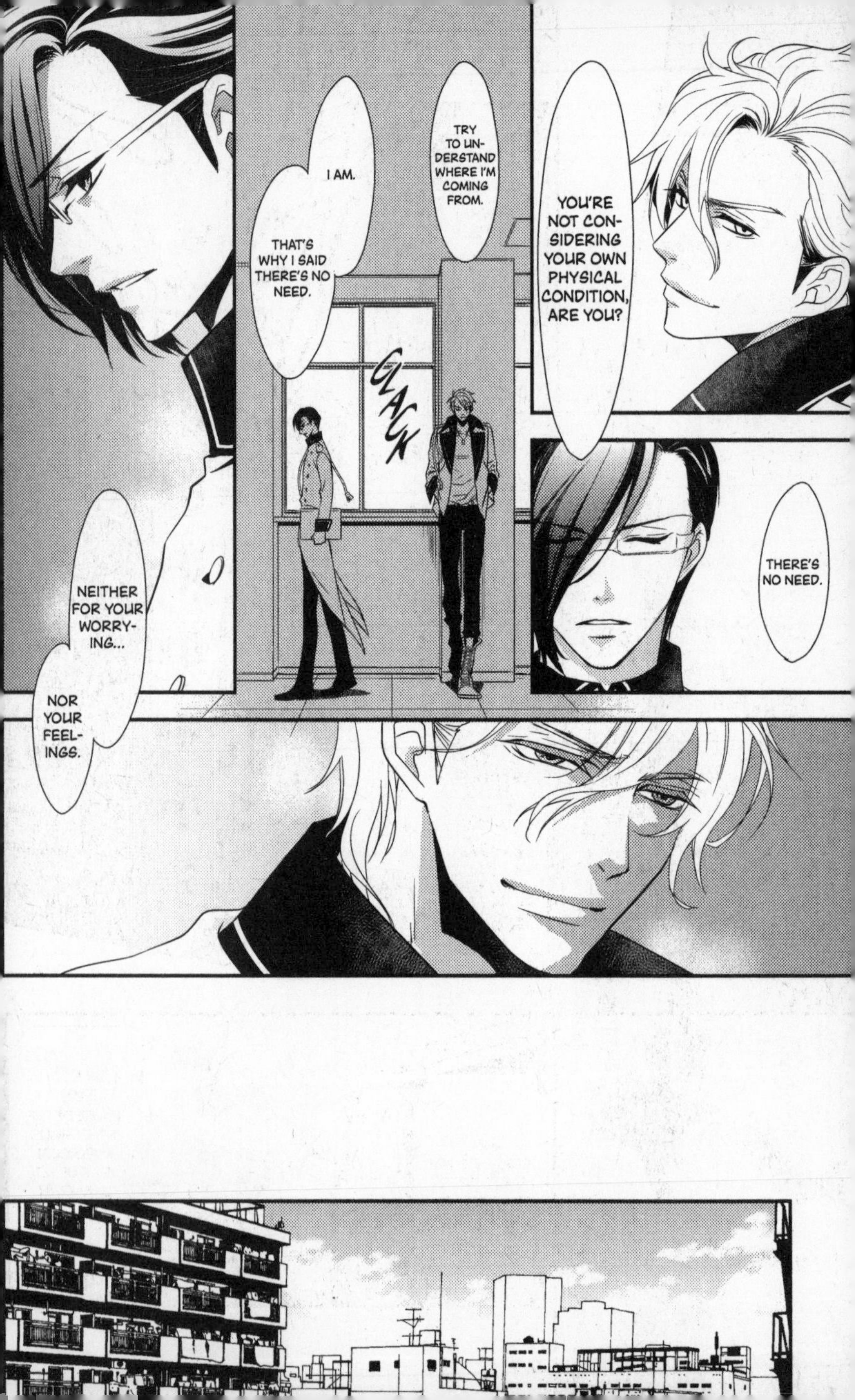
YOU'RE NOT CONSIDERING YOUR OWN PHYSICAL CONDITION, ARE YOU?
THERE'S NO NEED.
TRY TO UNDERSTAND WHERE I'M COMING FROM.
I AM.
THAT'S WHY I SAID THERE'S NO NEED.
CLACK
NEITHER FOR YOUR WORRYING...
NOR YOUR FEELINGS.

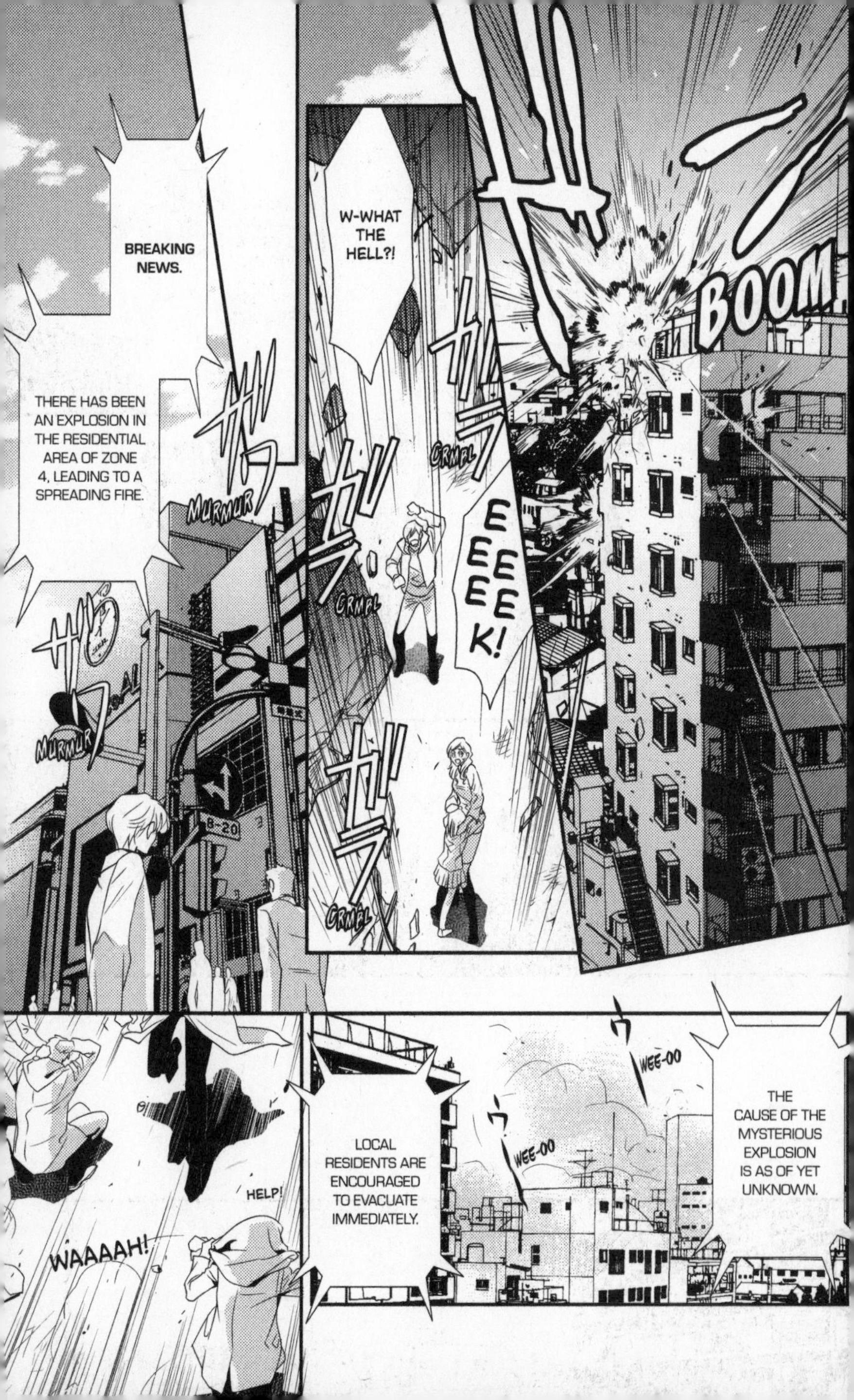
BOOM
W-WHAT THE HELL?!
GRMPL
EEEEEK!
GRMPL
GRMPL
BREAKING NEWS.
THERE HAS BEEN AN EXPLOSION IN THE RESIDENTIAL AREA OF ZONE 4, LEADING TO A SPREADING FIRE.
MURMUR
MURMUR
8-20
WEE-OO
THE CAUSE OF THE MYSTERIOUS EXPLOSION IS AS OF YET UNKNOWN.
WEE-OO
LOCAL RESIDENTS ARE ENCOURAGED TO EVACUATE IMMEDIATELY.
HELP!
WAAAAH!

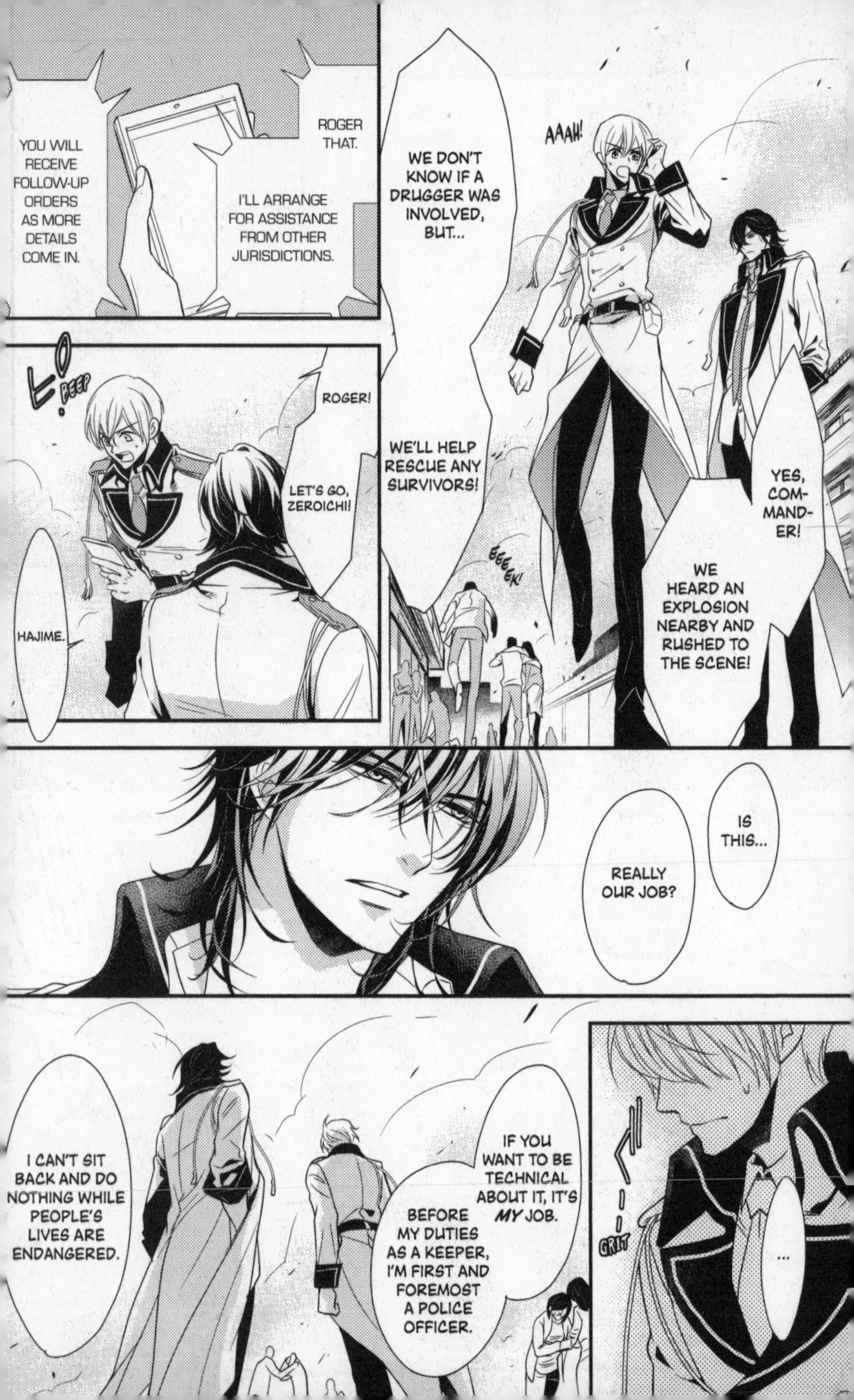
AAAH!
YES, COMMANDER!
WE HEARD AN EXPLOSION NEARBY AND RUSHED TO THE SCENE!
WE DON'T KNOW IF A DRUGGER WAS INVOLVED, BUT...
WE'LL HELP RESCUE ANY SURVIVORS!
EEEEK!
ROGER THAT.
I'LL ARRANGE FOR ASSISTANCE FROM OTHER JURISDICTIONS.
YOU WILL RECEIVE FOLLOW-UP ORDERS AS MORE DETAILS COME IN.
BEEP
ROGER!
LET'S GO, ZEROICHI!
HAJIME.
IS THIS...
REALLY OUR JOB?
GRIT
...
IF YOU WANT TO BE TECHNICAL ABOUT IT, IT'S *MY* JOB.
BEFORE MY DUTIES AS A KEEPER, I'M FIRST AND FOREMOST A POLICE OFFICER.
I CAN'T SIT BACK AND DO NOTHING WHILE PEOPLE'S LIVES ARE ENDANGERED.

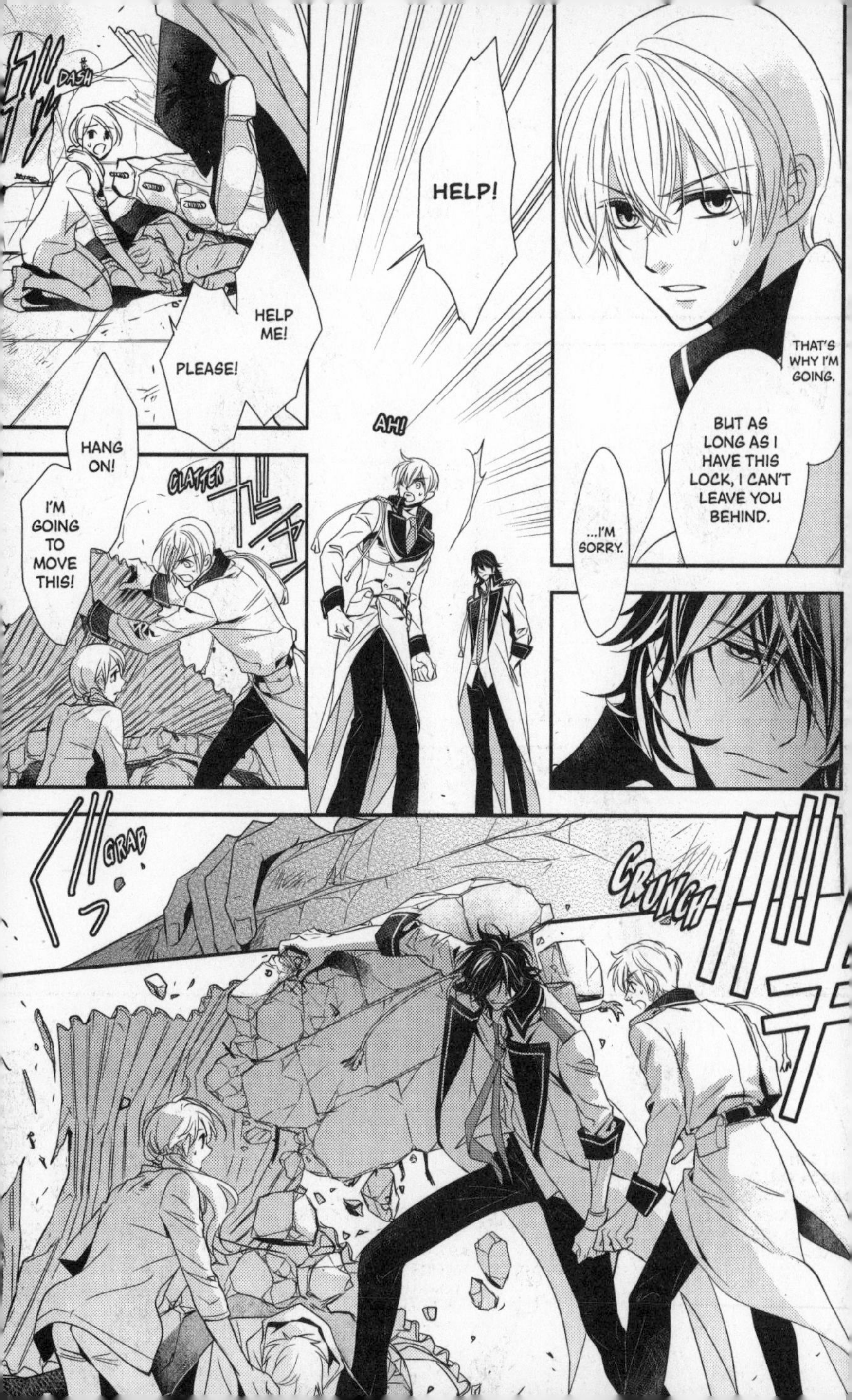
THAT'S WHY I'M GOING.
BUT AS LONG AS I HAVE THIS LOCK, I CAN'T LEAVE YOU BEHIND.
...I'M SORRY.
HELP!
AH!
DASH
HELP ME!
PLEASE!
HANG ON!
I'M GOING TO MOVE THIS!
CLATTER
CRUNCH
GRAB

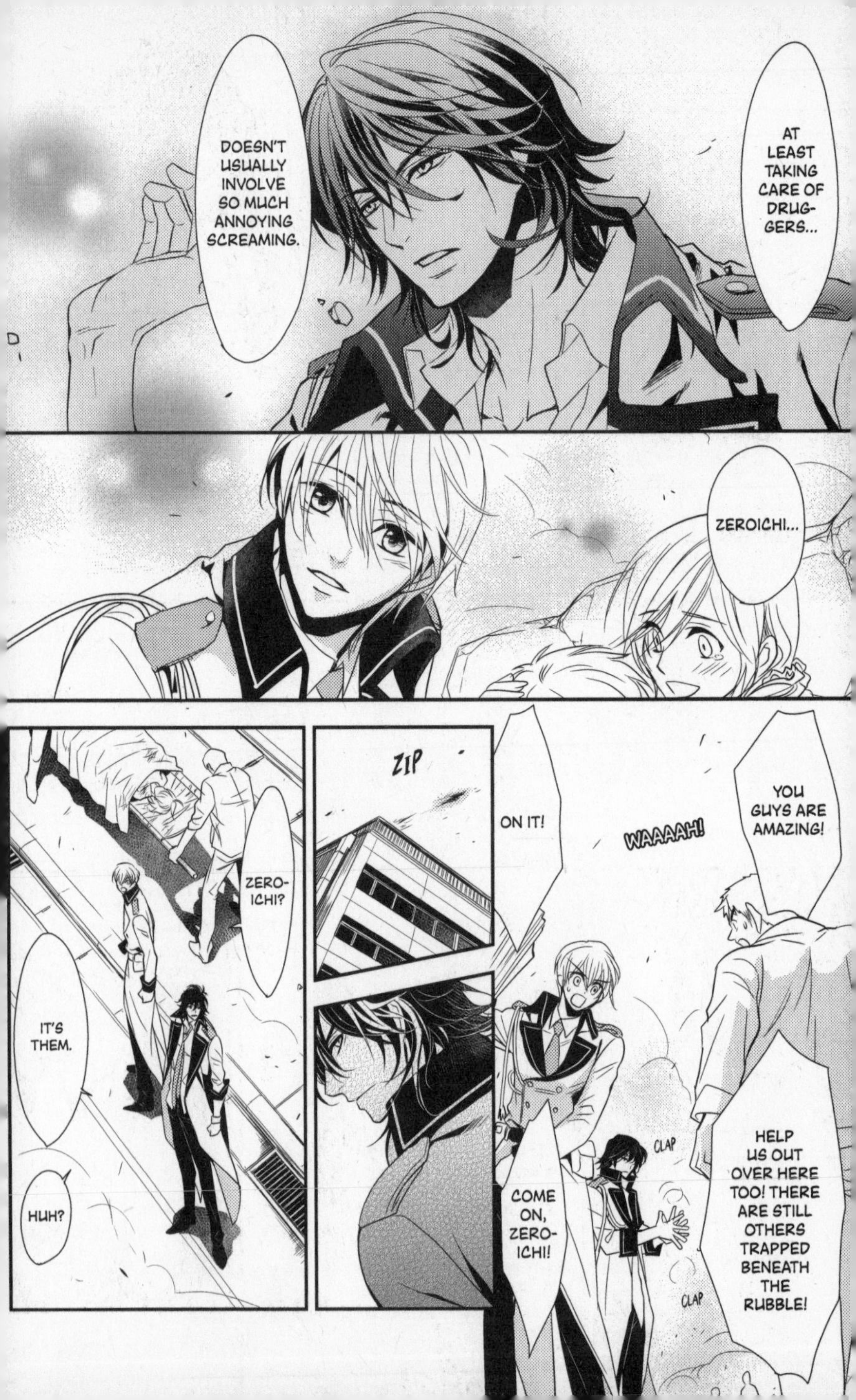
AT LEAST TAKING CARE OF DRUG-GERS...
DOESN'T USUALLY INVOLVE SO MUCH ANNOYING SCREAMING.
ZEROICHI...
YOU GUYS ARE AMAZING!
WAAAAH!
ON IT!
HELP US OUT OVER HERE TOO! THERE ARE STILL OTHERS TRAPPED BENEATH THE RUBBLE!
CLAP
CLAP
COME ON, ZERO-ICHI!
ZIP
ZERO-ICHI?
IT'S THEM.
HUH?

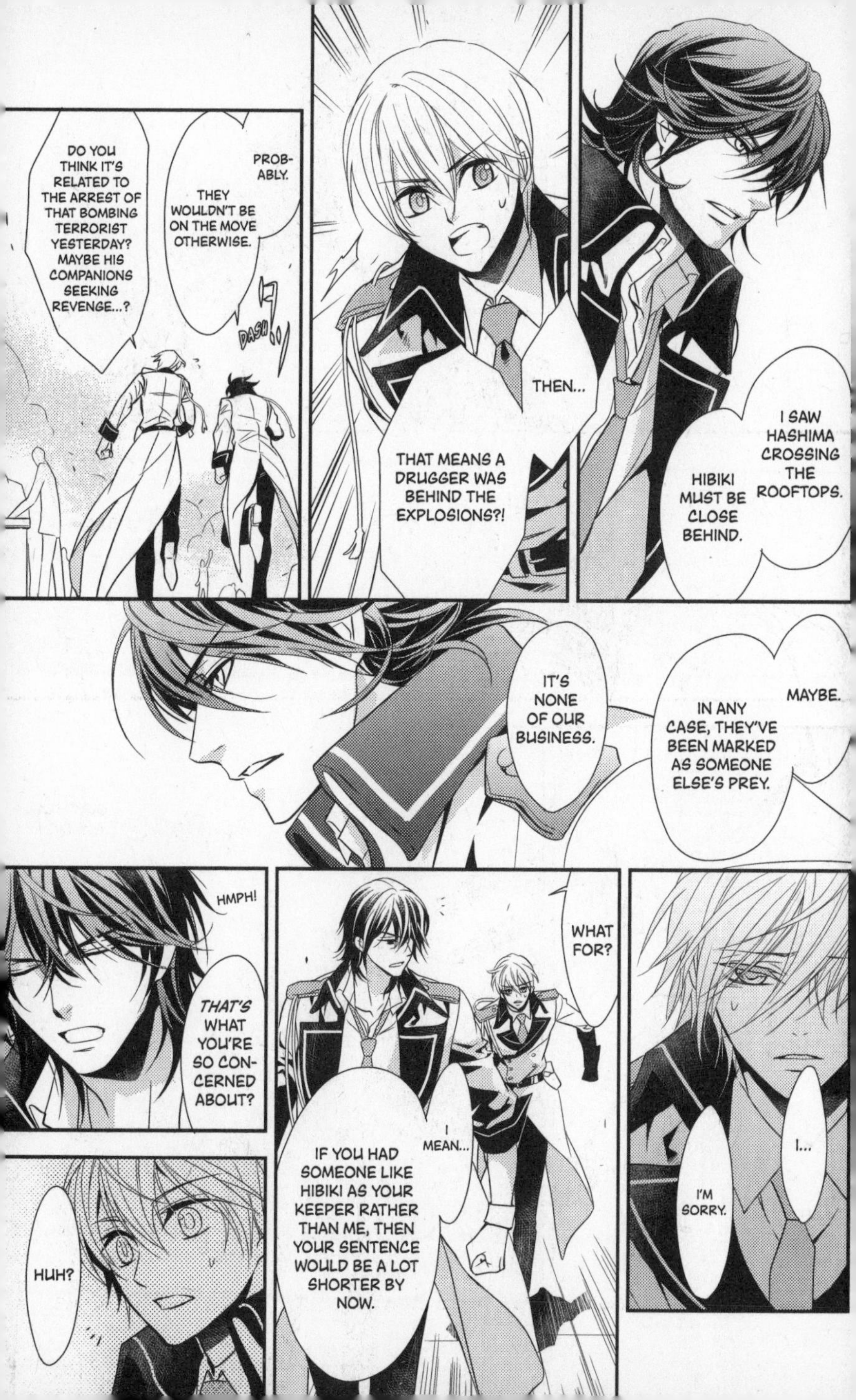
I SAW HASHIMA CROSSING THE ROOFTOPS.
HIBIKI MUST BE CLOSE BEHIND.
THEN...
THAT MEANS A DRUGGER WAS BEHIND THE EXPLOSIONS?!
PROB-ABLY.
THEY WOULDN'T BE ON THE MOVE OTHERWISE.
DO YOU THINK IT'S RELATED TO THE ARREST OF THAT BOMBING TERRORIST YESTERDAY? MAYBE HIS COMPANIONS SEEKING REVENGE...?
DASH
MAYBE.
IN ANY CASE, THEY'VE BEEN MARKED AS SOMEONE ELSE'S PREY.
IT'S NONE OF OUR BUSINESS.
I...
I'M SORRY.
WHAT FOR?
I MEAN...
IF YOU HAD SOMEONE LIKE HIBIKI AS YOUR KEEPER RATHER THAN ME, THEN YOUR SENTENCE WOULD BE A LOT SHORTER BY NOW.
HMPH!
THAT'S WHAT YOU'RE SO CON-CERNED ABOUT?
HUH?

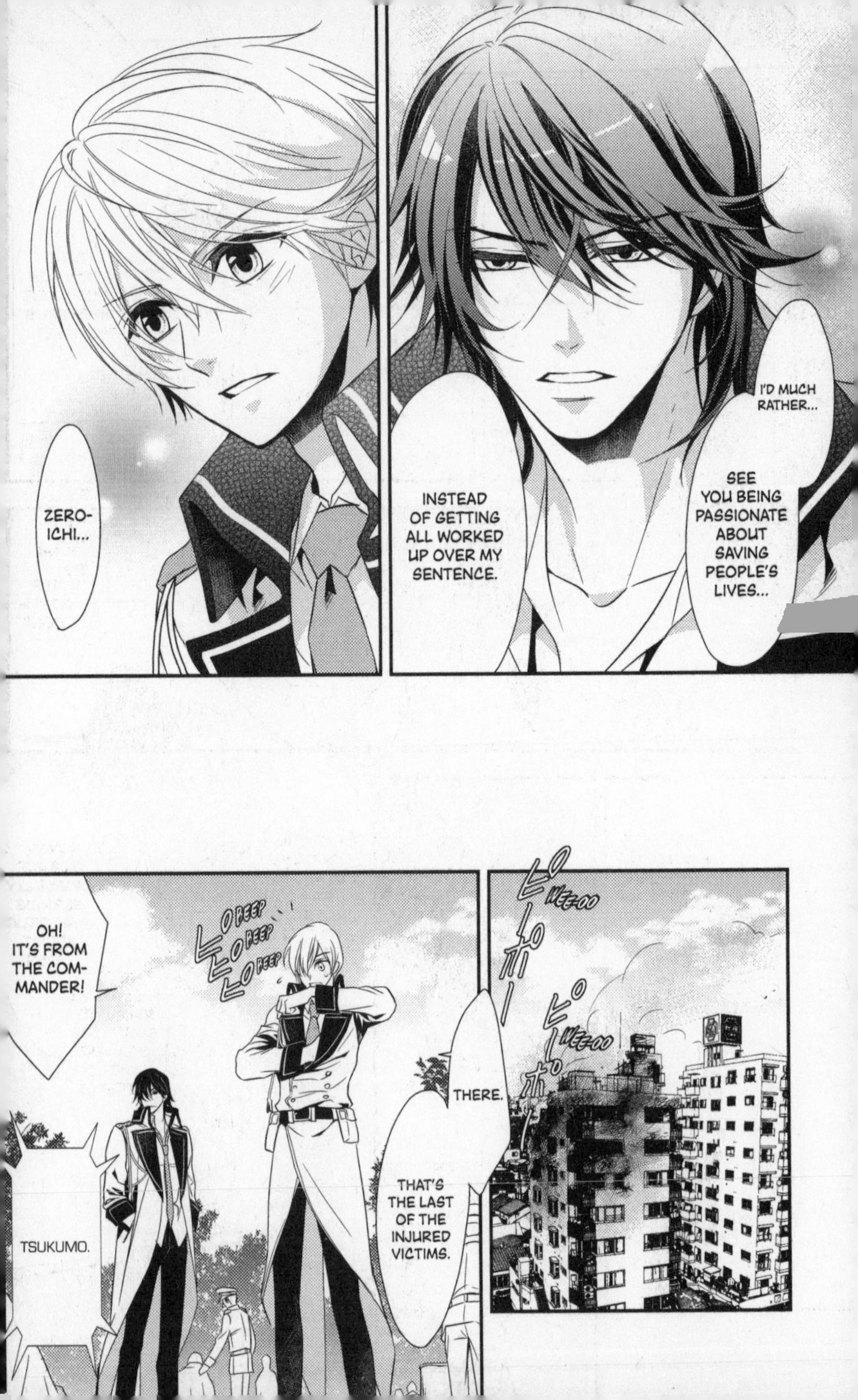
I'D MUCH RATHER...
SEE YOU BEING PASSIONATE ABOUT SAVING PEOPLE'S LIVES...
INSTEAD OF GETTING ALL WORKED UP OVER MY SENTENCE.
ZERO-ICHI...
WEE-OO
WEE-OO
THERE.
THAT'S THE LAST OF THE INJURED VICTIMS.
BEEP BEEP BEEP
OH! IT'S FROM THE COMMANDER!
TSUKUMO.

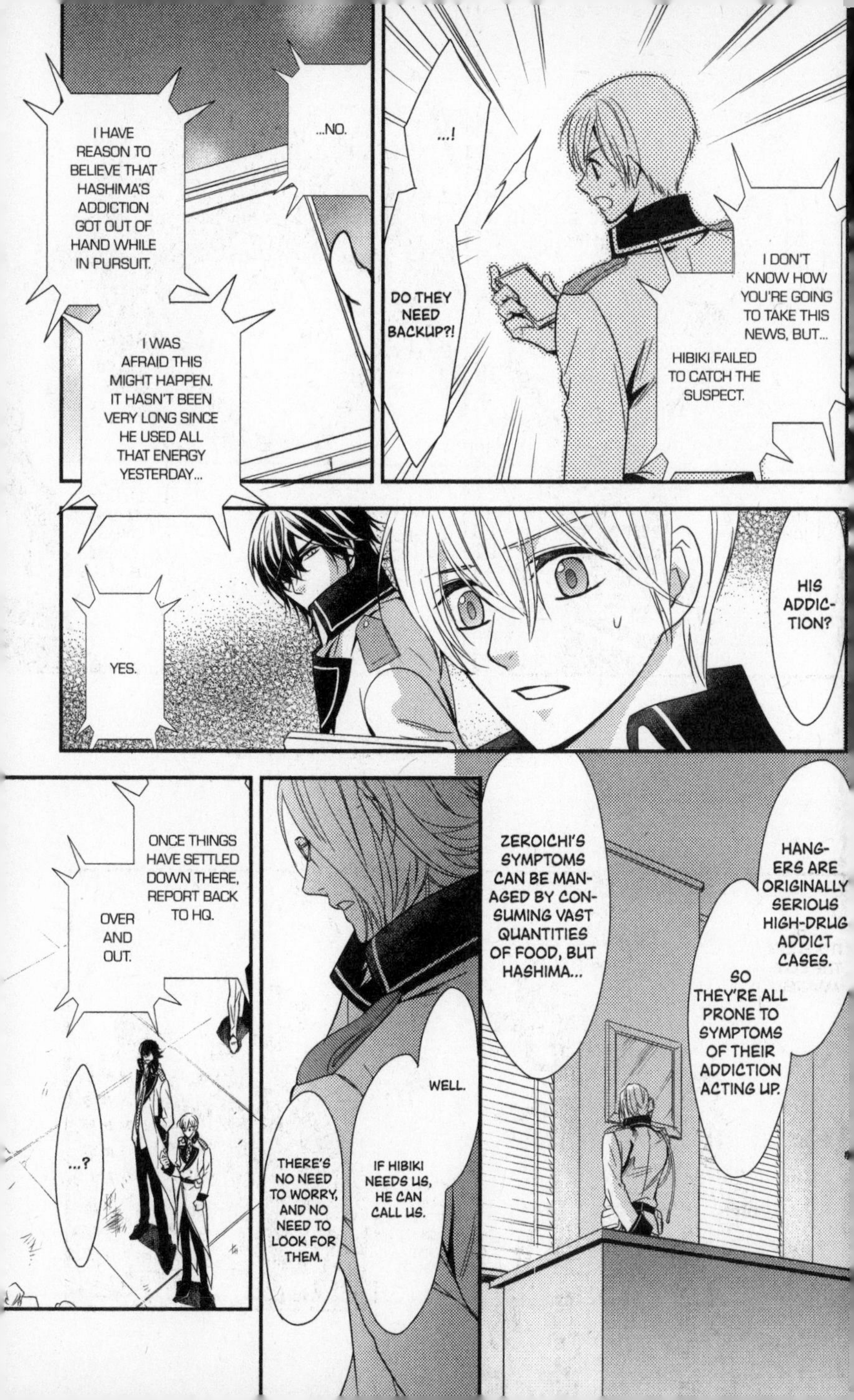
I DON'T KNOW HOW YOU'RE GOING TO TAKE THIS NEWS, BUT...
HIBIKI FAILED TO CATCH THE SUSPECT.
...!
DO THEY NEED BACKUP?!
...NO.
I HAVE REASON TO BELIEVE THAT HASHIMA'S ADDICTION GOT OUT OF HAND WHILE IN PURSUIT.
I WAS AFRAID THIS MIGHT HAPPEN. IT HASN'T BEEN VERY LONG SINCE HE USED ALL THAT ENERGY YESTERDAY...
HIS ADDICTION?
YES.
HANGERS ARE ORIGINALLY SERIOUS HIGH-DRUG ADDICT CASES.
SO THEY'RE ALL PRONE TO SYMPTOMS OF THEIR ADDICTION ACTING UP.
ZEROICHI'S SYMPTOMS CAN BE MANAGED BY CONSUMING VAST QUANTITIES OF FOOD, BUT HASHIMA...
WELL.
IF HIBIKI NEEDS US, HE CAN CALL US.
THERE'S NO NEED TO WORRY, AND NO NEED TO LOOK FOR THEM.
ONCE THINGS HAVE SETTLED DOWN THERE, REPORT BACK TO HQ.
OVER AND OUT.
...?

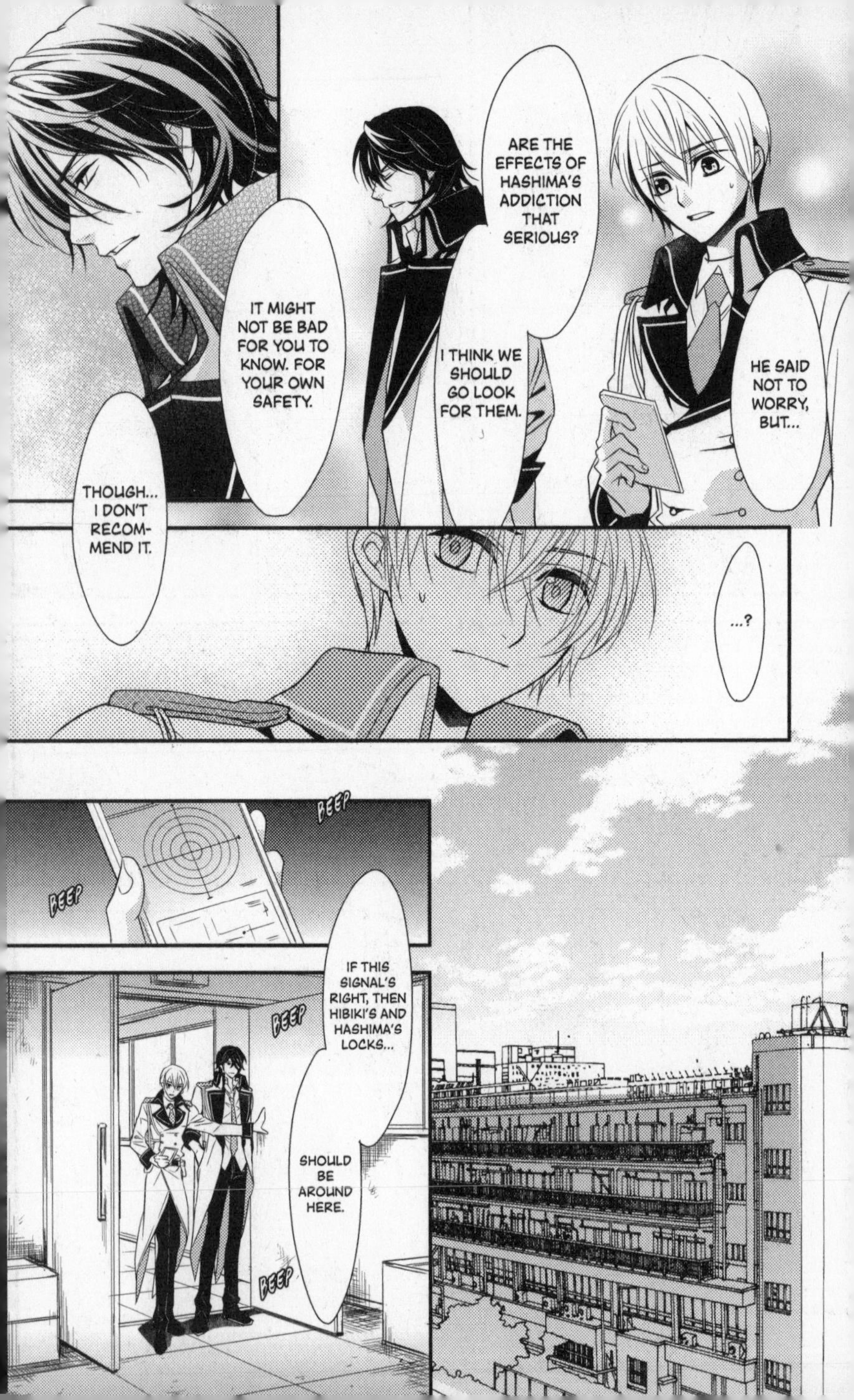
HE SAID NOT TO WORRY, BUT...
I THINK WE SHOULD GO LOOK FOR THEM.
ARE THE EFFECTS OF HASHIMA'S ADDICTION THAT SERIOUS?
IT MIGHT NOT BE BAD FOR YOU TO KNOW. FOR YOUR OWN SAFETY.
THOUGH... I DON'T RECOM-MEND IT.
...?
BEEP
BEEP
BEEP
IF THIS SIGNAL'S RIGHT, THEN HIBIKI'S AND HASHIMA'S LOCKS...
SHOULD BE AROUND HERE.
BEEP

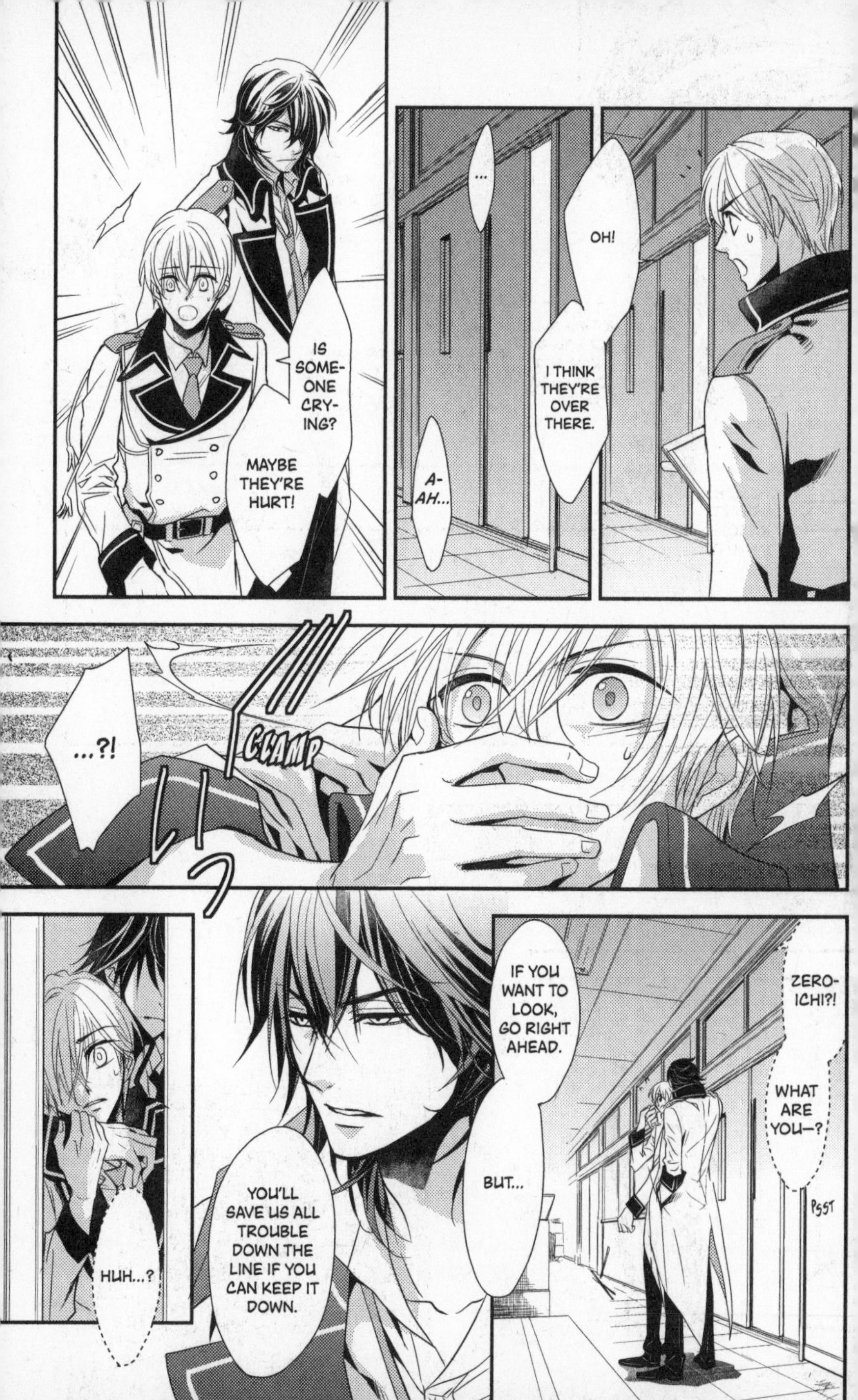
OH!
I THINK THEY'RE OVER THERE.
...
A-AH...
IS SOMEONE CRYING?
MAYBE THEY'RE HURT!
CLAMP
...?!
ZERO-ICHI?!
WHAT ARE YOU—?
PSST
IF YOU WANT TO LOOK, GO RIGHT AHEAD.
BUT...
YOU'LL SAVE US ALL TROUBLE DOWN THE LINE IF YOU CAN KEEP IT DOWN.
HUH...?

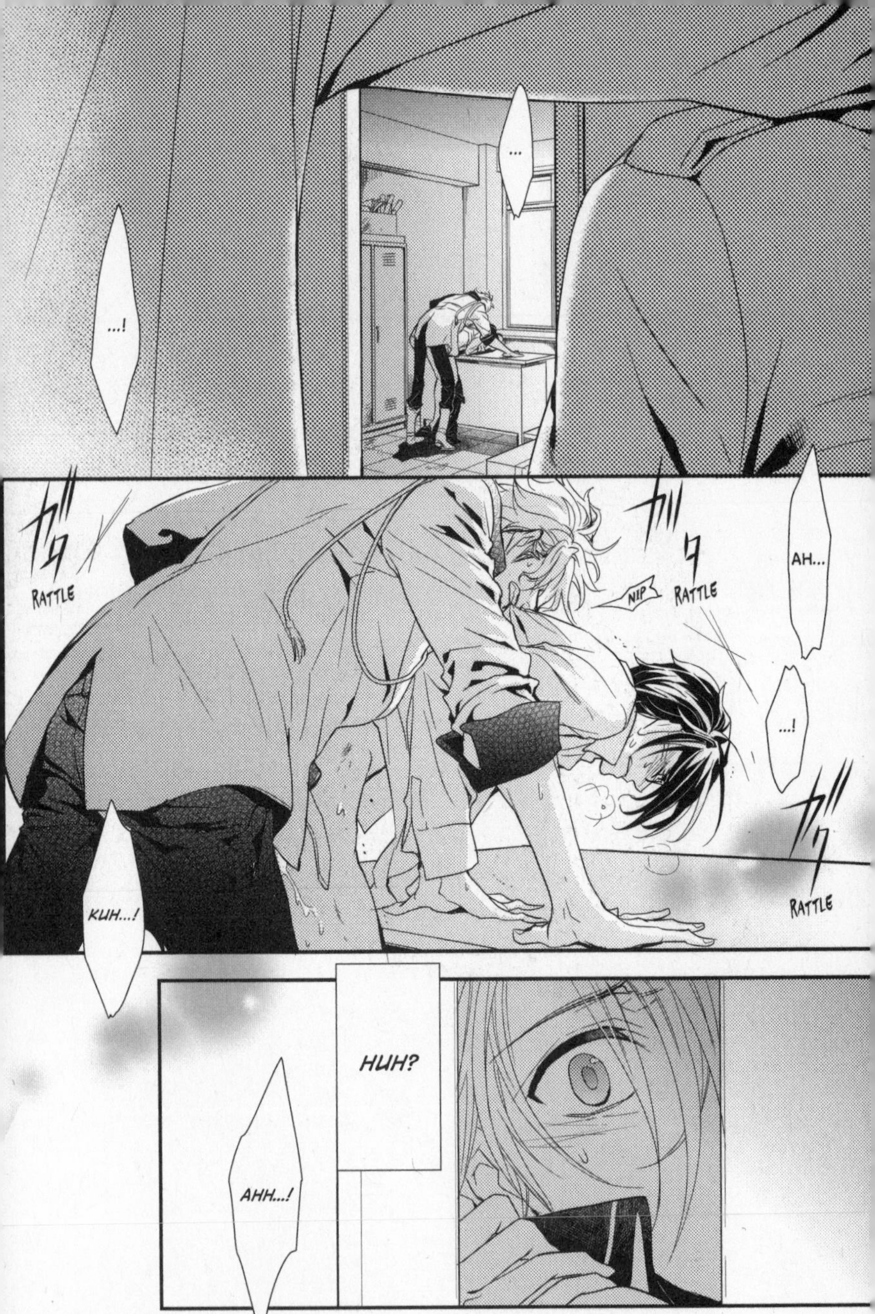
...
...!
AH...
...!
RATTLE
NIP
RATTLE
RATTLE
KUH...!
HUH?
AHH...!

Chapter 5

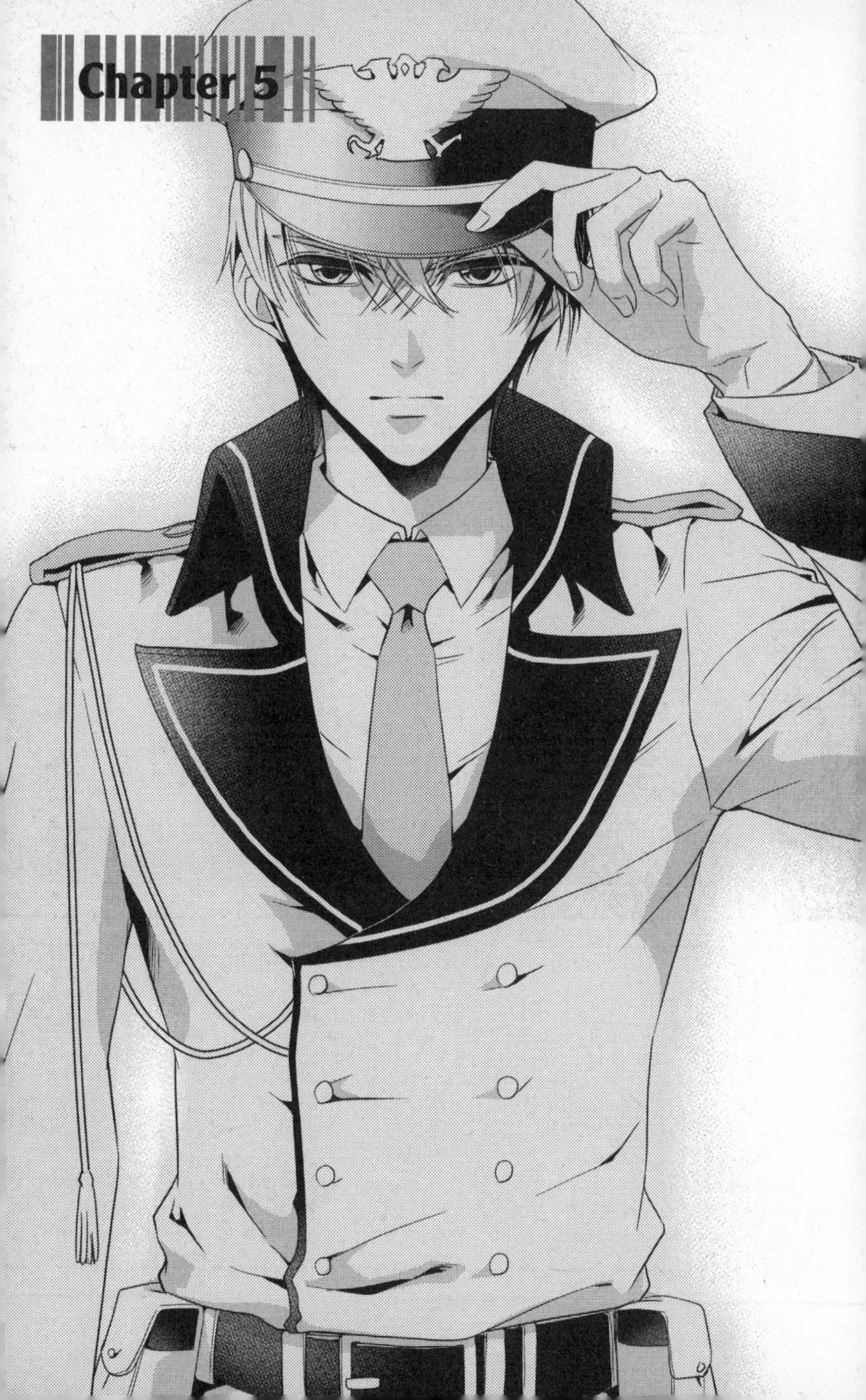

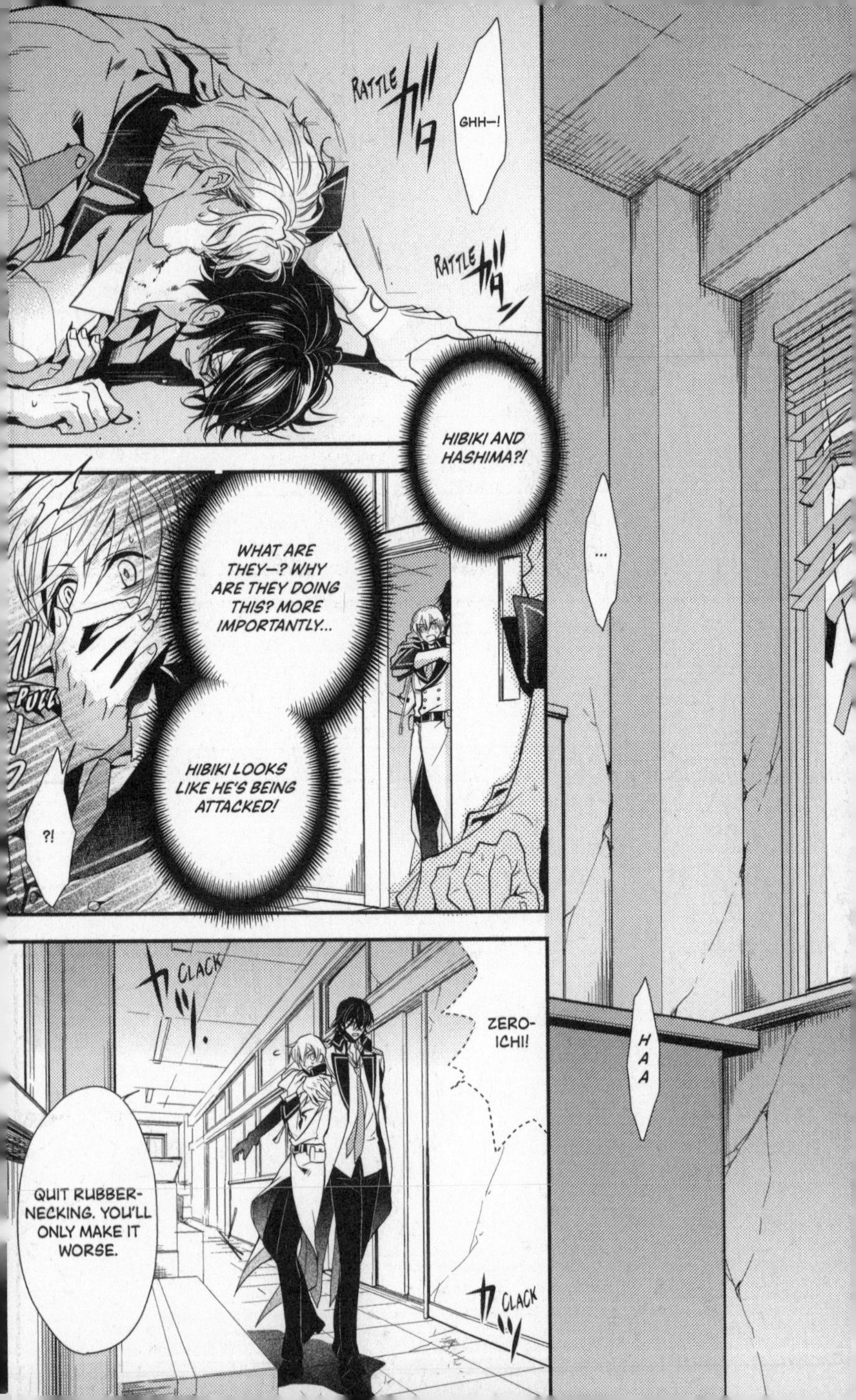
...
HAA
GHH—!
RATTLE
RATTLE
HIBIKI AND HASHIMA?!
WHAT ARE THEY—? WHY ARE THEY DOING THIS? MORE IMPORTANTLY...
HIBIKI LOOKS LIKE HE'S BEING ATTACKED!
PULL
?!
ZERO-ICHI!
CLACK
CLACK
QUIT RUBBER-NECKING. YOU'LL ONLY MAKE IT WORSE.

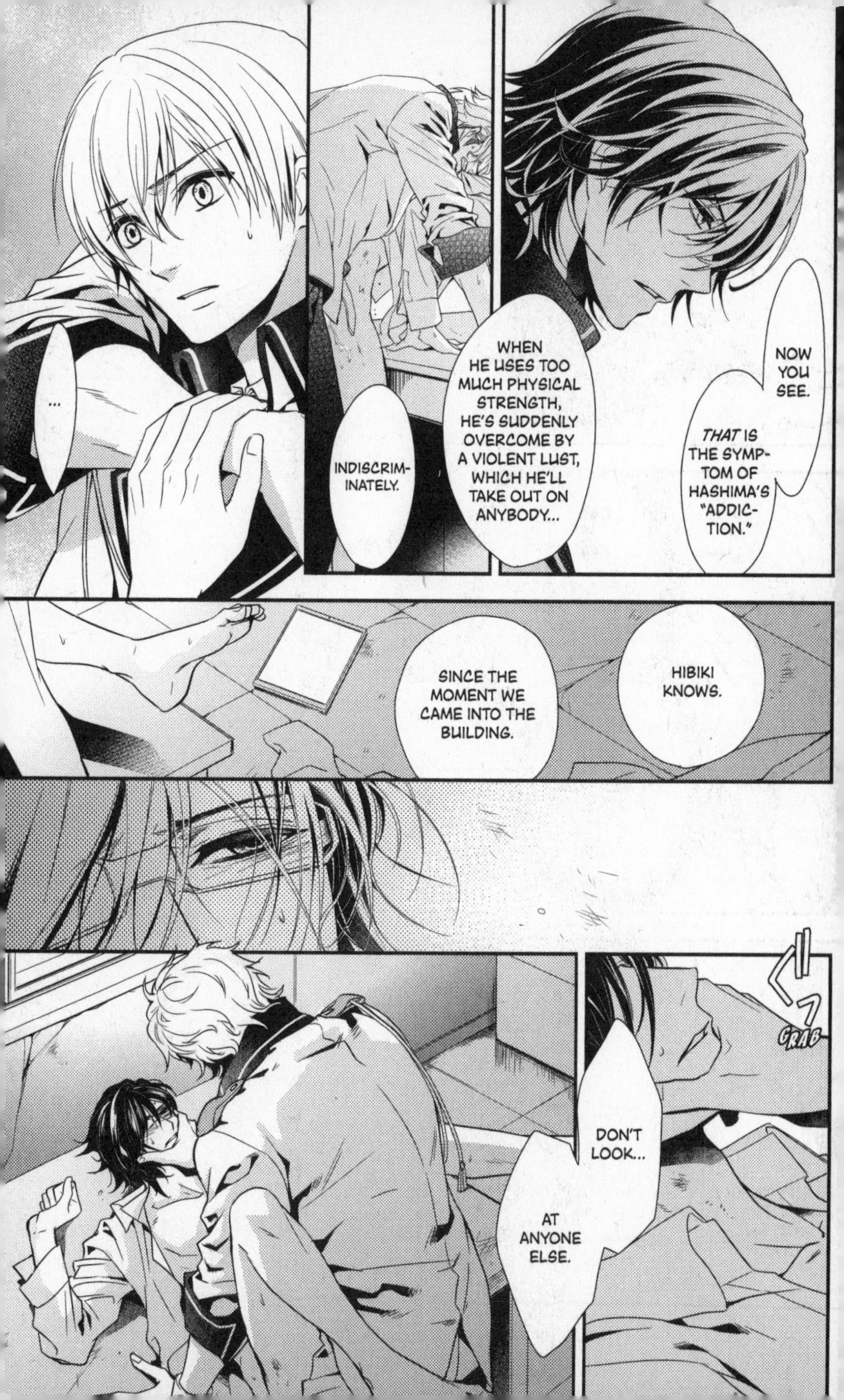
NOW YOU SEE.
THAT IS THE SYMPTOM OF HASHIMA'S "ADDICTION."
WHEN HE USES TOO MUCH PHYSICAL STRENGTH, HE'S SUDDENLY OVERCOME BY A VIOLENT LUST, WHICH HE'LL TAKE OUT ON ANYBODY...
INDISCRIMINATELY.
...
HIBIKI KNOWS.
SINCE THE MOMENT WE CAME INTO THE BUILDING.
GRAB
DON'T LOOK...
AT ANYONE ELSE.

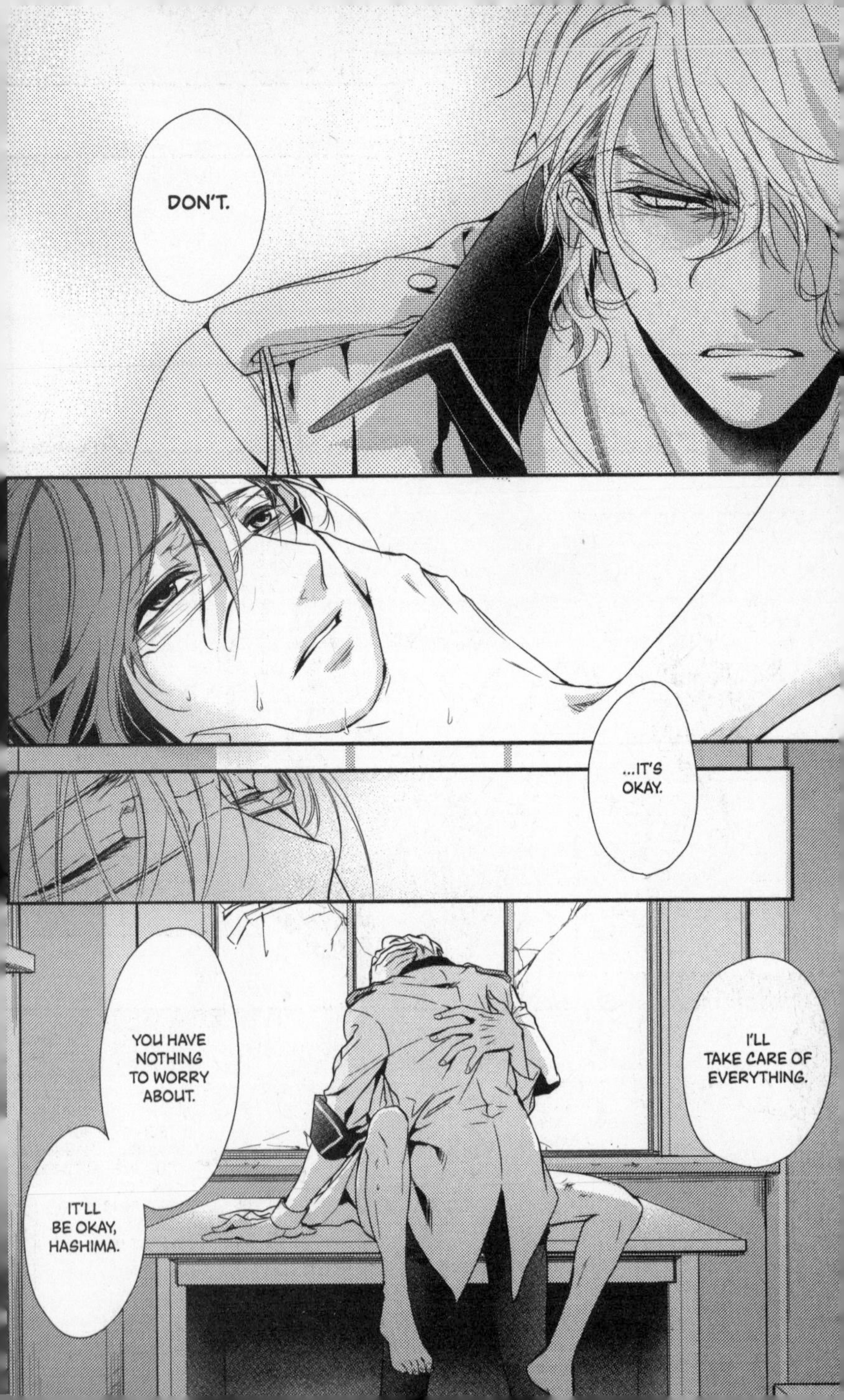
DON'T.
...IT'S OKAY.
I'LL TAKE CARE OF EVERYTHING.
YOU HAVE NOTHING TO WORRY ABOUT.
IT'LL BE OKAY, HASHIMA.

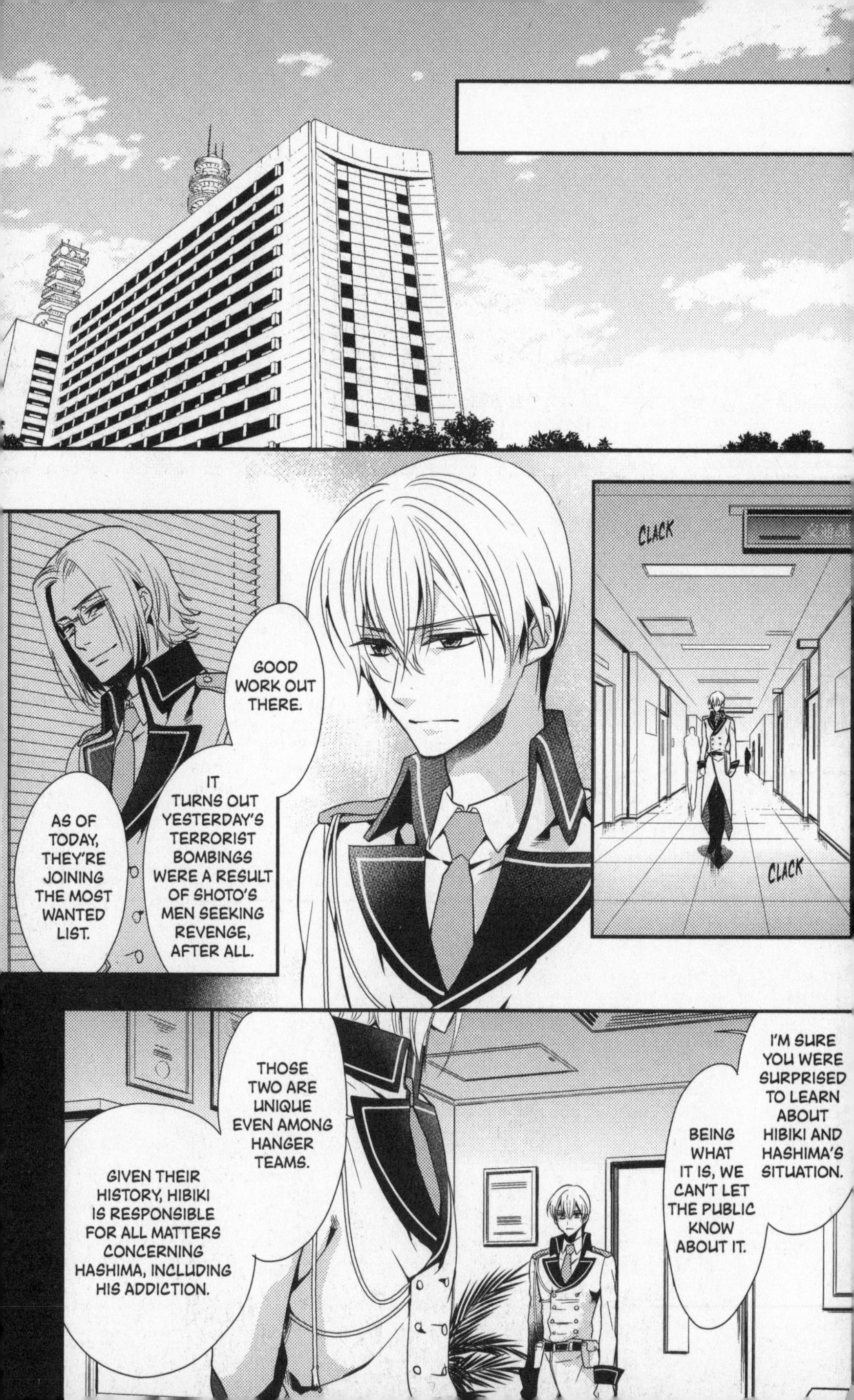
CLACK
CLACK
GOOD WORK OUT THERE.
IT TURNS OUT YESTERDAY'S TERRORIST BOMBINGS WERE A RESULT OF SHOTO'S MEN SEEKING REVENGE, AFTER ALL.
AS OF TODAY, THEY'RE JOINING THE MOST WANTED LIST.
I'M SURE YOU WERE SURPRISED TO LEARN ABOUT HIBIKI AND HASHIMA'S SITUATION.
BEING WHAT IT IS, WE CAN'T LET THE PUBLIC KNOW ABOUT IT.
THOSE TWO ARE UNIQUE EVEN AMONG HANGER TEAMS.
GIVEN THEIR HISTORY, HIBIKI IS RESPONSIBLE FOR ALL MATTERS CONCERNING HASHIMA, INCLUDING HIS ADDICTION.

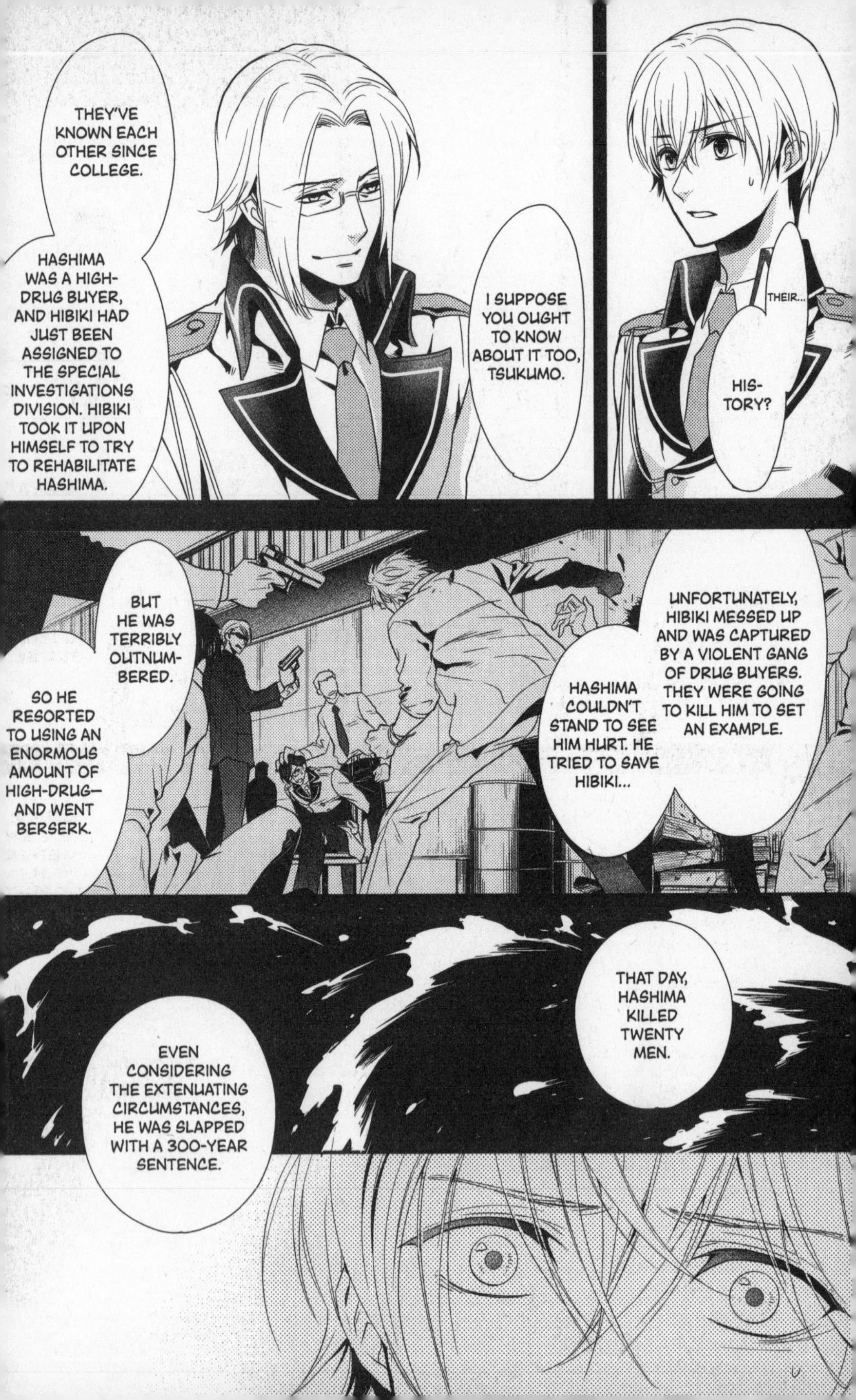
THEIR...
HIS-TORY?
I SUPPOSE YOU OUGHT TO KNOW ABOUT IT TOO, TSUKUMO.
THEY'VE KNOWN EACH OTHER SINCE COLLEGE.
HASHIMA WAS A HIGH-DRUG BUYER, AND HIBIKI HAD JUST BEEN ASSIGNED TO THE SPECIAL INVESTIGATIONS DIVISION. HIBIKI TOOK IT UPON HIMSELF TO TRY TO REHABILITATE HASHIMA.
UNFORTUNATELY, HIBIKI MESSED UP AND WAS CAPTURED BY A VIOLENT GANG OF DRUG BUYERS. THEY WERE GOING TO KILL HIM TO SET AN EXAMPLE.
HASHIMA COULDN'T STAND TO SEE HIM HURT. HE TRIED TO SAVE HIBIKI...
BUT HE WAS TERRIBLY OUTNUM-BERED.
SO HE RESORTED TO USING AN ENORMOUS AMOUNT OF HIGH-DRUG—AND WENT BERSERK.
THAT DAY, HASHIMA KILLED TWENTY MEN.
EVEN CONSIDERING THE EXTENUATING CIRCUMSTANCES, HE WAS SLAPPED WITH A 300-YEAR SENTENCE.

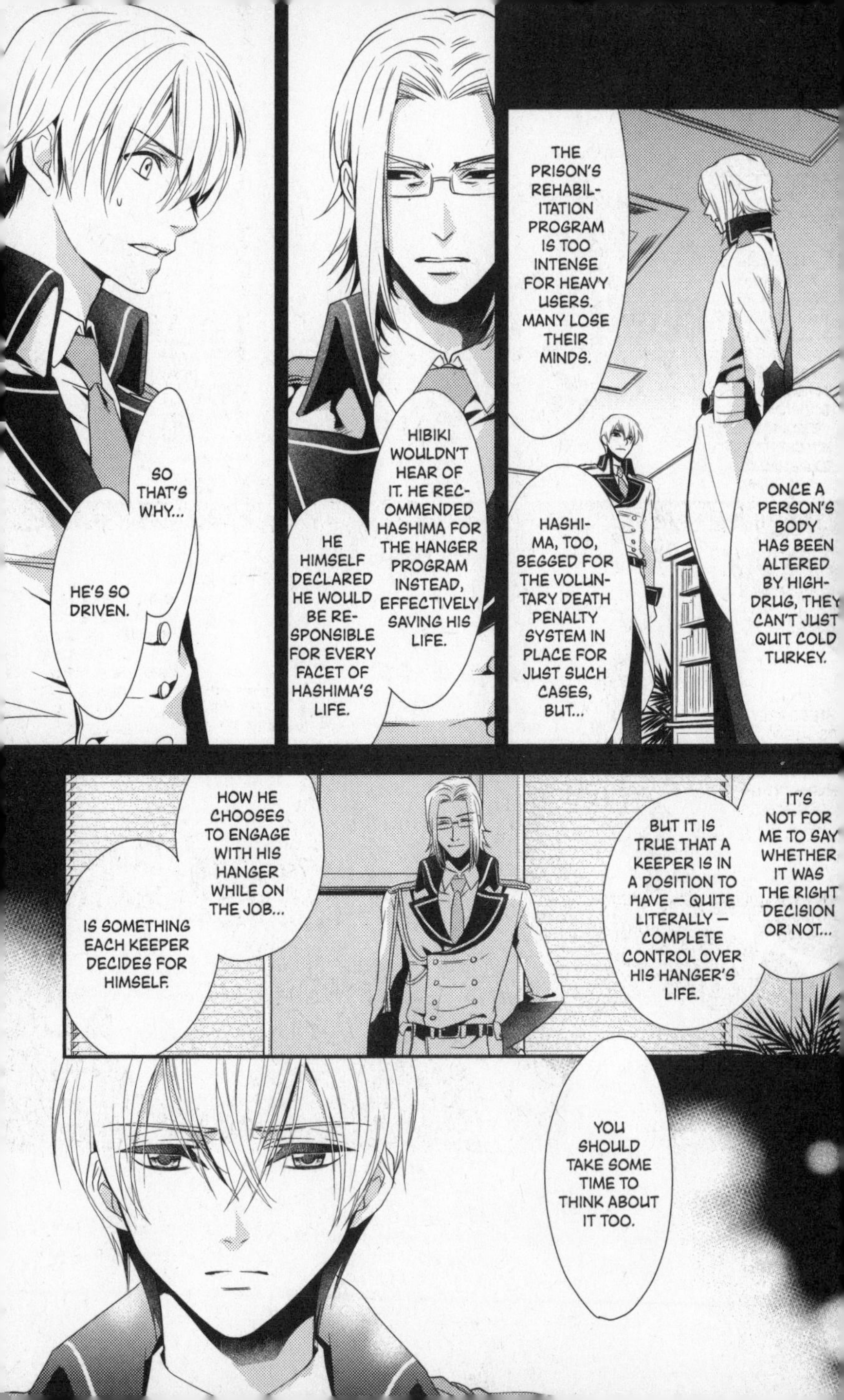
THE PRISON'S REHABILITATION PROGRAM IS TOO INTENSE FOR HEAVY USERS. MANY LOSE THEIR MINDS.
ONCE A PERSON'S BODY HAS BEEN ALTERED BY HIGH-DRUG, THEY CAN'T JUST QUIT COLD TURKEY.
HASHIMA, TOO, BEGGED FOR THE VOLUNTARY DEATH PENALTY SYSTEM IN PLACE FOR JUST SUCH CASES, BUT...
HIBIKI WOULDN'T HEAR OF IT. HE RECOMMENDED HASHIMA FOR THE HANGER PROGRAM INSTEAD, EFFECTIVELY SAVING HIS LIFE.
HE HIMSELF DECLARED HE WOULD BE RESPONSIBLE FOR EVERY FACET OF HASHIMA'S LIFE.
SO THAT'S WHY...
HE'S SO DRIVEN.
IT'S NOT FOR ME TO SAY WHETHER IT WAS THE RIGHT DECISION OR NOT...
BUT IT IS TRUE THAT A KEEPER IS IN A POSITION TO HAVE — QUITE LITERALLY — COMPLETE CONTROL OVER HIS HANGER'S LIFE.
HOW HE CHOOSES TO ENGAGE WITH HIS HANGER WHILE ON THE JOB...
IS SOMETHING EACH KEEPER DECIDES FOR HIMSELF.
YOU SHOULD TAKE SOME TIME TO THINK ABOUT IT TOO.

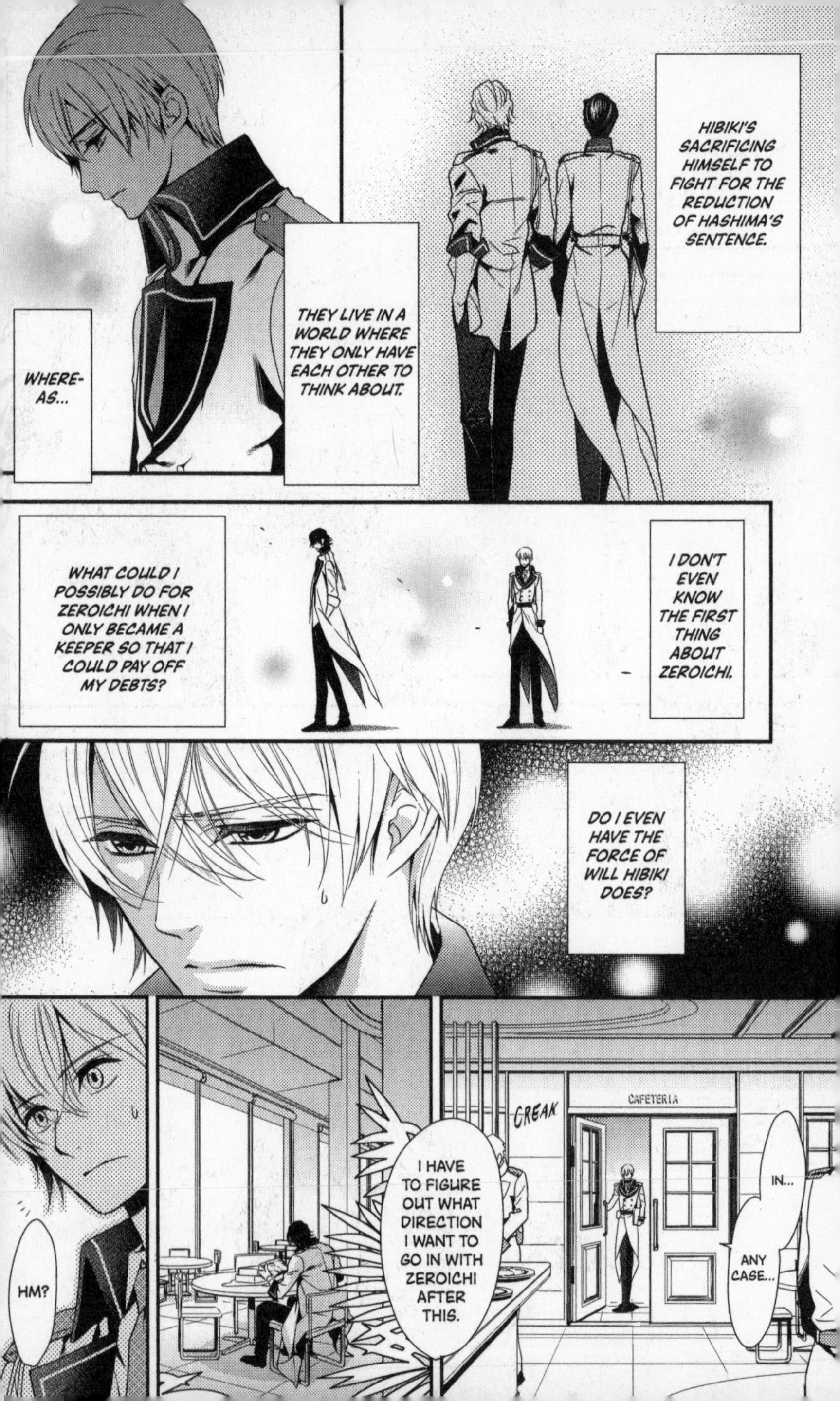
HIBIKI'S SACRIFICING HIMSELF TO FIGHT FOR THE REDUCTION OF HASHIMA'S SENTENCE.
THEY LIVE IN A WORLD WHERE THEY ONLY HAVE EACH OTHER TO THINK ABOUT.
WHERE-AS...
I DON'T EVEN KNOW THE FIRST THING ABOUT ZEROICHI.
WHAT COULD I POSSIBLY DO FOR ZEROICHI WHEN I ONLY BECAME A KEEPER SO THAT I COULD PAY OFF MY DEBTS?
DO I EVEN HAVE THE FORCE OF WILL HIBIKI DOES?
IN...
ANY CASE...
CAFETERIA
CREAK
I HAVE TO FIGURE OUT WHAT DIRECTION I WANT TO GO IN WITH ZEROICHI AFTER THIS.
HM?

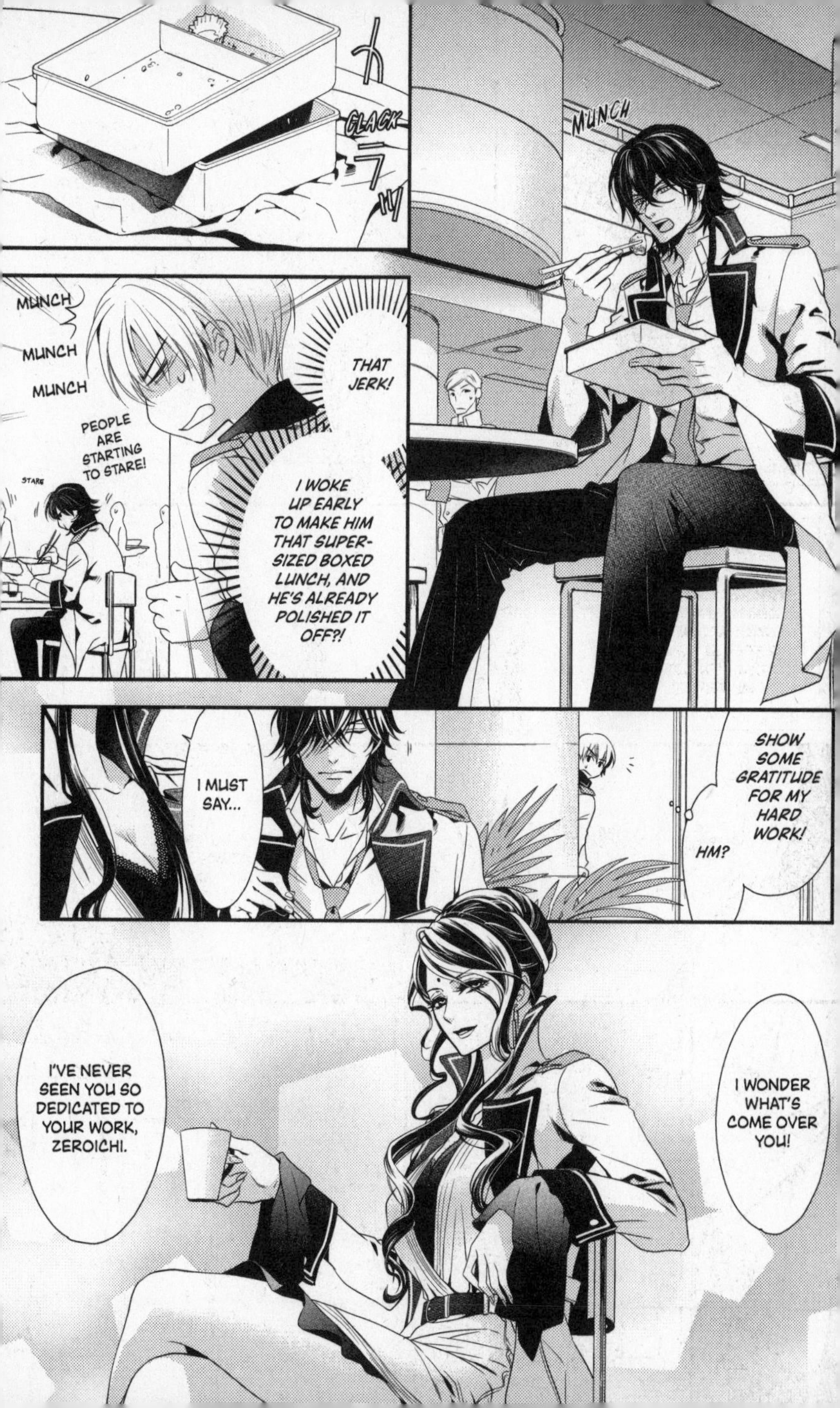
MUNCH
CLACK
THAT JERK!
I WOKE UP EARLY TO MAKE HIM THAT SUPER-SIZED BOXED LUNCH, AND HE'S ALREADY POLISHED IT OFF?!
PEOPLE ARE STARTING TO STARE!
MUNCH
MUNCH
MUNCH
STARE
SHOW SOME GRATITUDE FOR MY HARD WORK!
HM?
I MUST SAY...
I WONDER WHAT'S COME OVER YOU!
I'VE NEVER SEEN YOU SO DEDICATED TO YOUR WORK, ZEROICHI.

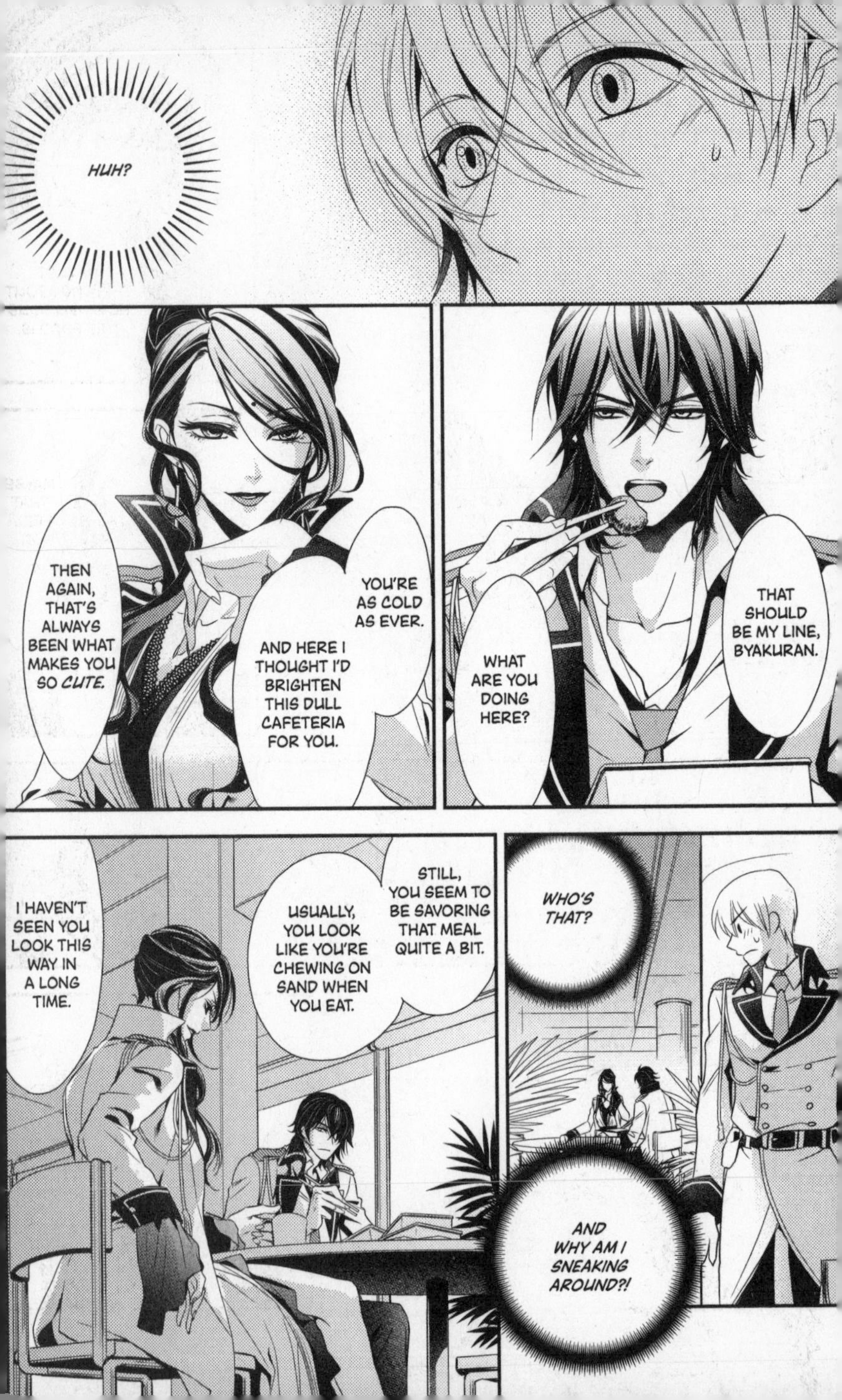
HUH?
THAT SHOULD BE MY LINE, BYAKURAN.
WHAT ARE YOU DOING HERE?
YOU'RE AS COLD AS EVER.
AND HERE I THOUGHT I'D BRIGHTEN THIS DULL CAFETERIA FOR YOU.
THEN AGAIN, THAT'S ALWAYS BEEN WHAT MAKES YOU SO *CUTE.*
WHO'S THAT?
AND WHY AM I SNEAKING AROUND?!
STILL, YOU SEEM TO BE SAVORING THAT MEAL QUITE A BIT.
USUALLY, YOU LOOK LIKE YOU'RE CHEWING ON SAND WHEN YOU EAT.
I HAVEN'T SEEN YOU LOOK THIS WAY IN A LONG TIME.

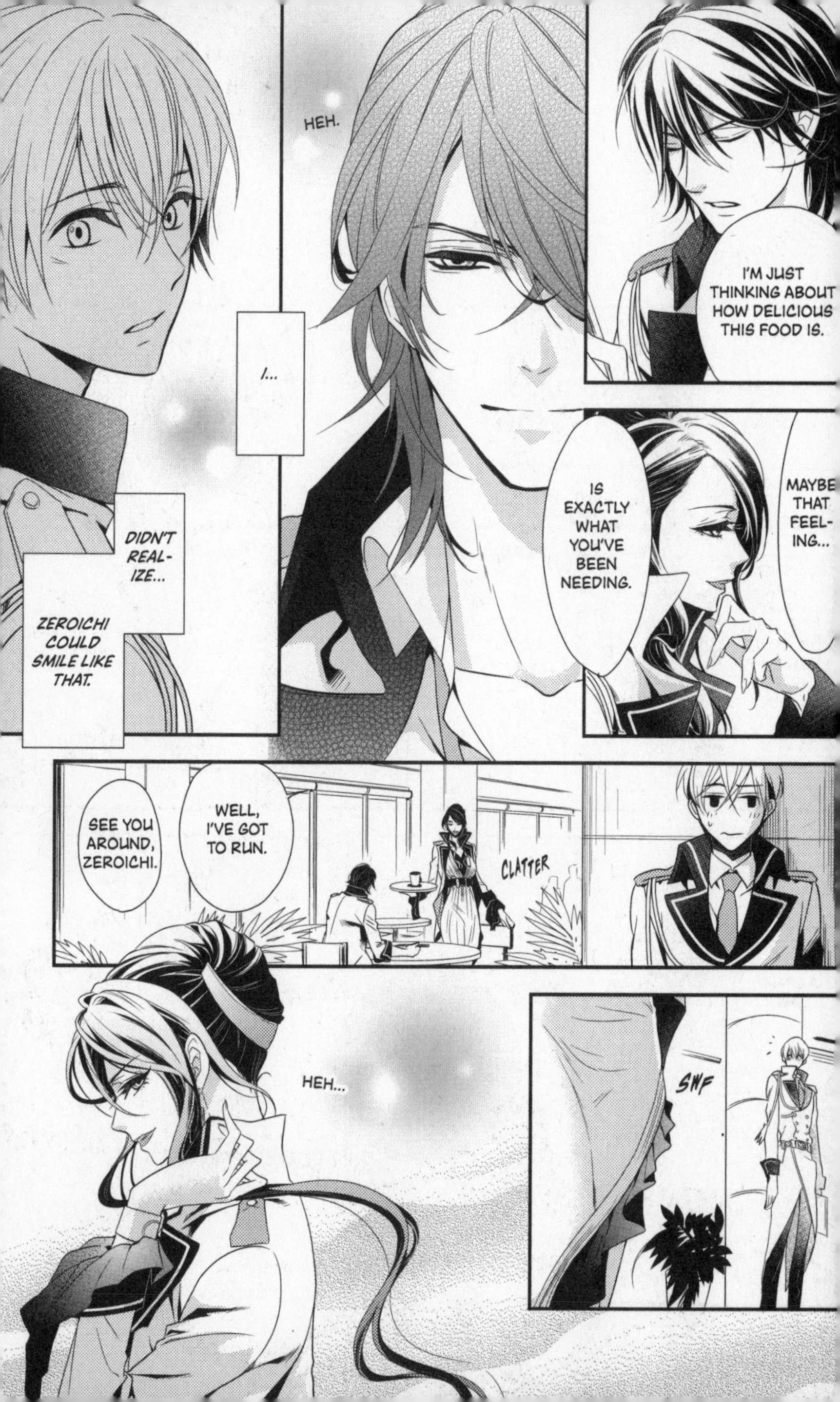
I'M JUST THINKING ABOUT HOW DELICIOUS THIS FOOD IS.
MAYBE THAT FEEL-ING...
IS EXACTLY WHAT YOU'VE BEEN NEEDING.
HEH.
I...
DIDN'T REAL-IZE...
ZEROICHI COULD SMILE LIKE THAT.
CLATTER
WELL, I'VE GOT TO RUN.
SEE YOU AROUND, ZEROICHI.
SWF
HEH...

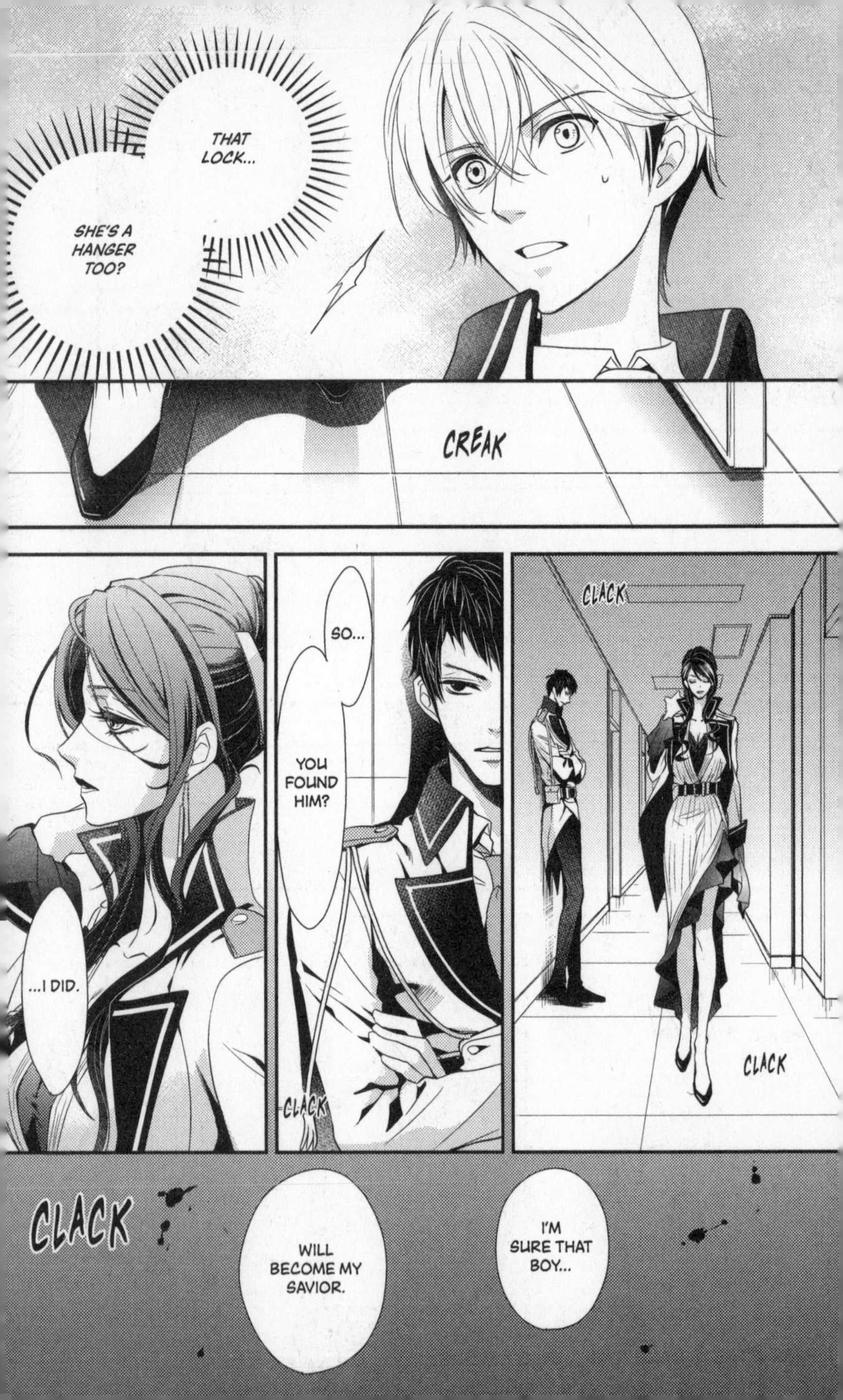
THAT LOCK...
SHE'S A HANGER TOO?
CREAK
CLACK
CLACK
SO...
YOU FOUND HIM?
CLACK
...I DID.
I'M SURE THAT BOY...
WILL BECOME MY SAVIOR.
CLACK

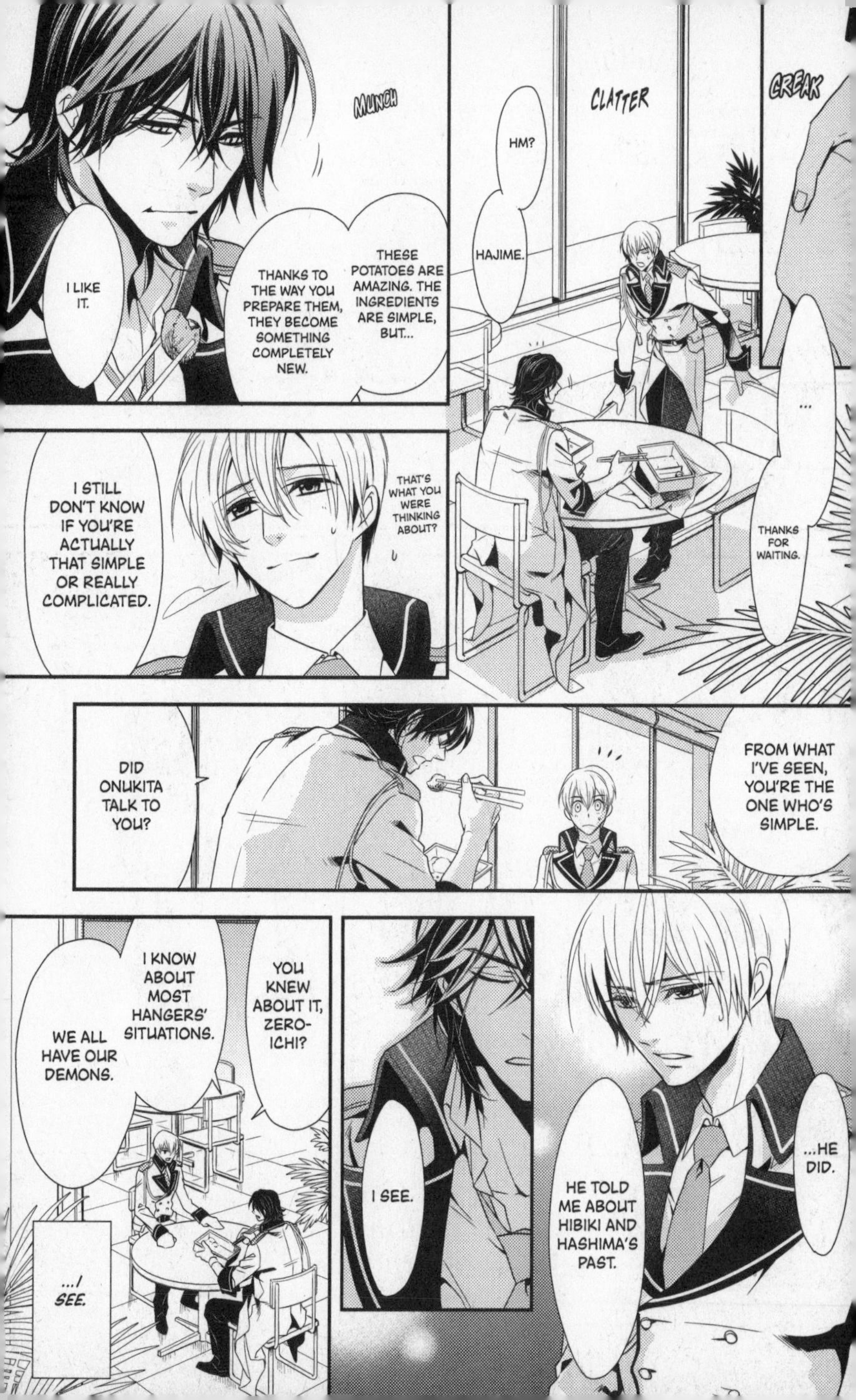
CREAK
...
THANKS FOR WAITING.
CLATTER
HM?
HAJIME.
MUNCH
THESE POTATOES ARE AMAZING. THE INGREDIENTS ARE SIMPLE, BUT...
THANKS TO THE WAY YOU PREPARE THEM, THEY BECOME SOMETHING COMPLETELY NEW.
I LIKE IT.
THAT'S WHAT YOU WERE THINKING ABOUT?
I STILL DON'T KNOW IF YOU'RE ACTUALLY THAT SIMPLE OR REALLY COMPLICATED.
FROM WHAT I'VE SEEN, YOU'RE THE ONE WHO'S SIMPLE.
DID ONUKITA TALK TO YOU?
...HE DID.
HE TOLD ME ABOUT HIBIKI AND HASHIMA'S PAST.
I SEE.
YOU KNEW ABOUT IT, ZERO-ICHI?
I KNOW ABOUT MOST HANGERS' SITUATIONS.
WE ALL HAVE OUR DEMONS.
...I SEE.

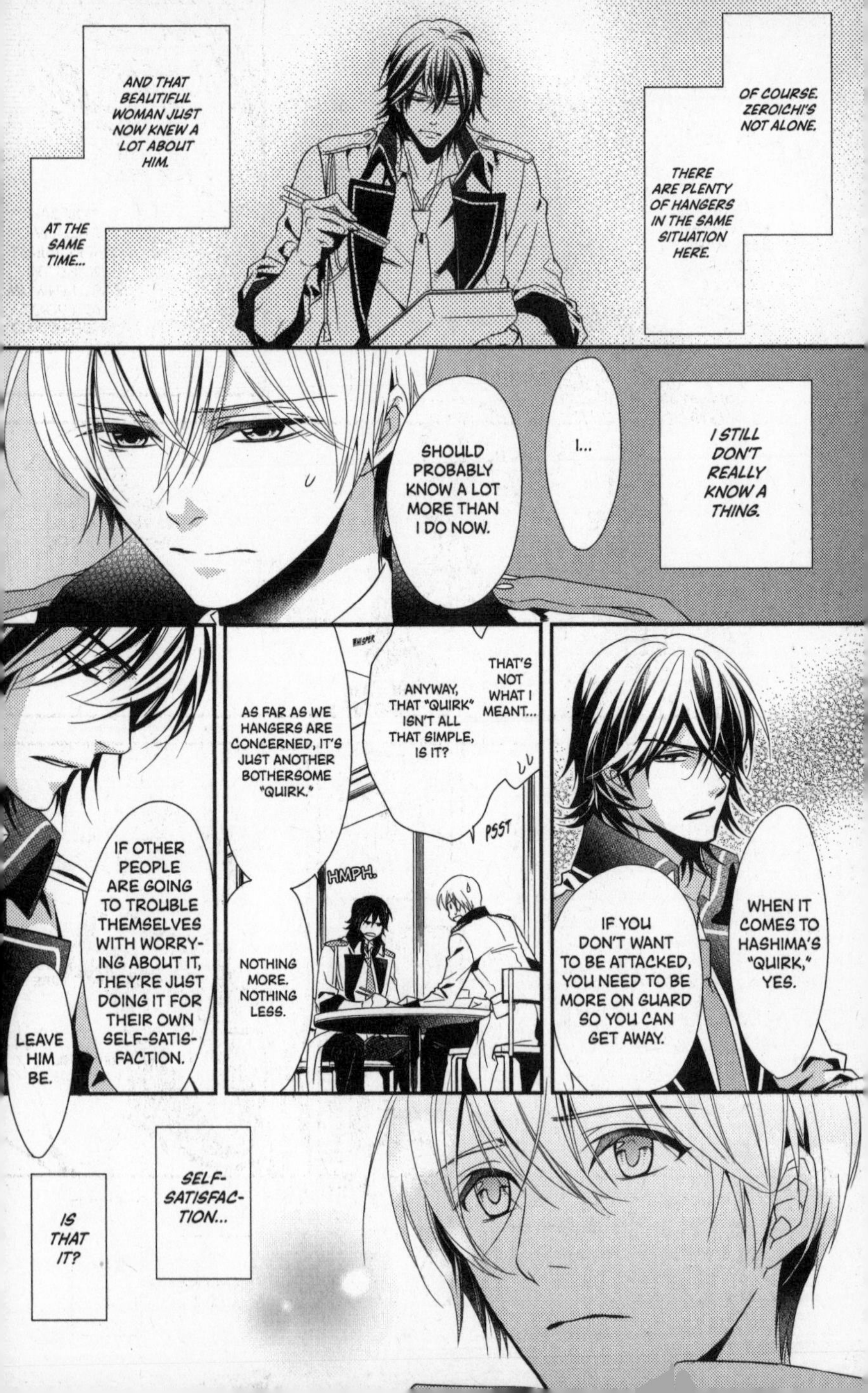
OF COURSE. ZEROICHI'S NOT ALONE.
THERE ARE PLENTY OF HANGERS IN THE SAME SITUATION HERE.
AND THAT BEAUTIFUL WOMAN JUST NOW KNEW A LOT ABOUT HIM.
AT THE SAME TIME...
I STILL DON'T REALLY KNOW A THING.
I...
SHOULD PROBABLY KNOW A LOT MORE THAN I DO NOW.
WHEN IT COMES TO HASHIMA'S "QUIRK," YES.
IF YOU DON'T WANT TO BE ATTACKED, YOU NEED TO BE MORE ON GUARD SO YOU CAN GET AWAY.
WHISPER
THAT'S NOT WHAT I MEANT...
ANYWAY, THAT "QUIRK" ISN'T ALL THAT SIMPLE, IS IT?
PSST
AS FAR AS WE HANGERS ARE CONCERNED, IT'S JUST ANOTHER BOTHERSOME "QUIRK."
HMPH.
NOTHING MORE. NOTHING LESS.
IF OTHER PEOPLE ARE GOING TO TROUBLE THEMSELVES WITH WORRY-ING ABOUT IT, THEY'RE JUST DOING IT FOR THEIR OWN SELF-SATIS-FACTION.
LEAVE HIM BE.
SELF-SATISFAC-TION...
IS THAT IT?

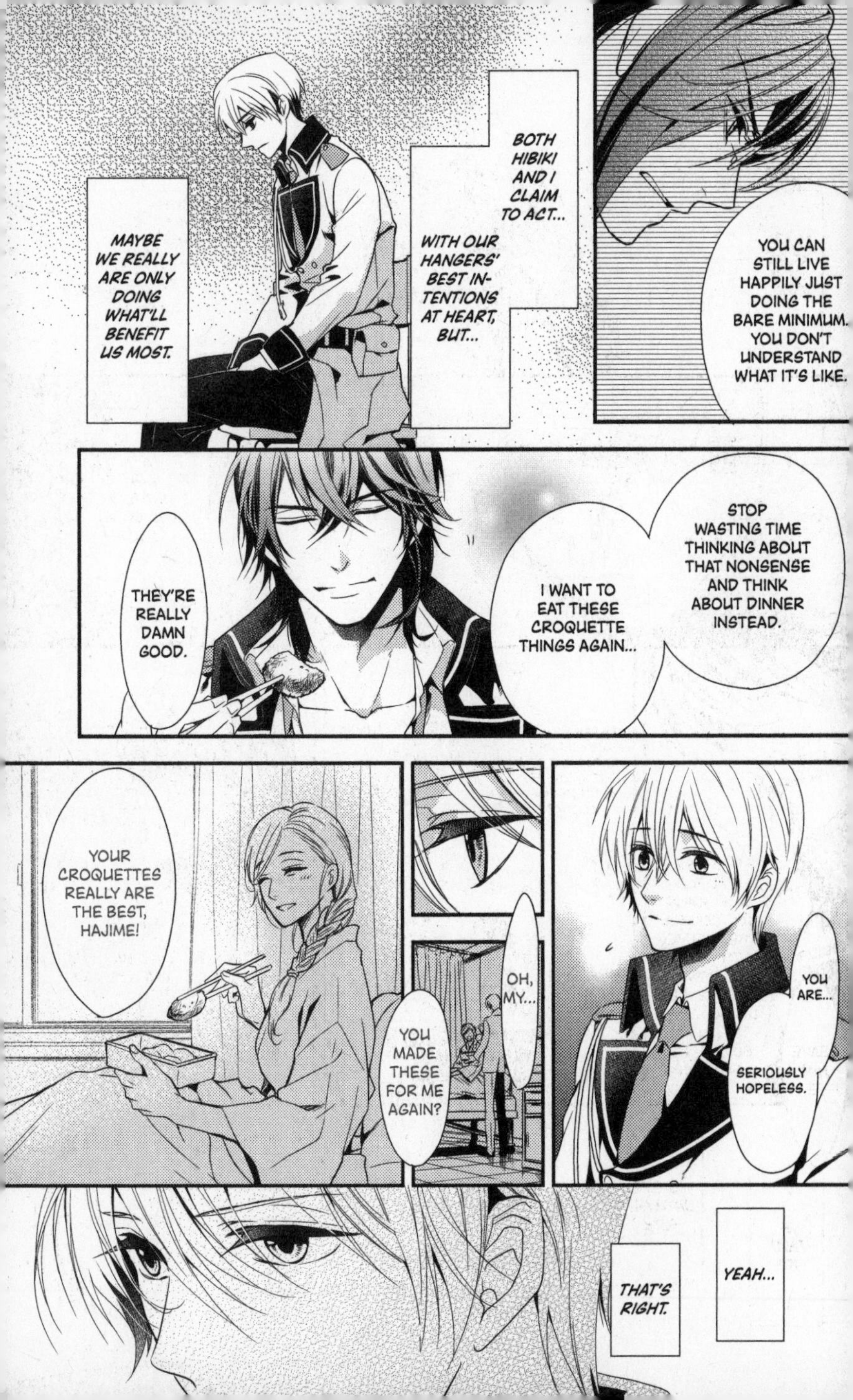
YOU CAN STILL LIVE HAPPILY JUST DOING THE BARE MINIMUM. YOU DON'T UNDERSTAND WHAT IT'S LIKE.
BOTH HIBIKI AND I CLAIM TO ACT...
WITH OUR HANGERS' BEST IN-TENTIONS AT HEART, BUT...
MAYBE WE REALLY ARE ONLY DOING WHAT'LL BENEFIT US MOST.
STOP WASTING TIME THINKING ABOUT THAT NONSENSE AND THINK ABOUT DINNER INSTEAD.
I WANT TO EAT THESE CROQUETTE THINGS AGAIN...
THEY'RE REALLY DAMN GOOD.
YOU ARE...
SERIOUSLY HOPELESS.
OH, MY...
YOU MADE THESE FOR ME AGAIN?
YOUR CROQUETTES REALLY ARE THE BEST, HAJIME!
YEAH...
THAT'S RIGHT.

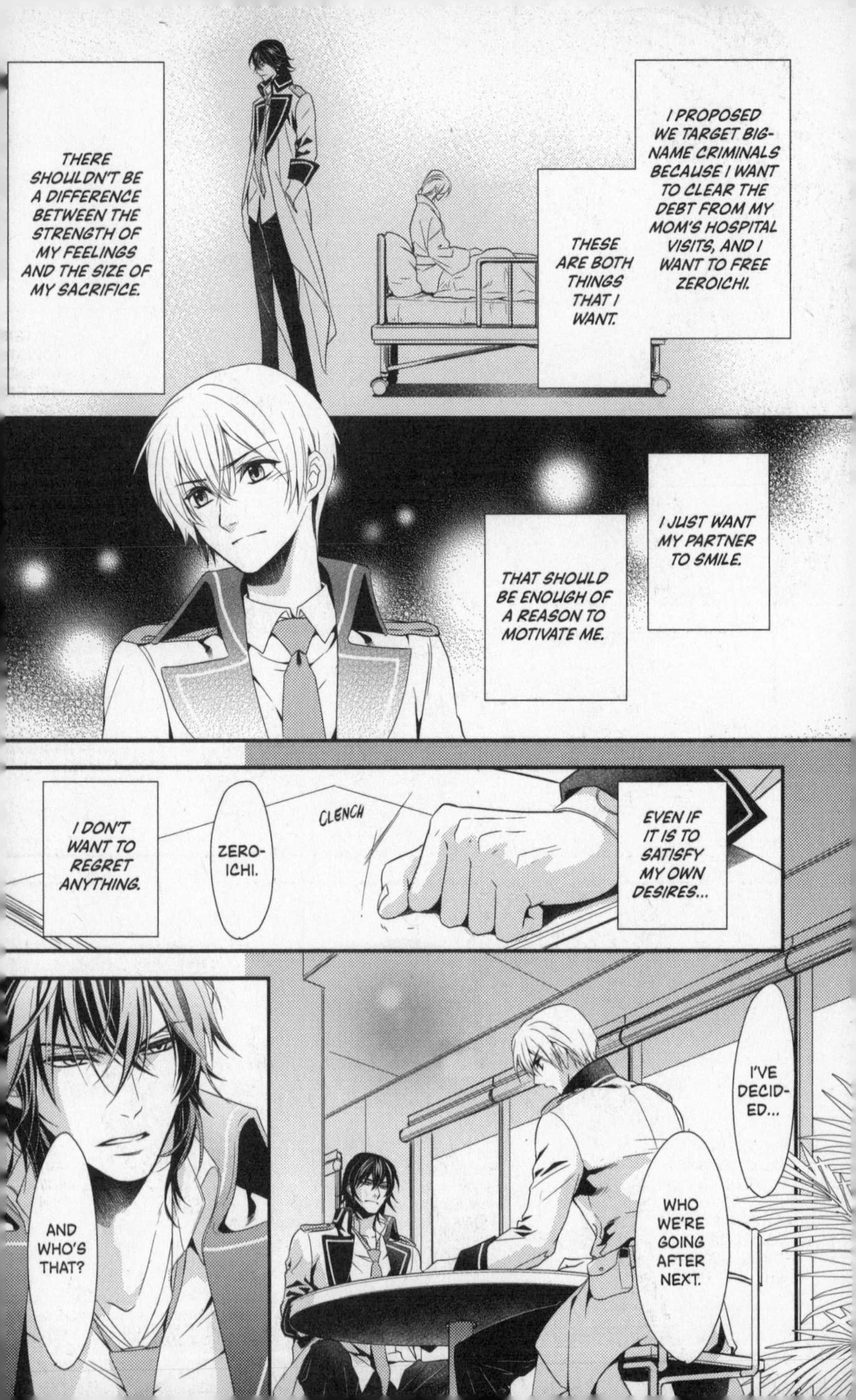
I PROPOSED WE TARGET BIG-NAME CRIMINALS BECAUSE I WANT TO CLEAR THE DEBT FROM MY MOM'S HOSPITAL VISITS, AND I WANT TO FREE ZEROICHI.
THESE ARE BOTH THINGS THAT I WANT.
THERE SHOULDN'T BE A DIFFERENCE BETWEEN THE STRENGTH OF MY FEELINGS AND THE SIZE OF MY SACRIFICE.
I JUST WANT MY PARTNER TO SMILE.
THAT SHOULD BE ENOUGH OF A REASON TO MOTIVATE ME.
EVEN IF IT IS TO SATISFY MY OWN DESIRES...
CLENCH
ZERO-ICHI.
I DON'T WANT TO REGRET ANYTHING.
I'VE DECID-ED...
WHO WE'RE GOING AFTER NEXT.
AND WHO'S THAT?

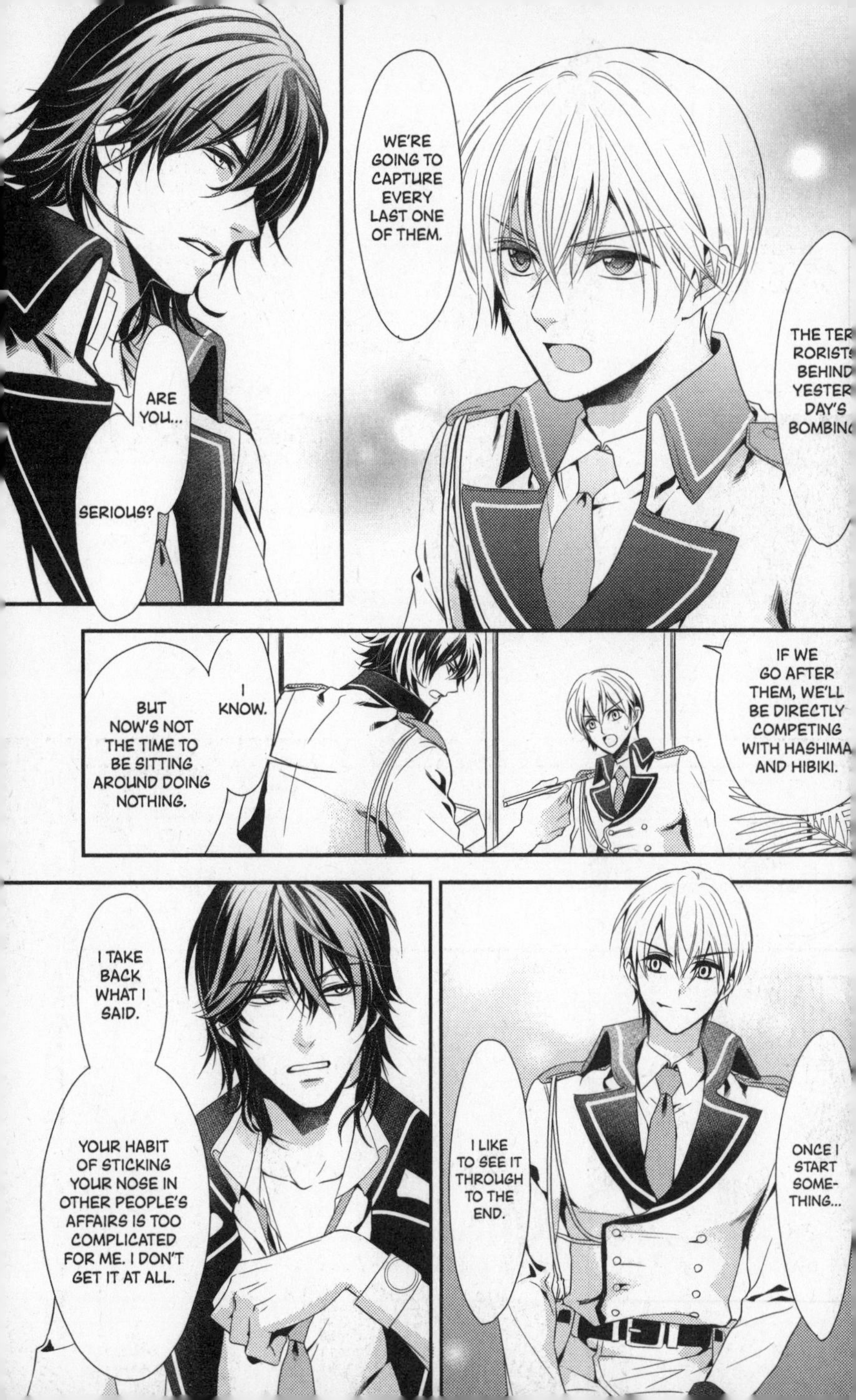
THE TER RORISTS BEHIND YESTER DAY'S BOMBIN
WE'RE GOING TO CAPTURE EVERY LAST ONE OF THEM.
ARE YOU...
SERIOUS?
IF WE GO AFTER THEM, WE'LL BE DIRECTLY COMPETING WITH HASHIMA AND HIBIKI.
I KNOW.
BUT NOW'S NOT THE TIME TO BE SITTING AROUND DOING NOTHING.
ONCE I START SOME-THING...
I LIKE TO SEE IT THROUGH TO THE END.
I TAKE BACK WHAT I SAID.
YOUR HABIT OF STICKING YOUR NOSE IN OTHER PEOPLE'S AFFAIRS IS TOO COMPLICATED FOR ME. I DON'T GET IT AT ALL.

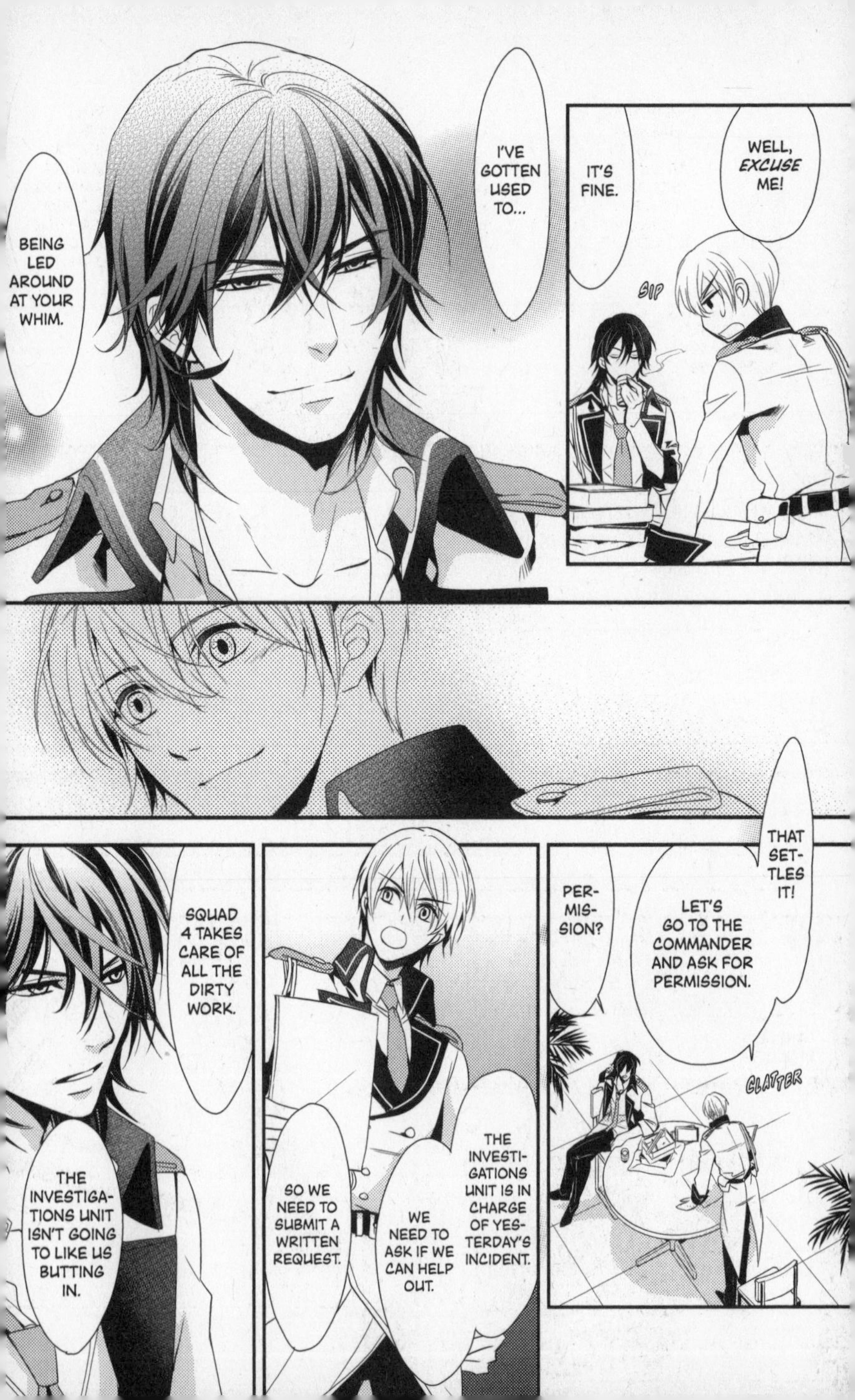
WELL, *EXCUSE* ME!
IT'S FINE.
SIP
I'VE GOTTEN USED TO...
BEING LED AROUND AT YOUR WHIM.
THAT SETTLES IT!
LET'S GO TO THE COMMANDER AND ASK FOR PERMISSION.
CLATTER
PERMISSION?
THE INVESTIGATIONS UNIT IS IN CHARGE OF YESTERDAY'S INCIDENT.
WE NEED TO ASK IF WE CAN HELP OUT.
SO WE NEED TO SUBMIT A WRITTEN REQUEST.
SQUAD 4 TAKES CARE OF ALL THE DIRTY WORK.
THE INVESTIGATIONS UNIT ISN'T GOING TO LIKE US BUTTING IN.

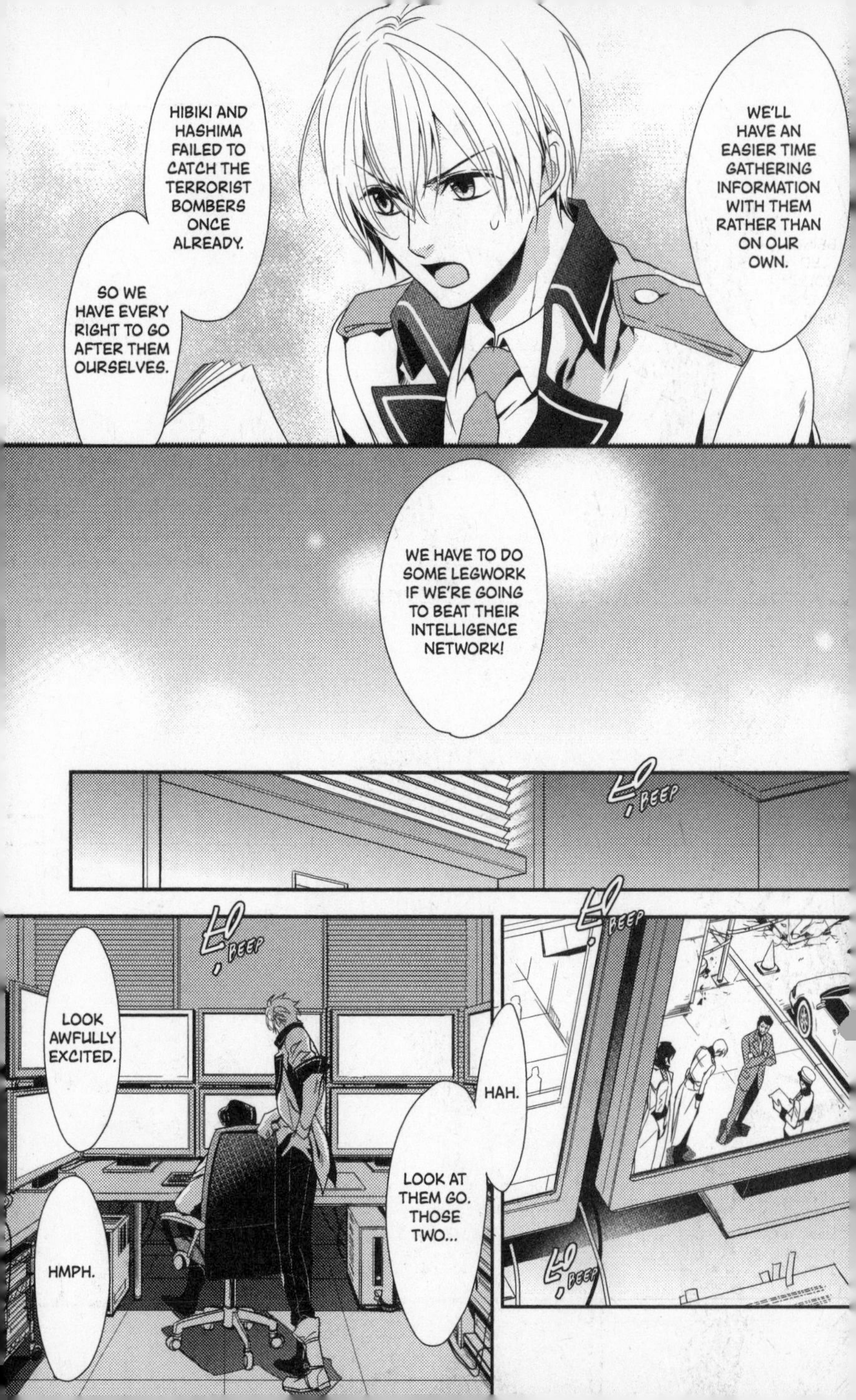
WE'LL HAVE AN EASIER TIME GATHERING INFORMATION WITH THEM RATHER THAN ON OUR OWN.
HIBIKI AND HASHIMA FAILED TO CATCH THE TERRORIST BOMBERS ONCE ALREADY.
SO WE HAVE EVERY RIGHT TO GO AFTER THEM OURSELVES.
WE HAVE TO DO SOME LEGWORK IF WE'RE GOING TO BEAT THEIR INTELLIGENCE NETWORK!
BEEP
BEEP
BEEP
HAH.
LOOK AT THEM GO. THOSE TWO...
LOOK AWFULLY EXCITED.
HMPH.
BEEP

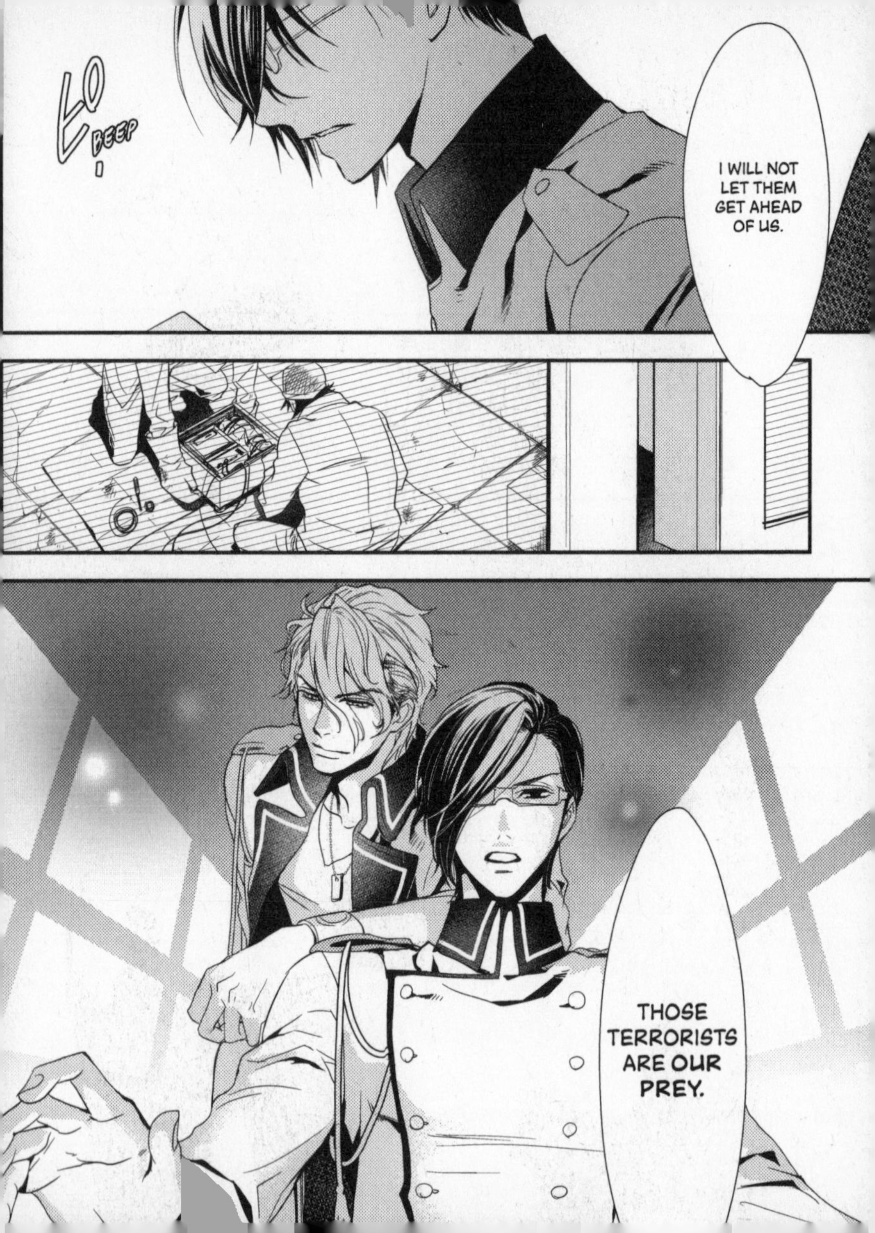
I WILL NOT LET THEM GET AHEAD OF US.
BEEP
THOSE TERRORISTS ARE OUR PREY.

Chapter 6

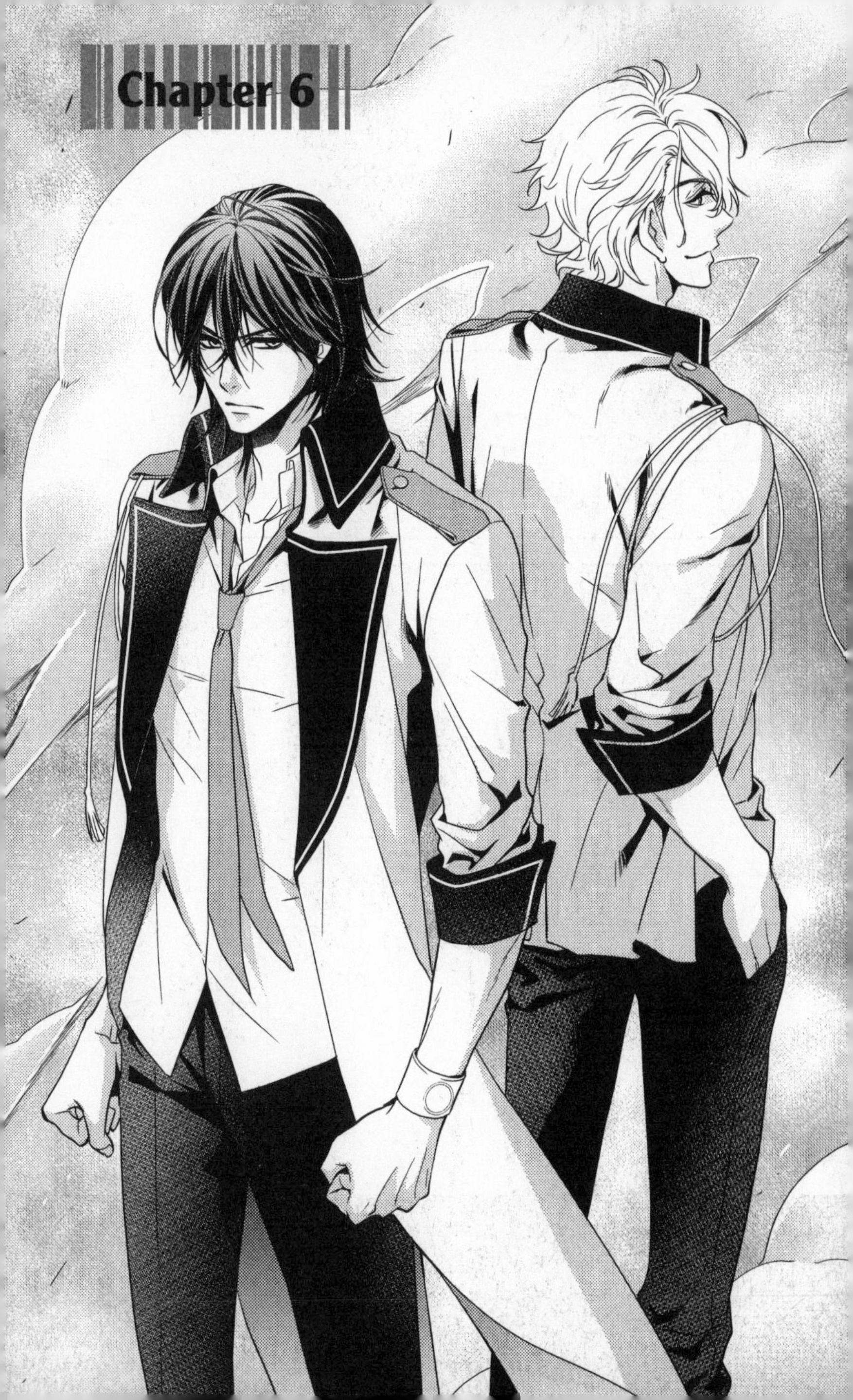

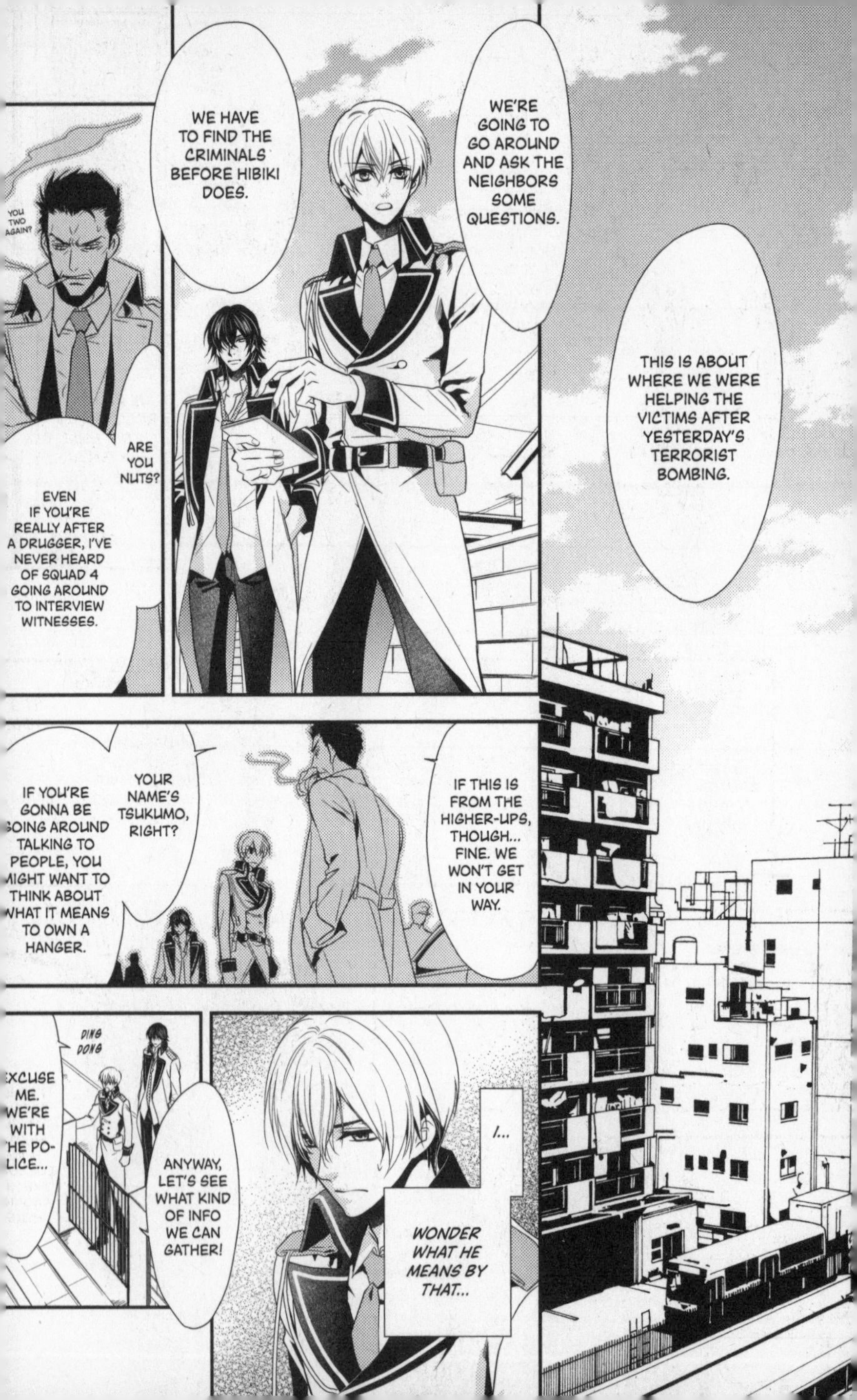
THIS IS ABOUT WHERE WE WERE HELPING THE VICTIMS AFTER YESTERDAY'S TERRORIST BOMBING.
WE'RE GOING TO GO AROUND AND ASK THE NEIGHBORS SOME QUESTIONS.
WE HAVE TO FIND THE CRIMINALS BEFORE HIBIKI DOES.
YOU TWO AGAIN?
ARE YOU NUTS?
EVEN IF YOU'RE REALLY AFTER A DRUGGER, I'VE NEVER HEARD OF SQUAD 4 GOING AROUND TO INTERVIEW WITNESSES.
IF THIS IS FROM THE HIGHER-UPS, THOUGH... FINE. WE WON'T GET IN YOUR WAY.
YOUR NAME'S TSUKUMO, RIGHT?
IF YOU'RE GONNA BE GOING AROUND TALKING TO PEOPLE, YOU MIGHT WANT TO THINK ABOUT WHAT IT MEANS TO OWN A HANGER.
I...
WONDER WHAT HE MEANS BY THAT...
ANYWAY, LET'S SEE WHAT KIND OF INFO WE CAN GATHER!
DING DONG
EXCUSE ME. WE'RE WITH THE POLICE...

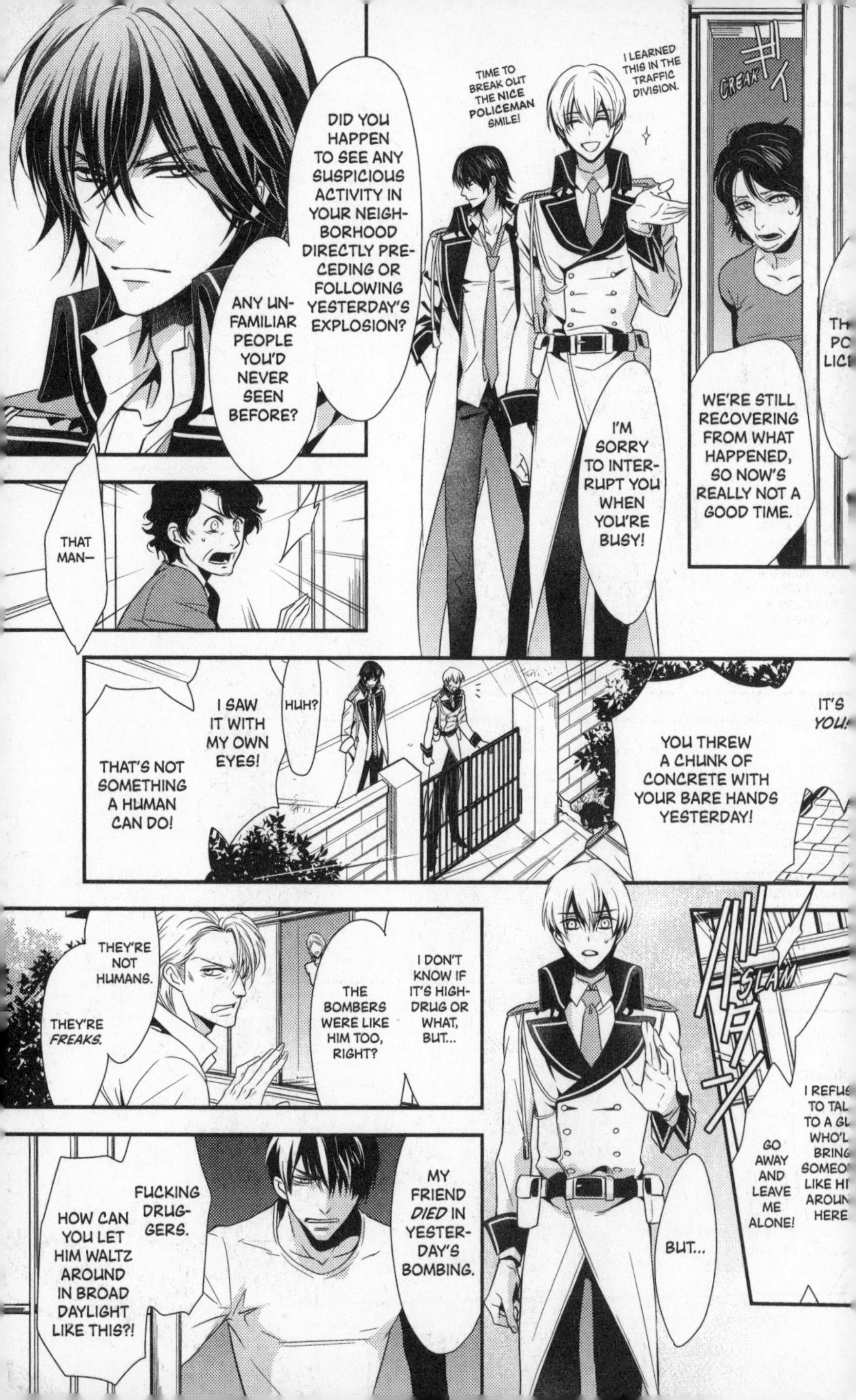
CREAK
WE'RE STILL RECOVERING FROM WHAT HAPPENED, SO NOW'S REALLY NOT A GOOD TIME.
I LEARNED THIS IN THE TRAFFIC DIVISION.
TIME TO BREAK OUT THE NICE POLICEMAN SMILE!
I'M SORRY TO INTERRUPT YOU WHEN YOU'RE BUSY!
DID YOU HAPPEN TO SEE ANY SUSPICIOUS ACTIVITY IN YOUR NEIGH-BORHOOD DIRECTLY PRE-CEDING OR FOLLOWING YESTERDAY'S EXPLOSION?
ANY UN-FAMILIAR PEOPLE YOU'D NEVER SEEN BEFORE?
THAT MAN—
IT'S *YOU!*
YOU THREW A CHUNK OF CONCRETE WITH YOUR BARE HANDS YESTERDAY!
HUH?
I SAW IT WITH MY OWN EYES!
THAT'S NOT SOMETHING A HUMAN CAN DO!
SLAM
GO AWAY AND LEAVE ME ALONE!
BUT...
I DON'T KNOW IF IT'S HIGH-DRUG OR WHAT, BUT...
THE BOMBERS WERE LIKE HIM TOO, RIGHT?
THEY'RE NOT HUMANS.
THEY'RE *FREAKS.*
MY FRIEND *DIED* IN YESTER-DAY'S BOMBING.
FUCKING DRUG-GERS.
HOW CAN YOU LET HIM WALTZ AROUND IN BROAD DAYLIGHT LIKE THIS?!

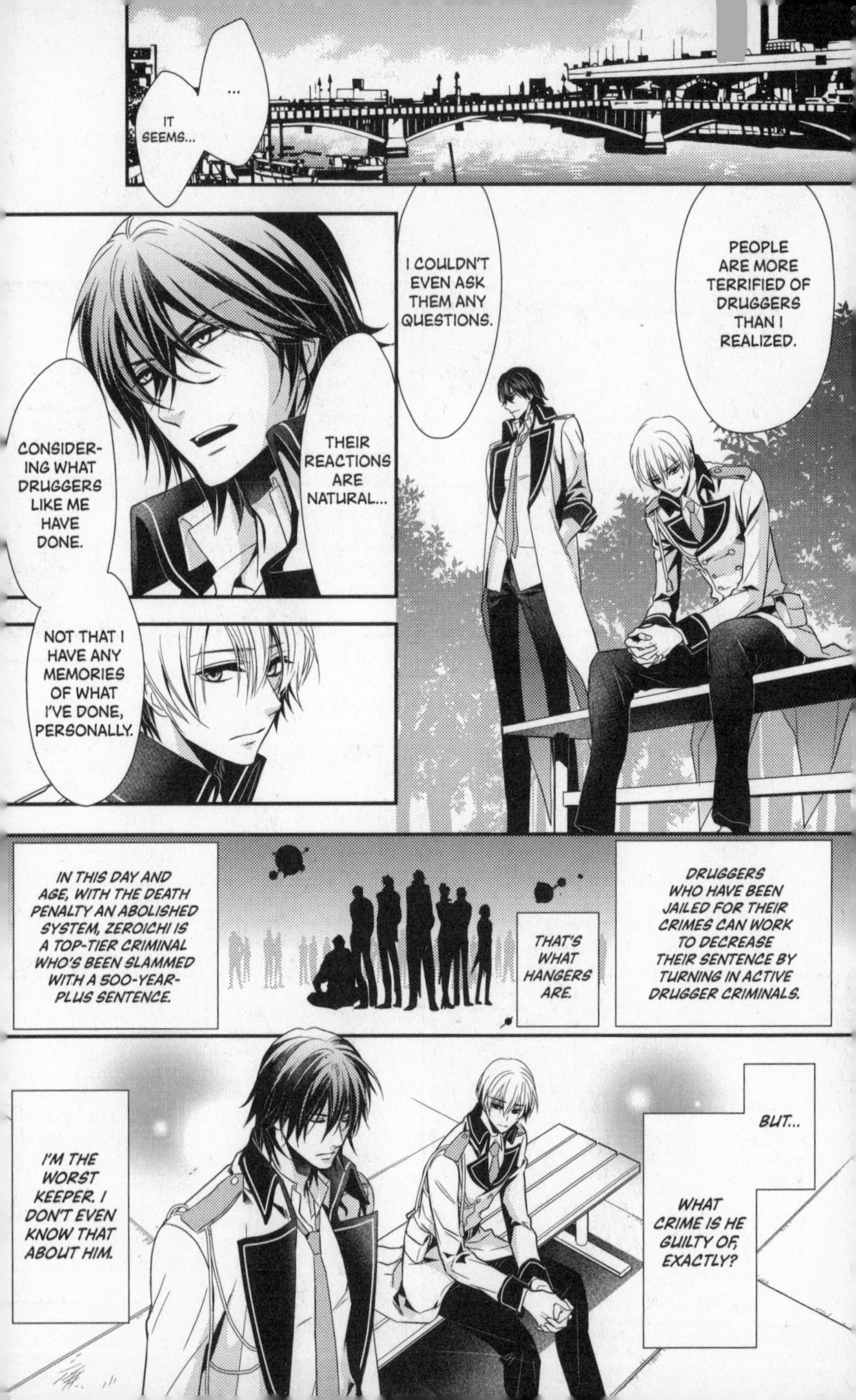
...
IT SEEMS...
PEOPLE ARE MORE TERRIFIED OF DRUGGERS THAN I REALIZED.
I COULDN'T EVEN ASK THEM ANY QUESTIONS.
THEIR REACTIONS ARE NATURAL...
CONSIDER-ING WHAT DRUGGERS LIKE ME HAVE DONE.
NOT THAT I HAVE ANY MEMORIES OF WHAT I'VE DONE, PERSONALLY.
DRUGGERS WHO HAVE BEEN JAILED FOR THEIR CRIMES CAN WORK TO DECREASE THEIR SENTENCE BY TURNING IN ACTIVE DRUGGER CRIMINALS.
THAT'S WHAT HANGERS ARE.
IN THIS DAY AND AGE, WITH THE DEATH PENALTY AN ABOLISHED SYSTEM, ZEROICHI IS A TOP-TIER CRIMINAL WHO'S BEEN SLAMMED WITH A 500-YEAR-PLUS SENTENCE.
BUT...
WHAT CRIME IS HE GUILTY OF, EXACTLY?
I'M THE WORST KEEPER. I DON'T EVEN KNOW THAT ABOUT HIM.

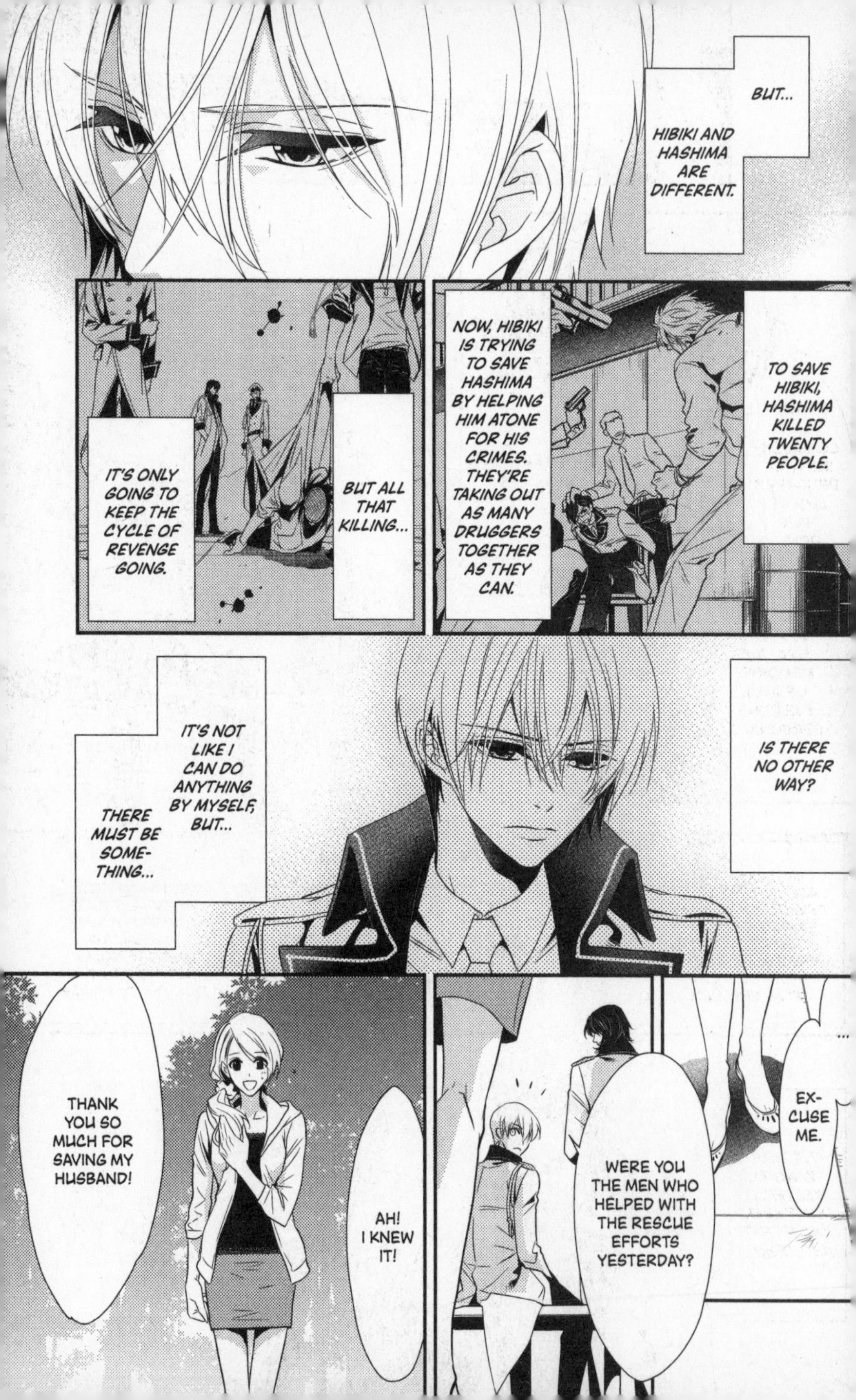
BUT...
HIBIKI AND HASHIMA ARE DIFFERENT.
TO SAVE HIBIKI, HASHIMA KILLED TWENTY PEOPLE.
NOW, HIBIKI IS TRYING TO SAVE HASHIMA BY HELPING HIM ATONE FOR HIS CRIMES. THEY'RE TAKING OUT AS MANY DRUGGERS TOGETHER AS THEY CAN.
BUT ALL THAT KILLING...
IT'S ONLY GOING TO KEEP THE CYCLE OF REVENGE GOING.
IS THERE NO OTHER WAY?
IT'S NOT LIKE I CAN DO ANYTHING BY MYSELF, BUT...
THERE MUST BE SOME-THING...
...
EX-CUSE ME.
WERE YOU THE MEN WHO HELPED WITH THE RESCUE EFFORTS YESTERDAY?
AH! I KNEW IT!
THANK YOU SO MUCH FOR SAVING MY HUSBAND!

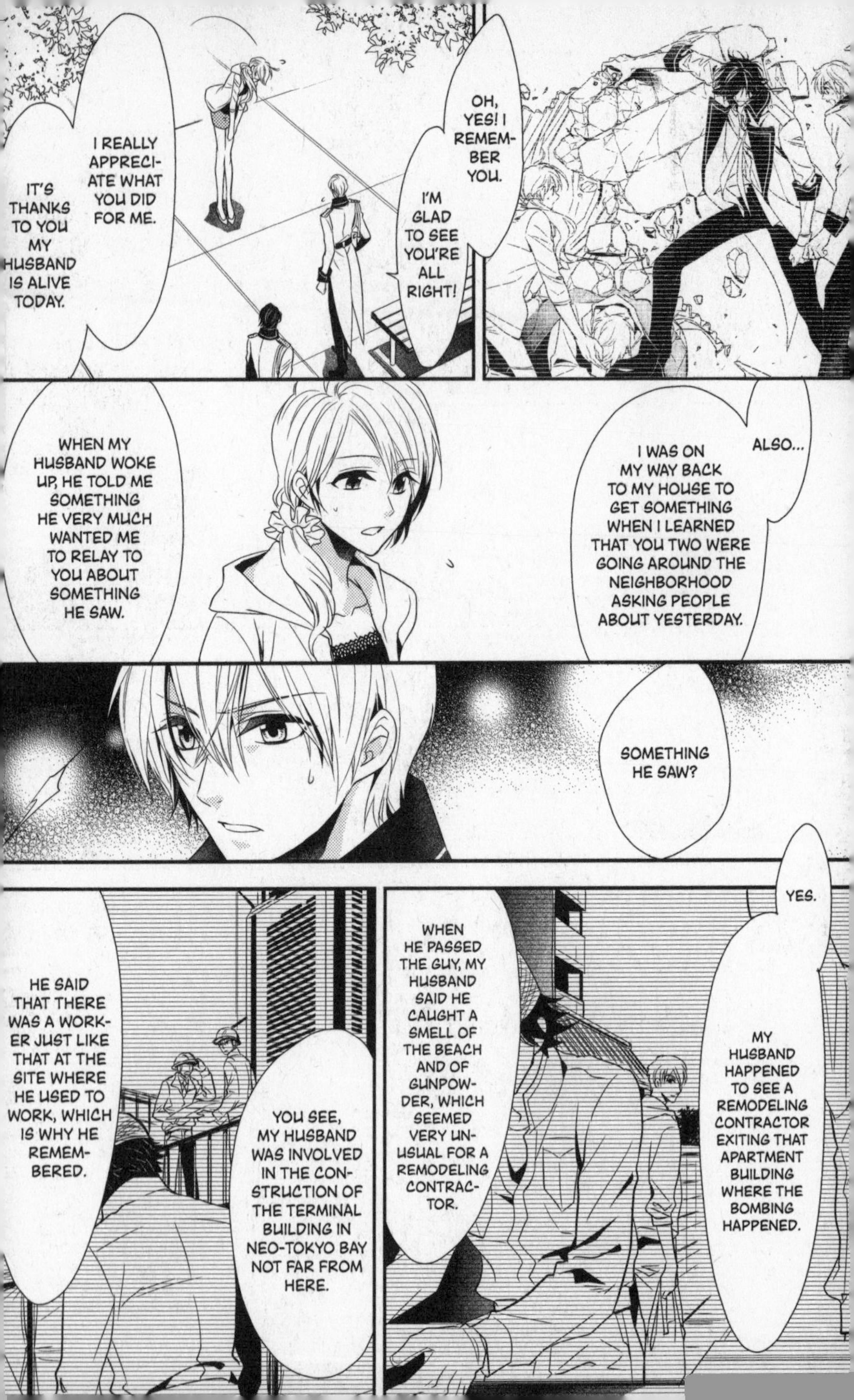

OH, YES! I REMEMBER YOU.
I'M GLAD TO SEE YOU'RE ALL RIGHT!
I REALLY APPRECIATE WHAT YOU DID FOR ME.
IT'S THANKS TO YOU MY HUSBAND IS ALIVE TODAY.
ALSO...
I WAS ON MY WAY BACK TO MY HOUSE TO GET SOMETHING WHEN I LEARNED THAT YOU TWO WERE GOING AROUND THE NEIGHBORHOOD ASKING PEOPLE ABOUT YESTERDAY.
WHEN MY HUSBAND WOKE UP, HE TOLD ME SOMETHING HE VERY MUCH WANTED ME TO RELAY TO YOU ABOUT SOMETHING HE SAW.
SOMETHING HE SAW?
YES.
MY HUSBAND HAPPENED TO SEE A REMODELING CONTRACTOR EXITING THAT APARTMENT BUILDING WHERE THE BOMBING HAPPENED.
WHEN HE PASSED THE GUY, MY HUSBAND SAID HE CAUGHT A SMELL OF THE BEACH AND OF GUNPOWDER, WHICH SEEMED VERY UNUSUAL FOR A REMODELING CONTRACTOR.
YOU SEE, MY HUSBAND WAS INVOLVED IN THE CONSTRUCTION OF THE TERMINAL BUILDING IN NEO-TOKYO BAY NOT FAR FROM HERE.
HE SAID THAT THERE WAS A WORKER JUST LIKE THAT AT THE SITE WHERE HE USED TO WORK, WHICH IS WHY HE REMEMBERED.

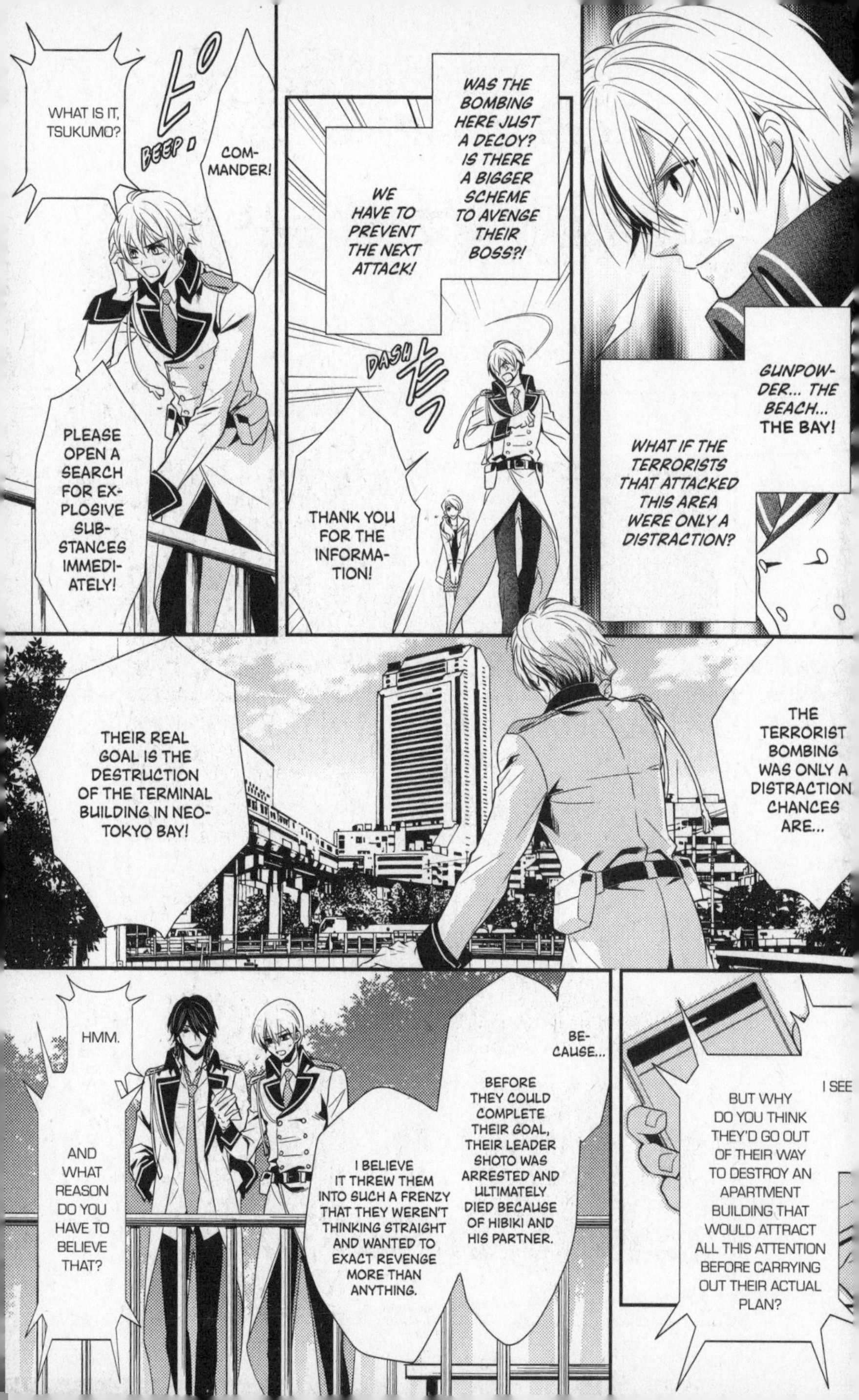
GUNPOWDER... THE BEACH... THE BAY!
WHAT IF THE TERRORISTS THAT ATTACKED THIS AREA WERE ONLY A DISTRACTION?
WAS THE BOMBING HERE JUST A DECOY? IS THERE A BIGGER SCHEME TO AVENGE THEIR BOSS?!
WE HAVE TO PREVENT THE NEXT ATTACK!
DASH
THANK YOU FOR THE INFORMATION!
BEEP
COMMANDER!
WHAT IS IT, TSUKUMO?
PLEASE OPEN A SEARCH FOR EXPLOSIVE SUBSTANCES IMMEDIATELY!
THE TERRORIST BOMBING WAS ONLY A DISTRACTION. CHANCES ARE...
THEIR REAL GOAL IS THE DESTRUCTION OF THE TERMINAL BUILDING IN NEO-TOKYO BAY!
I SEE
BUT WHY DO YOU THINK THEY'D GO OUT OF THEIR WAY TO DESTROY AN APARTMENT BUILDING THAT WOULD ATTRACT ALL THIS ATTENTION BEFORE CARRYING OUT THEIR ACTUAL PLAN?
BECAUSE...
BEFORE THEY COULD COMPLETE THEIR GOAL, THEIR LEADER SHOTO WAS ARRESTED AND ULTIMATELY DIED BECAUSE OF HIBIKI AND HIS PARTNER.
I BELIEVE IT THREW THEM INTO SUCH A FRENZY THAT THEY WEREN'T THINKING STRAIGHT AND WANTED TO EXACT REVENGE MORE THAN ANYTHING.
HMM.
AND WHAT REASON DO YOU HAVE TO BELIEVE THAT?

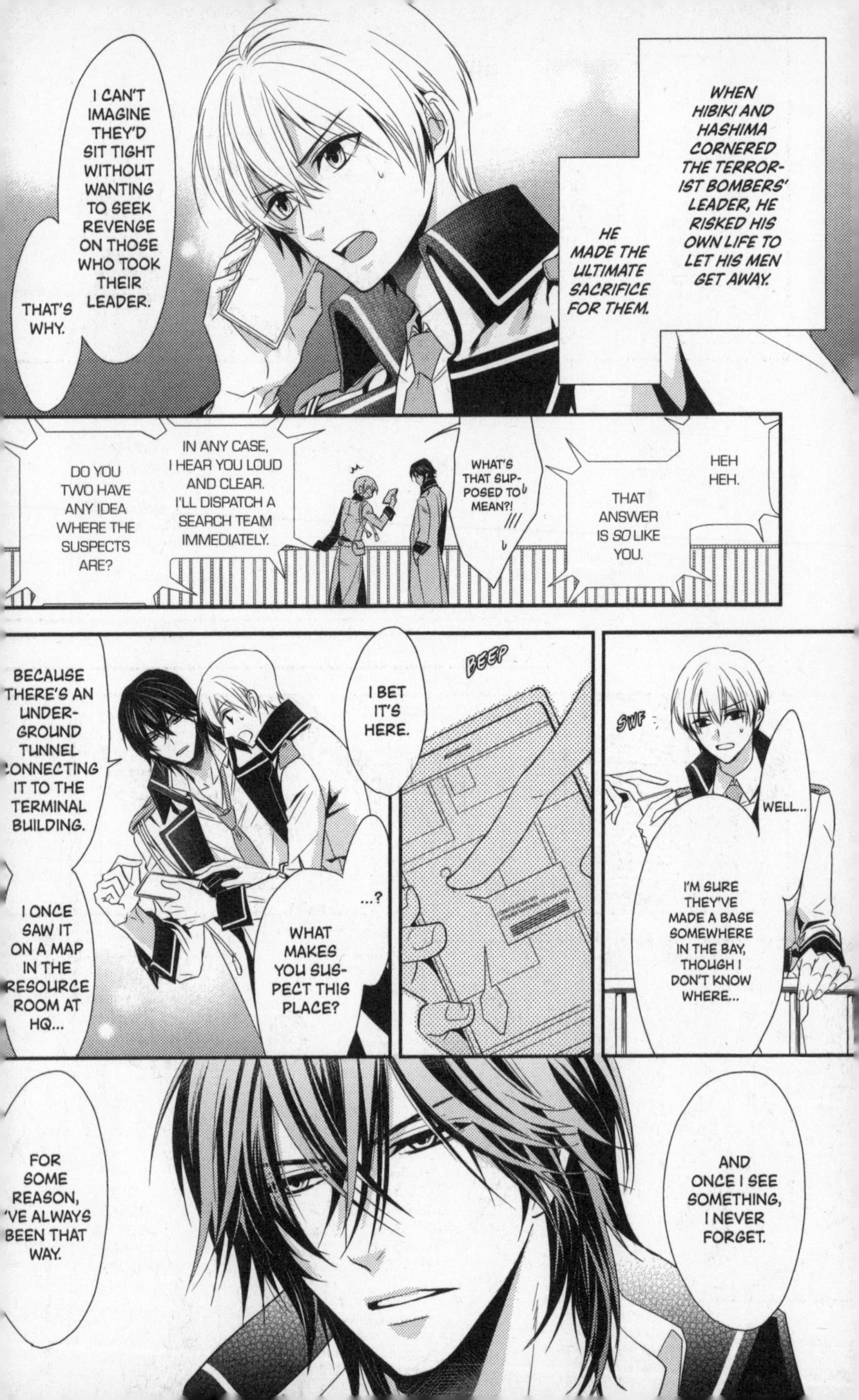
WHEN HIBIKI AND HASHIMA CORNERED THE TERROR-IST BOMBERS' LEADER, HE RISKED HIS OWN LIFE TO LET HIS MEN GET AWAY.
HE MADE THE ULTIMATE SACRIFICE FOR THEM.
I CAN'T IMAGINE THEY'D SIT TIGHT WITHOUT WANTING TO SEEK REVENGE ON THOSE WHO TOOK THEIR LEADER.
THAT'S WHY.
HEH HEH.
THAT ANSWER IS *SO* LIKE YOU.
WHAT'S THAT SUP-POSED TO MEAN?!
IN ANY CASE, I HEAR YOU LOUD AND CLEAR. I'LL DISPATCH A SEARCH TEAM IMMEDIATELY.
DO YOU TWO HAVE ANY IDEA WHERE THE SUSPECTS ARE?
SWF
WELL...
I'M SURE THEY'VE MADE A BASE SOMEWHERE IN THE BAY, THOUGH I DON'T KNOW WHERE...
BEEP
I BET IT'S HERE.
...?
WHAT MAKES YOU SUS-PECT THIS PLACE?
BECAUSE THERE'S AN UNDER-GROUND TUNNEL CONNECTING IT TO THE TERMINAL BUILDING.
I ONCE SAW IT ON A MAP IN THE RESOURCE ROOM AT HQ...
AND ONCE I SEE SOMETHING, I NEVER FORGET.
FOR SOME REASON, 'VE ALWAYS BEEN THAT WAY.

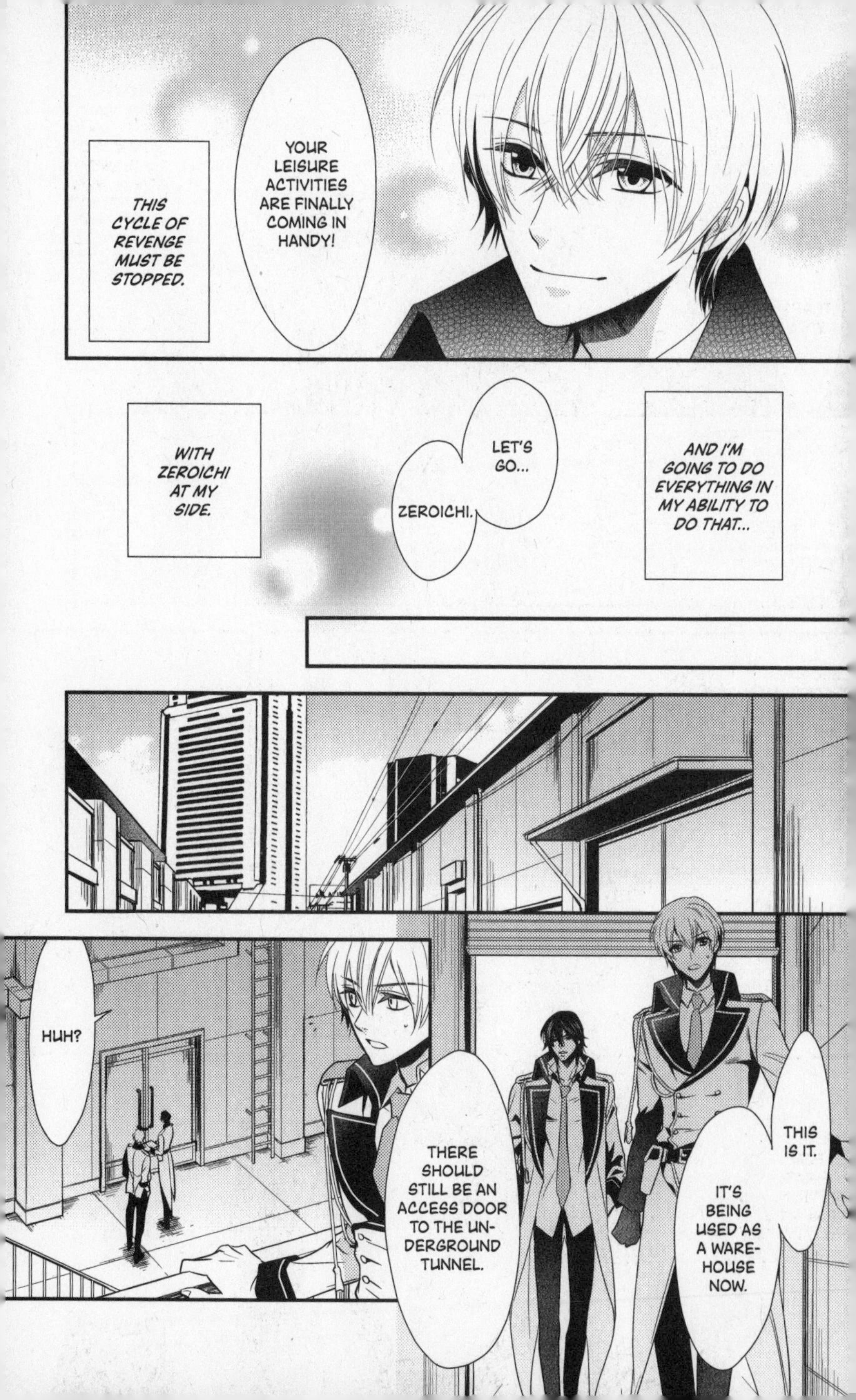
YOUR LEISURE ACTIVITIES ARE FINALLY COMING IN HANDY!
THIS CYCLE OF REVENGE MUST BE STOPPED.
AND I'M GOING TO DO EVERYTHING IN MY ABILITY TO DO THAT...
LET'S GO...
ZEROICHI.
WITH ZEROICHI AT MY SIDE.
THIS IS IT.
IT'S BEING USED AS A WARE-HOUSE NOW.
THERE SHOULD STILL BE AN ACCESS DOOR TO THE UN-DERGROUND TUNNEL.
HUH?

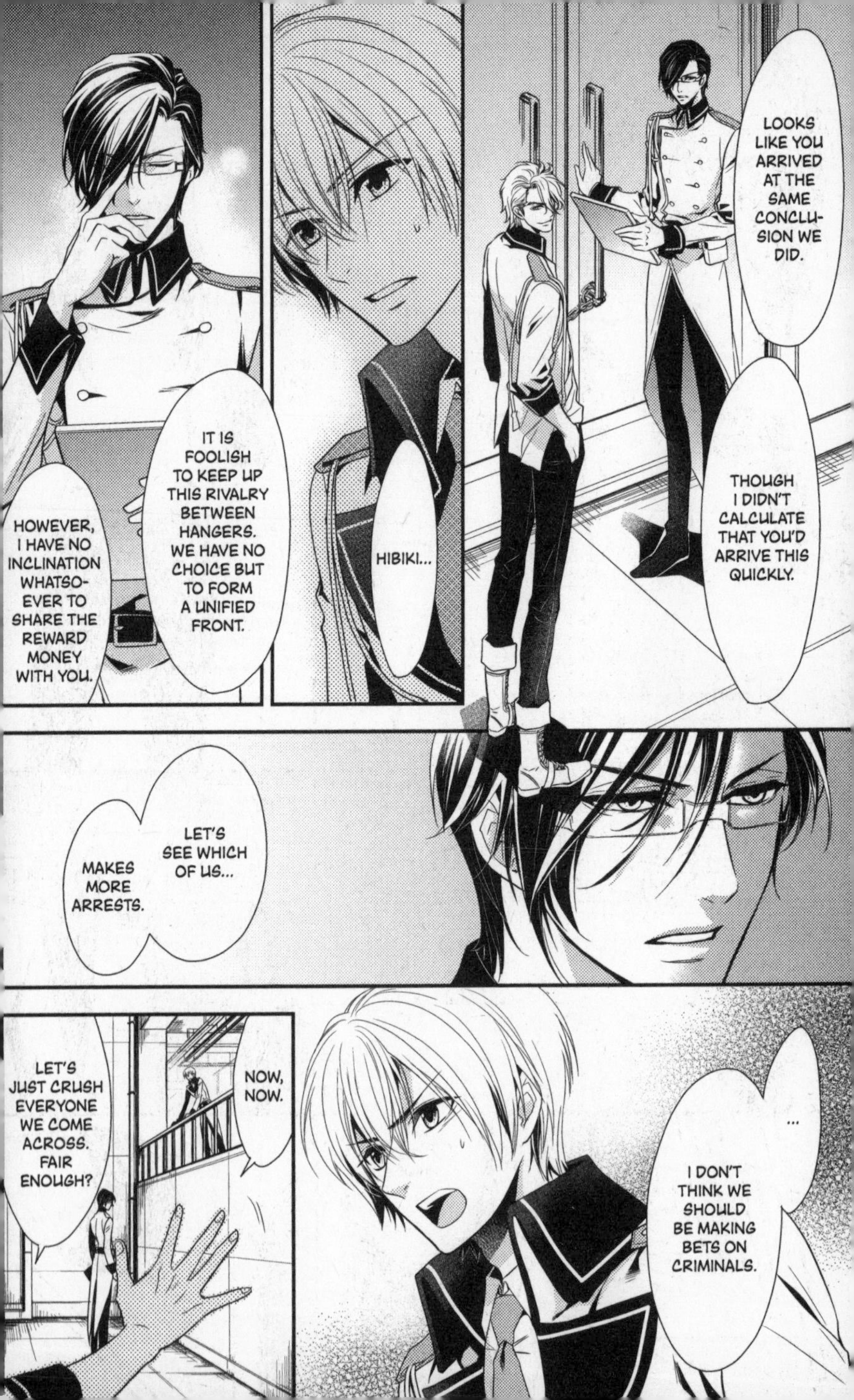
LOOKS LIKE YOU ARRIVED AT THE SAME CONCLUSION WE DID.
THOUGH I DIDN'T CALCULATE THAT YOU'D ARRIVE THIS QUICKLY.
HIBIKI...
IT IS FOOLISH TO KEEP UP THIS RIVALRY BETWEEN HANGERS. WE HAVE NO CHOICE BUT TO FORM A UNIFIED FRONT.
HOWEVER, I HAVE NO INCLINATION WHATSOEVER TO SHARE THE REWARD MONEY WITH YOU.
LET'S SEE WHICH OF US...
MAKES MORE ARRESTS.
...
I DON'T THINK WE SHOULD BE MAKING BETS ON CRIMINALS.
NOW, NOW.
LET'S JUST CRUSH EVERYONE WE COME ACROSS. FAIR ENOUGH?

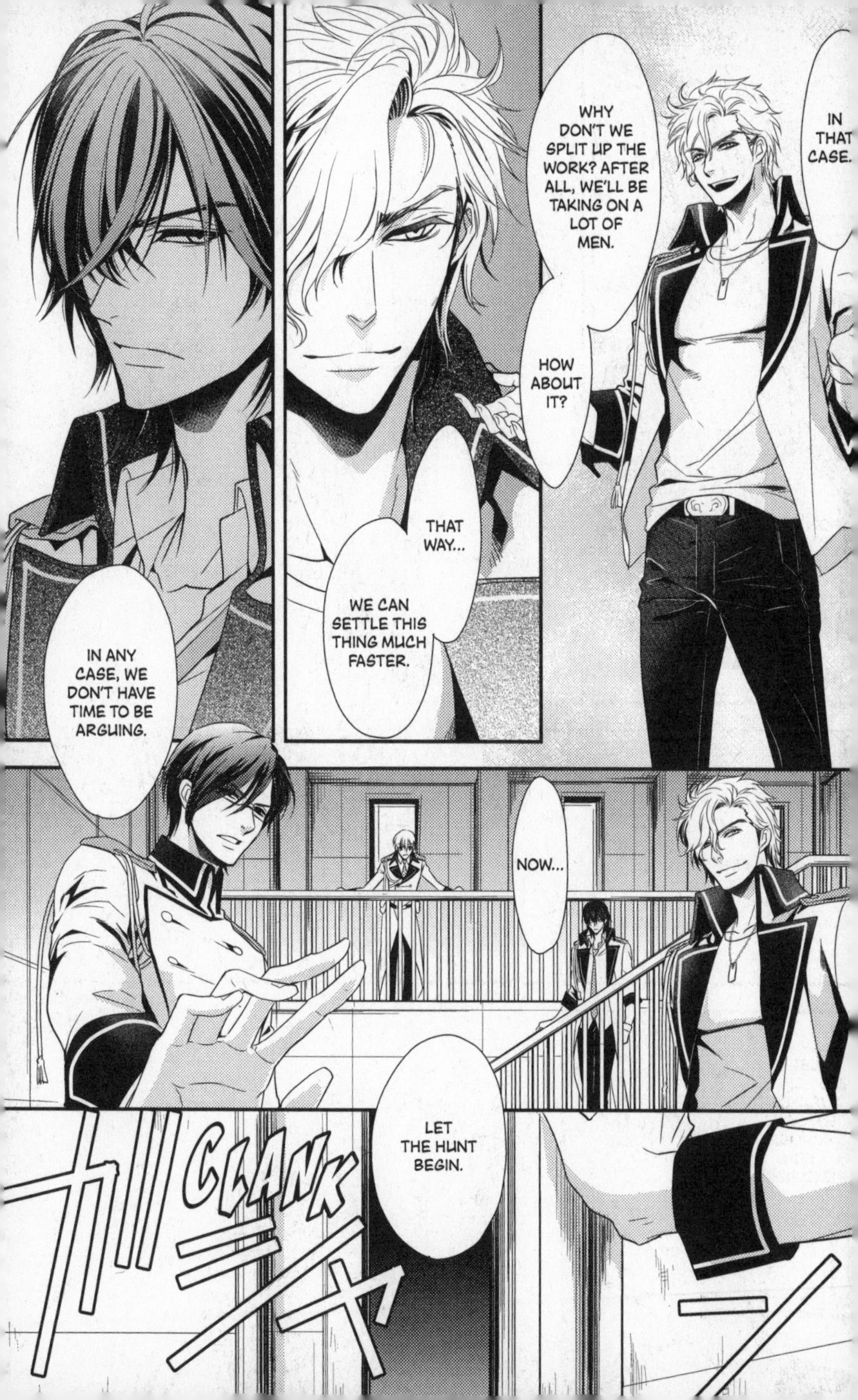
IN THAT CASE.
WHY DON'T WE SPLIT UP THE WORK? AFTER ALL, WE'LL BE TAKING ON A LOT OF MEN.
HOW ABOUT IT?
THAT WAY...
WE CAN SETTLE THIS THING MUCH FASTER.
IN ANY CASE, WE DON'T HAVE TIME TO BE ARGUING.
NOW...
LET THE HUNT BEGIN.
CLANK

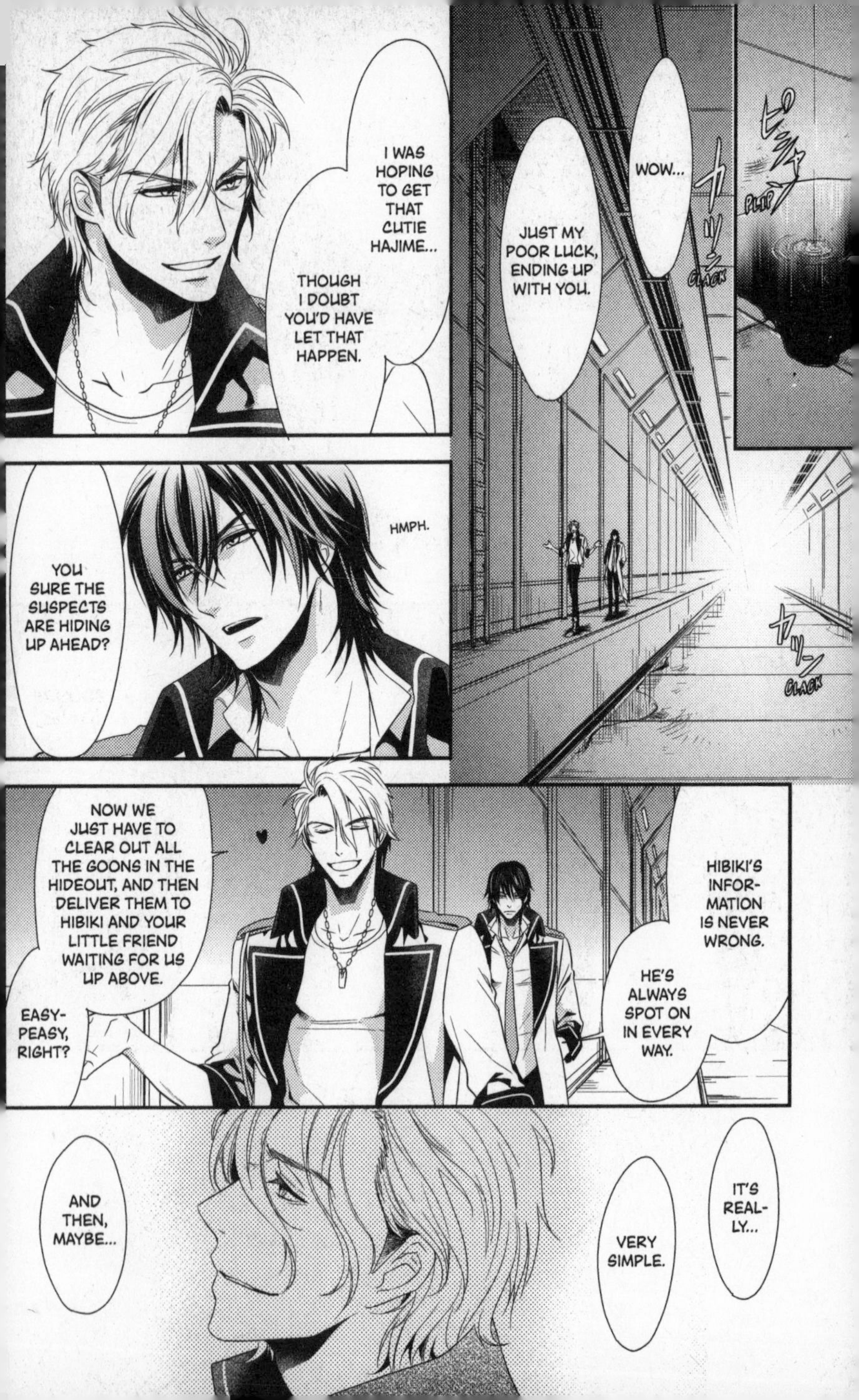
PLIP
CLACK
WOW...
JUST MY POOR LUCK, ENDING UP WITH YOU.
CLACK
I WAS HOPING TO GET THAT CUTIE HAJIME...
THOUGH I DOUBT YOU'D HAVE LET THAT HAPPEN.
HMPH.
YOU SURE THE SUSPECTS ARE HIDING UP AHEAD?
HIBIKI'S INFORMATION IS NEVER WRONG.
HE'S ALWAYS SPOT ON IN EVERY WAY.
NOW WE JUST HAVE TO CLEAR OUT ALL THE GOONS IN THE HIDEOUT, AND THEN DELIVER THEM TO HIBIKI AND YOUR LITTLE FRIEND WAITING FOR US UP ABOVE.
EASY-PEASY, RIGHT?
IT'S REALLY...
VERY SIMPLE.
AND THEN, MAYBE...

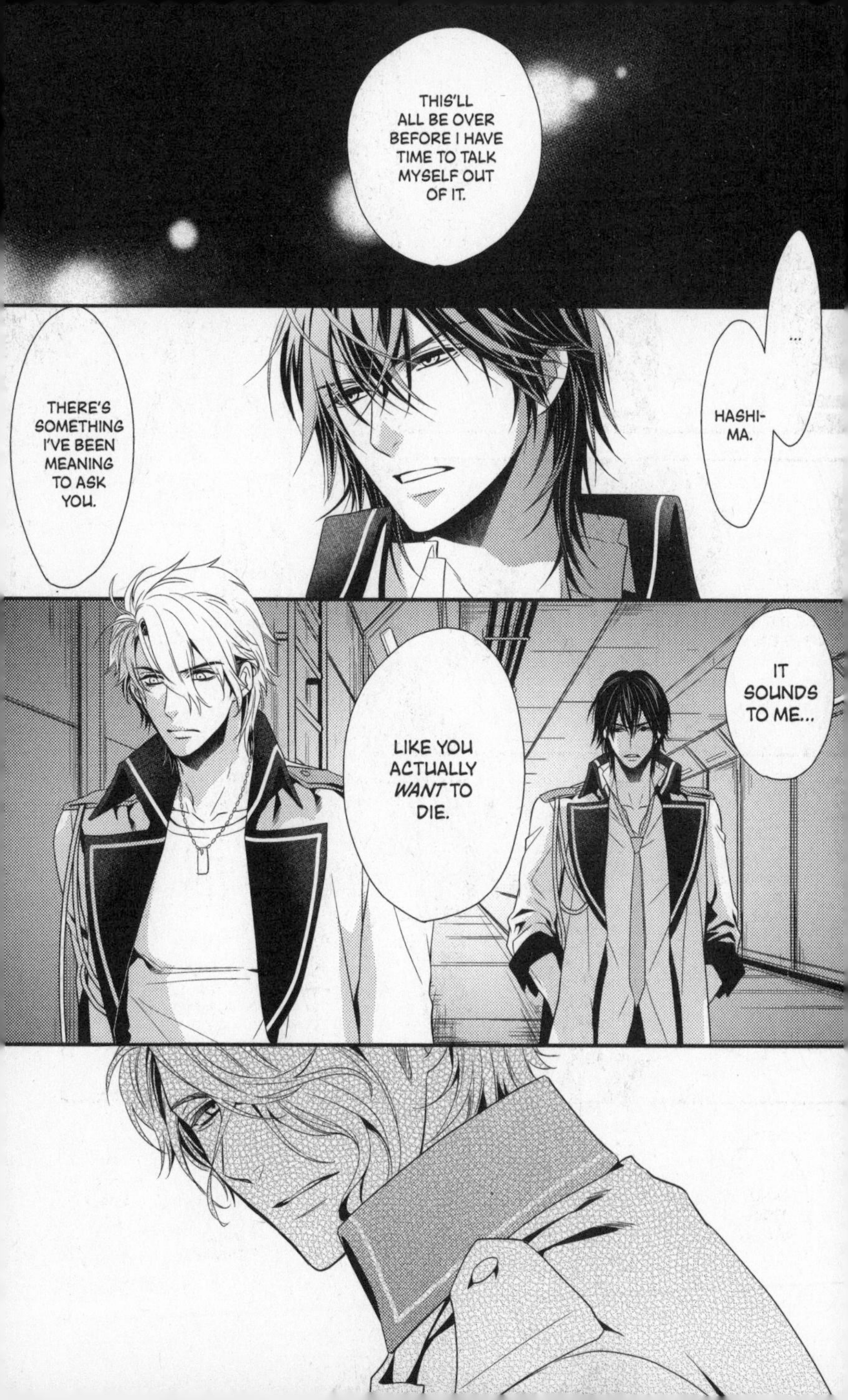
THIS'LL ALL BE OVER BEFORE I HAVE TIME TO TALK MYSELF OUT OF IT.
... HASHIMA.
THERE'S SOMETHING I'VE BEEN MEANING TO ASK YOU.
IT SOUNDS TO ME...
LIKE YOU ACTUALLY *WANT* TO DIE.

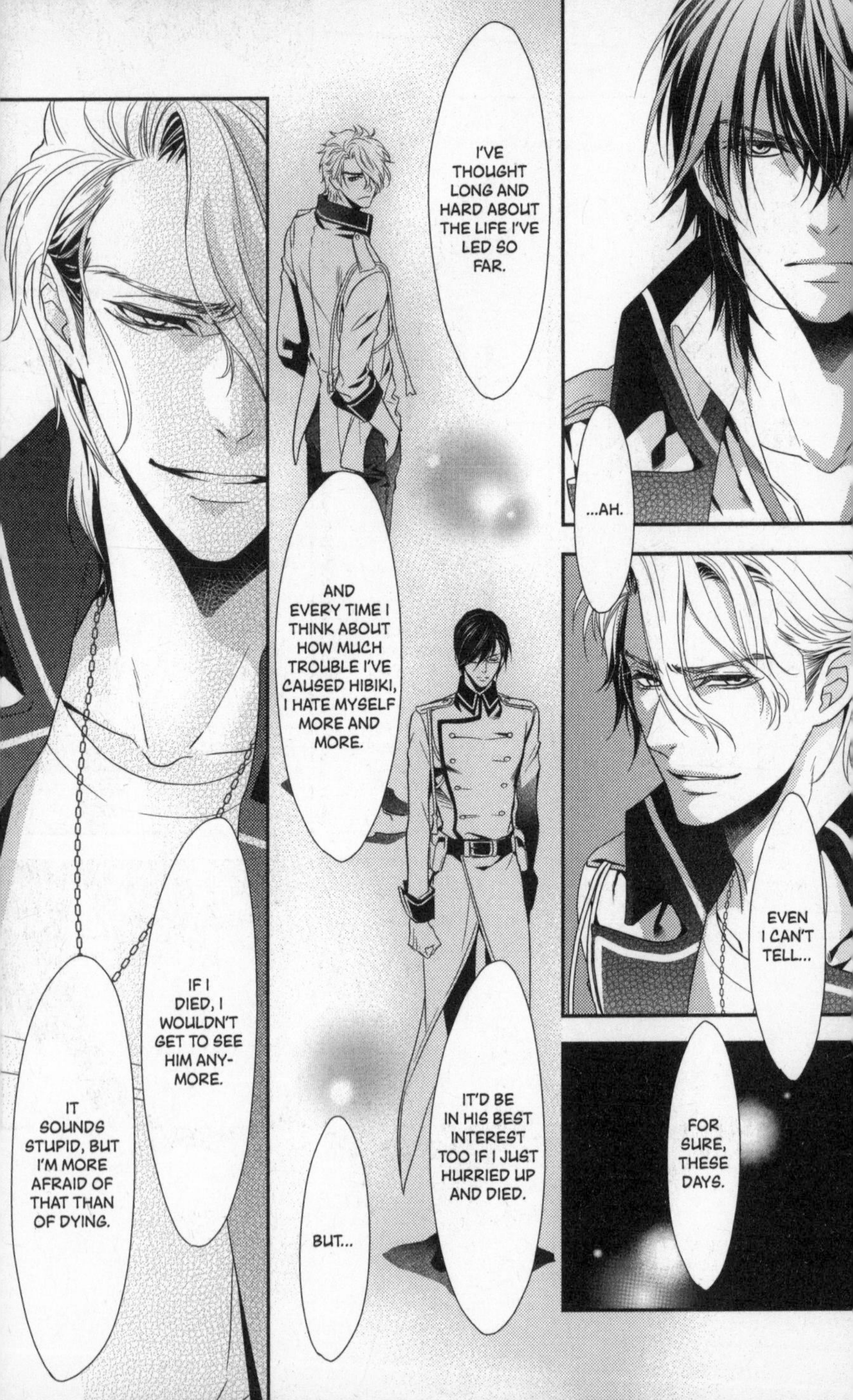
...AH.
EVEN I CAN'T TELL...
FOR SURE, THESE DAYS.
I'VE THOUGHT LONG AND HARD ABOUT THE LIFE I'VE LED SO FAR.
AND EVERY TIME I THINK ABOUT HOW MUCH TROUBLE I'VE CAUSED HIBIKI, I HATE MYSELF MORE AND MORE.
IT'D BE IN HIS BEST INTEREST TOO IF I JUST HURRIED UP AND DIED.
BUT...
IF I DIED, I WOULDN'T GET TO SEE HIM ANY-MORE.
IT SOUNDS STUPID, BUT I'M MORE AFRAID OF THAT THAN OF DYING.

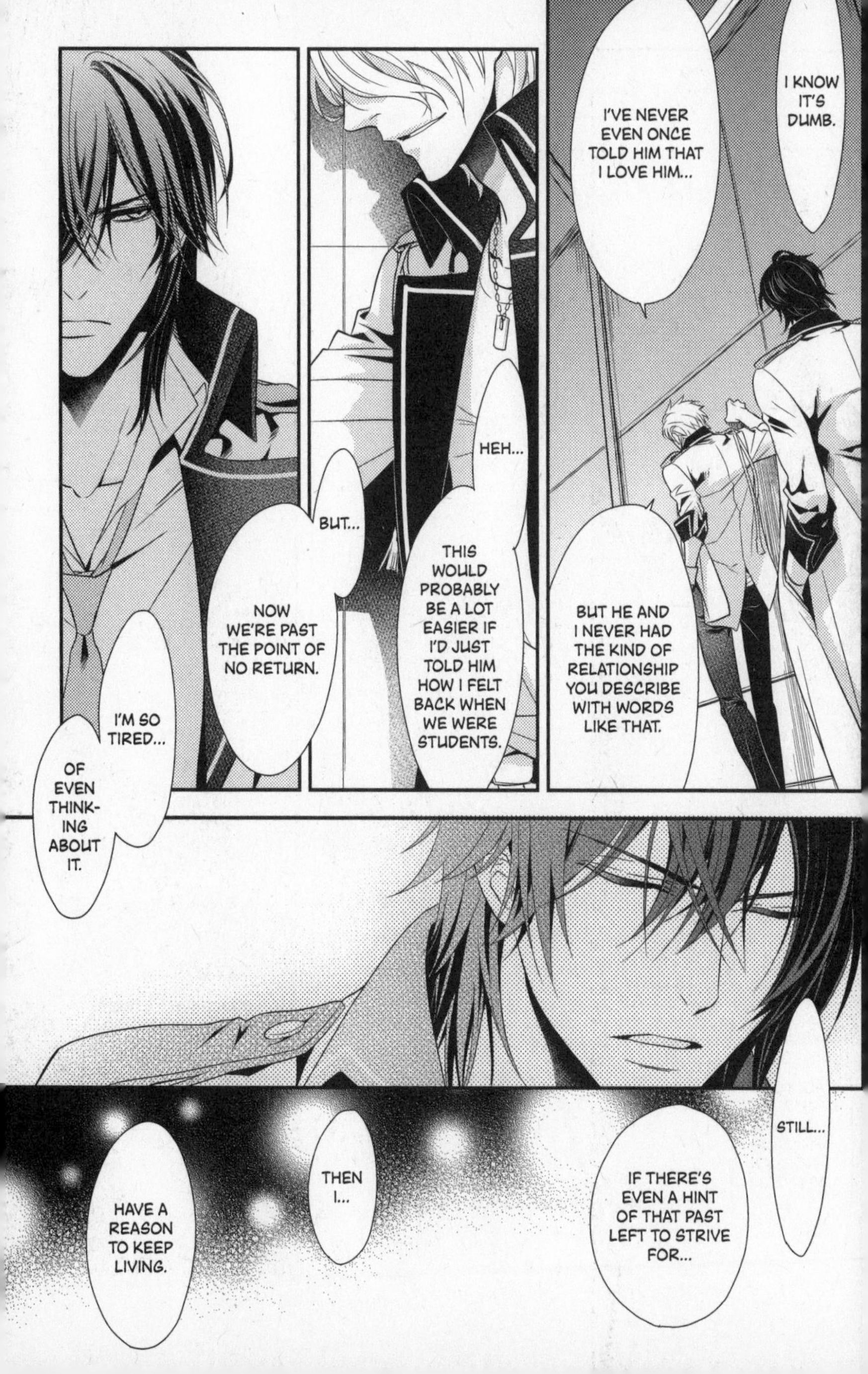
I KNOW IT'S DUMB.
I'VE NEVER EVEN ONCE TOLD HIM THAT I LOVE HIM...
BUT HE AND I NEVER HAD THE KIND OF RELATIONSHIP YOU DESCRIBE WITH WORDS LIKE THAT.
HEH...
THIS WOULD PROBABLY BE A LOT EASIER IF I'D JUST TOLD HIM HOW I FELT BACK WHEN WE WERE STUDENTS.
BUT...
NOW WE'RE PAST THE POINT OF NO RETURN.
I'M SO TIRED...
OF EVEN THINKING-ING ABOUT IT.
STILL...
IF THERE'S EVEN A HINT OF THAT PAST LEFT TO STRIVE FOR...
THEN I...
HAVE A REASON TO KEEP LIVING.

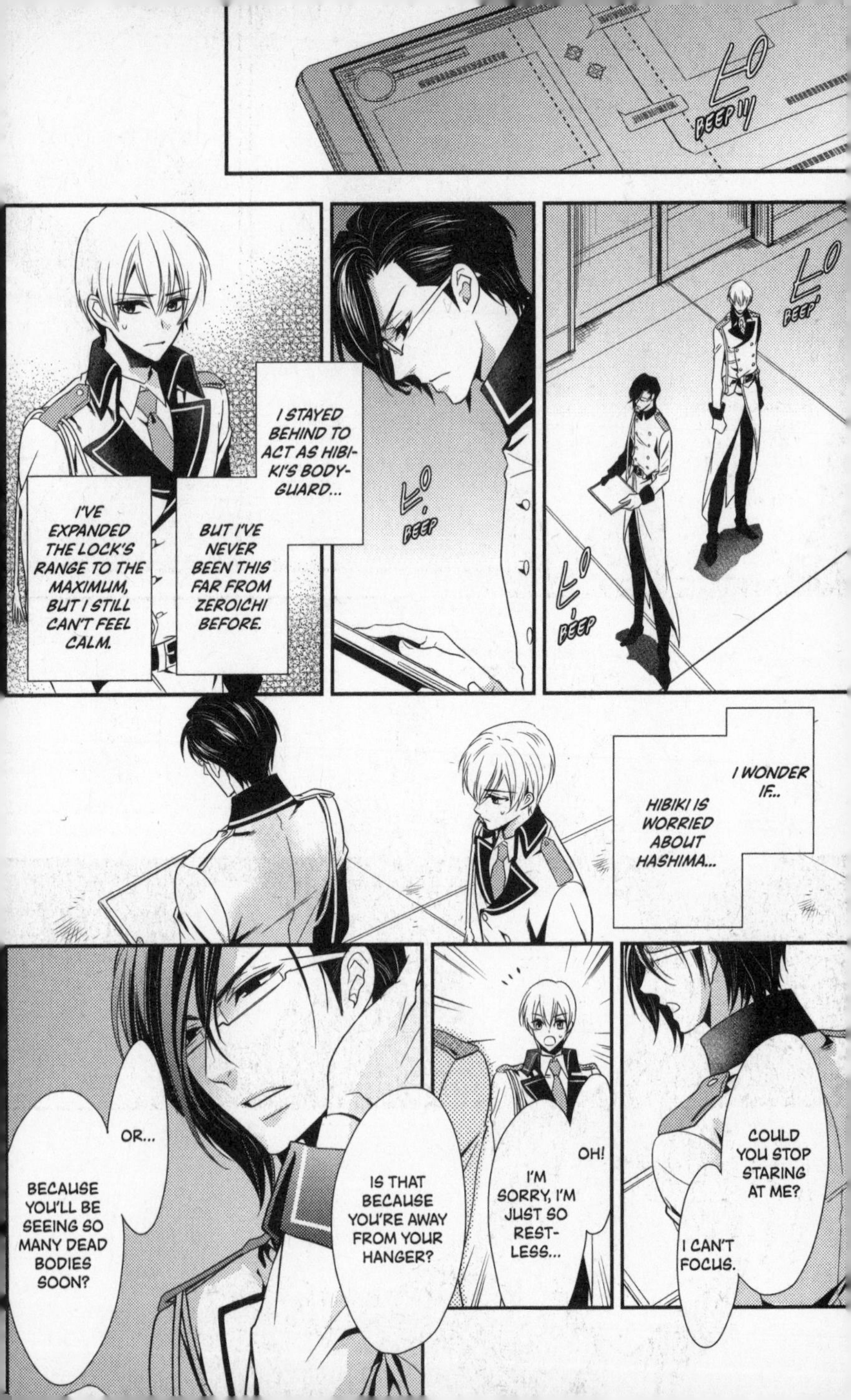
BEEP
BEEP
BEEP
I STAYED BEHIND TO ACT AS HIBIKI'S BODY-GUARD...
BEEP
BUT I'VE NEVER BEEN THIS FAR FROM ZEROICHI BEFORE.
I'VE EXPANDED THE LOCK'S RANGE TO THE MAXIMUM, BUT I STILL CAN'T FEEL CALM.
I WONDER IF...
HIBIKI IS WORRIED ABOUT HASHIMA...
COULD YOU STOP STARING AT ME?
I CAN'T FOCUS.
OH!
I'M SORRY, I'M JUST SO REST-LESS...
IS THAT BECAUSE YOU'RE AWAY FROM YOUR HANGER?
OR...
BECAUSE YOU'LL BE SEEING SO MANY DEAD BODIES SOON?

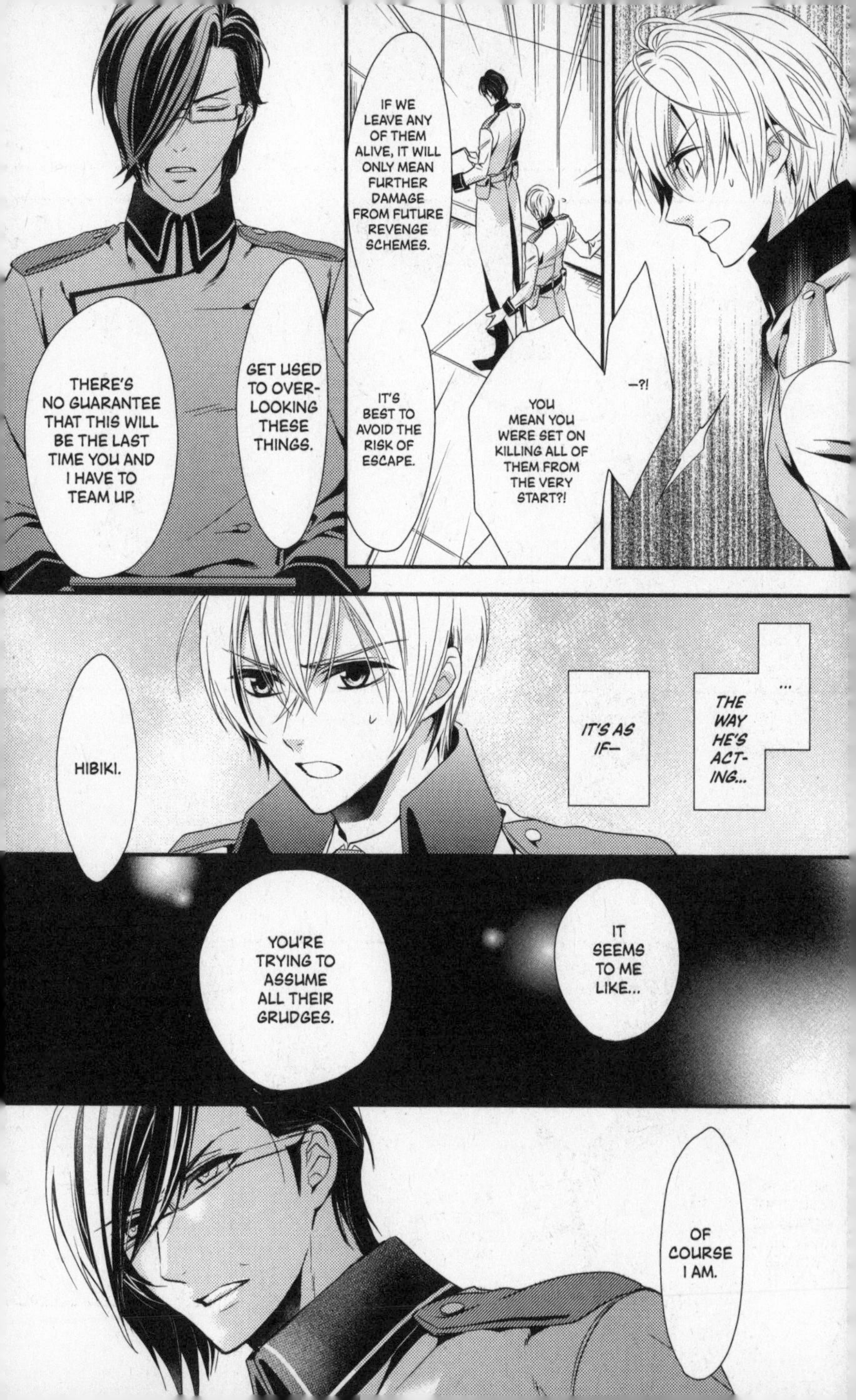
—?!
YOU MEAN YOU WERE SET ON KILLING ALL OF THEM FROM THE VERY START?!
IF WE LEAVE ANY OF THEM ALIVE, IT WILL ONLY MEAN FURTHER DAMAGE FROM FUTURE REVENGE SCHEMES.
IT'S BEST TO AVOID THE RISK OF ESCAPE.
GET USED TO OVER-LOOKING THESE THINGS.
THERE'S NO GUARANTEE THAT THIS WILL BE THE LAST TIME YOU AND I HAVE TO TEAM UP.
...
THE WAY HE'S ACT-ING...
IT'S AS IF—
HIBIKI.
IT SEEMS TO ME LIKE...
YOU'RE TRYING TO ASSUME ALL THEIR GRUDGES.
OF COURSE I AM.

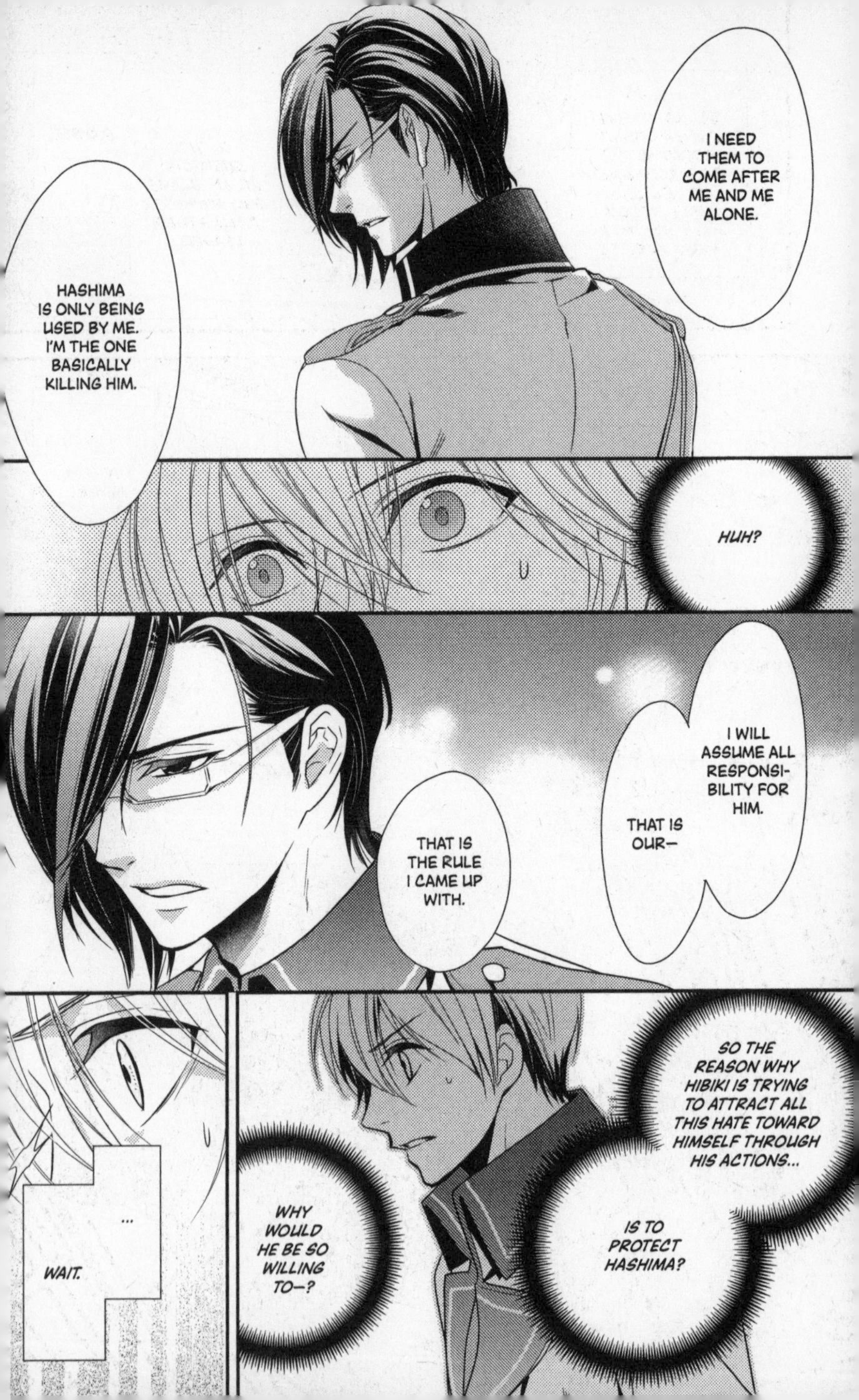
I NEED THEM TO COME AFTER ME AND ME ALONE.
HASHIMA IS ONLY BEING USED BY ME. I'M THE ONE BASICALLY KILLING HIM.
HUH?
I WILL ASSUME ALL RESPONSI-BILITY FOR HIM.
THAT IS OUR—
THAT IS THE RULE I CAME UP WITH.
SO THE REASON WHY HIBIKI IS TRYING TO ATTRACT ALL THIS HATE TOWARD HIMSELF THROUGH HIS ACTIONS...
IS TO PROTECT HASHIMA?
WHY WOULD HE BE SO WILLING TO—?
...
WAIT.

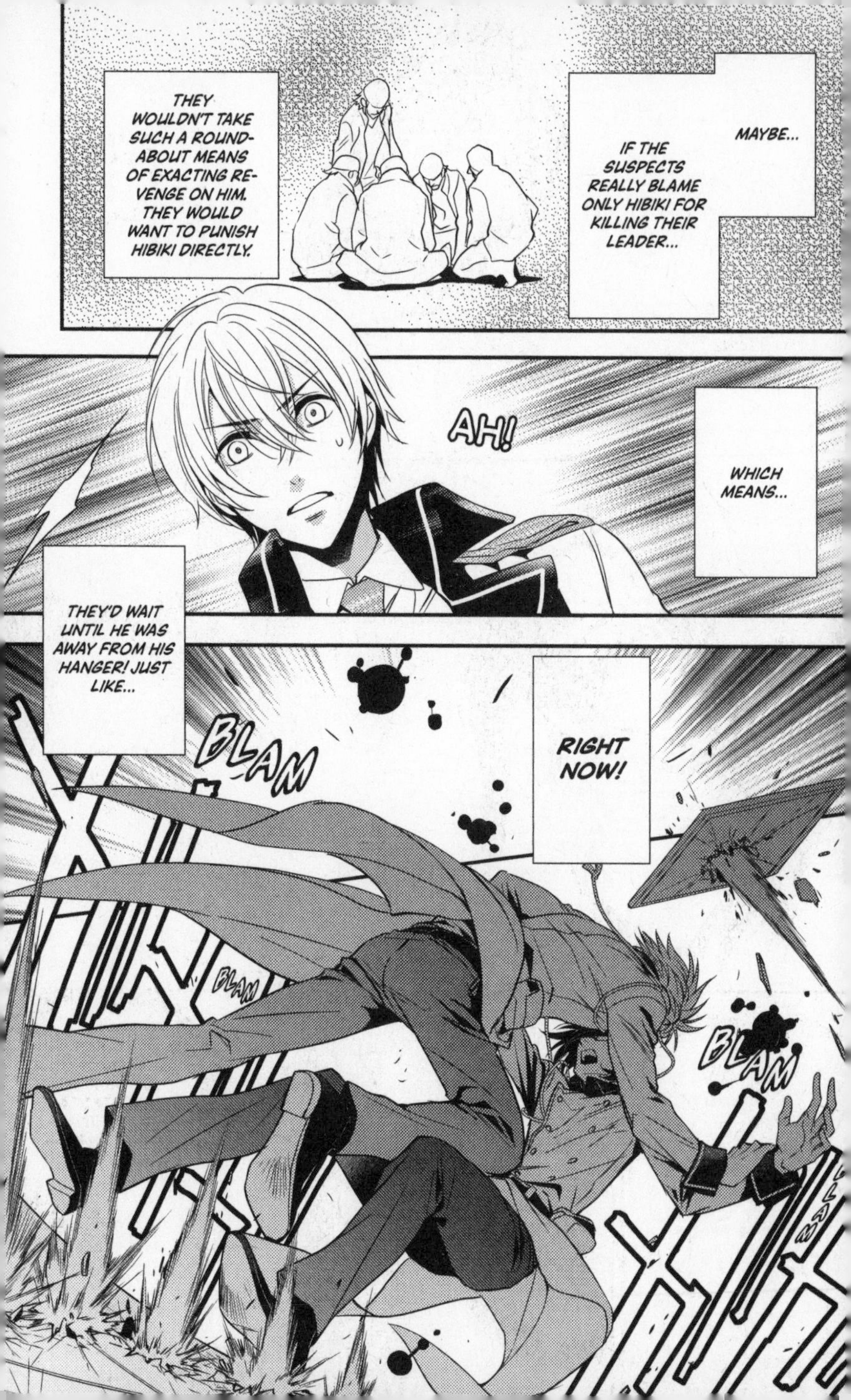
MAYBE...
IF THE SUSPECTS REALLY BLAME ONLY HIBIKI FOR KILLING THEIR LEADER...
THEY WOULDN'T TAKE SUCH A ROUND-ABOUT MEANS OF EXACTING RE-VENGE ON HIM. THEY WOULD WANT TO PUNISH HIBIKI DIRECTLY.
WHICH MEANS...
AH!
THEY'D WAIT UNTIL HE WAS AWAY FROM HIS HANGER! JUST LIKE...
RIGHT NOW!
BLAM
BLAM
BLAM

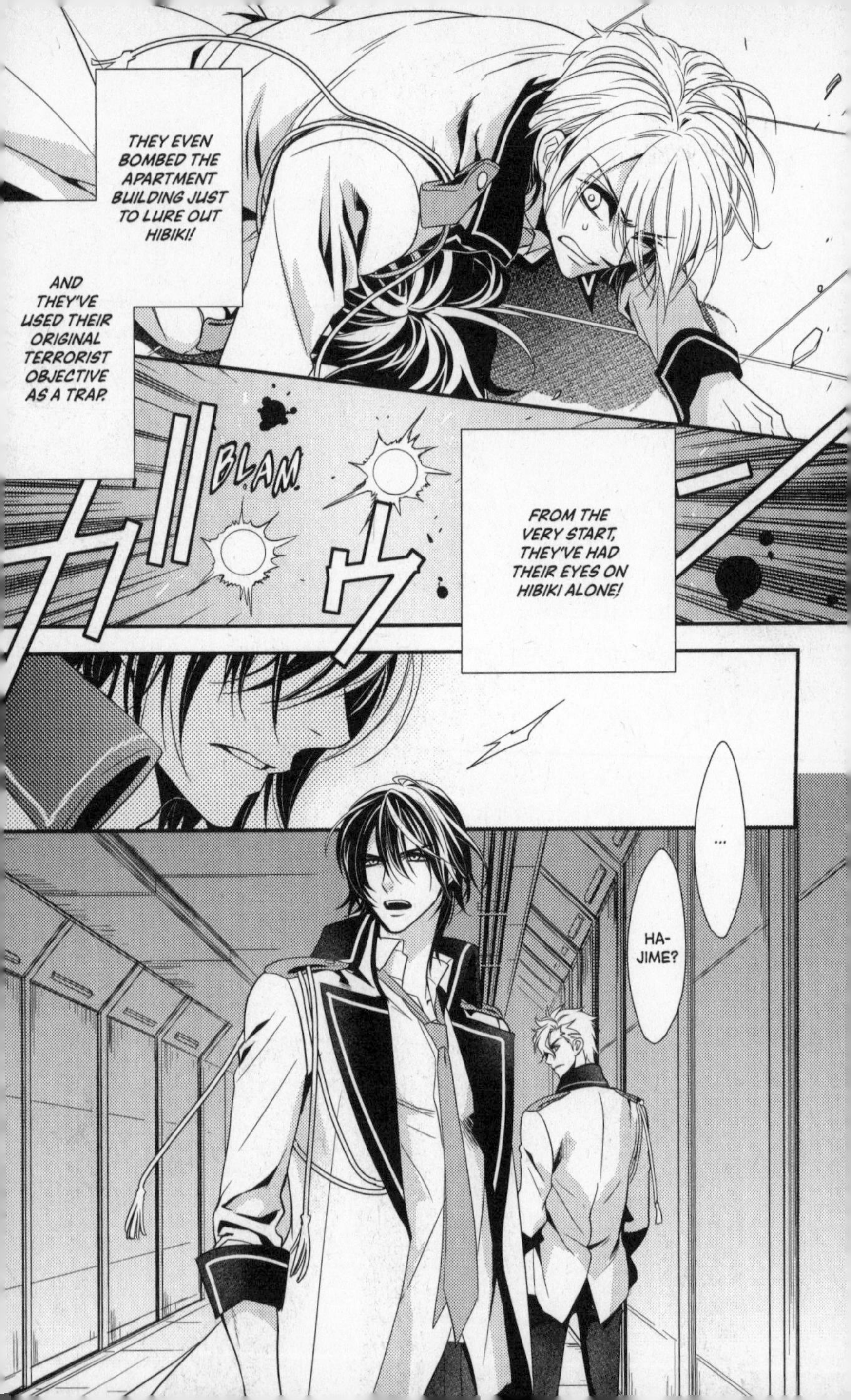
THEY EVEN BOMBED THE APARTMENT BUILDING JUST TO LURE OUT HIBIKI!
AND THEY'VE USED THEIR ORIGINAL TERRORIST OBJECTIVE AS A TRAP.
FROM THE VERY START, THEY'VE HAD THEIR EYES ON HIBIKI ALONE!
BLAM
...
HA-JIME?

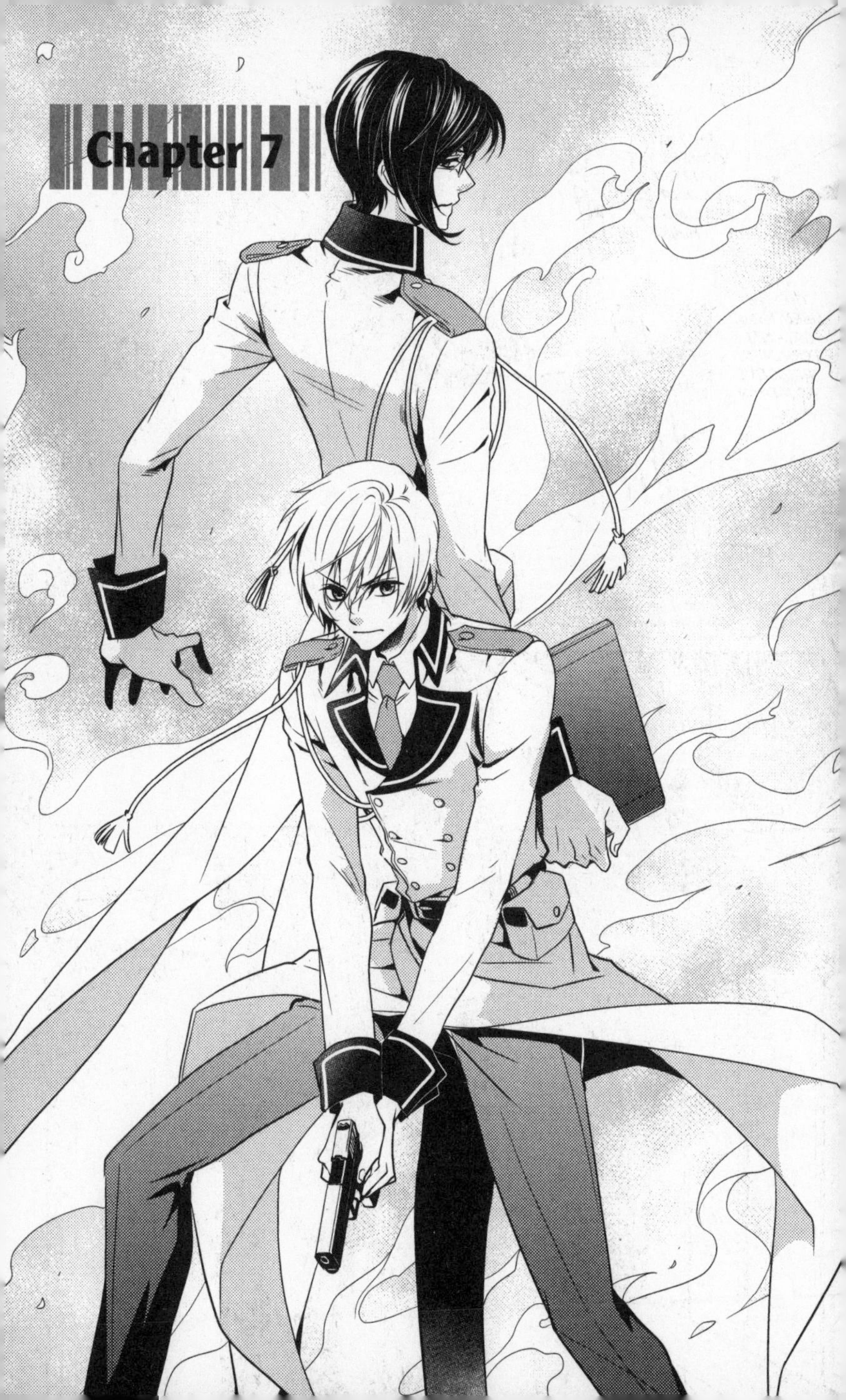
Chapter 7

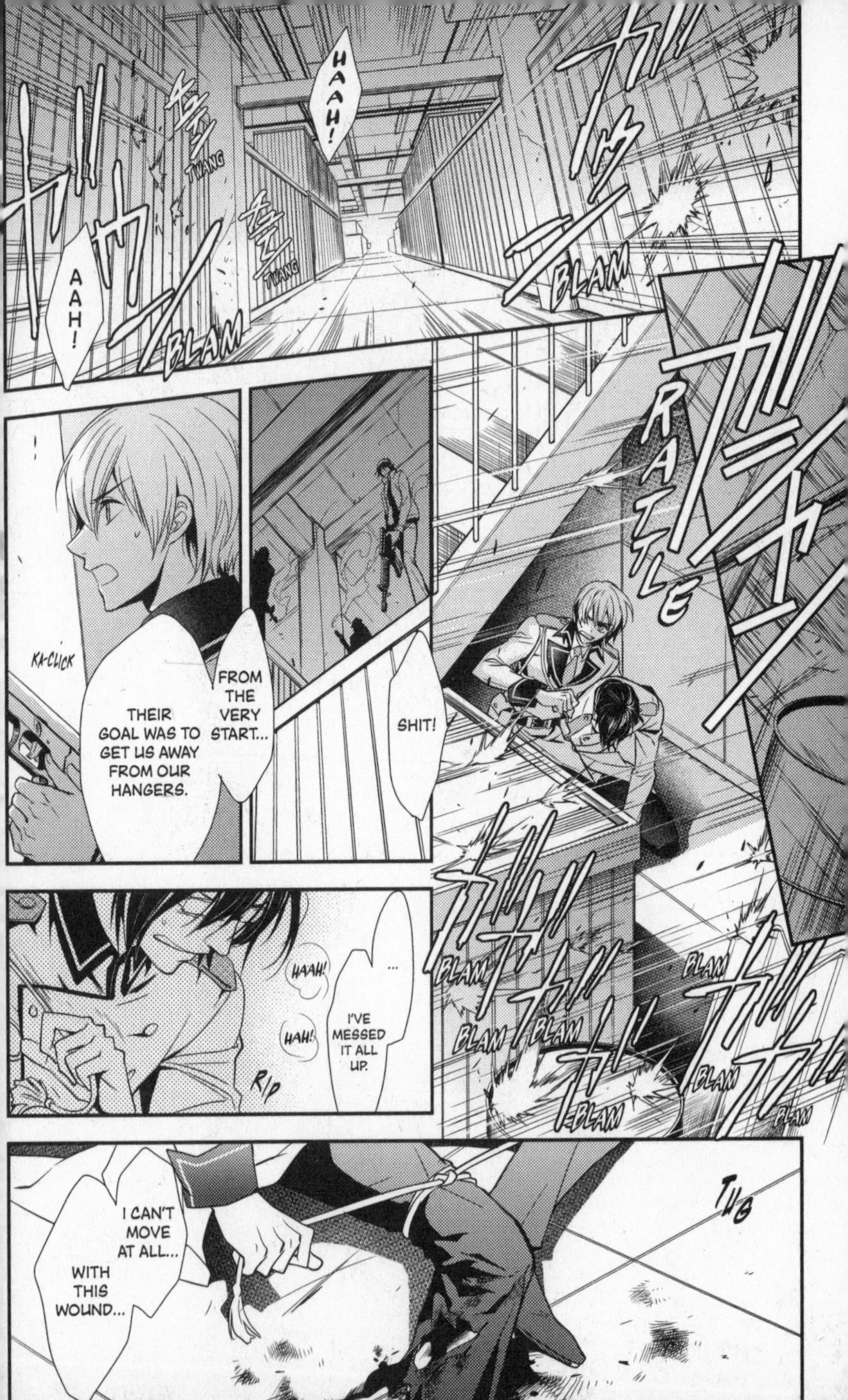
BLAM
HAAH!
TWANG
TWANG
BLAM
AAH!
RATTLE
SHIT!
BLAM
BLAM
BLAM
BLAM
BLAM
BLAM
BLAM
FROM THE VERY START...
!
THEIR GOAL WAS TO GET US AWAY FROM OUR HANGERS.
KA-CLICK
...
I'VE MESSED IT ALL UP.
HAAH!
HAAH!
RIP
TUG
I CAN'T MOVE AT ALL...
WITH THIS WOUND...

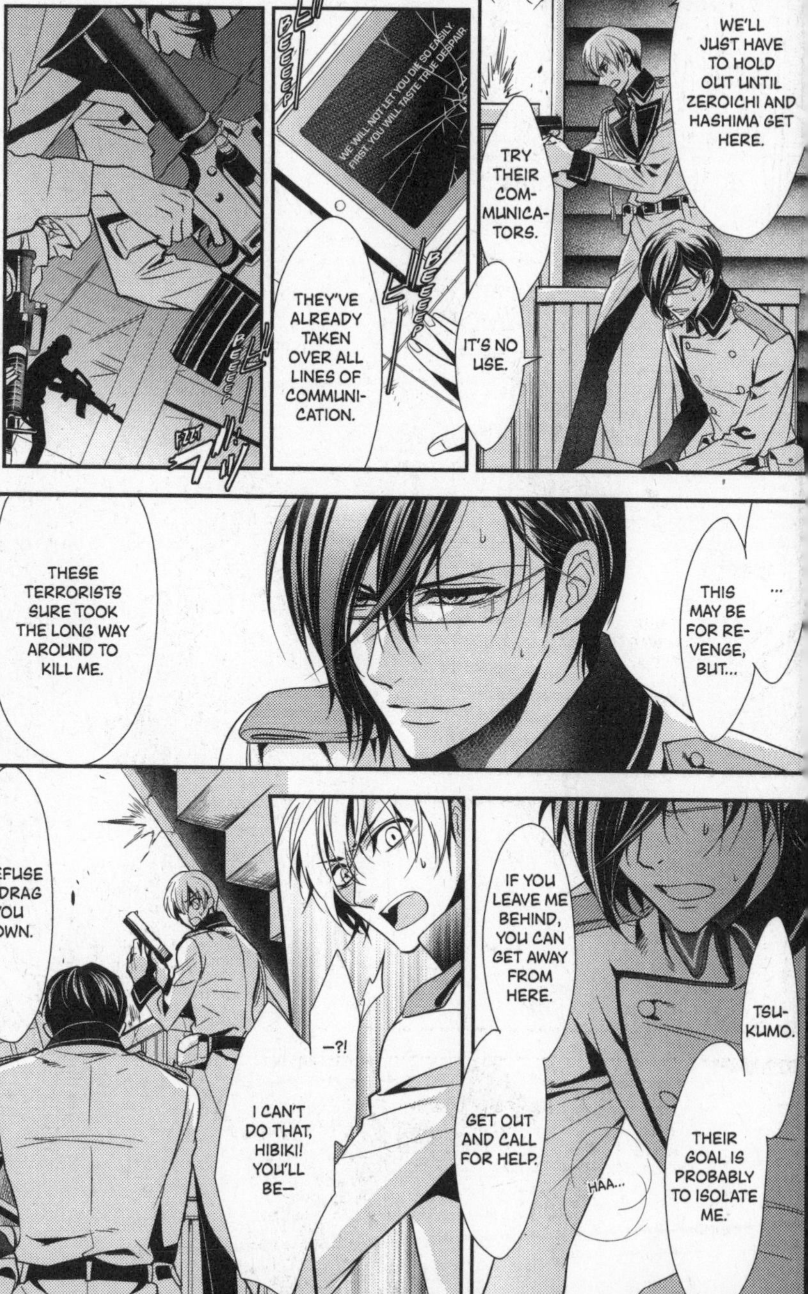
WE'LL JUST HAVE TO HOLD OUT UNTIL ZEROICHI AND HASHIMA GET HERE.
TRY THEIR COMMUNICATORS.
IT'S NO USE.
WE WILL NOT LET YOU DIE SO EASILY. FIRST, YOU WILL TASTE TRUE DESPAIR.
BEEEEP
BEEEEP
THEY'VE ALREADY TAKEN OVER ALL LINES OF COMMUNICATION.
BEEEEP
FZZT
...
THIS MAY BE FOR REVENGE, BUT...
THESE TERRORISTS SURE TOOK THE LONG WAY AROUND TO KILL ME.
TSUKUMO.
THEIR GOAL IS PROBABLY TO ISOLATE ME.
HAA...
IF YOU LEAVE ME BEHIND, YOU CAN GET AWAY FROM HERE.
GET OUT AND CALL FOR HELP.
—?!
I CAN'T DO THAT, HIBIKI! YOU'LL BE—
I REFUSE TO DRAG YOU DOWN.

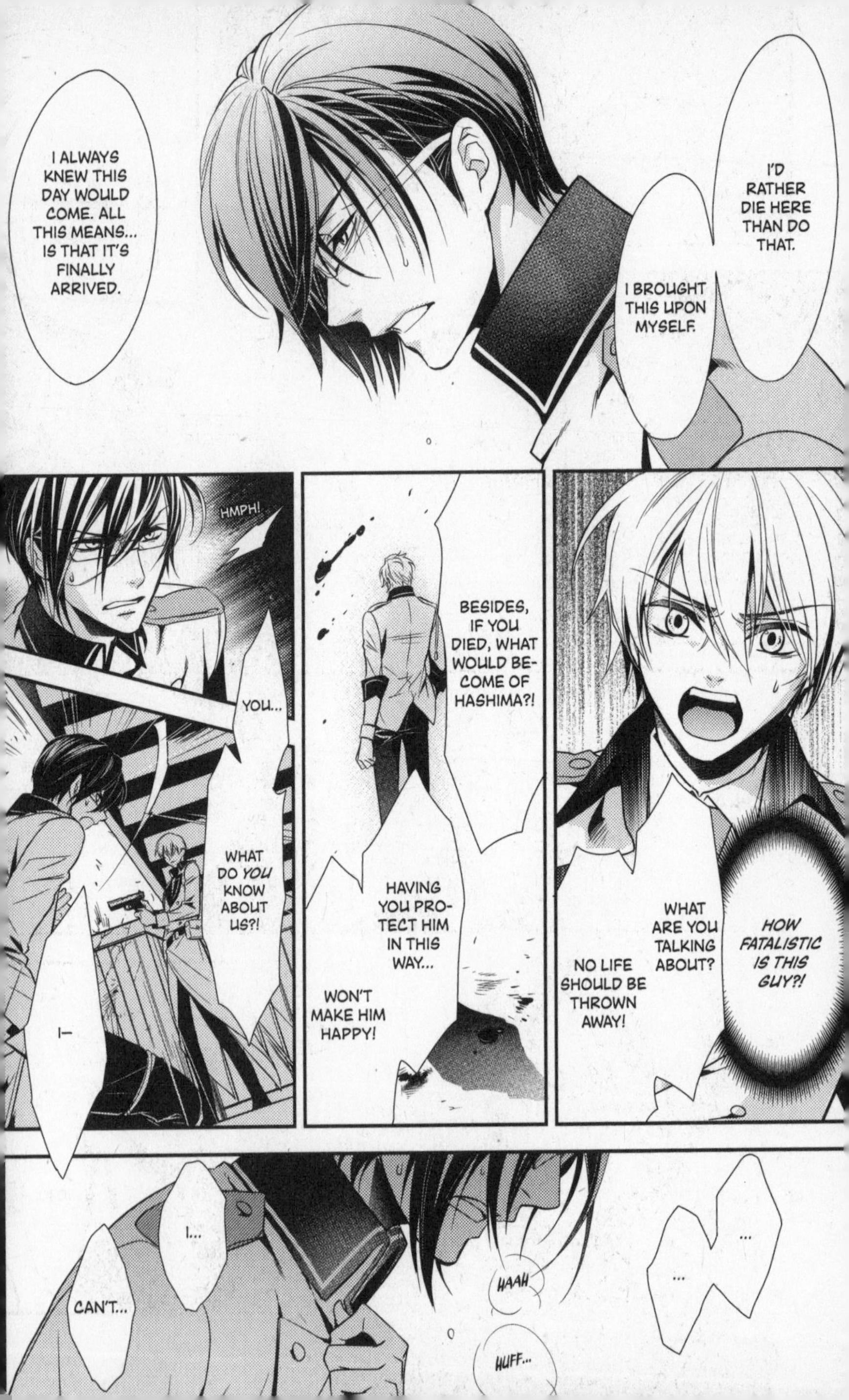
I'D RATHER DIE HERE THAN DO THAT.
I BROUGHT THIS UPON MYSELF.
I ALWAYS KNEW THIS DAY WOULD COME. ALL THIS MEANS... IS THAT IT'S FINALLY ARRIVED.
HOW FATALISTIC IS THIS GUY?!
WHAT ARE YOU TALKING ABOUT?
NO LIFE SHOULD BE THROWN AWAY!
BESIDES, IF YOU DIED, WHAT WOULD BE-COME OF HASHIMA?!
HAVING YOU PRO-TECT HIM IN THIS WAY...
WON'T MAKE HIM HAPPY!
HMPH!
YOU...
WHAT DO YOU KNOW ABOUT US?!
I—
...
...
HAAH
HUFF...
I...
CAN'T...

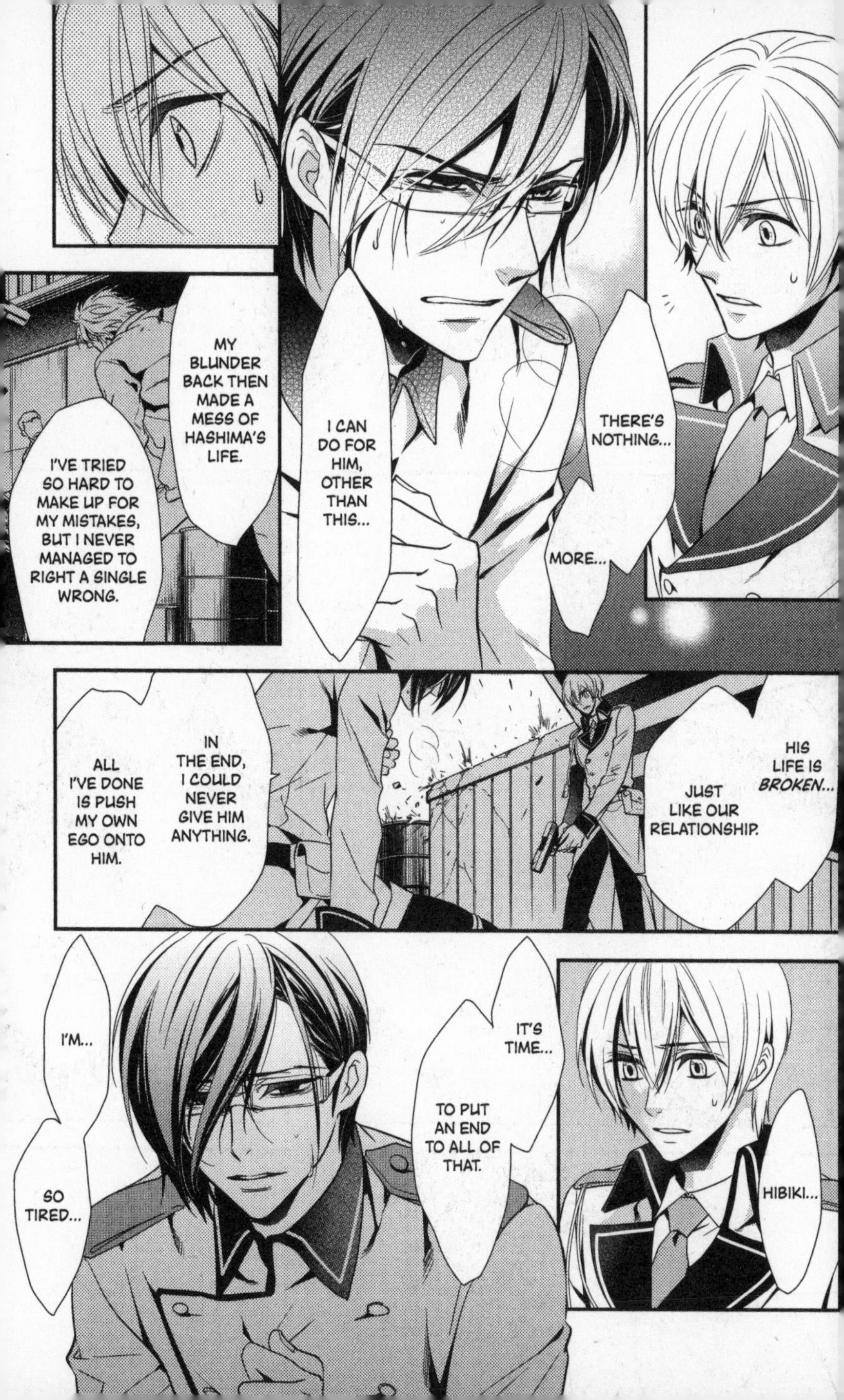
THERE'S NOTHING...
MORE...
I CAN DO FOR HIM, OTHER THAN THIS...
MY BLUNDER BACK THEN MADE A MESS OF HASHIMA'S LIFE.
I'VE TRIED SO HARD TO MAKE UP FOR MY MISTAKES, BUT I NEVER MANAGED TO RIGHT A SINGLE WRONG.
HIS LIFE IS *BROKEN*...
JUST LIKE OUR RELATIONSHIP.
IN THE END, I COULD NEVER GIVE HIM ANYTHING.
ALL I'VE DONE IS PUSH MY OWN EGO ONTO HIM.
HIBIKI...
IT'S TIME...
TO PUT AN END TO ALL OF THAT.
I'M...
SO TIRED...

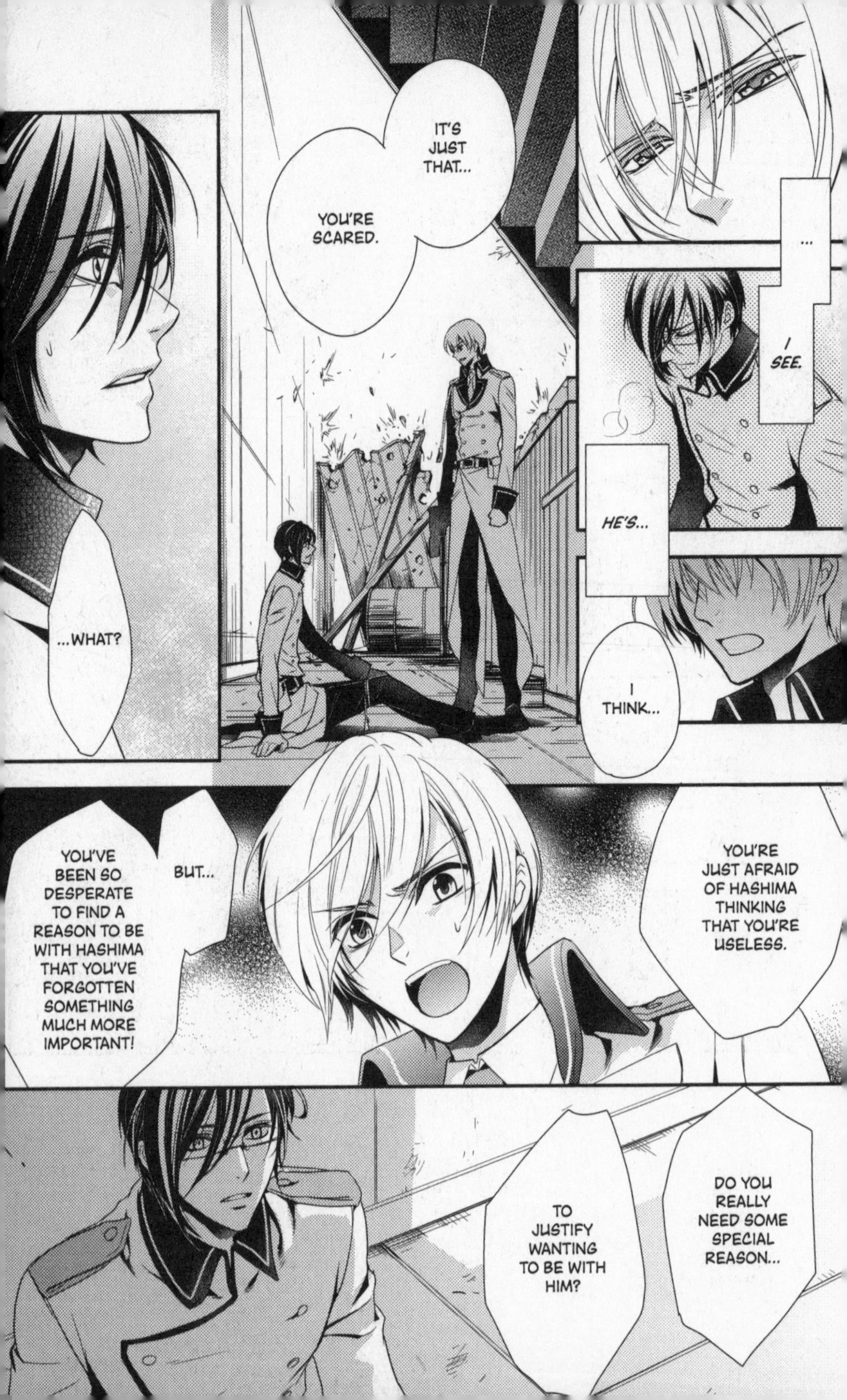
...
I SEE.
HE'S...
I THINK...
IT'S JUST THAT...
YOU'RE SCARED.
...WHAT?
YOU'RE JUST AFRAID OF HASHIMA THINKING THAT YOU'RE USELESS.
BUT...
YOU'VE BEEN SO DESPERATE TO FIND A REASON TO BE WITH HASHIMA THAT YOU'VE FORGOTTEN SOMETHING MUCH MORE IMPORTANT!
DO YOU REALLY NEED SOME SPECIAL REASON...
TO JUSTIFY WANTING TO BE WITH HIM?

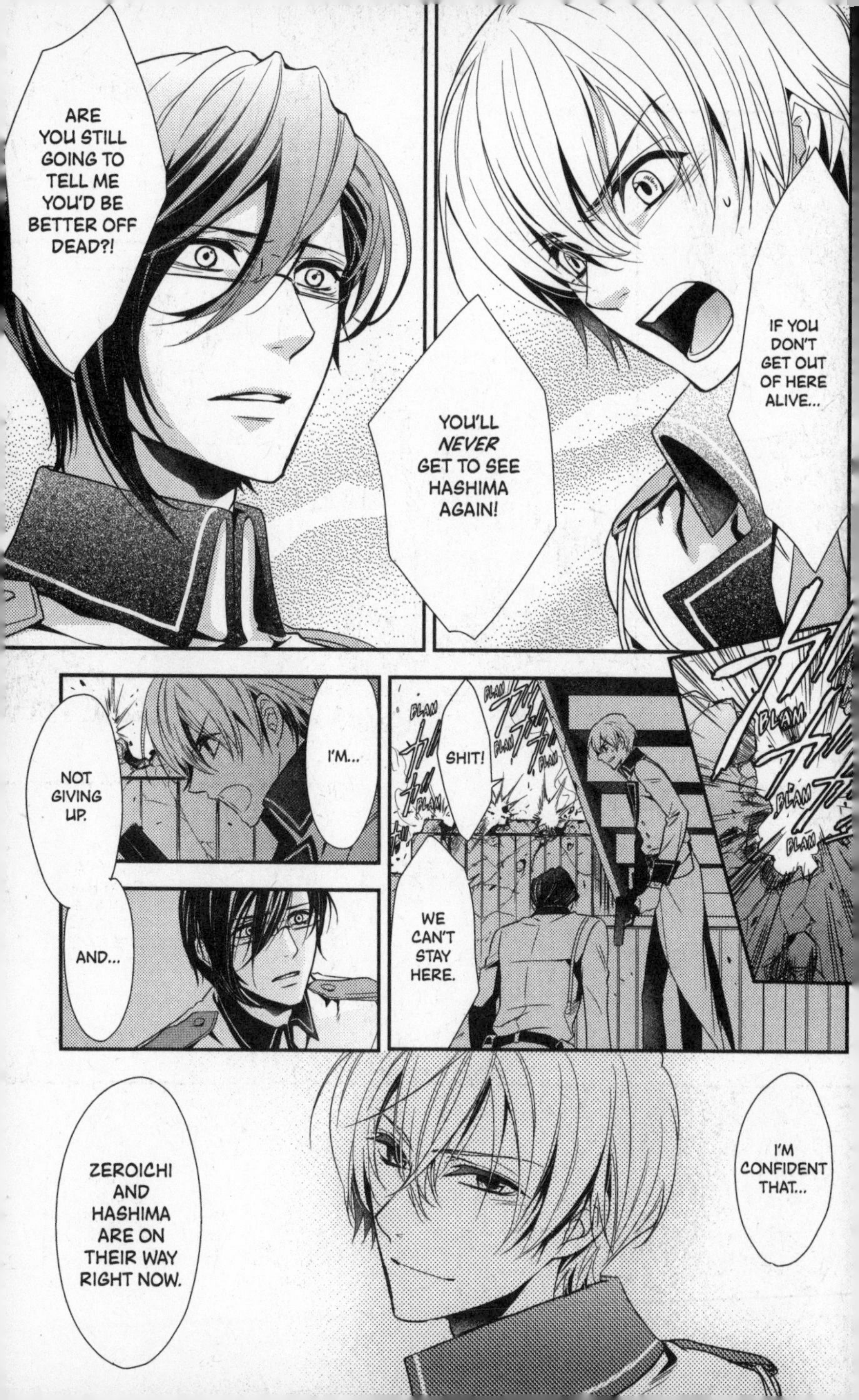
IF YOU DON'T GET OUT OF HERE ALIVE...
YOU'LL *NEVER* GET TO SEE HASHIMA AGAIN!
ARE YOU STILL GOING TO TELL ME YOU'D BE BETTER OFF DEAD?!
BLAM
BLAM
BLAM
BLAM
BLAM
BLAM
SHIT!
BLAM
BLAM
BLAM
WE CAN'T STAY HERE.
I'M...
NOT GIVING UP.
AND...
I'M CONFIDENT THAT...
ZEROICHI AND HASHIMA ARE ON THEIR WAY RIGHT NOW.

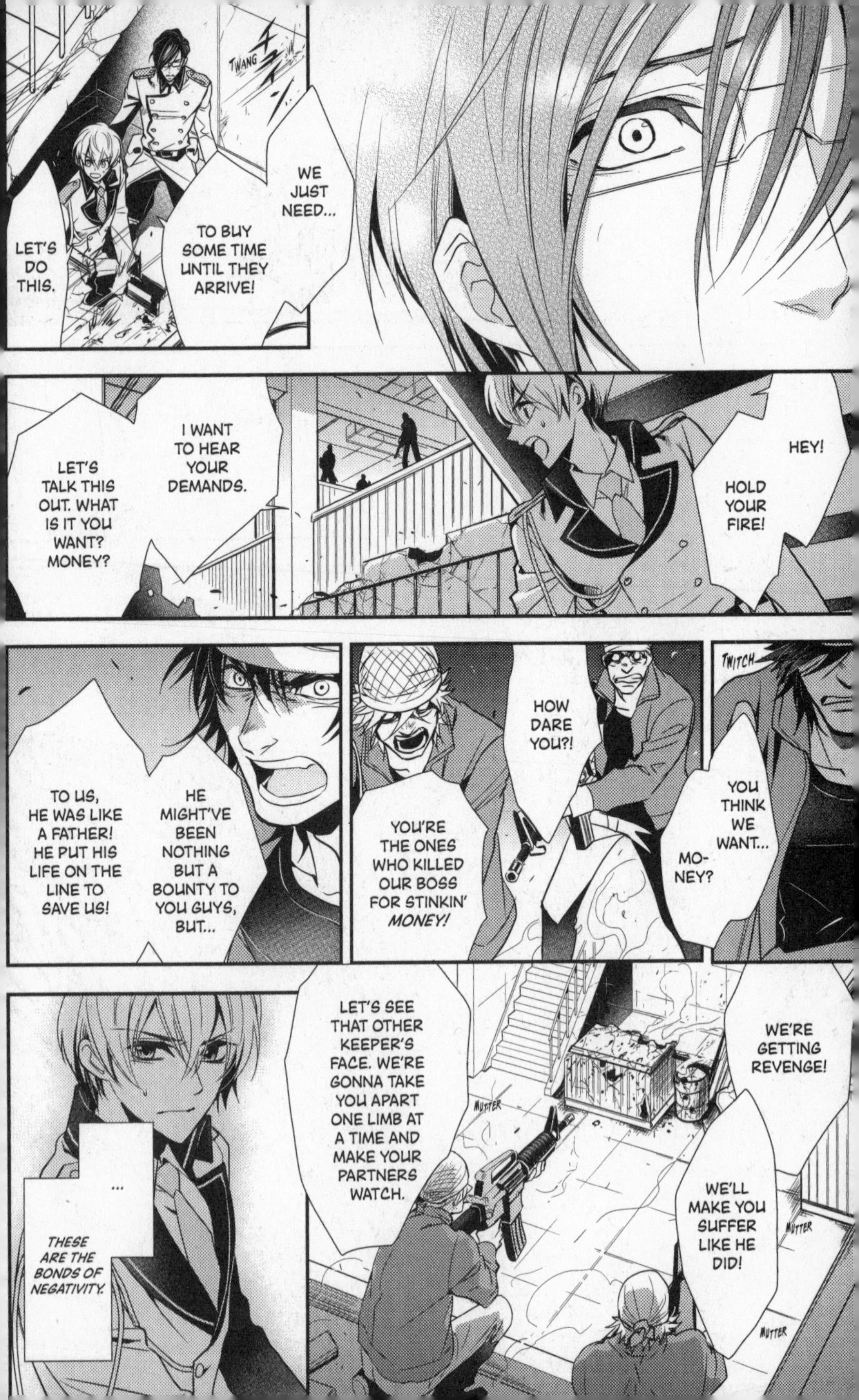
TWANG
WE JUST NEED...
TO BUY SOME TIME UNTIL THEY ARRIVE!
LET'S DO THIS.
HEY!
HOLD YOUR FIRE!
I WANT TO HEAR YOUR DEMANDS.
LET'S TALK THIS OUT. WHAT IS IT YOU WANT? MONEY?
TWITCH
YOU THINK WE WANT...
MO-NEY?
HOW DARE YOU?!
YOU'RE THE ONES WHO KILLED OUR BOSS FOR STINKIN' *MONEY!*
HE MIGHT'VE BEEN NOTHING BUT A BOUNTY TO YOU GUYS, BUT...
TO US, HE WAS LIKE A FATHER! HE PUT HIS LIFE ON THE LINE TO SAVE US!
WE'RE GETTING REVENGE!
WE'LL MAKE YOU SUFFER LIKE HE DID!
MUTTER
MUTTER
LET'S SEE THAT OTHER KEEPER'S FACE. WE'RE GONNA TAKE YOU APART ONE LIMB AT A TIME AND MAKE YOUR PARTNERS WATCH.
MUTTER
...
THESE ARE THE BONDS OF NEGATIVITY.

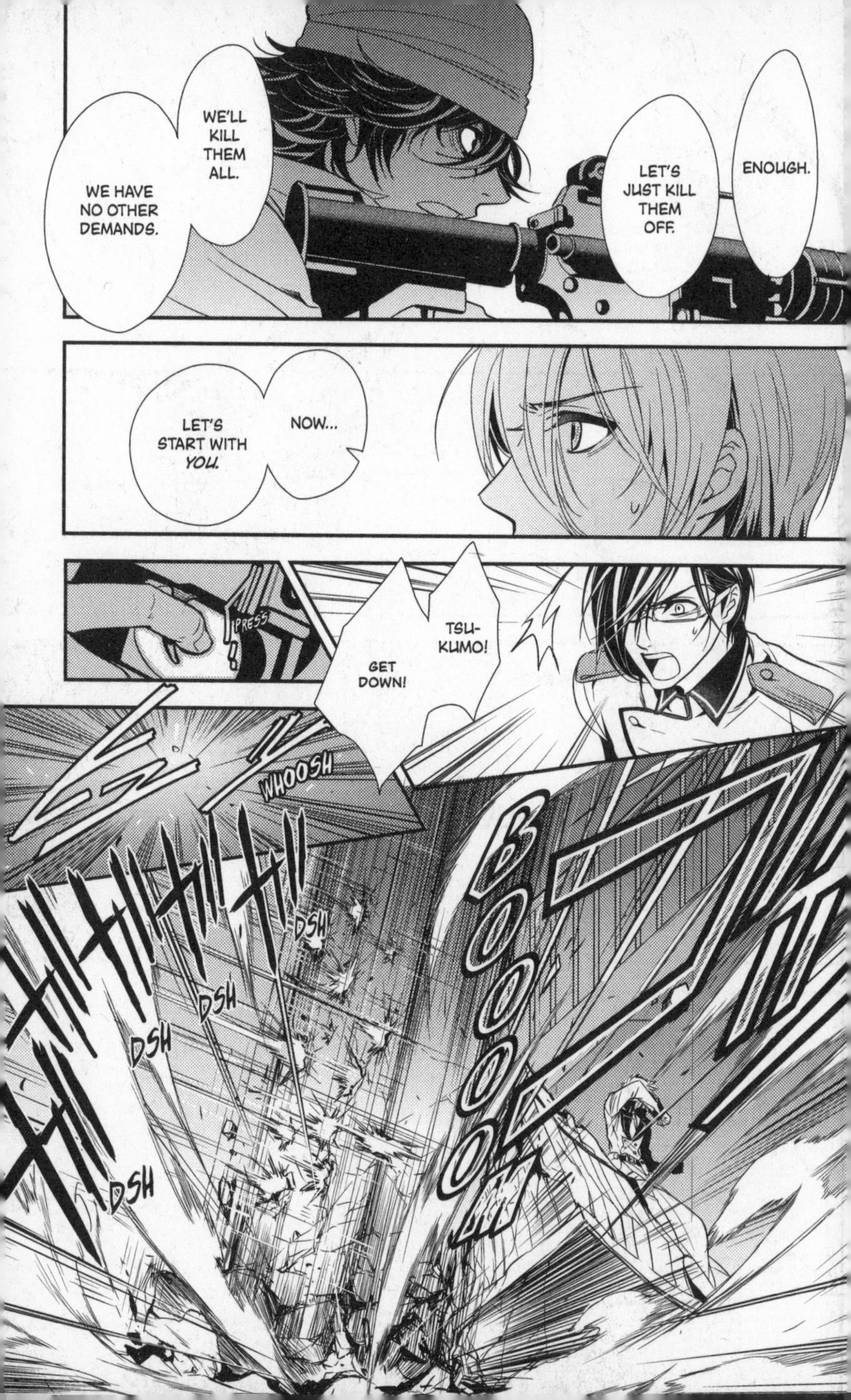
ENOUGH.
LET'S JUST KILL THEM OFF.
WE'LL KILL THEM ALL.
WE HAVE NO OTHER DEMANDS.
NOW...
LET'S START WITH YOU.
TSU-KUMO!
GET DOWN!
PRESS
BOOOOOM
WHOOSH
DSH
DSH
DSH
DSH

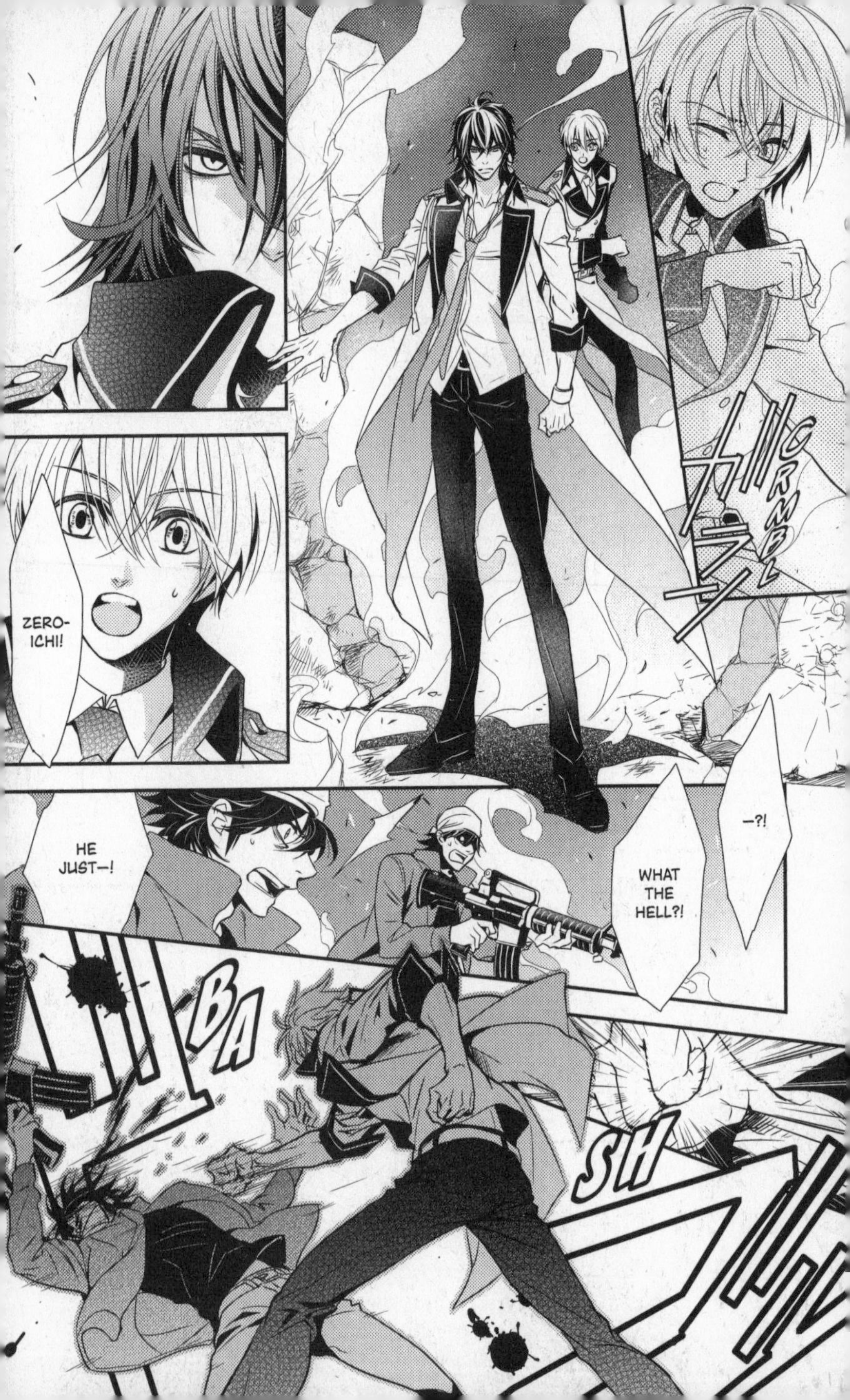

GRMBL
ZERO-ICHI!
—?!
WHAT THE HELL?!
HE JUST—!
SH
BA

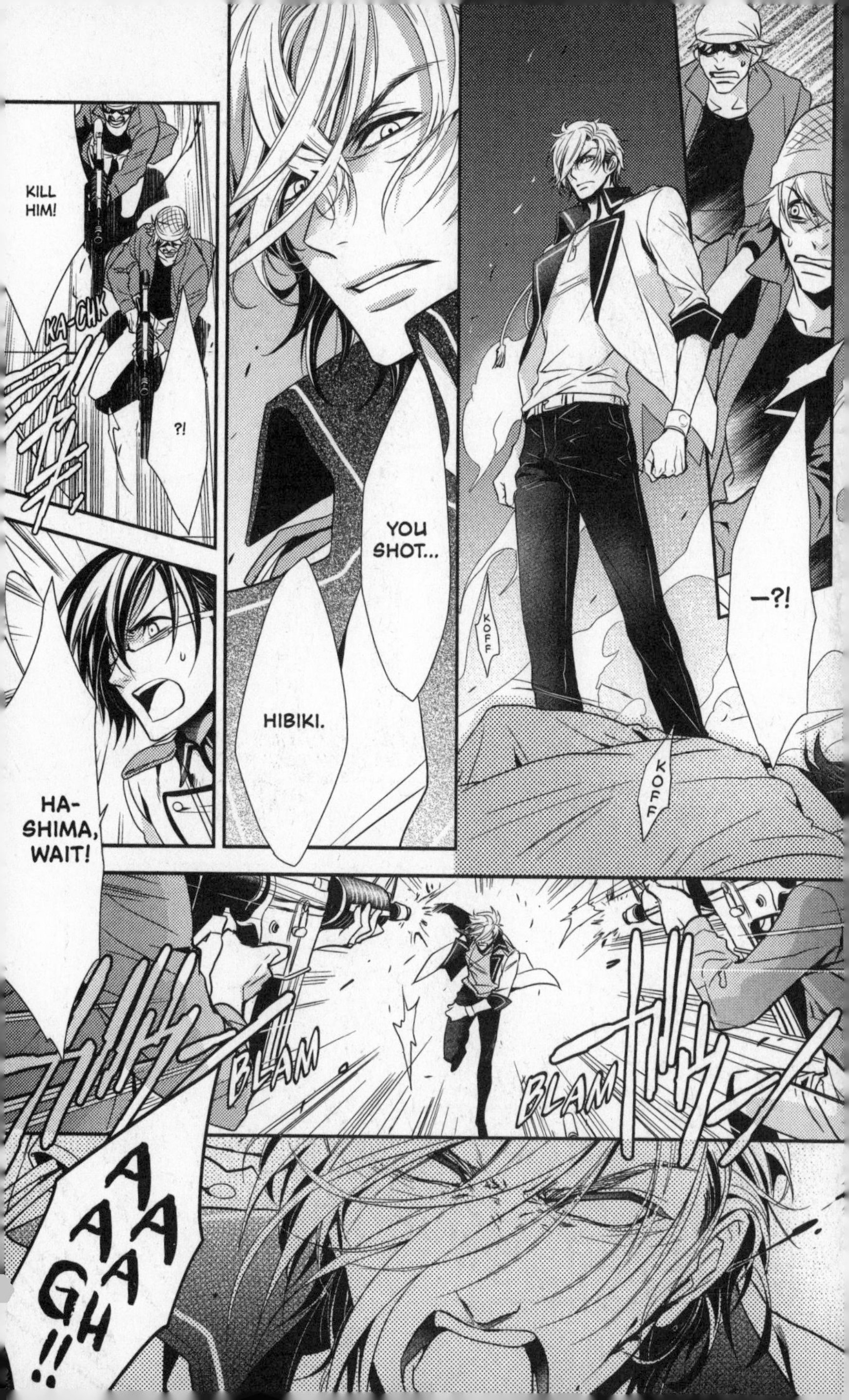
—?!
KOFF
KOFF
YOU SHOT...
HIBIKI.
KILL HIM!
KA-CHK
?!
HA-SHIMA, WAIT!
BLAM
BLAM
AAAAGH!!

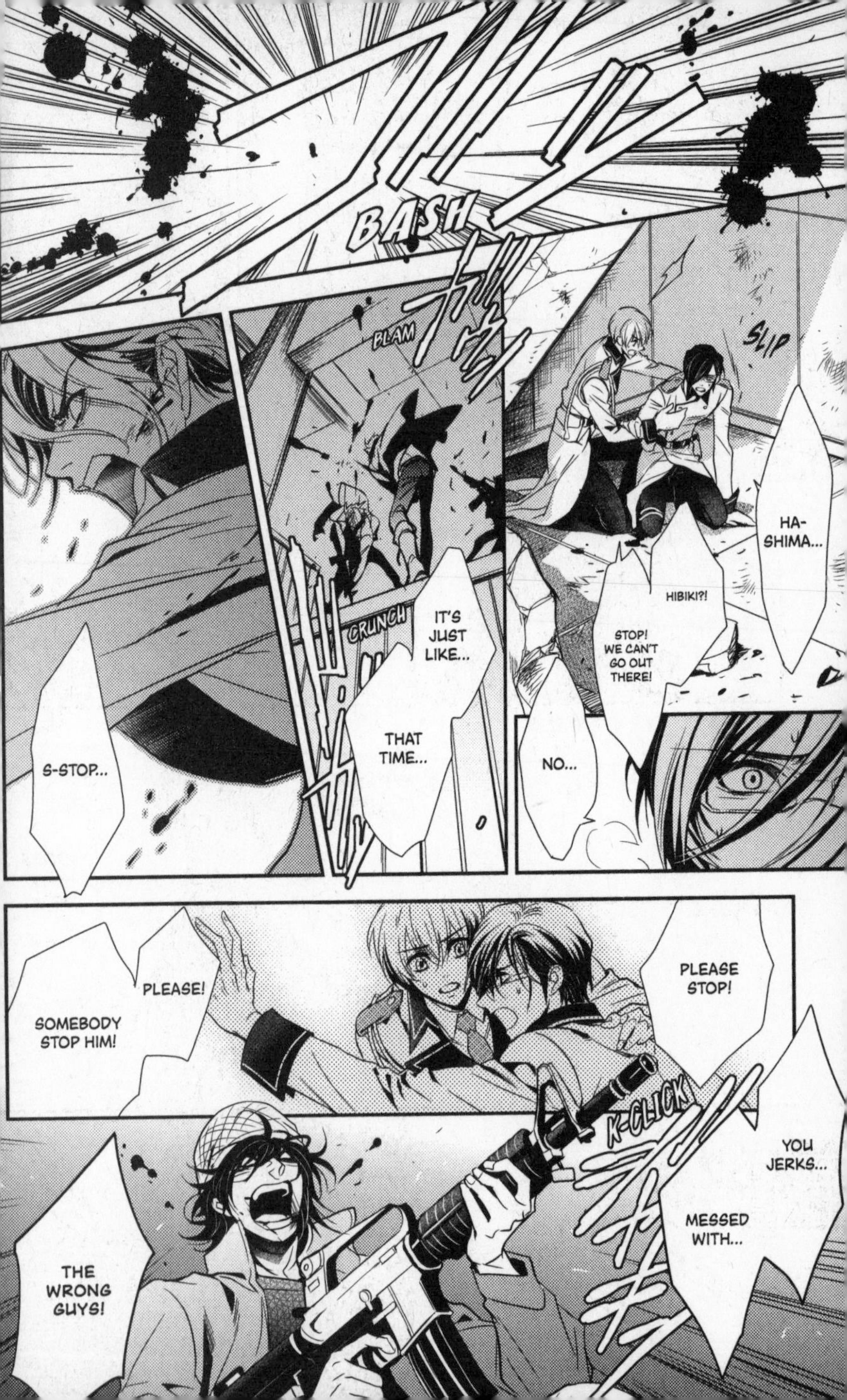
BASH
SLIP
HA-SHIMA...
HIBIKI?!
STOP! WE CAN'T GO OUT THERE!
NO...
BLAM
CRUNCH
IT'S JUST LIKE...
THAT TIME...
S-STOP...
PLEASE STOP!
PLEASE!
SOMEBODY STOP HIM!
K-CLICK
YOU JERKS...
MESSED WITH...
THE WRONG GUYS!

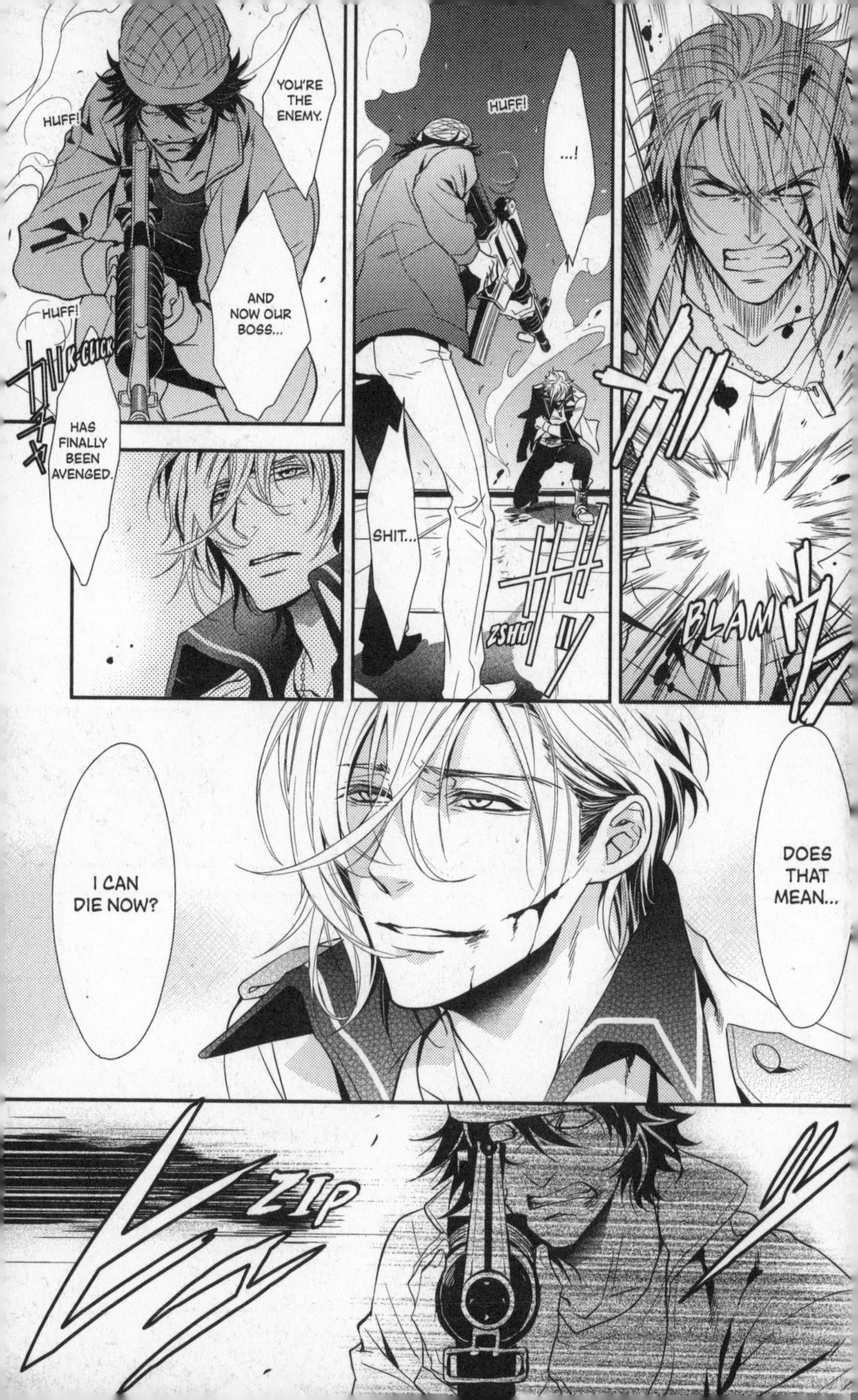
BLAM
HUFF!
...!
SHIT...
ZSHH
YOU'RE THE ENEMY.
HUFF!
HUFF!
AND NOW OUR BOSS...
K-CLICK
HAS FINALLY BEEN AVENGED.
DOES THAT MEAN...
I CAN DIE NOW?
ZIP

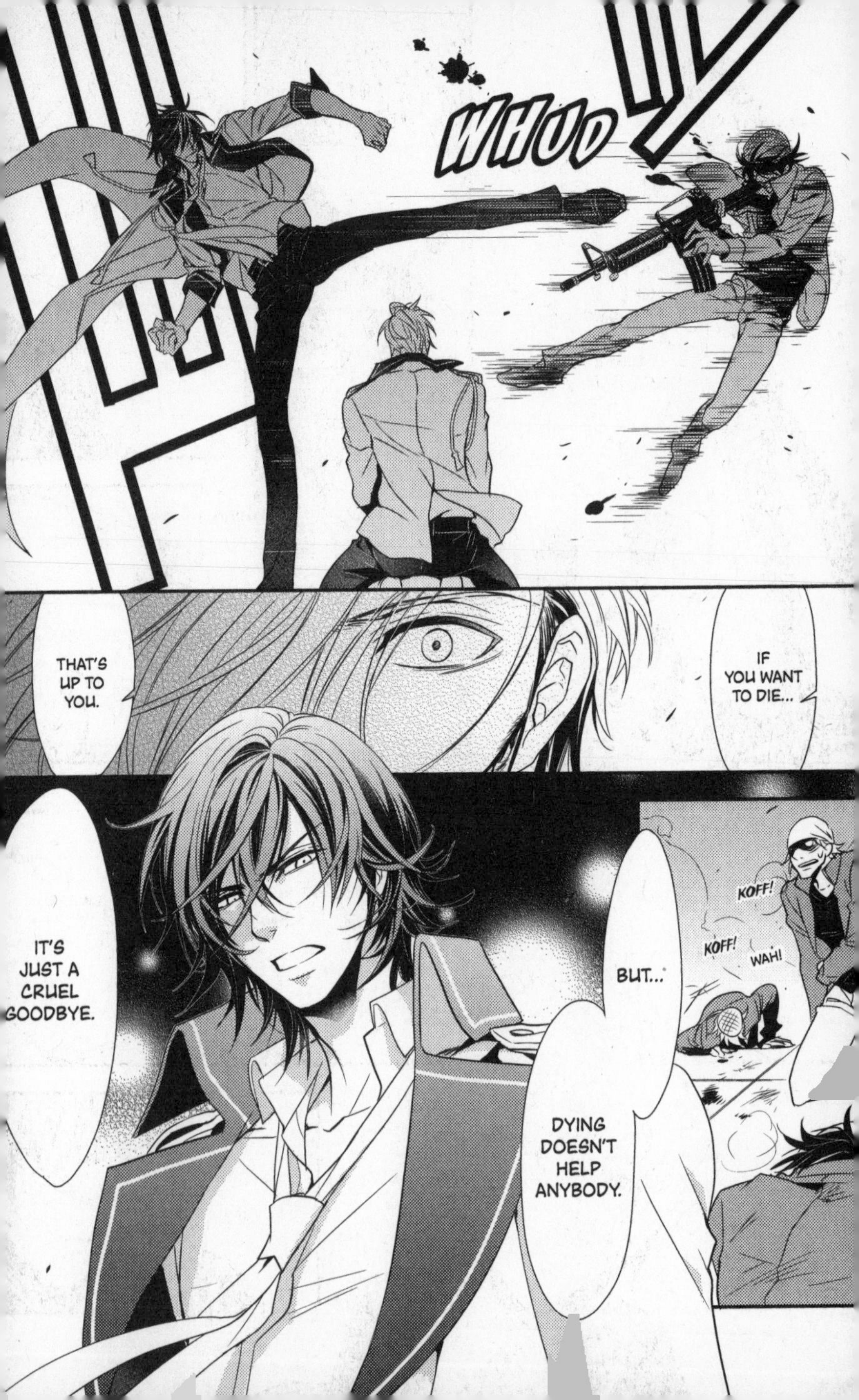
WHUD
IF YOU WANT TO DIE...
THAT'S UP TO YOU.
KOFF!
KOFF!
WAH!
BUT...
DYING DOESN'T HELP ANYBODY.
IT'S JUST A CRUEL GOODBYE.

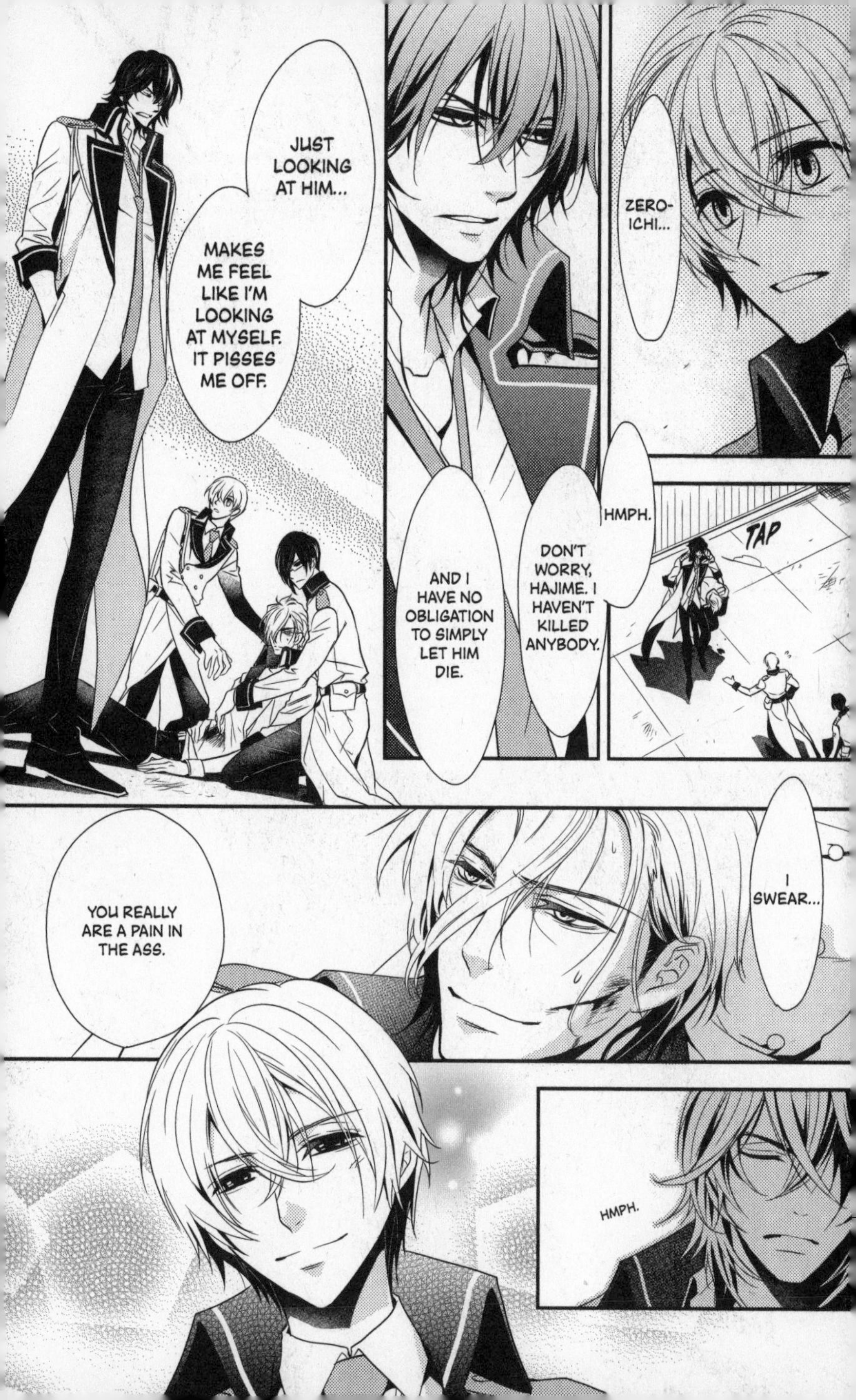
ZERO-ICHI...
TAP
HMPH.
DON'T WORRY, HAJIME. I HAVEN'T KILLED ANYBODY.
AND I HAVE NO OBLIGATION TO SIMPLY LET HIM DIE.
JUST LOOKING AT HIM...
MAKES ME FEEL LIKE I'M LOOKING AT MYSELF. IT PISSES ME OFF.
I SWEAR...
YOU REALLY ARE A PAIN IN THE ASS.
HMPH.

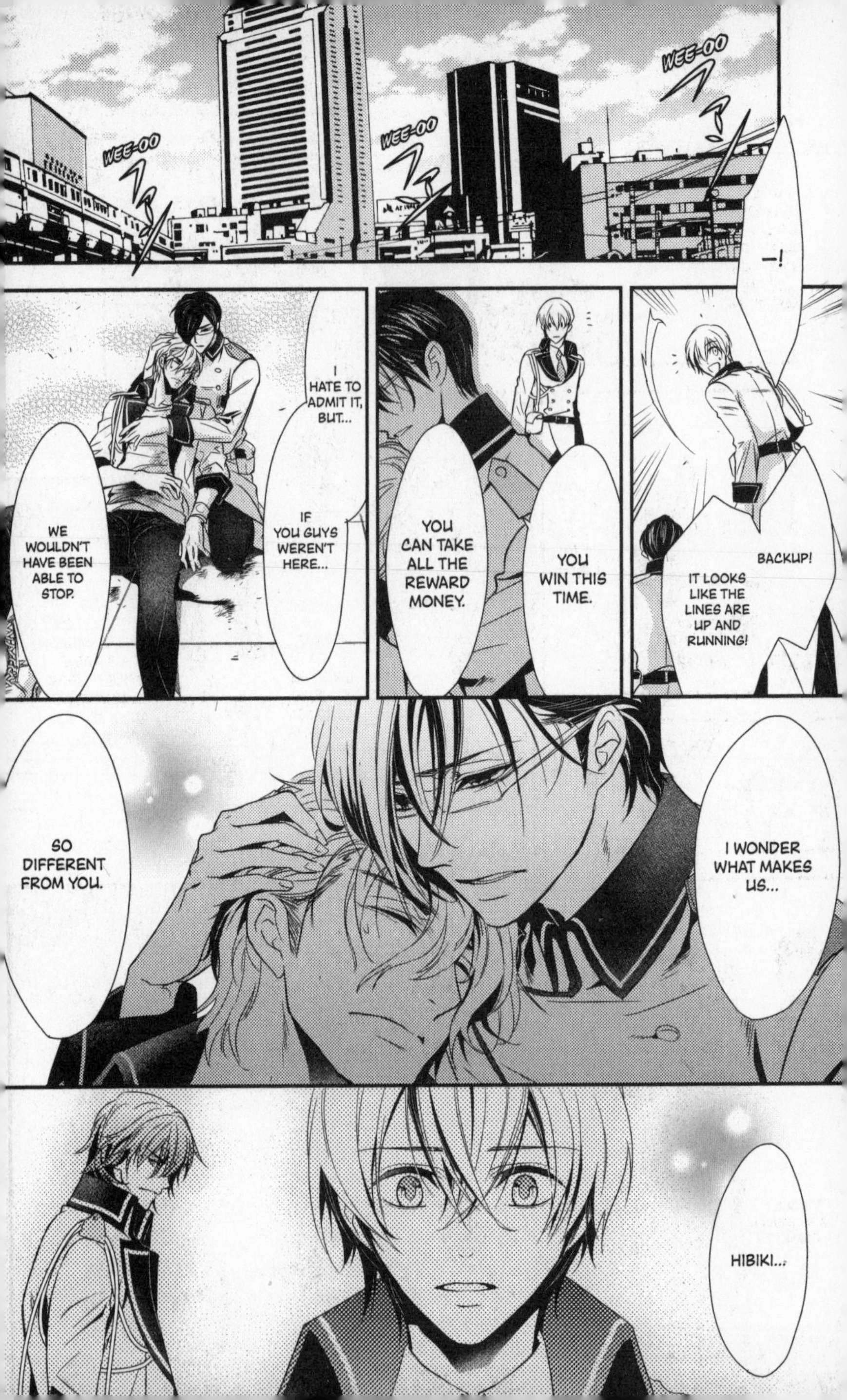
WEE-OO
WEE-OO
WEE-OO
—!
BACKUP!
IT LOOKS LIKE THE LINES ARE UP AND RUNNING!
YOU WIN THIS TIME.
YOU CAN TAKE ALL THE REWARD MONEY.
I HATE TO ADMIT IT, BUT...
IF YOU GUYS WEREN'T HERE...
WE WOULDN'T HAVE BEEN ABLE TO STOP.
I WONDER WHAT MAKES US...
SO DIFFERENT FROM YOU.
HIBIKI...

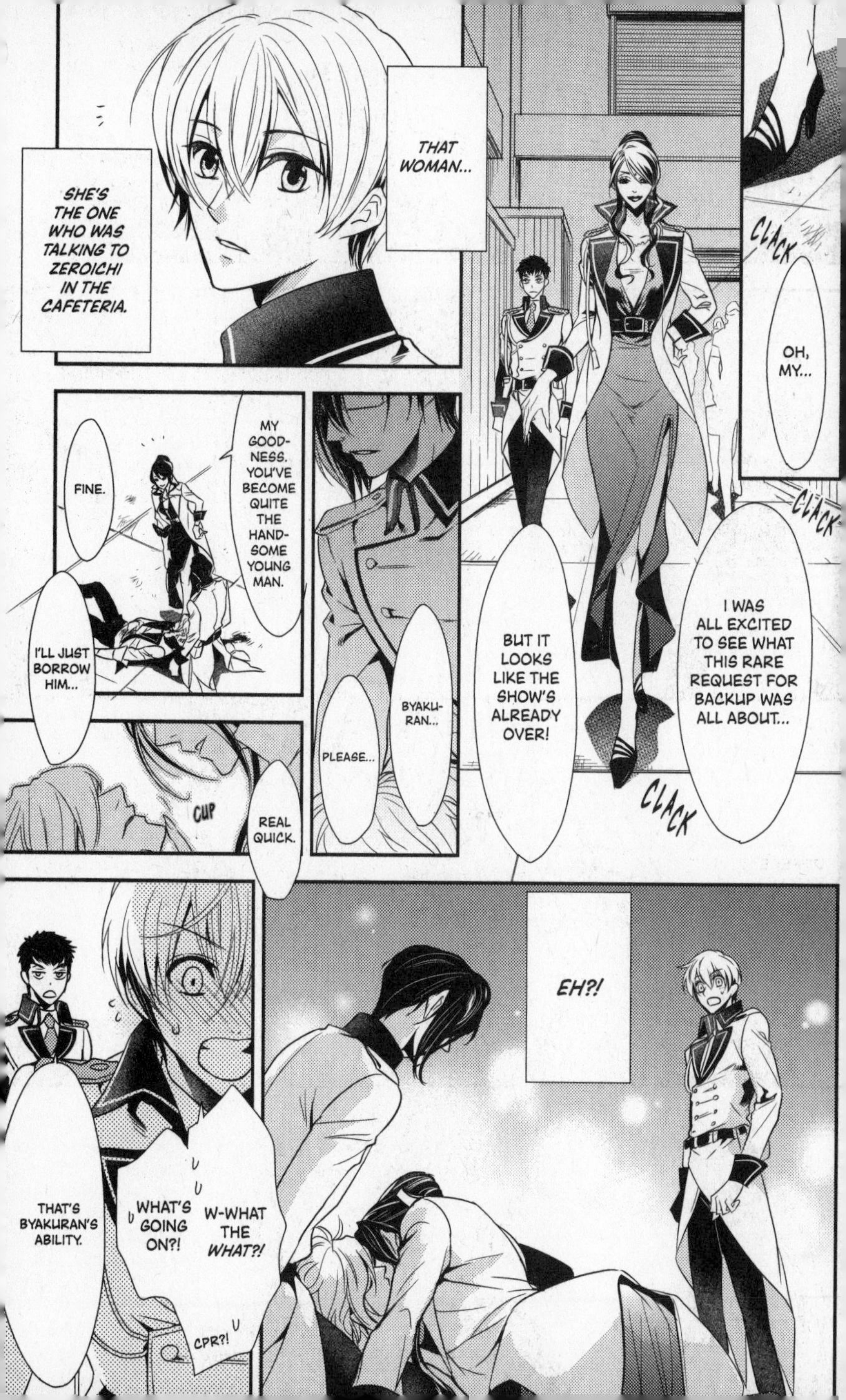
CLACK
OH, MY...
CLACK
THAT WOMAN...
SHE'S THE ONE WHO WAS TALKING TO ZEROICHI IN THE CAFETERIA.
I WAS ALL EXCITED TO SEE WHAT THIS RARE REQUEST FOR BACKUP WAS ALL ABOUT...
BUT IT LOOKS LIKE THE SHOW'S ALREADY OVER!
CLACK
BYAKURAN...
PLEASE...
MY GOODNESS. YOU'VE BECOME QUITE THE HANDSOME YOUNG MAN.
FINE.
I'LL JUST BORROW HIM...
REAL QUICK.
CUP
EH?!
W-WHAT THE WHAT?!
WHAT'S GOING ON?!
THAT'S BYAKURAN'S ABILITY.
CPR?!

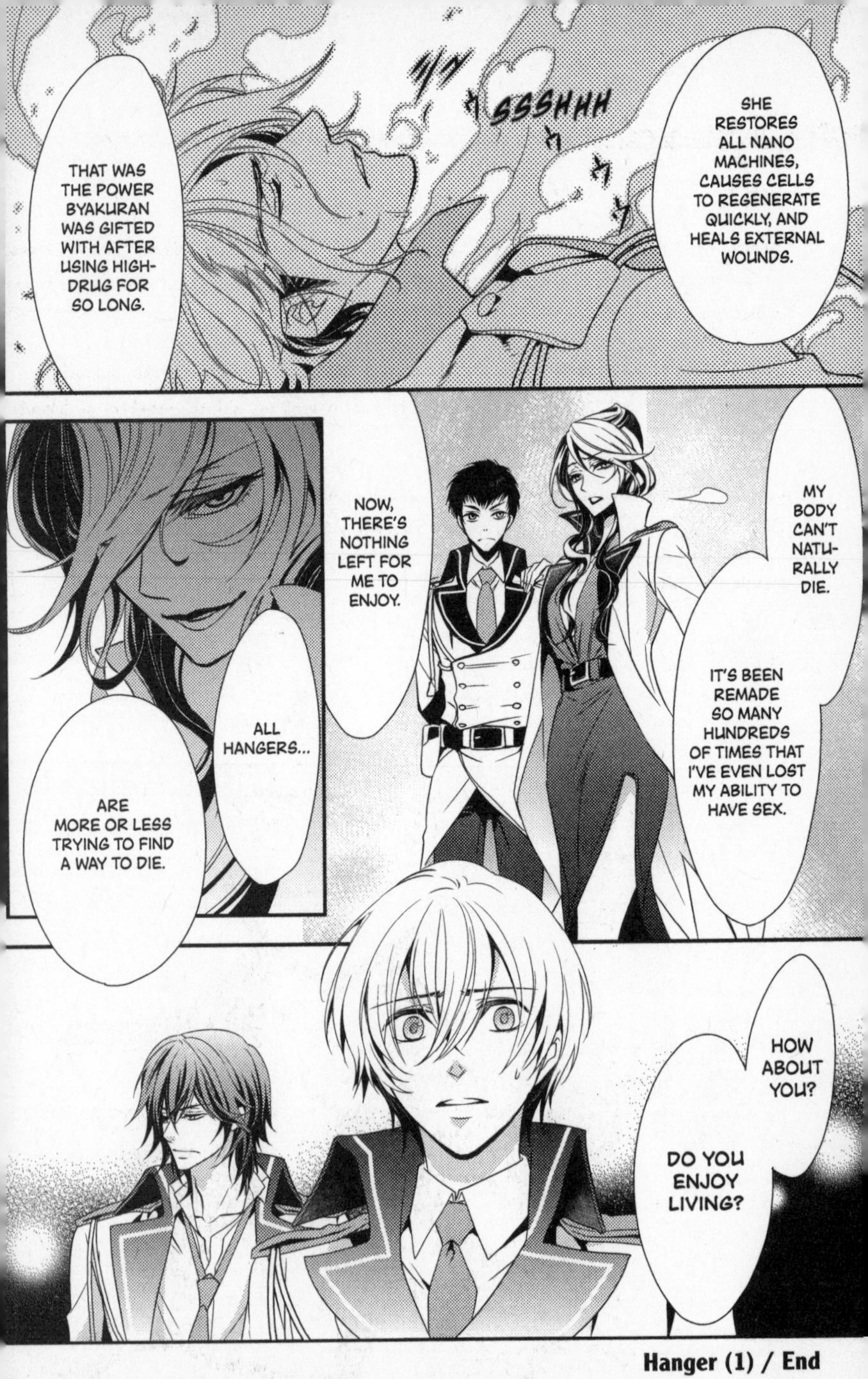
SHE RESTORES ALL NANO MACHINES, CAUSES CELLS TO REGENERATE QUICKLY, AND HEALS EXTERNAL WOUNDS.
SSSHHH
THAT WAS THE POWER BYAKURAN WAS GIFTED WITH AFTER USING HIGH-DRUG FOR SO LONG.
MY BODY CAN'T NATU-RALLY DIE.
IT'S BEEN REMADE SO MANY HUNDREDS OF TIMES THAT I'VE EVEN LOST MY ABILITY TO HAVE SEX.
NOW, THERE'S NOTHING LEFT FOR ME TO ENJOY.
ALL HANGERS...
ARE MORE OR LESS TRYING TO FIND A WAY TO DIE.
HOW ABOUT YOU?
DO YOU ENJOY LIVING?

Hanger (1) / End

Afterword

Hello, this is Hirotaka Kisaragi.

Thank you so much for reading Volume 1 of HANGER! At the start of this serialization, I was so generously told to build a world that I liked, so I went with uniforms and a near-future type of buddy cop story.♡

Basically, this is what happens when I throw in every kind of self-indulgent trope and get to draw whatever I want! I hope you look forward to more adventures with the members of Squad 4 and all their unique quirks!

I would like to thank everyone in the editorial department who helped me so much, and more than anything, everyone who read this book. Thank you from the very bottom of my heart!

Hirotaka Kisaragi

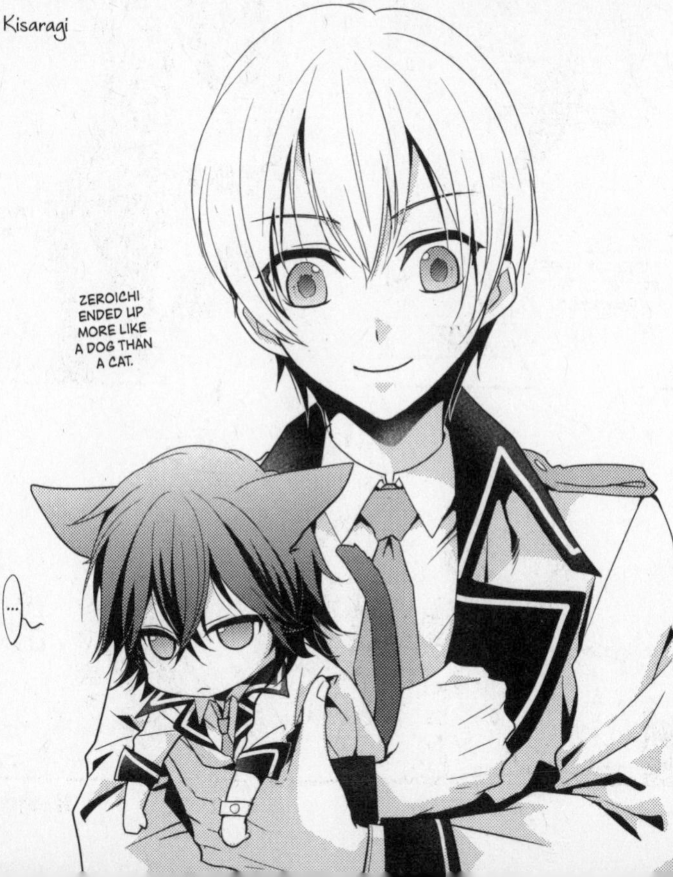
ZEROICHI ENDED UP MORE LIKE A DOG THAN A CAT.
...

HANGER

IN THE NEXT VOLUME OF

HANGER

AFTER SO MANY RECENT CLOSE CALLS, ZEROICHI STRUGGLES TO ACCEPT HAJIME'S DETERMINATION TO KEEP WORKING ALONGSIDE HIM. IN HIS DESPERATION TO KEEP HAJIME FROM MEETING THE SAME TRAGIC FATE AS HIS PREVIOUS KEEPER, ZEROICHI PULLS FURTHER AWAY, PUTTING EVEN MORE EMOTIONAL DISTANCE BETWEEN THEM... AND LEAVING HAJIME TO WONDER WHAT KIND OF RELATIONSHIP THEY REALLY HAVE.

UNFORTUNATELY, IT SEEMS THEY WON'T HAVE THE LUXURY OF TIME TO FIGURE IT OUT— NOT WITH THE TERRORIST ORGANIZATION THAT TOOK THE LIFE OF ZEROICHI'S FORMER KEEPER ON THE LOOSE IN NEO-TOKYO ONCE MORE. IN THE FACE OF EVEN GREATER DANGER AND HIGHER THAN EVER STAKES, ZEROICHI MUST LEARN TO MOVE PAST THE FEAR THAT HAS BEEN DRIVING THEM APART AND RELY ON HAJIME AS A TRUE PARTNER.

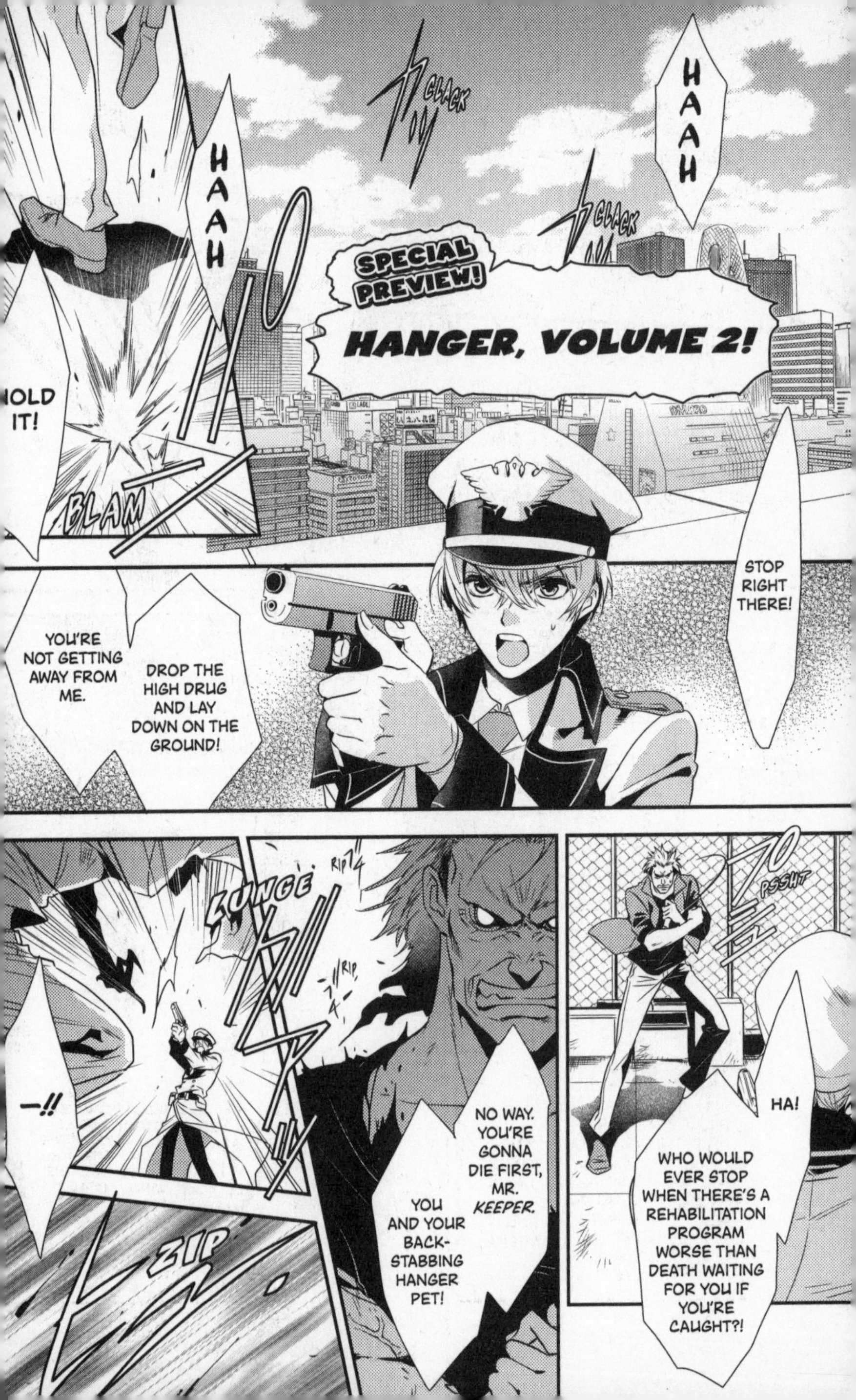
HAAAH
CLACK
CLACK
SPECIAL PREVIEW!
HANGER, VOLUME 2!
HAAAH
OLD IT!
BLAM
STOP RIGHT THERE!
DROP THE HIGH DRUG AND LAY DOWN ON THE GROUND!
YOU'RE NOT GETTING AWAY FROM ME.
PSSHT
HA!
WHO WOULD EVER STOP WHEN THERE'S A REHABILITATION PROGRAM WORSE THAN DEATH WAITING FOR YOU IF YOU'RE CAUGHT?!
NO WAY. YOU'RE GONNA DIE FIRST, MR. *KEEPER*.
YOU AND YOUR BACK-STABBING HANGER PET!
RIP
RIP
LUNGE
—!!
ZIP

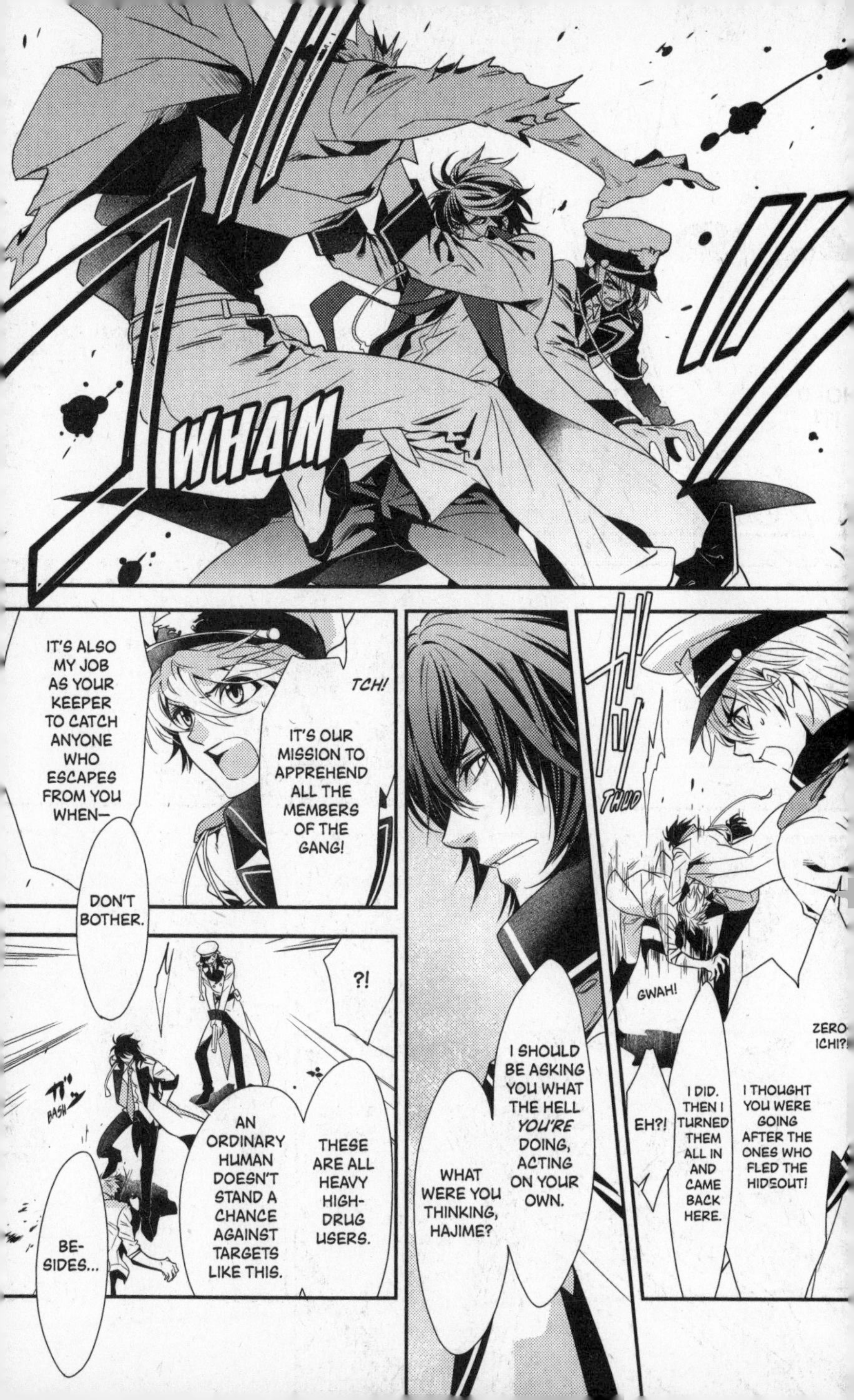
WHAM
THUD
GWAH!
ZERO-ICHI?!
I THOUGHT YOU WERE GOING AFTER THE ONES WHO FLED THE HIDEOUT!
I DID. THEN I TURNED THEM ALL IN AND CAME BACK HERE.
EH?!
I SHOULD BE ASKING YOU WHAT THE HELL *YOU'RE* DOING, ACTING ON YOUR OWN.
WHAT WERE YOU THINKING, HAJIME?
TCH!
IT'S OUR MISSION TO APPREHEND ALL THE MEMBERS OF THE GANG!
IT'S ALSO MY JOB AS YOUR KEEPER TO CATCH ANYONE WHO ESCAPES FROM YOU WHEN—
DON'T BOTHER.
?!
BASH
THESE ARE ALL HEAVY HIGH-DRUG USERS.
AN ORDINARY HUMAN DOESN'T STAND A CHANCE AGAINST TARGETS LIKE THIS.
BE-SIDES...

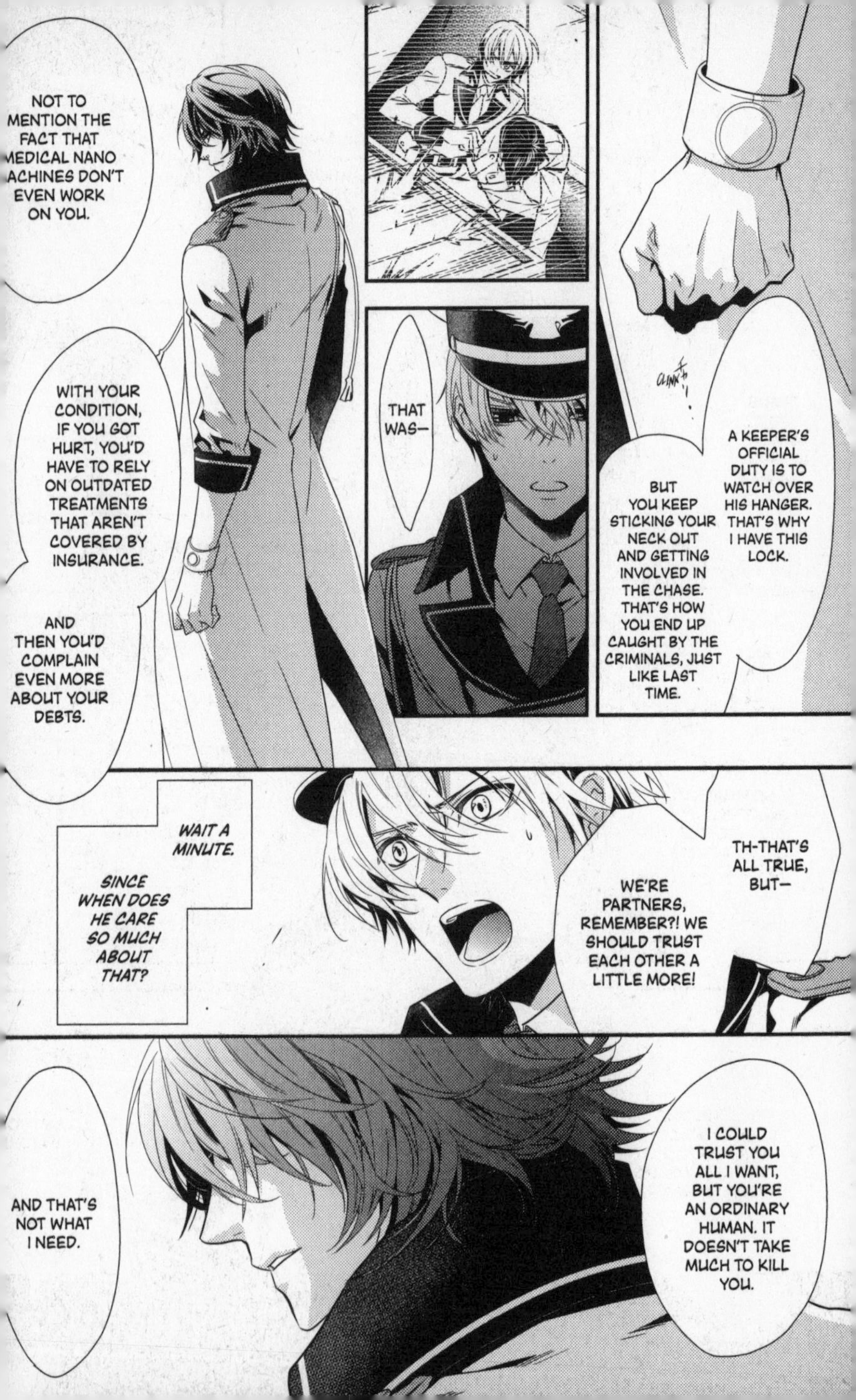
CLINK
A KEEPER'S OFFICIAL DUTY IS TO WATCH OVER HIS HANGER. THAT'S WHY I HAVE THIS LOCK.
BUT YOU KEEP STICKING YOUR NECK OUT AND GETTING INVOLVED IN THE CHASE. THAT'S HOW YOU END UP CAUGHT BY THE CRIMINALS, JUST LIKE LAST TIME.
THAT WAS—
NOT TO MENTION THE FACT THAT MEDICAL NANO ACHINES DON'T EVEN WORK ON YOU.
WITH YOUR CONDITION, IF YOU GOT HURT, YOU'D HAVE TO RELY ON OUTDATED TREATMENTS THAT AREN'T COVERED BY INSURANCE.
AND THEN YOU'D COMPLAIN EVEN MORE ABOUT YOUR DEBTS.
TH-THAT'S ALL TRUE, BUT—
WE'RE PARTNERS, REMEMBER?! WE SHOULD TRUST EACH OTHER A LITTLE MORE!
WAIT A MINUTE.
SINCE WHEN DOES HE CARE SO MUCH ABOUT THAT?
I COULD TRUST YOU ALL I WANT, BUT YOU'RE AN ORDINARY HUMAN. IT DOESN'T TAKE MUCH TO KILL YOU.
AND THAT'S NOT WHAT I NEED.

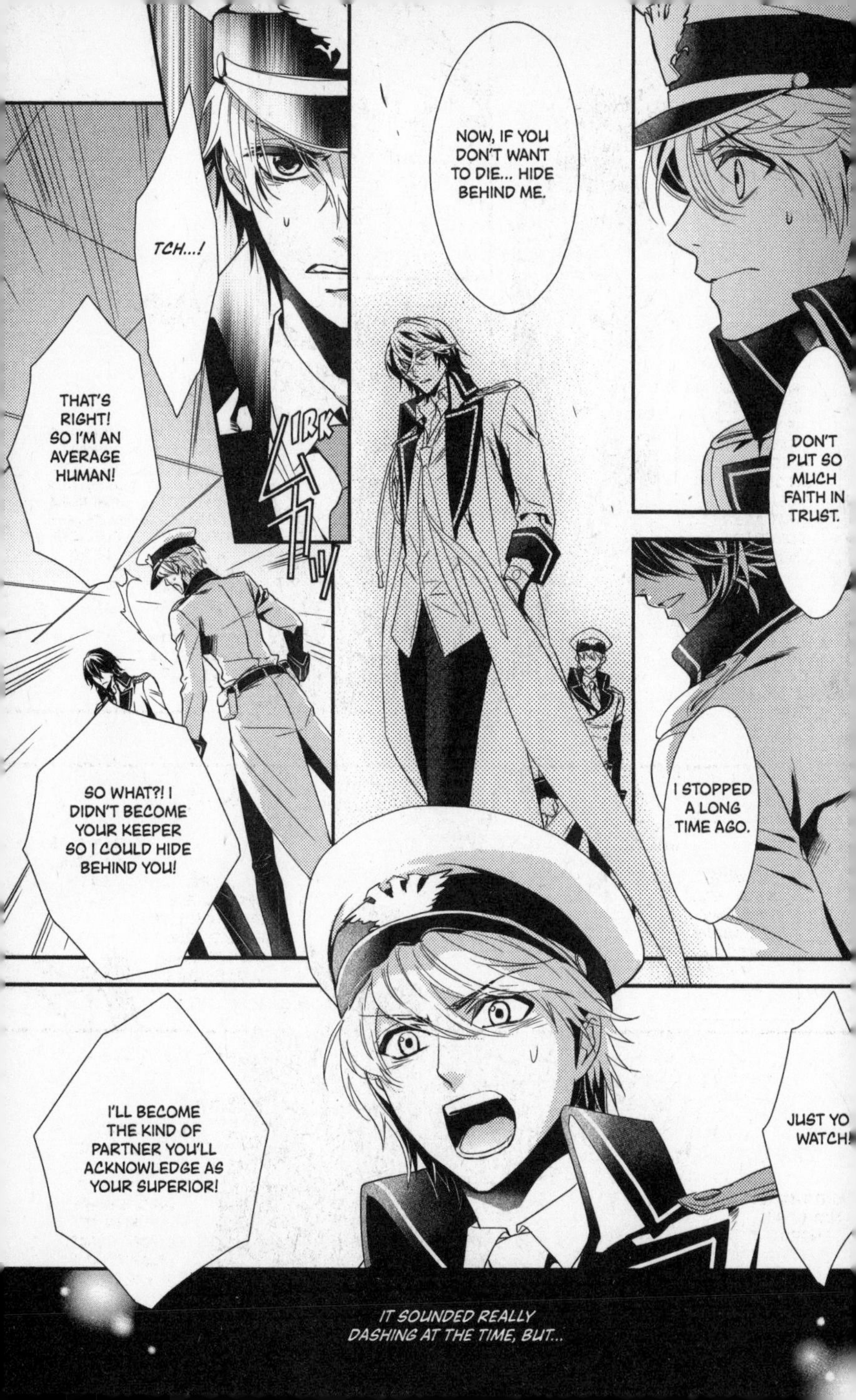
DON'T PUT SO MUCH FAITH IN TRUST.
I STOPPED A LONG TIME AGO.
NOW, IF YOU DON'T WANT TO DIE... HIDE BEHIND ME.
TCH...!
IRK
THAT'S RIGHT! SO I'M AN AVERAGE HUMAN!
SO WHAT?! I DIDN'T BECOME YOUR KEEPER SO I COULD HIDE BEHIND YOU!
JUST YO WATCH!
I'LL BECOME THE KIND OF PARTNER YOU'LL ACKNOWLEDGE AS YOUR SUPERIOR!
IT SOUNDED REALLY DASHING AT THE TIME, BUT...

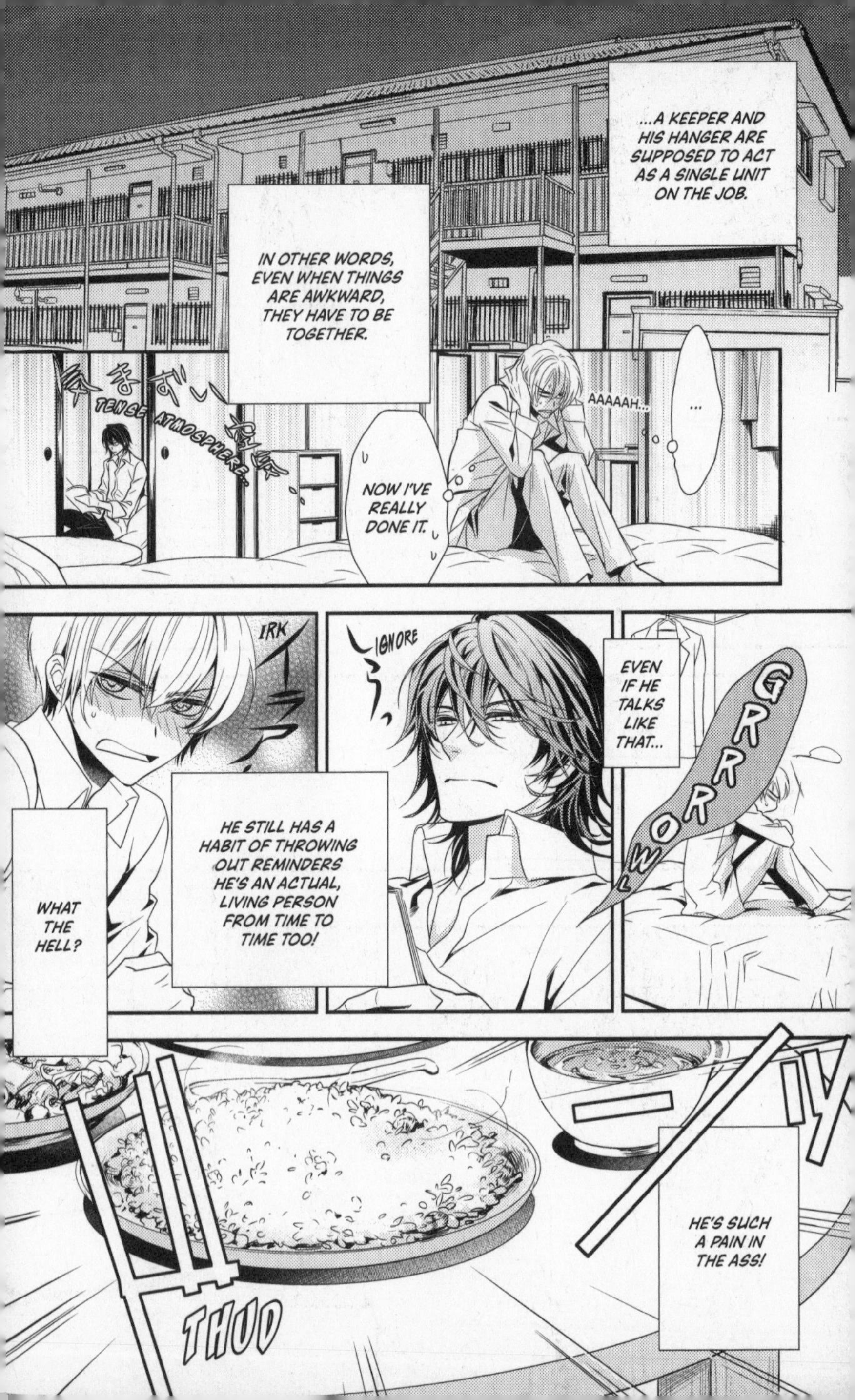
...A KEEPER AND HIS HANGER ARE SUPPOSED TO ACT AS A SINGLE UNIT ON THE JOB.
IN OTHER WORDS, EVEN WHEN THINGS ARE AWKWARD, THEY HAVE TO BE TOGETHER.
...
AAAAAH...
NOW I'VE REALLY DONE IT.
TENSE ATMOSPHERE...
EVEN IF HE TALKS LIKE THAT...
GRRROWL
IGNORE
HE STILL HAS A HABIT OF THROWING OUT REMINDERS HE'S AN ACTUAL, LIVING PERSON FROM TIME TO TIME TOO!
IRK
WHAT THE HELL?
HE'S SUCH A PAIN IN THE ASS!
THUD

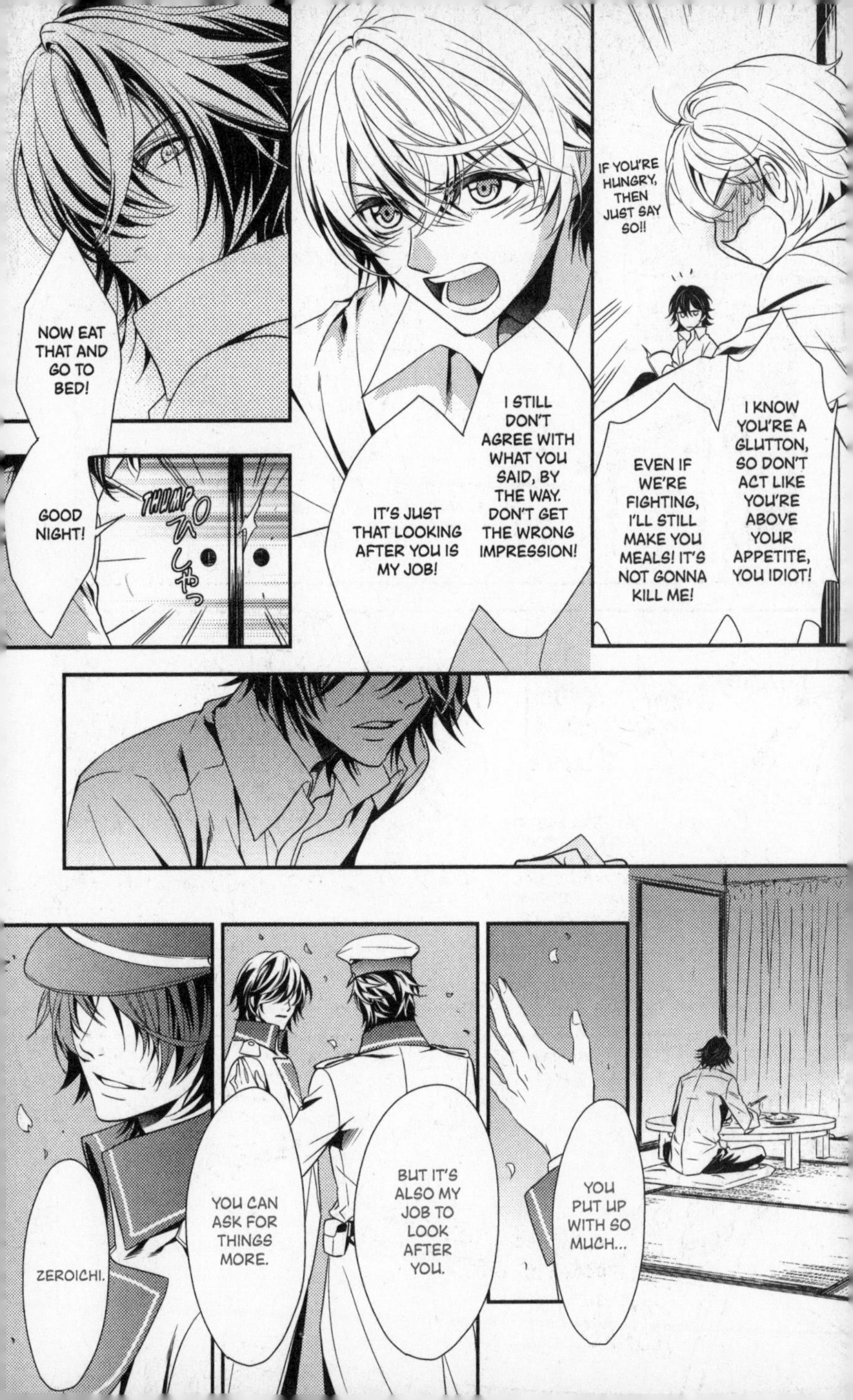
IF YOU'RE HUNGRY, THEN JUST SAY SO!!
I KNOW YOU'RE A GLUTTON, SO DON'T ACT LIKE YOU'RE ABOVE YOUR APPETITE, YOU IDIOT!
EVEN IF WE'RE FIGHTING, I'LL STILL MAKE YOU MEALS! IT'S NOT GONNA KILL ME!
I STILL DON'T AGREE WITH WHAT YOU SAID, BY THE WAY. DON'T GET THE WRONG IMPRESSION!
IT'S JUST THAT LOOKING AFTER YOU IS MY JOB!
NOW EAT THAT AND GO TO BED!
GOOD NIGHT!
THUMP
ぴしゃっ
YOU PUT UP WITH SO MUCH...
BUT IT'S ALSO MY JOB TO LOOK AFTER YOU.
YOU CAN ASK FOR THINGS MORE.
ZEROICHI.

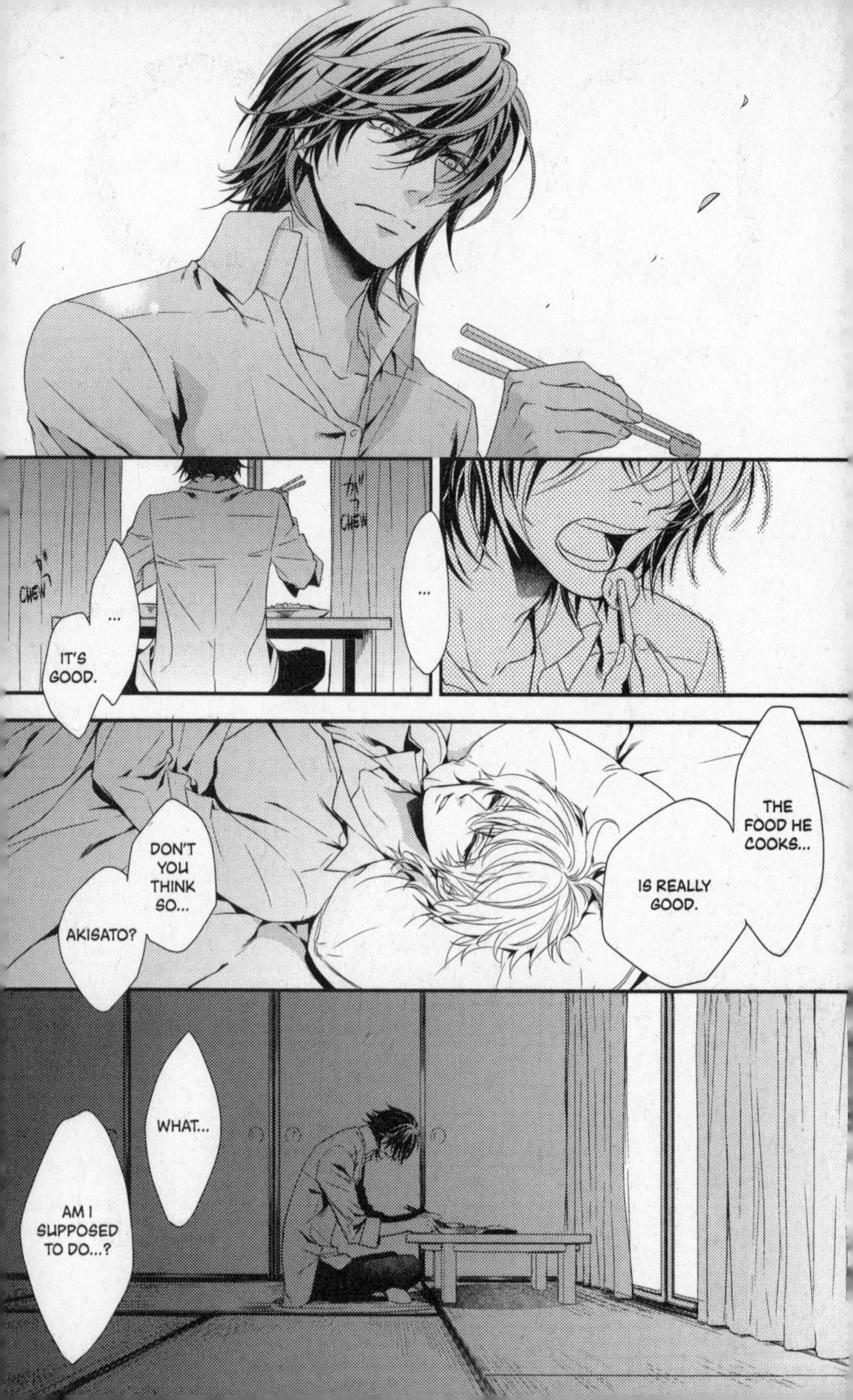
...
CHEW
CHEW
...
IT'S GOOD.
THE FOOD HE COOKS...
IS REALLY GOOD.
DON'T YOU THINK SO...
AKISATO?
WHAT...
AM I SUPPOSED TO DO...?

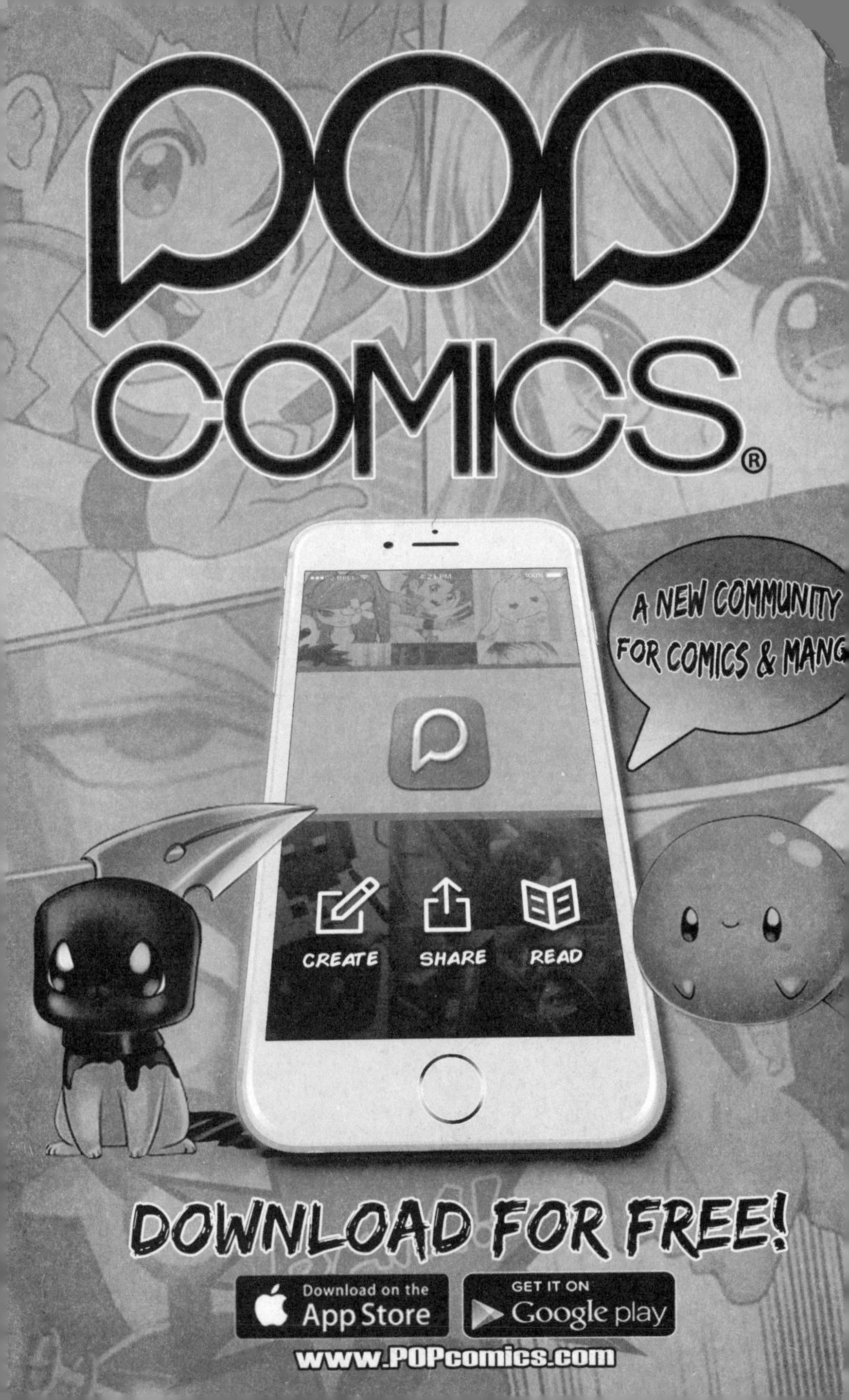
POP
COMICS®
A NEW COMMUNITY
FOR COMICS & MANG
CREATE
SHARE
READ
DOWNLOAD FOR FREE!
Download on the App Store
GET IT ON Google play
www.POPcomics.com

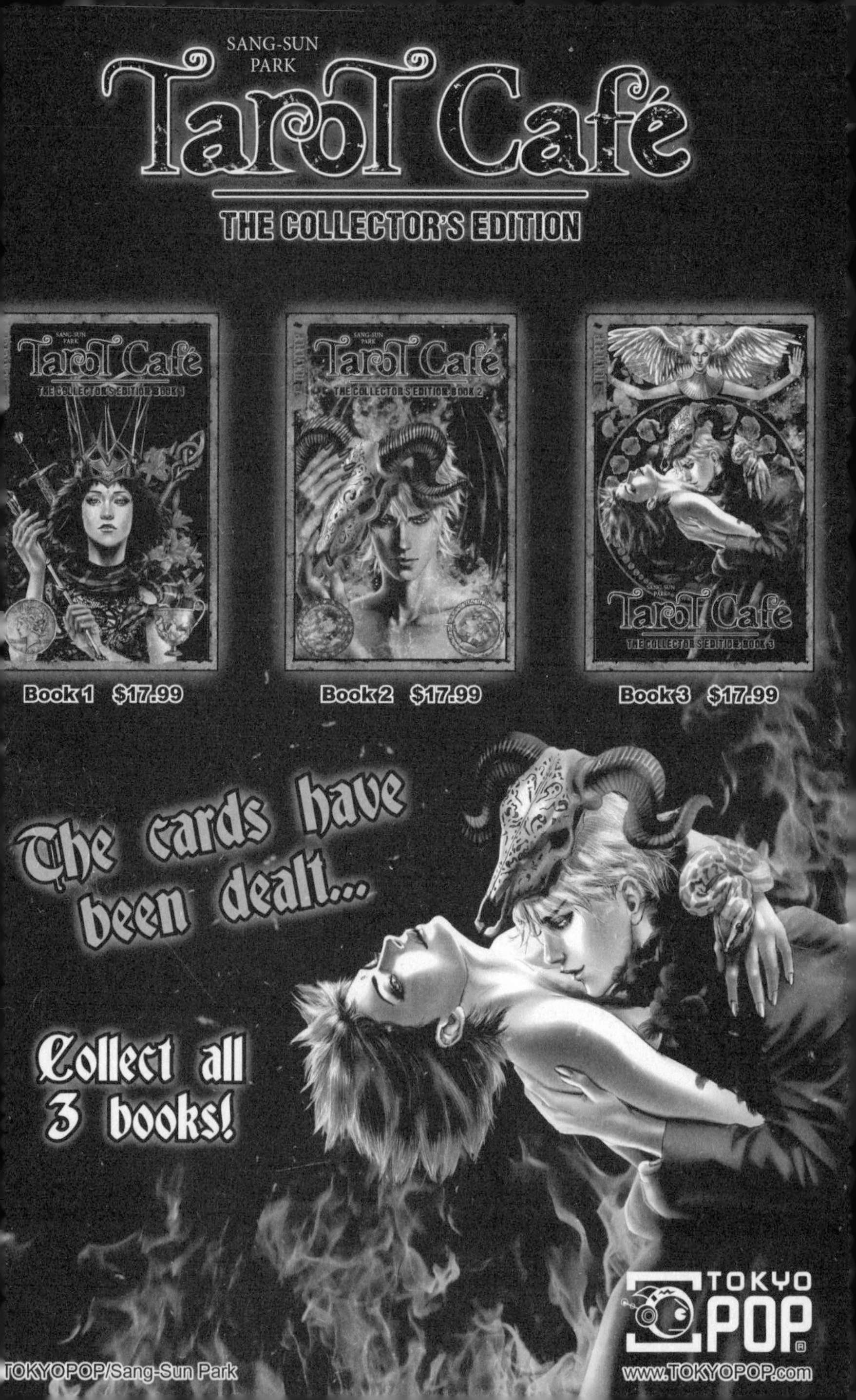
SANG-SUN PARK
Tarot Café
THE COLLECTOR'S EDITION
Book 1 $17.99
Book 2 $17.99
Book 3 $17.99
The cards have been dealt...
Collect all 3 books!
TOKYO POP
TOKYOPOP/Sang-Sun Park
www.TOKYOPOP.com